Systems

Volume 3

Beyond Alignment
Applying Systems Thinking in
Architecting Enterprises

Volume 1
A Journey Through the Systems Landscape
Harold "Bud" Lawson

Volume 2
A Discipline of Mathematical Systems Modelling
Matthew Collinson, Brian Monahan, and David Pym

Volume 3
Beyond Alignment. Applying Systems Thinking in Architecting Enterprises
John Gøtze and Anders Jensen-Waud, eds.

Beyond Alignment
Applying Systems Thinking in Architecting Enterprises

Edited by

John Gøtze

and

Anders Jensen-Waud

ISBN 978-1-84890-116-2

College Publications
Scientific Director: Dov Gabbay
Managing Director: Jane Spurr
Department of Computer Science
King's College London, Strand, London WC2R 2LS, UK

http://www.collegepublications.co.uk

Printed by Lightning Source, UK

Contents

Part 3: Practicing Systems Thinking

Part 4: Systems Thinking in the Enterprise

Foreword

Peter Bernus

In 1976 I was invited to join the Computer and Automation Institute of the Hungarian Academy of Sciences as a research scientist, and lead a systems engineering group in the Division of Manufacturing Automation. The reason for the establishment of this group was a massive project to create a computer integrated manufacturing system for the Csepel Machine Tool Factory.

By the time I joined (6 months into the project) Joe Hatvany, the head of the division, told me: "we already have such a massive amount of documentation, minutes of meetings and decisions, that they have grown to a half a meter tall paper pile – I need you to develop a method to deal with such complexity"! Indeed over a hundred engineers worked for five years (from the institute and the factory) on this project, comprising mechanical engineering, computer numerical control, software and electronics hardware, computer aided design / computer graphics, process planning, automated measurement, scheduling, and many other subsystems, designed and created by people who traditionally did not talk too much to one another.

The 'obvious' decision was to adopt methods that could capture a model of this system of systems on a level of abstraction that made the functions, the information and material flow among these functions explicit, as well as described how the system's elements and its connections implemented the system's functions. The level of abstraction used to understand the inherent complexity was much higher than that of the usual drawings used in mechanical, electronic, or production engineering, and was met with suspicion by many engineers. However, to align the decisions made by managers and engineers of different disciplinary background, it was necessary to understand the *system as a whole*, and use the models created by the systems engineering group as a means of identifying inconsistencies and incompleteness in the original designs. Such an understanding allowed us to ask the right questions from managers and engineers, but eventually the questions needed to be answered by *them*. Our work was not very visible – after all we *only asked* the questions, and the answers were provided by the *'real engineers'* ...

Today we know that it was the *systems view* that allowed us ask the right questions.

After the initial efforts to model the complete integrated manufacturing system, someone told to me: well – the next step is to model the complete enterprise!

What became clear from this and subsequent projects during the following ten years was that we needed methods to architect very large-scale systems, and that due to their complexity, there is actually no single person who has a full understanding of these systems!

From similar projects in the US, Japan, France and Germany in the machine-tool-, aircraft-, and electronics manufacturing area grew out a field called 'enterprise integration', that preceded – or grew in parallel – to similar developments in Information Systems and Software Engineering, and Systems Engineering.

The first four years of the 1990s saw a major effort by the IFIP-IFAC Task Force to review all efforts that were at the time known to systematize the knowledge necessary to architect a complete manufacturing company (Bernus, Nemes and Williams, 1996). The outcome, called the 'Generalised Enterprise Reference Architecture and Methodology (GERAM)' (Chapter 2 in Bernus *et al*, 2003), and the related ISO standard ISO 15704, is a generalization of what an architecture framework should be able to explain (the list below is only illustrative). Fundamental requirements include:

(i)   beyond a level of complexity, man-made systems are invariably socio-technical, therefore any architecture framework must equally treat the human and automated aspects of these systems,

(ii)   the 'life cycle' and 'life cycle process' concepts of systems is fundamental to the understanding of the evolution of any system, and related 'enterprise entities', and this is so on all levels of systems decomposition, and for every type of enterprise entity (e.g. organization, product, project, program, etc.),

(iii)   a system can only be understood if both its operations and its control are understood (including how these relate to other systems and to the environment),

(iv)   the framework must have concepts to be able to describe the dynamics and temporal trajectories of evolution, including the dependency between evolutionary stages (for example be able to describe both emergent and deliberate change, and how they relate),

(v)   the framework must account for the relationship between normative and descriptive models, because systems of large complexity are never created from scratch. For example, the understanding of good and bad models is a prerequisite for the adoption of tried and tested reference models that exist on all levels of abstraction (expressed as principles, architectures, requirements, and designs), and these abstract models embody human knowledge, including theories of useful classes of systems.

As of today, a similar effort to define requirements for architecture frameworks is currently being conducted by the ISO working group that developed ISO 42010, so as to incorporate requirements as above into the software and systems engineering suite of standards.

Today we are at the crossroads, because the evolution of the Enterprise Architecture (EA) discipline requires that the multiple origins of EA (from manufacturing, information systems, software- and systems engineering) be synthesized and harmonized. This is a challenging task due to the path dependencies that exist within the discipline-based communities behind their respective standards, therefore the system concepts inherited from these origins need to be re-expressed in an interdisciplinary language of systems both acceptable and useful for all.

The development of an interdisciplinary theory of systems understood by theoreticians *and* practitioners of all constituent disciplines is a very important agenda. I believe that the great challenge of the century is now beyond being 'only' the problem of enterprise architecture or the problem of systems engineering: we are now faced with the problem of the management of complexity of systems of systems that cross the boundaries between three layers, the social system, the economy and the ecosystem.

Therefore the harmonization and systematization of system concepts must encompass all three system-layers, and consequently we need a theory that can express the concerns of all the respective disciplines, all with their own current views of systems, of how they evolve, and what it means to manage them.

But where do we start? As of today there is no agreement yet, which makes this book a very timely attempt to organize many important systems concepts that could contribute to the development of a grand unified theory of system of systems of all kind, and that explains the fundamental life processes of systems in a manner that allows the theory to be used to (in some way) manage the complex systems around us.

The term 'in some way' refers to the fact that the manageability of complex systems has theoretical limitations, thus the management of a system's life trajectory is not a strict control task: often all we can contend with is partial control, in an attempt to ensure that the system during its life is not faced with critical obstacles, – even though we can not predict which possible life trajectory will actually realize.

The reader should not expect from this book the final word on the problem – that would be far too ambitious. However, in the following chapters, some important and fundamental concepts, models and methods are laid out for the reader to contemplate, and the book demonstrates their use showing the way to a *new way of thinking* about enterprise architecture, instead of trying to rely on 'heavy' architecture frameworks. (Heavy frameworks are those, which do not separate well the conceptual framework of enterprise architecture [which is usually light, and generally applicable], and prescriptive meta-models, models and methodologies [usually heavy on content and limited in the scope of applicability]).

I like the approach of using light frameworks (Lawson, 2010), because they are very powerful: this is precisely why I always tell my Master of Enterprise Architecture students, many of them practicing mangers, that the course will *not* teach them a particular EA methodology, because at the end of the course they must be equipped with abstract and generally applicable concepts, tools and methods to consider practically *any* current and future EA problem, and go on to develop their own method to solve it (of course abstract frameworks are only useful if we demonstrate how they can be used).

The theory I am calling for must be agnostic of system type, and must be limited to a set of fundamental system concepts and associated axioms, it should refrain from prescribing a particular model, methodology, or ontology.

The reader may notice that this objective is very close to the objective of General Systems Theory (GST). However, GST has never been developed fully enough to be of practical use in EA – except for raising awareness of fundamental systems characteristics that the architect of the enterprise (and of the larger system of systems around it) must be aware of, and contemplate.

Once we have such a theory, it will be possible to express many problems of complex systems management in a unified set of terms, giving rise to new theories, as well as re-state (or re-interpret) numerous known solution models and combine them into better ones.

Part 1 of this book is exposing the importance of systems thinking in Enterprise Architecture, and rightly argues that the results of great systems thinkers of the XXth century have not been used to their fullest potential. Thus the work of Bertalanffy (1968), Wiener (1948), Ackoff (1972), Ashby (1956), and Beer (1972) – to name some of the notable authors – needs re-examining and Part I takes an important step in this direction.

Such a re-examination and subsequent attempts to apply them will probably reveal some limitations of the original models, but this is expected according to the usual trajectory of a discipline's evolution (Kandjani and Bernus, 2013).

Part 2 points out that Enterprise Architecture can be seen as the 'consciousness' of the intelligent enterprise, and should therefore be central concern to management. Chapters in this part explore the possible uses of Beer's Viable Systems Model (VSM) (Beer, 1972; Espejo and Harnden, 1989), which is a reference model of a class of systems that exhibit desirable survival and self-referential characteristics.

VSM uses fundamental cybernetic concepts to layout a useful model to organize the management of a system that is viable, but in some respects its exposition has been obscure, until made more accessible by Hoverstadt (2008).

It is to be noted for future research, that VSM does not account for two important characteristic properties of complex living systems, namely life and death of the individual, and the evolution of the species, therefore to follow the work that this book is starting, more research will have to be done on formulating VSM using the concepts of General Systems Theory.

Further combinations are also possible, using reference models pioneered in the 1990s, such as the Bionic Manufacturing Systems (Okino, 1989, cited by Tharumarajah *et al*, 1996), Warnecke's Fractal Factory model (1993), and Holonic Manufacturing systems architecture (Mathews, 1995), or more recently the work on Self Designing Enterprises in my laboratory (Kandjani and Bernus, 2011), – each offering desirable system characteristics, and I am sure that other useful reference models will emerge as more candidates are considered.

Parts 3 and **4** of this book are of particular interest to practicing managers and consultants, because through the examples the authors demonstrate the insight that systems thinking can offer so as the system's architecture becomes meaningful in the context to stakeholders who need answer to their concerns.

These chapters show how systems thinking can be used on multiple levels, from the overall enterprise level, to the level of analyzing individual processes and their influencing factors. In addition, Part 3 gives a good introduction to important systems thinking concepts and their origins, and is an illustration of systems knowledge that one would expect all levels of management to be familiar with and be able to competently apply.

The variety of these chapters is important, because it illustrates the many ways in which incorporating systems thinking into EA practice can enhance its effectiveness, after all it is by today clear that EA is not a function that can be relegated to a single enterprise architect, but rather a discipline that management of all levels needs to be familiar with.

I would like to congratulate the Editors both to the idea of producing this book, and to the choice of authors that make this book a very enjoyable reading.

Brisbane, August 2013

About the Author

Dr Bernus is a Hungarian Australian scientist and Associate Professor of Enterprise Architecture at the School of Information and Communication Technology, and director of the Centre for Enterprise Architecture Research and Management at Griffith University, Brisbane, Australia.

References

Ackoff, R., Emery, F.E. (1972) On Purposeful Systems. Chicago: Aldine-Atherton.

Ashby, W. R. (1956) An Introduction to Cybernetics. London: Chapman & Hall.

Beer, S. (1972) Brain of the Firm. London Allen Lane, The Penguin Press.

Bernus, P., Nemes, L., Williams, T.J. (Eds) (1996) Architectures for Enterprise Integration . London : Chapman and Hall.

Bernus, P., Nemes, L., Schmidt, G. (2003) Handbook on Enterprise Architecture. Berlin : Springer.

Bertalanffy, L. (1968) General System theory: Foundations, Development, Applications. New York: Braziller.

Espejo, R., Harnden, R. (Eds.) (1989) The viable system model: interpretations and applications of Stafford Beer's VSM. Chichester: Wiley.

Hoverstadt, P. (2008). The Fractal Organization: Creating Sustainable Organizations with the Viable Systems Model. Chichester: Wiley & Sons.

ISO15704:2000/Amd1:2005 Industrial automation systems – Requirements for enterprise-reference architectures and methodologies.

ISO/IEC/IEEE 42010:2011, Systems and software engineering – Architecture description.

Kandjani, H. and Bernus, P. (2011). Engineering Self-Designing Enterprises as Complex Systems Using Extended Axiomatic Design Theory. IFAC Papers On Line , IFAC-WCC18(1). Amsterdam : Elsevier. pp11943-11948.

Kandjani, H., Bernus, P. (2013). The Enterprise Architecture Body of Knowledge as an Evolving Discipline. In Saha, P. (Ed) A Systemic Perspective to Managing Complexity with Enterprise Architecture. Hershey : IGI Global.

Lawson, H. (2010) A Journey Through the Systems Landscape. London: College Publications.

Mathews, J. (1995) Organizational foundations of intelligent manufacturing systems – the holonic viewpoint. *Computer Integrated Manufacturing Systems* 8(4). pp237–243.

Okino, N. (1992) A Prototyping of Bionic Manufacturing System. In Norrie, D.H. (Ed), Proc. Int Conf on Object-Oriented Manufacturing Systems. Div. Mfg. Sys. Alberta : U Calgary. pp297-302.

Tharumarajah A., Wells A.J., Nemes, L. 1996. A Comparison of the Bionic, Fractal and Holonic Manufacturing Concepts, *International Journal of Computer Integrated Manufacturing.* 9(3): 217-226.

Warnecke, H. J. (1993) The Fractal Company. Heidelberg : Springer

Wiener, N. (1948) Cybernetics, or Communication and Control in the Animal and the Machine. Cambridge: MIT Press.

Foreword

Dirk Baecker

The function of any architecture is to both separate and connect inside and outside, relying in both respects on highly specific conditions. Architecture is chiefly about the management of the asymmetry between inside and outside. Usually it is easier to go out than to re-enter. Equally, it is different to live inside and monitor the outside from roaming outside and peeking inside. There is a protected area usually marked by roofs, walls, windows and doors where people can live undisturbed by changing conditions outside or unwelcome people. And there is an undefined outdoor world, which can be searched for opportunities but at the same time poses a threat to people inside with the prospect of facing to possibly being released to this unknown territory.

Issues of architecture are non-trivial. It is easy to forget this because we take our rooms, houses, halls and walls for granted. But any look at how the boundaries between inside and outside are managed, and how the inside is differentiated to grant unequal access to the outside, and at how different doors and back doors are used to let different issues and people in or keep them out – just think of the cat flap – instantly makes us aware of the complexity of even the most simple architecture.

This book is an answer to one of the most pertinent challenges of the last sixty years or so of the reorganization of organizations, be they enterprises, offices, churches, universities, schools, armies or hospitals. For certainly more than 5 000 or 6 000 years – since we have known about Babylonian hospitals, for instance, managed as they were by veteran army officers – the rule has been to restrict access to inside and outside on an all levels of the organization save the uppermost to an absolute minimum. Organization meant to make sure that technical and social routines inside went undisturbed, whether it concerned the treatment of patients, teaching a school class, preparing a campaign or the fabrication of pins. Members of the organization had to be kept unaware of changing environments, and people outside had to be prevented from even the most minimal interfering with people inside. Only the top of the organization had full access to the outside world but had so much authority governing the rest of the organization that it - the top - had itself become almost inaccessible to anybody else. Even when this hierarchy architecture had to be supplemented by middle levels to address problems of cooperation and even when the very differentiation of the levels themselves made sure that different work styles, modes of communication and even frames of awareness could be employed, there was still a hierarchy translating the asymmetry of inside and outside into an asymmetry of top and bottom.

Today's network organization is different. There is still one overall hierarchy, to be sure, and there are many sub-hierarchies in divisions, departments and teams. Yet the whole architecture is heterarchic, which means that it is, in principle, able to pass the lead to people or jobs having the most reliable information, respectively. In his architecture of buildings, Frank Lloyd Wright in the 1920s and 1930s proclaimed the destruction of the box,

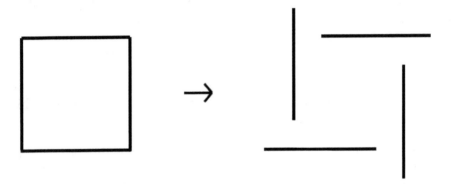

Frank Lloyd Wright, The Destruction of the Box

thereby asking for a fluid, or organic, connection between inside and outside. In the architecture of organizations, however, such an easy, even if by residents and colleagues equally contested, move was and is not possible. You cannot just open the box, let people roam freely both inside and between outside and inside without first asking yourself what to do about your venerable old hierarchy and then searching for substitutes to still organize the way how differentiations inside the organizations deal with, or even produce, the turbulences outside.

It may come as some kind of comfort that, as Niklas Luhmann showed in his classic *Zweckbegriff und Systemrationalität*, his contribution to the landmark year 1968, workflow and hierarchy never were or could be in concord. But that concerned the current practices in any organization and never put its dominant semantics of hierarchical unity in jeopardy. What is more, the lacking concord that was never addressed by semantics made sure that a kind of organizational culture emerged which let people always outwit official language regimes. That proved rather beneficial to the living organization, which in fact is drawing much more on tensions, unsolved problems and secret dissonances than on the famous one purpose rationally informing all sub-goals.

Thus, unity through an overall hierarchy never existed and is just an imagination the new and rather stressful network organization is only dreaming of. But this insight does not help. It makes matters worse since now organization architects know that they do not only have to design a new formal organization but also provide for new and still mostly unknown informal aspects of the organization to emerge and flourish. How do you design an informal organization? By definition, you cannot.

This is why this book about enterprise architecture is one to be distinguished from any living organization just as the plans of architects are to be distinguished from the very buildings they are planning. The designs presented here are not meant to model or picture the real organization. They are meant to make readers aware of how to look at organizations and detect possible causes for their smooth or otherwise bumpy working. They are even meant to let readers look at the working of an organization first and design it only later, following the lead the spontaneous self-organization of its working provides for its possible design. There is an ancient saying in the theory of urban planning, which says to let people first walk and then build the ways and streets exactly where they already have chosen to walk. Unfortunately, the saying in this case is wiser than the practice, since with streets and more important ways this is rarely possible. But the saying makes one aware of an important insight. And in gardens and parks it is often actually done, be it only to protect the flowers and the grass.

This book, moreover, is timely because it addresses the question of enterprise architecture when promises are around that IT will solve the riddles of organization anyhow. Just let IT have its way, both in terms of hardware and software. Wetware will follow suit. The articles of this book show readers why this is an illusion, and a dangerous one at that. The computer is more restrictive in its procedures than the venerable old hierarchies proved to be. To align computer and organization would mean to kill the latter. To let the organization live means to learn how and where to introduce what kind of computational thinking into the organization. We know that the usual computer is tremendously useful in letting us run forceful algorithms. Its Achilles' heel, though, are its interfaces. Yet any kind of architecture is about interfaces. So let ideas about a network of interfaces take the lead in thinking about how to use IT in organizations.

As Immanuel Kant said, both matter and form are categories of reflection about processes that link people to the world and people to people. Reflection means that any person should be aware of a change of perspective changing the idea you have of any matter or form. Architecture should go with that insight. Organizations should align with possible changes of perspective.

Friedrichshafen, August 2013

About the Author

Professor Dr. rer. soc. Dirk Baecker leads the Lehrstuhl für Kulturtheorie und –analyse at Zeppelin University in Friedrichshafen, Germany.

Acknowledgment: English language editing by Adelheid Baker.

Introducing
Beyond Alignment

John Gøtze and Anders Jensen-Waud

Abstract

This chapter is an introduction to the book. The editors explain why enterprise architects must move beyond having alignment of "business" and "IT" as their focal point. Instead, the editors suggest, enterprise architects should apply Systems Thinking.

Keywords

Enterprise Architecture, Systems Thinking, alignment

The Alignment Debate

There has been a longstanding debate in the literature about what alignment means. Some of the definitions used in peer-reviewed articles specific to an IT-context are the following:

> *The degree of fit and integration among business strategy, IT strategy, business infrastructure, and IT infrastructure. Henderson and Venkatraman (1989)*

> *The degree to which the mission, objectives, and plans contained in the business strategy are shared and supported by the IT strategy. Reich and Benbasat (1996)*

> *The basic principle is that IT should be managed in a way that mirrors management of the business. Sauer and Yetton (1997)*

> *Good alignment means that the organization is applying appropriate IT in given situations in a timely way, and that these actions stay congruent with the business strategy, goals, and needs. Luftman and Brier (1999)*

> *Strategic alignment of IT exists when an organization's goals and activities and the information systems that support them remain in harmony. McKeen and Smith (2003)*

> *Alignment is the business and IT working together to reach a common goal. Campbell (2005)*

In May 2013, a research library database counts 281.152 peer-reviewed articles about "alignment", and 21.199 about "business-IT alignment". Alignment in an IT-context is today generally understood as the ability of the IT department to support the business department's mission, vision and plans. When aligned, employees in IT act in such a way that their actions stay congruent with the business strategy, goals, and needs.

Since 2010, alignment researchers even have a dedicated journal, the *International Journal of IT/Business Alignment and Governance* (IJITBAG), which puts emphasis on "how organizations enable both businesses and IT people to execute their responsibilities in support of business/IT alignment and the creation of business value from IT-enabled investments".

Henderson and Ventrakaman (1989) developed a strategic alignment model to delineate alignment between IT and business. The model features two types of integration: strategic integration and functional integration. Strategic integration is about alignment between strategy and operations, and is the alignment between the external and internal organizational domains. As Figure 1 illustrates, strategic integration exists for the business and IT units. Functional integration involves two types of alignment: One between business and IT strategy, and one between organizational infrastructure and processes and IT infrastructure and processes.

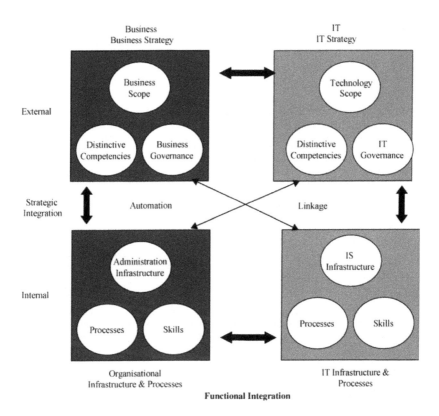

Figure 1. Strategic Alignment Model
(Henderson & Ventrakaman, 1989)

The functional integration on the strategy level is concerned with the integration about the position of the firm for both domains. On the infrastructure level, functional integration is about the relationship between organizational processes, skills and infrastructure and the IT infrastructure, processes, and skills. Also, cross-domain alignment is the relationship between the IT strategy level and the organizational infrastructure and processes level, and the business strategy and the IT infrastructure and processes level. Strategic alignment at an organizational level can only occur when three of the four domains are in alignment. The underlying premise is that change cannot happen in one domain without impacting on at least two of the remaining three domains in some way (Avison et al., 2004). The distributions of domains that are either anchor, pivot, or impacted determine the organization's alignment perspective. The anchor domain is the strongest domain and will be the initiator of change and provide the majority of requests for IT resources. The pivot domain will ultimately be affected by the change initiated within the anchor domain. The impacted domain is impacted the greatest by the change initiated in the anchor domain. The strategic alignment model provides a more nuanced conceptualization of alignment. The IT-business relationship can take different alignment perspectives. Further, the model proposes that effective strategic IT management process must address both functional and strategic integration (Henderson & Ventrakaman, 1989).

Maas (1999) and Maes et al. (2000) extended the strategic alignment model to a unified framework that incorporates layers into the model to reflect the need for information and communication. The unified framework refines the alignment model to reflect the fact that IT and business strategies are moving closer together as technology evolves and becomes more integrated (Avison et al, 2004). The unified framework deals with the relationship between business, information, communication and technology at three distinct levels: strategy, structure, and operations (Maes et al., 2000). Strategy is constituted by core competencies, governance and scope; structure is constituted by architecture, communication processes and information models; and operations are constituted by processes, modeling and skills.

A stream of research has investigated the antecedents of IT-business alignment to improve understanding of the alignment process. Weiss & Anderson (2004) found four common themes they found were repeated in organizations with a good level of IT/business alignment. These themes are shown in Figure 2.

Similar thinking can be found in MIT CISRs research. Fonstad and Robertson (2006) argue that in order to get alignment the enterprise needs to have both a top-down organizational view and a bottom-up project view. This is reflected in MIT CISR's IT Engagement Model, Figure 3:

Figure 2: Path to alignment, the Four Cs (Weiss & Anderson, 2004)

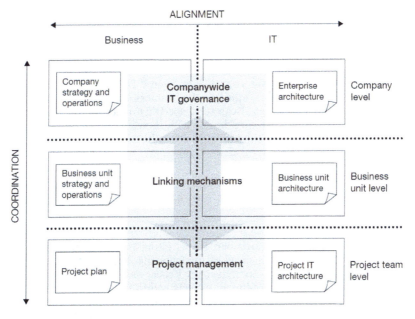

**Figure 3. MIT CISR's IT Engagement Model
(Ross, Weill and Robertson, 2006)**

There are studies showing that when organizations adopt a proven framework for alignment early in the planning process, these organizations save time and resources in the long run (Kearns and Sabherwal, 2007). Based on an empirical study of 63 firms, Tallon & Kraemer (2003) find that there is a significant IT payoff for firms that practice strategic alignment, and other studies have shown that a strategic fit between

19

business and IT strategies positively affect sales growth, profitability, and reputation (Tallon & Pinsonneault, 2011; Thatcher & Pingry, 2007; Watson, 2007). Other research has focused on the challenges and issues organizations are facing when creating alignment. Chan & Reich (2007) summarize some of the challenges with alignment:

Alignment challenge description	Alignment challenge elaboration
Knowledge and awareness	IT executives are not always privy to corporate strategy, and that organizational leaders are not always knowledgeable about IT. Also, managers are not always knowledgeable about key business and industry drivers.
Corporate strategy is unknown	Corporate strategy is unknown or, if known, is unclear and/or difficult to adapt. This poses a significant challenge because most models of alignment presuppose an existing business strategy to which an IT organization can align itself. Formal business strategies are often too ambiguous for business managers to adapt. Managers face ambiguity surrounding the differences between espoused strategies, strategies in use, and managerial actions, many of which may be in conflict with one another.
Lack of awareness or belief in the importance of alignment	Many business managers are unaware of the importance of IT alignment and/or have little belief that IT can solve important business problems. Even if IT issues are perceived to have a strong effect on the business objectives, there is no clear belief that IT can solve specific problems. Managers are typically more comfortable with their ability to comprehend business positioning choices rather than IT positioning choices (i.e., critical technology to support business strategies). Strategy has typically been viewed as something applied to the output market, while IT has been viewed as an internal response.
Lack of industry and business knowledge	IT alignment was hindered by a lack of knowledge about an industry. In particular, it was found that IT alignment was negatively influenced by the following industry factors: when awareness of an industry's issues was low and when the interaction of different aspects within the corporate strategy was not well known to managers. Therefore, before managers could use IT solutions to help solve their problems, a deeper knowledge of the banking industry itself was required. A multiple case study showed that shared domain knowledge between business and IT executives was the strongest predictor of the social dimension of alignment.
Alignment challenges related to locus of control and	When managers are confronted with a business challenge, they make decisions based on their locus of understanding and their locus of control (authority to make decisions). These constraints impact alignment. From this perspective, strategic alignment can be seen as an array of bounded

the status of IT	choices made in order to resolve strategic ambiguity. Another contributing factor in the attainment of alignment is the status of IT within the business unit or organization.
Alignment challenges related to organization al change	The business environment is constantly changing, and thus there may be no such thing as a 'state' of alignment. Alignment is thus the time lag between business and IT planning processes. That is, given that the business environment and technology change so quickly, once an IT plan is enacted, there is a high probability that the plan and the technology are already obsolete.

Table 1: Alignment challenges (Chan & Reich, 2007)

Critics of alignment emphasize that organizations constantly change and therefore alignment will never be fully achieved (Chan & Reich, 2007). In many organizations the IT department is always struggling to keep up with the business department's demands and changes. Luftman et al. (1999) did an exhaustive study of inhibitors and enablers for creating IT-business alignment in big companies. Respondents were asked to rank factors enabling and factors hindering IT-business alignment. The top five enablers were "Senior executives support IT", "IT involved in strategy development", "IT understands business", "IT/non-IT have close relationship", and "IT shows strong leadership". The top five inhibitors were "IT/non-IT lack close relationship", "IT does not prioritize well", "IT fails to meet the commitments", "IT does not understand business", and "Senior executives do not support IT".

The Alignment Trap

Alignment enablers and inhibitors are more often than not described at such an abstract level that they apply to most organizations, yet are very difficult to operationalize. Essentially, alignment theory is difficult to apply and utilize in today's enterprises. As expressed in Doucet et al (2009):

> *Infosys recently published a survey in which the major finding is that "Alignment of business and IT organization is the #1 objective of enterprise architecture ..." That is certainly goodness, but how about assuring that all parts of the business are aligned with each other? How about ensuring all the oars are pulling together?*

Alignment is essentially to the ability of the organization to operate as one by working towards a common shared vision supported by a well-orchestrated set of strategies and actions (Doucet et al, 2009). It covers the need for all parts of an organization to be working together, and is an important concept for complex enterprises that are composed of a number of lines of business and business functions with competing priorities and limited resources.

It is not that IT doesn't matter, but we need to reconsider the way we work with IT:

> *It is time for a major transformation of IT. It is time for a quantum leap. For years, the way we have run IT, as a CIO, was to command an army of ordertaking specialist workers, an underground army hidden away in the basement of our companies. These reactive armies of craftsmen are a thing of the past. In a Fusion concept, we need a new breed of professionals, with a new blend of capabilities. The challenge becomes how to crack the culture code in IT transformation? (Hinssen, 2011)*

This "culture code" is not about IT, but about management:

> *A thousand facts and no information, such is the case as we sit in this period of incoherency. Incoherency makes enterprises less manageable. As Gary Hamel said in The Future of Management, "Management is out of date. Like the combustion engine, it's a technology that has largely stopped evolving, and that's not good."* (Doucet et al 2009)

The whole idea of business-IT alignment is out of date. In fact, we consider it a trap.

This Book

The idea of publishing this book was originally conceived by John as a textbook for an advanced level masters course named *Enterprise Strategy, Business and Technology* at the IT University of Copenhagen. The course was created to build on top of John's *Enterprise Architecture* course, and the course's design criterion number one was that it should appeal to John's "elite students", a group of highly motivated full-time students at the MSc in Business and Information Technology program at the IT University of Copenhagen and the MSc in Business Administration and Computer Science at Copenhagen Business School, including Anders.

Teaching business strategy and technology alignment concepts at an *advanced* masters course requires much more than repeating the core curriculum of enterprise architecture. Whilst orthodox enterprise architecture frameworks usually provide in-depth tools and methodologies for taming the alignment of business and IT, very few approaches go further in considering and explaining how to avoid the alignment trap altogether. When teaching a course to elite students we asked ourselves the question – what should these aspiring enterprise architects learn? How could one provide a comprehensive theoretical foundation for thinking about any complex organization in a holistic, integrative manner? Systems thinking was the most compelling answer because it provides 1) a vibrant cross-disciplinary community of thinkers and practitioners and 2) an entire history of academic research, tradition, and frameworks.

In essence, systems thinking provides a plethora of generalized models and approaches to analyzing complex systems, be it human, biological, social, or mechanical, and how they respond to changing internal and external conditions (Jensen-Waud et al, 2012). Enterprise architecture is often employed as a tool to understand and manage the many moving parts of large-scale organizational change – and systems thinking therefore provides a viable theoretical basis for conceptualizing and reflecting upon how and why enterprise architecture is best applied in different situations so as to successfully execute organizational changes for better outcomes (Buckl et al 2009, Zadeh 2012).

A peer-reviewed paper recently published by John discusses how the scope and role of the enterprise architect is gradually changing from problem solving to problem finding and from dialectic to dialogic skills (Gøtze, 2013). The former is expressed in the way in which enterprise architecture has gradually transitioned from the "classic" domain of business drivers and IT requirements into dealing with many different domains of the enterprise, e.g. business strategy, operations, capability development, etc. These non-IT areas typically deal with "wicked", ill-defined problems, which are very hard to solve with traditional engineering methods (Jensen-Waud et al, 2012). Instead, skills such as continuous learning, exploration, collaboration, and enquiry are required. The latter is expressed in the increasing need for cross-departmental, cross-disciplinary collaboration and learning in the modern organization in order to solve complex business issues (Gøtze, 2013). In the light of this changing role, systems thinking again provides a compelling approach for framing and analyzing these challenges – relevant examples include Stafford Beer's viable systems model (VSM) (Beer, 1972), Peter Checkland's soft systems methodology (SSM), which focuses on the human content and enquiry of systemic problems (Checkland, 1985), and Karl Weick's (2001) concepts of organizational sense-making and loosely-coupled systems.

Beyond Alignment

In a turbulent macro environment and volatile global economy where successful change increasingly depends on systemic enquiry and cross-disciplinary collaboration, systems thinking has never been more relevant. With this book we hope to demonstrate how both aspiring and experience enterprise architecture practitioners can go beyond alignment and implement better and more holistic change initiatives by applying systems thinking to existing work processes and practices.

Many of these concepts are discussed in this book. The book, in essence, discusses the many new issues faced by enterprise architects and suggests how systems thinking can be applied to frame, understand, and resolve them.

After this introduction, the book falls in four parts:

- Part I: Enterprise Architecture and Systems Thinking
- Part 2: The Brain and the Heart of the Enterprise
- Part 3: Practicing Systems Thinking
- Part 4: Systems Thinking in the Enterprise

Part 1 has five chapters about how enterprise architecture and systems thinking work together. Part 2 has six chapters about using the Viable Systems Model in enterprise architecture. Part 3 has five chapters about using systems thinking as a practice framework. Part 4 has five chapters that positions systems thinking in the enterprise.

Contributing authors are (in order of appearance):

- Sally Bean
- Tue Westmark Steensen
- Janne J. Korhonen
- Jan Hoogervorst and Jan Dietz
- Leo Laverdure and Alex Conn
- Mesbah Khan
- Patrick Hoverstadt
- Adrian Campbell
- Mikkel Stokbro Holst
- Olusola O. Oduntan and Namkyu Park
- Tom Graves
- James Lapalme and Don deGuerre
- Harold "Bud" Lawson
- James Martin
- Dennis Sherwood
- Rasmus Fischer Frost and Linda Clod Præstholm
- Olov Östberg, Per Johannisson and Per-Arne Persson
- Peter Sjølin
- Ilia Bider, Gene Bellinger and Erik Perjons
- Jack Ring
- John Morecroft

The book hopefully stimulates, perhaps even provokes, the reader. Those who would like to comment can make reviews and comments on the book's website: *BeyondAlignment.com*.

About the Editors

Dr John Gøtze has worked with the interplay between strategy, business and technology since the early 1980s. With over 12 years of experience in the enterprise architecture discipline, John is today CEO of EA Fellows where he runs Carnegie Mellon University Enterprise Architecture Certification Program in Europe. John also leads the Professional Master in IT Leadership program at the IT University of Copenhagen, and teaches at Copenhagen Business School. John co-founded the Association of Enterprise Architects and was Chief Editor of the Journal of Enterprise Architecture from 2010-2013. He holds an MSc in systems engineering and a PhD in urban planning, both from the Technical University of Denmark.

Anders Jensen-Waud is a Managing Consultant and consulting architect within the Architecture & Technology Transformation practice of Capgemini Australia. With more than six years of general consulting experience and a background in defense systems engineering, Anders has deep experience as a consulting enterprise architect within government, defense, energy, utilities, oil and gas, and financial services. He has delivered a variety of architecture and business transformation engagements through Scandinavia and Australia. He is furthermore a published author in a number of international peer-reviewed journals and books. Anders holds an MSc in Business Administration and Computer Science and BSc in Business Administration and Computer Science from Copenhagen Business School.

References

Avison, D., J. Jones, P. Powell and D. Wilson (2004) Using and validating the strategic alignment model. Journal of Strategic Information Systems 13, pp. 223–246.

Beer, S. (1972). Brain of the Firm – The Managerial Cybernetics of Organization. Allan Lane and Penguin Press, London, UK.

Buckl, S., Schweda, CM, and Matthes, F. (2009) A Viable System Perspective on Enterprise Architecture Management. In Proceedings of SMC, 1pp. 483-1488.

Campbell, B. (2005). Alignment: Resolving ambiguity within bounded choices, PACIS 2005, Bangkok, Thailand, pp. 1–14.

Chan, Y. E. and B. H. Reich (2007). IT alignment: what have we learned? Journal of Information Technology (2007) 22, pp. 297–315.

Checkland, P. (1985). From Optimizing to Learning: A Development of Systems Thinking for the 1990s. The Journal of the Operational Research Society, 36(9), pp. 757-767.

Doucet, G., Gøtze, J., Saha, P., Bernard, S., 2009, Coherency Management: Architecting the Enterprise for Alignment, Agility, and Assurance, AuthorHouse.

Fonstad, N. and D. Robertson (2006) Transforming a Company, Project by Project: The IT Engagement Model. MIS Quarterly Executive. 5:1. pp. 1-14.

Gøtze, J., 2013, The Changing Role of the Enterprise Architect. Proceedings of the

2013 17th IEEE International Enterprise Distributed Object Computing Conference Workshops (EDOCW 2013), 9-13 September 2013, Vancouver, British Columbia, Canada

Henderson, J., Venkatramen, N. (1989) Strategic Alignment: A Model for Organisational Transformation, in Kochan, T., Unseem, M. (Eds.), 1992. Transforming Organisations. OUP, New York.

Hinssen, P. (2011) Business/IT Fusion. 2nd Ed.

Jensen-Waud, A.Ø. & J. Gøtze (2012) A Systemic-Discursive Framework for Enterprise Architecture. Journal of Enterprise Architecture, 8 (3) pp 35-44.

Kearns, G. S., & Sabherwal, R. (2007). Strategic Alignment Between Business and Information Technology: A Knowledge-Based View of Behaviors, Outcome, and Consequences. Journal of Management Information Systems, 23(3), 129–162.

Luftman, J., Brier, T. (1999) Achieving and Sustaining Business IT Alignment. California Management Review, Fall, 1999, Vol.42(1), p.109.

Luftman, J.A., Papp, R. and Brier, T. (1999). Enablers and Inhibitors of Business–IT Alignment, Communications of the Association for Information Systems 1(Article 11), pp. 1–33.

Maes, R., 1999. A Generic Framework for Information Management. Prime Vera Working Paper, Universiteit van Amsterdam

Maes, R., Rijsenbrij, D., Truijens, O., Goedvolk, H., 2000. Redefining Business–IT Alignment Through A Unified Framework. Universiteit Van Amsterdam/Cap Gemini White Paper.

McKeen, J.D. and Smith, H. (2003). Making IT Happen: Critical issues in IT management, Chichester, Hoboken, NJ: Wiley.

Reich, B. and I. Benbasat (2000). "Factors that influence the social dimension of alignment between business and information technology objectives." MIS quarterly 24(1): 81-113.

Ross, J.W., Weil, P. & Robertson, D.C., 2006, Enterprise architecture as strategy: Creating a foundation for business execution, Harvard Business School Press.

Sauer and Yetton (1997) (eds.) Steps to the Future: Fresh thinking on the management of IT-based organizational transformation, 1st edn, San Francisco: Jossey-Bass, pp. 1–21.

Tallon, P. P., & Kraemer, K. L. (2003). Investigating the relationship between strategic alignment and IT business value: the discovery of a paradox. (N. Shin, Ed.)Business, 12, 1–22.

Tallon, P. P., & Pinsonneault, A. (2011). Competing perspectives on the link between strategic information technology alignment and organizational agility: insights from a mediation model. MIS Quarterly, 35(2), 463–486.

Thatcher, M. E., & Pingry, D. E. (2007). Modeling the IT value paradox. Communications of the ACM, 50(8), 41–45.

Watson, B. P. (2007). Is Strategic Alignment Still a Priority? CIO Insight, (86), 36–39.

Weick, K. E. (2001). Making Sense of the Organization. Blackwell Publishing, Malden, MA.

Weiss, J.W. and D. Anderson (2004) Aligning Technology and Business Strategy: Issues & Frameworks, A Field Study of 15 Companies. Proceedings 37th Hawaii International Conference on System Sciences.

Part 1

Enterprise Architecture and Systems Thinking

Positioning Enterprise Architecture as a Strategic Discipline in Organizations

Sally Bean

Abstract

Enterprise Architecture has the potential to integrate many different aspects of business design, and Systems Practice can play a significant role in extending EA modeling capability to help achieve this aim. It can also help to shift the current rather mechanistic practice of EA in a direction that allows for the more organic approach to change that is required in today's increasingly complex environment. This chapter describes the limitations of the architecture metaphor when applied too rigidly to organizations, looks at the value and applicability of more systemic metaphors, and presents a simple model to help position EA as a strategic discipline that facilitates the design, planning and delivery of business change in a way that enhances the long-term viability of the organization.

Keywords

Enterprise Architecture, Business Design, Strategic Planning, Organization Design, Mental Models, Organizational Metaphors

Enterprise Architecture is in a State of Transition

Enterprise Architecture is an emerging discipline that aspires to improve enterprise coherence, yet is itself often perceived as incoherent. There is frequent confusion over its meaning, purpose and scope, and also the role of the EA function within organizations.

The majority of EA efforts to date have been directed at organizing IT systems from an enterprise-wide perspective, ensuring that these are both adaptable and consistent with business strategy. However, it's becoming increasingly difficult to separate thinking about 'IT' from thinking about 'business', since information systems and technology are increasingly interwoven into business activity in complex ways. So there is an opportunity for EA to help understand how to tie together all the different facets of change (e.g. strategy, process, behavior, information, technology) and consider wider, longer-term issues in the interests of long-term viability.

These advanced aspirations for EA are ambitious and challenging, given the current state of EA practice, and many EA teams currently struggle to demonstrate the value of their efforts. They may fail to achieve the right degree of business involvement, may be out of touch with what's happening on the ground, and can be viewed as barriers to progress, rather than enablers of change. Relatively few people have the skills, experience and behavioral qualities required to be effective in this role. The models and diagrams produced by EA teams may not be effectively promulgated and are not always appropriate or easily consumable by their intended audiences. Often several iterations of EA programs are required before an organization finds an approach that works effectively in its particular context.

However, some EA groups are starting to execute this more comprehensive form of EA and are delivering real value to their organizations. They have a broad understanding of their business and its external influences, what information systems and technologies are capable of doing, and a varied repertoire of useful models and frameworks to structure discussion about business changes such as product/service innovation or organizational restructuring. As Patrick Hoverstadt points out in his chapter, the time now seems right to help executives appreciate and exploit the potential of EA as a strategic 'meta-discipline' that can enable better-informed and more coordinated enterprise change.

The most significant challenge to establishing a more comprehensive approach to EA is making the key concepts and ideas understandable and accessible to a wider range of stakeholders. The reality is that there are already numerous specialists in and around organizations who contribute to performance improvement and business change in different ways, working in fields like Organizational Development, Operational Research or Business Process Management. So this extended form of EA must support trans-disciplinary work by providing a common frame of reference to help these groups to work together more coherently to achieve more than they could do by working independently. It is not about usurping their roles or absorbing all of them into a centralized planning department. It requires the organization as a whole to carefully examine its current business change capabilities and then explore the concept of enterprise architecture as a vehicle for creating coherence; what it means for that organization, whether it's appropriate, how it might make a difference, and who contributes to it.

A second challenge is that of extending EA modeling and design capability to encompass truly coherent business and IT change. This is where Systems Practice can play a significant role, as described by Hoverstadt, and it is not surprising that some EA practitioners are starting to pick up on its potential. Like EA, Systems Practice values a holistic perspective and creates a variety of models to understand inter-relationships and consider how situations are likely to evolve over time. It utilizes natural laws such as feedback and requisite variety as basic principles of design and can help to highlight information needed in support of decision-making and action. Techniques such as Systems Dynamics, Soft Systems Methodology and the Viable Systems Model provide tools that can be used to:

- reason about conditions in the real world from a range of perspectives
- provide reference models against which organizational elements can be mapped and their inter-relationships understood
- provide a basis for planning information systems

Finally, some people perceive EA as being mechanistic and unwieldy and it may not be a good fit with the cultural and political environment of the organization, though it may work effectively in more structured fields such as manufacturing and logistics.

Strengths and Weaknesses of the 'Architecture' Metaphor

The term 'Enterprise Architecture' is somewhat misleading, since even those people who are part of a business-facing EA team are rarely designing enterprises; they are more likely to be acting in an advisory role, usually through the creation and facilitated exploitation of a structured knowledge base that provides decision support for designing, planning and executing business change in a coherent way.

Existing frameworks and methodologies for EA are generally very conceptual in nature. They don't make it easy for business people to grasp what an 'EA approach' is or how it will benefit them or their organization. So it is not surprising that the 'architecture' metaphor has been deployed quite creatively by many thought-leaders and practitioners to promote EA and its benefits. Considering this metaphor with respect to enterprise, we can see a number of aspects that are very useful. The term Enterprise Architecture became popular after John Zachman developed the Zachman Framework™ empirically from comparing enterprise systems with large complex objects such as buildings and aircraft which can be successfully maintained over a long period of time. The architecture of great buildings can be an inspirational way to communicate the idea of enterprise coherence, contrasting the integrity of an iconic building to the somewhat disjointed way that both customers and employees experience the average business. Layered, modular designs can improve flexibility and agility, not only of IT systems, but also other elements of a business by differentiating areas of stability from areas of change. Enduring models or blueprints can enable the visualization of different perspectives by key stakeholders and help manage business and technology evolution in a more controlled way.

Insights into the design of enterprises can be drawn from the work of architects such as Christopher Alexander (1979) who has inspired much interest with his work on architectural patterns and Stewart Brand, whose book 'How Buildings Learn ' (Brand 1994) describes how the architecture embodied in some buildings allows them to change and evolve gracefully over their lifetime.

However, metaphors can also 'conceal as much as they reveal' (Lakoff and Johnson 2003) and it's easy to identify ways in which the architecture metaphor breaks down. Enterprises have important physical differences from buildings. Enterprises are complex, geographically distributed collections of tangible elements (e.g. products, equipment and facilities), and less tangible ones, (e.g. relationships and brands) which are brought to life by people. The relationship of a building with its environment is relatively stable and well-understood, unlike that of an enterprise, which is increasingly part of a complex organizational ecosystem as activities and processes are outsourced, and customers are increasingly drawn into more complex interactions through the proliferation of channels and consumer devices.

The role of the architect is very different in the case of a building, with a clear separation between the client as owner of a relatively well-understood need, and the architect as an expert in the art and science of building design. There's a very different dynamic in the current field of EA. Many people currently occupying the EA role tend to be more like draughtsmen, map-makers, or planners than designers, while some business leaders may already be natural enterprise architects who have mastered the art of creating and refining new business models and orchestrating all the resources of their organization to support their vision. Buildings do not have the same dimension of human complexity as enterprises, since the people who use the building are not seen as part of the building. Nor do buildings exchange information with each other or exhibit the rapid dynamics of change in the way that enterprises do.

So we can see that, while the idea of architecture has a lot to offer enterprises, it's important not to stretch the metaphor too far, as the comparison with physical objects will become less relevant as organizations become more networked and/or digitized. In particular, it's important to distinguish architecture from engineering. Architecture is concerned with overall purpose, conceptual integrity, style and structure. It tends to focus on critical structural elements and the relationships that really matter. In addition to these, engineering is concerned with ensuring that all the different elements fit together properly and that they function as expected to meet a particular set of requirements.

It may be realistic to 'architect' an enterprise, but it is not realistic to 'engineer' one. The engineering metaphor assumes that an enterprise functions like a machine and is made up of interchangeable parts. This has significant limitations. 'Mechanistically structured organizations have great difficulty adapting to changing circumstances because they are designed to achieve predetermined goals, they are not designed for innovation' (Morgan, 1997). Any business has to be able to strike the right balance between adaptation and execution. Adaptation typically places greater emphasis on the social architecture of an enterprise, which cannot be engineered in a mechanistic way. Most current EA practice does not address the social aspects of organizations, since the scope of the role has been historically oriented more towards rational, ordered analysis of business issues, although this is starting to change.

Morgan describes the strengths and weaknesses of several other metaphors, and shows how applying different metaphors in turn to view organizations can help to generate insights while avoiding the traps and limitations of taking individual metaphors too far. Two of these metaphors provide valuable insights on how the biological world and systems theory can help us to think about organizations in a way that supports effective adaptation.

The 'Organization as Organism' metaphor considers organizations as living entities which are part of an ecosystem. Viewing organizations in this way reduces emphasis on pre-determined goals, and increases emphasis on understanding the current landscape and adapting organically to changes in the environment. This way of looking at the world suggests that a degree of diversity to handle external complexities is beneficial, rather than undesirable. Processes are not necessarily linear sequences of well-understood activities with predictable results, but may be ongoing activities aimed at achieving whatever is necessary to ensure survival. Within organizations, the needs and motivations of individuals should be considered along with the interplay between them and technology.

The 'Organization as Brain' metaphor is also based on biology, but this time looks at what we can learn from the work of cyberneticians, based on how the brain and central nervous system process information, apply intuition, handle complexity, and develop learning capability. The key ideas of value that emerge from this perspective are distribution of decision-making, feedback, double-loop learning, early detection of trends and patterns, and the ability to reach out into the environment and develop 'new ways of seeing', in order to create insight and knowledge. This way of looking at the world suggests that some redundancy of function is desirable to create space for learning and self-organization to occur.

Current EA practice (and indeed much management theory) is predicated on an assumption that organizations would be more effective if they operated like machines and exhibited a greater degree of order. This is unlikely to be true in a rapidly changing world that is becoming more networked and diverse. The reality is that organizations need to be able to deploy a richer set of ways of looking at how they operate in order to get the balance right between execution and adaptability. While the architecture metaphor is helpful to promote the key ideas of coherence, EA needs to adopt some of other approaches from systems and complexity science in order to ensure that the resulting organization can survive in the long term. As Hoverstadt has indicated, this requires a change to the way that enterprise architects approach modeling. We also need a simple model of the enterprise to help us explore how EA can be positioned as a business discipline (and not just a departmental function).

A Simple Model of Enterprise Activity Types

Some systems practitioners draw an important distinction between ontological models of a reasonably well-understood domain that purport to represent parts of the 'real world', and epistemological models that are used to explore perceptions of the real world (Checkland 2004). Ontological models require the application of extensive domain knowledge and modeling expertise. Epistemological models are not necessarily models of actual reality and have limited predictive capability. They are conceptual illustrations, designed to support discussion, debate and argument about people's perceptions of reality, where the real nature of the problems to be tackled is unclear. Such a process can be very valuable, as otherwise, 'mental models slide undetected into discussions and then dominate the way that managers think about their situation' (Hoverstadt 2008).

EA is currently subject to many such assumptions, many of them stemming from the metaphorical considerations described above. Figure 1 provides a very simple epistemological model of how a business operates and changes over time.

This is designed to help understand the potential role of EA within organizations, based on the author's extensive practical experience as a business systems architect and consultant. (Here, the term enterprise is taken to be roughly equivalent to organization. Some authors (e.g. Graves 2009) assert with justification that there are differences between the two terms, but they are not too significant in this context. Public sector organizations, while not businesses, can also be conceptualized in a similar way). While there are many management models available in business literature, most of them are either too complicated for this purpose, or have significant limitations (e.g. Porter's Value Chain does not handle the activities related to innovation and learning particularly well, and is restricted in its applicability to more production-oriented organizations).

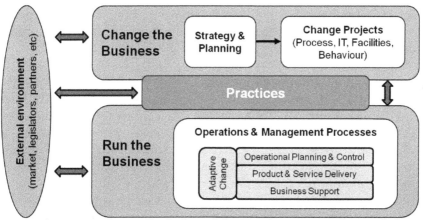

Figure 1. Epistemological model of business operation and change.

The model in Figure 1 is intended to enable a discussion about the balance and interplay between different key types of activity in an organization. It makes no assumptions about how the activities are resourced, so should not be in any sense regarded as an organizational design model and the same people can participate in many different types of activity. It also makes no assumptions about the balance between IT-related activity and other business activity, which are assumed to be woven together as required. The model has some similarities to the Viable System Model (Beer), including being fractal in nature, so it could be applied at different levels in the organization. We will start by describing it independently of enterprise architecture and then use it to discuss how EA's contribution could be maximized in a particular context.

Firstly, the model distinguishes between 'Changing the Business' (through strategy/change portfolio definition and projects) and 'Running the Business' (the activities the business does routinely, including planning, control and operational change).

'Running the Business' activities are generally reasonably well understood and readily describable. They may be viewed as linked sets of processes (e.g. manufacturing or logistics) or as configurations of capabilities (e.g. military organizations or professional services firms) or a mixture of these. The activities required to solve operational problems or make minor changes are also included here. One goal of EA should be to make the 'Running the Business' activities and the IT to support them more inherently adaptive and thus reduce the need for large-scale project-based change.

'Changing the Business' is concerned with the less repeatable types of activity that are about setting a new direction for the organization, responding to significant problems, or instigating changes that require significant investment and coordination. This activity must be informed by sufficient knowledge of the 'Running the Business' activities. It further subdivides into:-

- Strategy & Planning (upstream change), which are somewhat loosely-defined episodic activities that explore the current business environment and performance, identify actions to respond to these or influence them, and draw up and resource plans for implementing them. Administratively, some of these activities may be run as projects, but they are different from the kinds of downstream projects that have clear scope and outcomes.
- Change Projects (downstream change), which are the activities that actually deliver the change into the organization (e.g. product and service innovation, procedural change, behavioral change, workplace change or information system change). They may be routine or very complicated. Some may be of a more experimental nature. Most projects will follow some kind of methodological framework in search of agreed outcomes, within agreed constraints, but will not be as structured, predictable and

repeatable as processes that have well defined trigger points, outcomes, and sequencing.

The final type of activity in this model is that of 'Practices', which are those activities, often less visible and of an adhoc nature, that are dedicated to the accumulation and dispersion of specialist knowledge required by people in the enterprise and continuous incremental improvement to the way that it works (Brown & Duguid 2002). As already mentioned, a balance needs to be struck between making the 'Running the Business' activities efficient and lean on the one hand, and on the other hand making them flexible to change, which requires a degree of learning and adaptiveness. 'Space' therefore needs to be made available in the organization for this activity. Practices may be formal or informal, and may occur within departmental groups, explicit communities of practice, or loose networks. Some of these groups retain their knowledge in a relatively closed community (e.g. salespeople); others may disperse their knowledge to other people in the organization to help them do their jobs more effectively (e.g. an HR person having an informal conversation with a manager about staff development); others may share interest across functions in a particular methodology (e.g. Lean). Practices can be cross-organizational and have fuzzy boundaries. They tend to generate specialized forms of language that require explanation and translation to make sense to people outside the group. Social media tools have the potential to help practices become more visible and effective.

All of these activities have many interactions with external entities outside the organization and with each other.

Positioning EA's Contribution Strategically Within Organizations

Enterprise Architecture is instantiated in an organization in a variety of ways. It can equally be viewed as a process, a practice, a strategic knowledge base and a departmental unit (or units), but fundamentally it is a vehicle for improving both agility and coherence at the same time.

Without EA, the following problems are commonplace:

- Lack of understanding about how the business actually works
- Inadequate information for strategic and operational decision-making
- Inability to optimize project investments in line with strategy
- Lack of awareness of conflicts and disconnects in business activity and in projects

- Adoption of an incomplete set of tactics for change, that only focus on one aspect of a problem
- Inability to identify critical requirements and interfaces in IT systems, leading to delay or failure
- IT systems that are inflexible

An organizational design for an EA function to address these problems needs to instigate EA practices and processes by considering the following questions, among others:

1. What is the primary purpose of EA in this organization?

2. What is the interplay between EA, Strategy and Portfolio Management? How well do we understand the current business? What new processes and responsibilities need to be established in order to create a future-oriented high-level business system design?

3. How will this EA content be used to initiate, govern and enable project delivery?

4. What can other practices contribute to the development and management of EA?

Initially, significant effort will need to be devoted to EA practice development, but this should always be balanced with active engagement in activities that add more direct value to management decision-making and project delivery.

Ideally, in future, EA will be positioned as a discipline that brings a new dimension to the design of organizations within Strategy and Planning and supports continuous organizational change through facilitating the sharing of models and information across other practices. There are 3 strands of activity, each of which may have behavioral, procedural, information and technology elements:-

- A Prescriptive strand – determining, agreeing and promulgating fundamental design principles, policies and standards in support of organizational strategies, risk reduction and key performance characteristics. These are developed as part of strategy work and then applied downstream to relevant decision-making in business/IT development projects and business operations. In this sense EA is partly a design activity and partly a governance activity.
- A Descriptive strand – creating an aligned set of models that define key elements of the business, its information systems and its technologies and managing these in such a way that the

relationships and dependencies between these different elements can be clearly understood. These models, at least to start with, are broad in scope and shallow in detail though can be elaborated further by specific change projects. They can be used to generate scenarios to facilitate understanding of what is involved in business or IT change and provide a common starting point for new business or IT development projects. Such models may also have practical utility in day-to-day business operations, as tools for training, or supporting business processes in other ways. An IT-focused EA group will also provide standards and patterns for project teams to exploit. In this sense, EA is partly a design activity and partly a knowledge management activity

- A Programmatic strand - designing a target state architecture and identifying and coordinating the significant projects, investments, commitments, and milestones needed to move towards it, including the development of core 'building blocks' that can be shared across different projects and the partition of work into manageable chunks where the interdependencies and risks are understood and optimized. In this sense EA is a planning and coordination activity. In some organizations, a portfolio management function fulfills this role, but architecture provides an essential tool to guide it.

The above categorization can usefully be applied to individual EA deliverables, many of which may need to contain elements of all three types of information. In addition to formal content that is stored in structured repositories, more narrative and visually appealing explanations of the architecture will also be essential in order to gain better understanding and appreciation of what it offers.

EA must also guide and support change projects, and the exact way in which this is achieved is very dependent on the specific organizational context. The most important guiding principles to consider are that EA should ensure that the right projects are initiated, establish favorable starting conditions and then facilitate them rather than hinder them. This means having appropriate EA engagement with architecturally significant projects and ensuring that more routine ones can exploit architectural assets, where available.

Conclusion

Enterprise Architecture must support an organization's requirement to adapt and innovate, as well as to execute. It is a non-linear process with wide participation that defines a coherent plan for business and IT change, that's appropriate to the business context and allows for experimentation and adaptation. Enterprise architects in organizations can become facilitators of this process through applying systems approaches and coordinating the maintenance of models and other knowledge assets. They can design multi-disciplinary participative processes, drawing on external ideas and a wide range of skills from different parts of the enterprise to identify patterns of behavior, explore different mental models and develop shared ones. They can develop a customized framework for managing and maintaining the strategic knowledge assets which are appropriate for the organization's context and maturity in EA. For this to be successful, the choice of knowledge assets must be carefully made, mindful of the effort required to maintain them, the importance of communicating them, and getting feedback. This needs to be treated as an iterative learning process, which evolves in the light of experience and changing priorities.

About the Author

Sally Bean is an independent Enterprise Architecture consultant. She advises large organizations in the private and public sector on how to develop their EA capability and embed EA approaches into their ways of working. She has 20 years experience in the field, with 10 years as a member of the EA team in British Airways. Here she championed many successful initiatives to improve processes, exploit technology and share data and applications more effectively across the organization. She also led a successful Architecture Community of Practice. She is particularly interested in systems thinking and complexity approaches and their applicability to enterprise architecture, as well as the human side of enterprise architecture.

References

Alexander, C. 1979. The Timeless Way of Building. New York, Oxford University Press

Brand, S. 1997 How Buildings Learn: What Happens After They're Built. London, Phoenix

Brown, J.S and P. Duguid 2002. The Social Life of Information. Boston, Mass., Harvard Business School

Checkland, P., Holwell, S. 2004. "Classic" OR and "Soft OR – an asymmetric complementarity. In Systems Modelling Theory and Practice. M Pidd (ed), Chichester, Wiley

Graves, T. 2009. Doing enterprise architecture: Process and practice in the real enterprise. Colchester, Tetradian Books

Hoverstadt, P. 2008. The Fractal Organization: Creating Sustainable Organizations with the Viable System Model. Hoboken, N.J., Wiley

Lakoff, G and Johnson, M 2003. Metaphors we live by. Chicago, Ill. ; London, University of Chicago Press

Kurtz. C.F. and Snowden, D.J. (2003), "The new dynamics of strategy: Sense-making in a complex and complicated world", IBM Systems Journal, Volume 42, Number 3, 46

Morgan, G. 1997. Images of Organization. Thousand Oaks, Calif., London, Sage

Enterprise Architecture in a Systemic Context

Tue Westmark Steensen

Abstract

The connection between Enterprise Architecture (EA) and Systems Theory is examined to determine in what way systems theory can contribute epistemologically to the discipline of EA. Parallels are discovered between modes of thinking in systems theory and EA, and the two disciplines are found to have a common holistic core. This leads to seeing both systems theory and EA as moving away from the reductionism dominating much of western philosophy and science, and instead as an operationalization of the holism of Aristotle. With the Aristotelian philosophical link between systems theory and EA established, its practical applications and possible future developments are examined.

Keywords

Enterprise Architecture, Systems Theory, Viable Systems Model, VSM, Complexity, Holism

Enterprise Architecture in a Systemic Context

It is the purpose of this chapter to examine what common ground the two academic disciplines of Enterprise Architecture (EA) and systems theory share, and how systems theory can contribute to the practice of EA. In the context of this chapter, systems theory is used as a wide term encompassing both formalized systemic models and systems thinking. It is also seen as closely tied to cybernetics, because of the mark made by the two disciplines on each other, which comes to expression in the scientists occupied with them.

One such academic is Stafford Beer who created the theory of the Viable Systems Model (VSM) (Beer 1981) and linked cybernetics and systems theory together. Another example is the cybernetician W. R. Ashby who stated the Law of Requisite Variety (Ashby 1957) and also influenced the work of Stafford Beer. The ideas of these men have further inspired a newer systems thinker and consultant by the name of Patrick Hoverstadt, who has applied the theories in practice and presented his method and results in the book The Fractal Organization. Hoverstadt's book, along with the work of Stafford Beer, has been the gateway of this author to systems theory and will as such be at the heart of the chapter.

In the systemic frame of reference of these academics, the organization is a system enveloped by an environment. This system can be divided into smaller systems and unified into larger ones. This frame is an objective one, in the sense that organizations are not judged as being "right" or "wrong". They simply are, and should be analyzed as such. Stafford Beer expresses it clearly with the following words:

> *"According to the cybernetician the purpose of a system is what it does. This is a basic dictum. It stands for bald fact, which makes a better starting point in seeking understanding than the familiar attributions of good intention, prejudices about expectations, moral judgment or sheer ignorance of circumstances." (Beer 2002)*

Another key issue in Beer's and Hoverstadt's systems approach, which is also expressed in the previous quote, is the understanding of the system. If one does not understand the system, one is not capable of leading it and much less of changing it with any kind of certainty or predictability. This leads to part of the foundation for the necessity of Beer's VSM; complexity. This is closely connected with the field of systems theory dismissing simple causal explanations as the root of problems, viewing them instead as part of the system, and thus not created randomly and unpredictably, but instead as a consequence of the structure of the system.

In this context complexity is not only viewed as a problem, but also as the very premise for a solution. An explanation of this and of how complexity must be balanced is given by Hoverstadt. He shows how the organization first attenuates the complexity of the environment, e.g. the market, by for example dividing customers into distinct groups. Then the complexity of the organization is attenuated by management, for example by introducing middle managers or merging units. However, as Ashby's Law of Requisite Variety teaches, only variety can absorb variety, and thus the system needs a way of increasing variety as well, in order to be able to balance the complexity of system and environment. This is done by the organization through amplifying its complexity, for example through new products or strategic partners and by management, for example by increasing the autonomy of the organization. The goal is for the system to constantly match the complexity of the environment (Hoverstadt 2008).

It is also this systemic structure which Beer's VSM concerns itself with. His is a universalistic model in the sense that Beer, even though his focus is on enterprises, also mentions animals, computers and economies, as complex systems which the VSM can handle (Beer 1981). The model consists of an environment and a system, which in turn consists of five subsystems; operations, coordination, delivery (including monitoring), development and policy. The names and characteristics of these subsystems are not random, but instead the very elements which make it possible for the system to observe and adapt. One example of this adaptation is the ability of the system to send output to the environment via operations, and receive input back through development. The system can then act on the input received and change its output to the environment in accordance with this, thus allowing the system to continuously match the complexity of the environment. This constant balancing of complexity is what helps the system attain viability – the purpose of Beer's VSM.

In stark contrast to the single purpose of VSM, stands EA, partly because this discipline is characterized by what can be seen as a series of different paradigms, with differing understandings of EA. One of these is the very IT-centric paradigm, which is expressed by for example Ross, Weill and Robertson in their book Enterprise Architecture as Strategy (Ross, Weill and Robertson 2006) and by Wagter et al. in their book Dynamic Enterprise Architecture (Wagter, et al. 2005). Another example of what can be viewed as a paradigm is the equally business and IT oriented mode of thinking advocated by Scott Bernard, exemplified by the formula: "Enterprise Architecture = Strategy + Business + Technology" (Bernard 2005). The third and last to be mentioned here is also the newest and most radical of the three, with consultant Chris Potts being one of the proponents (Potts 2008). His is an almost purist account, in which EA becomes a verb and is seen literally as enterprise architecting. Here the role of the architect is to support management in developing the enterprise, from his or her place in a staff function as close to the CEO as possible.

Having summarized the two disciplines it is now possible to begin contemplating their common ground and thereby how EA can be better understood through systems theory. One aspect shared by both disciplines is a common mindset regarding organizational comprehension. Hoverstadt considers how it is necessary to change organizational models of the enterprise from tacit to explicit and shared, in order to be able to lead and change the enterprise (Hoverstadt 2008). The same way of thinking can be recognized within EA, where work is done based on the realization, made by among others Zachman, that reality has become so complex that a meta model is needed in order to see dependencies (Zachmann 1987). Thus in this frame of reference both disciplines can be seen as having a holistic way of thinking in systems and analyzing them.

When looking at EA in a pure VSM-context, specifically concerning the previously mentioned balancing of complexity, one attains an understanding of the justification of EA as a tool for the handling of complexity. This especially applies to attenuation; reducing complexity, in order to make it more manageable for the decision makers of the enterprise. There are, however, differences in which kinds of complexity can be handled, depending on which understanding of EA the view on complexity is based on. One example of this would be the "EA = IT" stance, here the central issue would be complexity in things such as IT-systems and technical, information, and application architecture. Systems theory on the other hand, at least from Stafford Beer's point of view, focuses primarily on systemic complexity consisting of organizations, units, individuals, power, etc. The difference between these two viewpoints is apparent; the first view sees complexity primarily in hard systems, the second in soft systems. But if one exchanges the IT paradigm with Bernard's methodology, parallels are somewhat easier drawn, due to his focus on not only IT, but also lines of business, strategy and processes. The comparison is all the more interesting because Scott Bernard himself lists systems theory as one of the academic influences on EA (Bernard 2005).

Pointing out the different focuses of these two disciplines is in no way a critique of either of them. Instead it is a recognition of the fact that EA can diagnose and solve problems which systems theory is incapable of – and vice versa. This beckons the question of whether not the universalism of for example the VSM, is paid for with the inability to deal with problems of the organization at a more detailed level, such as business processes or IT-systems in an enterprise-context. It is equally worth consideration, whether the broader focus of EA contributes to the fact that there so far are no universal frameworks, such as the VSM. There are, however, signs that this may change, as CEO and enterprise architect Patrick Turner among others has expressed the need for a synthesis of the large body of EA frameworks (Turner 2010).

While systems theory applies itself very directly with complex causal relations, it is not something which is explicitly formulated in the same way within the EA discipline. There is however much to gain by adopting such a mind-set, regardless of which approach to EA one is a proponent for. This even though the systemic way of thinking is particularly eligible in those places where the focus of EA is more closely connected to the focus of the VSM, such as with the EA approaches of Scott Bernard or Chris Potts. No matter the approach to EA and whether it is viability, coherence, alignment, agility or something else which is promised as the prize, then it is still paramount to be able to handle complexity, if one desires the capability to deliver consistent and reliable results. And thus the systemic way of thinking comes into its own.

Taking a step back in the observation of the two disciplines and disregarding the differences evident up close, it seems clear that there still is something fundamentally the same. Something which connects the two disciplines more than it divides them. There is in systems theory and EA a shared purpose of wanting to create an overview of the connections and dependencies, born out of the increasing complexity of the world. The best examples available stem from the system models of systems theory and from the very basis for using frameworks in EA. Here can the dawning understanding be seen that there out of the complexity of a system can emerge something more, than if the system is divided and each part is considered separately. This is a viewpoint not only seen in systems theory and EA, but also in a strand of sociology called structural functionalism, formulated by sociologist Talcott Parsons, who sought to explain how social systems function (Parsons 1951). Interestingly enough Parsons also formulated a model for understanding organizational structure (Parsons 1960), which Scott Bernard later utilized by relating it to his EA3 Cube in order to better explain the structure of the enterprise and of his framework (Bernard 2005).

These preceding viewpoints stand opposite to the reductionism, which among others the philosopher, mathematician, and physicist René Descartes, was a key protagonist for and which has permeated western philosophy to a very high degree. One example of his viewpoint on complex systems, exemplified here with the human body, is that:

> *"if one knew well all the parts of the seed of a particular animal –*
> *man, for example - one could deduce from that alone, by reasons*
> *entirely mathematical and certain, the whole figure and*

conformation of each of its members" (Descartes, R. 1648. Description du corpse humain. Refered from Des Chene 2001)

These words show how the organismic is reduced to the mechanistic – a reduction which has spread to also be applied on organizations. The consequence of this is that complex systems within the frame of reference of Descartes, are seen as being nothing but the sum of their parts, and as such being fully explainable on the basis of their subsystems viewed separately.

The systemic mindset portrayed throughout this chapter, which dictates that this is not the case, is thus a break with reductionism and the simplification of the reality within organizations. This is however no new thought, but merely a return to a holism, which was already articulated by Aristotle in classical antiquity. In one of his works titled Metaphysica, he presents his thoughts on the relationship between part and whole, and states: "In the case of all things which have several parts and in which the totality is not, as it were, a mere heap, but the whole is something beside the parts" (W. D. Ross 1953). This statement along with the overall message of Aristotle's Metaphysica is often popularly summarized as being that the whole is more than the sum of its parts. This is an understanding quite similar to the previously mentioned one of systems theory and EA; that the contemplation of the whole of a system divulges more, than if it is divided and each part is considered by itself.

To return from antiquity to the purpose with which this chapter began, it can now be seen how systems theory contributes to EA the understanding of a shared common core rooted in holism. It is this core which leads from systems theory and EA back to Aristotle, because it shows us the underlying possibility for insight, which the two disciplines offer. Namely the fact that a system as a whole is more than the elements it can be divided into. Consequently it is through a kind of operationalization of Aristotle that the value promised by EA and systems theory is created. It is however only that; a promise and it can only be fulfilled if we as architects understand why we do EA, why it is important; because it gives us the whole, instead of just the parts.

Establishing the philosophical connection between systems theory and EA is one thing however, with the practical application and exploitation of this knowledge being entirely another matter. That being said, concrete examples of utilizing systems theory within EA do exist. One such is the Systemic Enterprise Architecture Methodology (SEAM), developed by Professor Alain Wegmann. Here systems theory is used as a theoretical foundation for EA and as a support in improving understanding of enterprise architects of the existing methodologies (Wegmann 2003). This allows for understanding the enterprise in the context of its environment and as a hierarchy of systems, thereby supporting IT-development in an enterprise-wide context (Wegmann, Regev, et al. 2007).

Systems theory spans wider than this though, and holds many methods not customized for EA unlike SEAM, which nonetheless are extremely useful. One example of this from the author's own experience is Stafford Beer's previously mentioned Viable Systems Model. In hands-on use it is a powerful tool for the EA practitioner, providing him or her with a much more advanced organizational analysis, than one could hope to achieve with a more traditional method. It is highly effective in locating problems with for example coordination or autonomy in the enterprise, both very crucial factors for the success of business process standardization and similar enterprise-encompassing initiatives. Such a proposition alone should be ample argument for the use of systems theory by practitioners of EA.

In contemplating my own experiences together with the now established link between EA and systems theory, I myself am convinced that it will only increase in strength and relevance in the future. I base this belief on two things. Firstly on the fact that more and more enterprise architects are moving from an IT-understanding towards a more "businessy" understanding of the enterprise, a development which according to the consultant company Gartner is already well underway (Burton and Allega 2011). Secondly on my own experience from tutoring and supervising "To Be" enterprise architects as a teaching assistant at the IT-University of Copenhagen. There I see more and more students not with a technical background, but with a background in the social sciences or humanities, and not exclusively focused on either business or IT, but instead on the link between them.

About the Author

At the time of writing Tue Westmark Steensen was a master student at the IT University of Copenhagen attending John Gøtze's Enterprise Architecture Program. Today Tue Westmark Steensen works as an enterprise architect and IT policy consultant for the Municipality of Copenhagen. He holds a BA in Library and Information Science from the Danish Royal School of Library and Information Science and an MSc in IT and Business from the IT University of Copenhagen.

References

Ashby, W. R. An Introduction To Cybernetics. London: Chapman & Hall, 1957.

Beer, Stafford. Brain of the firm. Whiley, 1981.

—. "What is Cybernetics?" Kybernetes, 2002: 209-219.

Bernard, Scott. An Introduction to Enterprise Architecture EA3. Linking Business and Technology. 2nd edition. AuthorHouse, 2005.

Burton, Betsy, and Philip Allega. Beyond the Tipping Point: EA Is Strateguc. Stamford: Gartner, 2011.

Des Chene, D. Spirits & Clocks : Machine & Organism in Descartes. New York: Cornelle University, 2001.

Doucet, G, J Gøtze, P Saha, and S Bernard. Coherency Management : Architecting the Enterprise for Alignment, Agility, and Assurance. AuthorHouse, 2009.

Hoverstadt, Patrick. The Fractal Organization : Creating Sustainable Organizations with the Viable Systems Model. Chichester, West Sussex: John Wiley & Sons, 2008.

Parsons, Talcott. Structure and Process in Modern Societies. Glencoe: The Free Press, 1960.

—. The Social System. London: Routledge & Kegan Paul Ltd., 1951.

Potts, Chris. "Enterprise Architecture Driving Business Innovation - Time to Break Out of IT." GEAO Journal of Enterprise Architecture Extract, no. 3 (1) (Marts 2008).

Ross, J. W., P. Weill, and D. C. Robertson. Enterprise Architecture As Strategy. Harvard Business Press, 2006.

Ross, W. D. Aristotle's Metaphysics. Vol. VIII. XIV vols. 1953.

Turner, Patrick. "Presentation on Next-Gen EA." Idre Fjäll Enterprise Architecture Student Conference. Idre Fjäll, 3 August 2010.

Wagter, Roel, Martin van den Berg, Joost Luijpers, and Marlies van Steenbergen. Dynamic Enterprise Architecture. John Wiley and Sons, 2005.

Wegmann, Alain. "On The Systemic Enterprise Architecture Methodology." International Conference on Enterprise Information Systems. Angers: EPFL/LAMS & ICEIS, 2003.

Wegmann, Alain, Gil Regev, Irina Rychkova, Lam-Son Lê, José Diego De La Cruz, and Philippe Julia. "Business and IT Alignment with SEAM for Enterprise Architecture." The 11th IEEE International EDOC Conference. Annapolis: EDOC, 2007.

Zachmann, J. A. "A framework for information systems architecture." IBM Systems Journal, 1987: 276-292.

Enterprise Architecture and EA Governance:

A Stratified Systems Approach

Janne J. Korhonen

Abstract

Increasingly complex business environments require sophisticated sense-making and behavior at all scales. This chapter investigates how the increasing complexity of business at all levels renders the traditional approach to Enterprise Architecture and its governance inadequate. Enterprise Architecture can longer be conceived as embracing mere IT architecture. Instead, Enterprise Architecture must be viewed as an encompassing aspect-system integrally intertwined with the overall design of the enterprise, which, holistically and systemically governed, enables more strategic, more effective, and more resilient enterprise engineering and – as a result – an improved capability to manage business change. As a consequence, Enterprise Architecture Governance must be conceptualized as a cross-sectional overlay, which distributes pertinent EA-related decision-making rights in the organization to a maximum degree. This change, the author argues, is crucial in order to make space for endogenous emergence of new ideas, creativity, and behaviors in order to increase the speed of adaption as well as to deploy principles of agile self-organization within the co-evolving business ecosystem.

Keywords

Systems thinking, enterprise architecture, governance, self-organization, stratification, circular governance, agile governance

Agility Imperative – Need for Enterprise Architecture Governance

The business environment of the 21st century is increasingly complex and characterized by continual change that is unprecedented both in pace and magnitude. Global competition and co-operation call for networked business ecosystems that pull together co-specialized capabilities in a nonlinear fashion, eliminating time and distance. In the increasingly interconnected and global world, discontinuities in the form of technological breakthroughs, new regulations and deregulation, geopolitical upheavals and nature disasters can change the game overnight and force organizations to find ways to reinvent their very essence without falling apart. The organizational systems and structures must be resilient in the face of unexpected and unpredictable changes and events and agile in readjusting to the constantly shifting value proposition of the enterprise.

In the last few decades, information technology has had fundamental consequences in organizations and the society at large: unprecedented computing power, infinity of virtual space and ubiquitous connectivity have presented enormous potential to create enterprise effectiveness, increase flexibility and enable entirely new business models. IT would certainly require more attention from the management than in the past to release this potential, but as Hoogervorst (2009) points out: "when it was possible to involve management heavily with IT developments, there was seemingly less need, and while at the moment there was a need to involve management heavily, it was apparently less possible".

As the vast complexity of the entire business-IT amalgam far exceeds the comprehension of any single individual, it is increasingly important to mediate knowledge and understanding of the underlying organizational system. Enterprise Architecture (EA) and Enterprise Architecture Governance (EAG) are essential vehicles to align the structure with enterprise strategy and to guide architecture-related decision-making, respectively.

Enterprise Architecture (EA) provides a comprehensive representation of the extant status and projected future status of the enterprise in terms of relevant components and their relationships. It is a discipline that addresses how the elements of an organization fit together, today and in the future, and how these elements transition to support the organization's strategic plans. Although enterprise architecture is often limited to an "as-is" description of existing organizational artifacts, its full potential can be unleashed through "to-be" and target views. While the representation alone helps the business decision-makers cope with the complexity, an advanced EA also comes with analytical methods that enable various kinds of impact analyses on hypothetical change scenarios, facilitate capital planning and help sequencing IT development. This is particularly important in dynamic environments, in which the forward-looking aspect of EA is emphasized. The bigger the intended business change, the more sophisticated the way in which the constituent entities and their spatial and temporal relationships should be represented.

Traditionally, the focus of enterprise architecture has been on technology and information systems architectures, but the increasing leverage of business change has recently put a greater emphasis on information and business architectures. Enterprise Architecture, in its recent and more encompassing conceptualization, extends traditional IT architecture with more business-related elements such as organizational goals, products and services, markets, and competitors. EA, as per this view, provides a comprehensive representation of the existing status and projected future status of the business in terms of its relevant components and component relationships. It can be concisely defined as follows (Korhonen et al., 2009):

> *Enterprise Architecture (EA) is a holistic, high-level approach to organizational design description and prescription.*

Whereas established IT governance frameworks define good management processes and control mechanisms for reliable and efficient IT control, they do not adequately address the strategic, forward-looking aspects of Enterprise Architecture. These frameworks tend to maintain the separate and subordinate role that is traditionally bestowed on IT. Consequently, EA is typically managed within the IT function of organizations. It does not have adequate business ownership and involvement, and the potential of EA cannot be fully realized on an enterprise scale.

The increasing complexity at all levels of scale renders the traditional approach to Enterprise Architecture and its governance inadequate. In this chapter, an alternative approach, based on a stratified system approach, is suggested. It is argued that Enterprise Architecture should be conceived as an integral aspect-system of the enterprise, which, holistically and systemically governed, enables more strategic, more effective and more resilient enterprise engineering.

"IT Follows Business" Paradigm Focuses on Short-Term

An enterprise architecture framework provides tools and methods to structure, classify and organize the enterprise architecture through a coherent set of views on relevant EA artifacts and their relationships. Enterprise-class description frameworks distinguish several architecture layers and architecture views to disentangle the vast complexity and to reduce the number of elements per model.

EA frameworks typically recognize three or four architectural dimensions that are used to structure architecture products. These dimensions typically include:

- Business Architecture
- Information Architecture
- Information Systems Architecture
- Technology Architecture

In many cases, these architectural dimensions are viewed as layers of the enterprise architecture, as depicted in Figure 1.

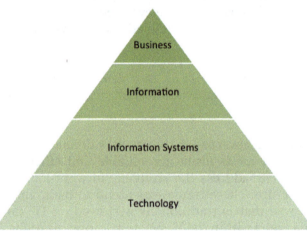

Figure 1. Layering the Enterprise Architecture by architectural dimensions.

The underlying basic assumption in this view is that business needs drive information needs, which drive technology decisions. Business processes and organizational structures follow the strategy, are implemented in and supported by information systems, which, in turn, are supported by technical infrastructure. While this "IT follows business" approach may be useful in categorizing IT assets, it falls short in aligning IT architecture with IT strategy and with business architecture elements. The business architecture may also fail to capture the technology dimension, although high-level IT decisions need to be made in consideration of both business and technology.

The "IT follows business" paradigm actually makes the business-IT divide worse by sharpening the distinction between the two. IT is seen as a separate function, isolated from overall organization and work design, relegated to a subordinate, supporting role that needs to be *aligned* with business. Such language implies support rather than unity: as if IT is asking for a permission to be on the board – or at least on board.

When IT is merely "aligned" with business, the focus of IT is on present-day value realization, cost containment, operational quality and reliability – on producing predictable outcomes on a consistent basis. Variance is eliminated through cascaded goals, metrics and controls that are ultimately passed down to the IT function in a top-down, deterministic manner. This results in sub-functions and sub-systems that have their own goals and ways of working and are challenging to integrate. IT may satisfy all the idiosyncratic and sometimes conflicting business requirements, but does not accommodate any future contingencies. Little consideration is given to IT effectiveness and enablement.

Do Not Turn EA Upside Down – Just 90 Degrees

The traditional approach of layering the Enterprise Architecture by architectural dimensions, as exhibited in Figure 1, does not adequately address higher-level IT considerations such as IT capabilities, systemic competencies, system and project portfolios, or strategic technology platforms. To enable enterprise strategies and (re-)engineering of value, Enterprise Architecture and its governance shall rather be built around natural organizational decision-making levels. Architectural dimensions would thereby be seen as vertical dimensions crossing abstraction levels rather than as forming abstraction levels themselves.

You do not have to turn Enterprise Architecture upside down to make it more effective. By changing the approach just by 90 degrees, as illustrated in Figure 2, the strategic aspects of IT are given due consideration and different facets of the enterprise are coherently co-designed. In its exalted role, technology creates enterprise flexibility and capability to change. The value of IT comes increasingly from how it is used rather than from the technology itself. It is possible to design IT in anticipation of changes, whose exact nature cannot be accurately predicted. The focus on reliability is balanced with focus on validity to create value, not only today, but also in the unfolding near future.

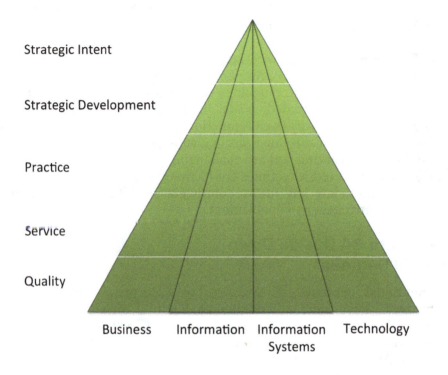

Figure 2. From Layers to Slices: Stratification by Decision-Making Levels.

By redirecting EA dimensions vertically, the inherent abstraction levels within architectural dimensions become more explicitly represented. These dimensions can also be linked laterally. As the same abstraction levels can be used to structure both architectural elements and governance, the ownership and stewardship for different architectural artifacts can be readily assigned to governance roles at respective levels. Also, governance processes can be more easily defined around clearly delineated decision-making and responsibility areas.

Fundamental Work Levels Can Be Identified

Every organization has its unique structure, with an idiosyncratic number of accountability levels. It may seem futile to identify any normative number of organizational levels that would provide a fundamental basis for Enterprise Architecture. However, the late organizational psychologist Elliott Jaques suggested such a prescriptive stratification of organizations. He recognized that organizations exhibit a hierarchical ordering of work complexity that reflects the discontinuous developmental stages in the nature of human capability. His conceptualization of Requisite Organization (Jaques, 1998) prescribes the "requisite" number of levels to organize human work. The role complexity increases in discontinuous steps, stratifying varying kinds of work into natural layers, or "requisite strata", in the organization.

In line with the strata I–V of Requisite Organization, five normative levels can be distinguished to arrange Enterprise Architecture and respective governance. This number of levels is typically requisite (i.e. not too few, not too many) in a self-governing organization such as a middle-size business or an independent business unit of a large corporation that is big and complex enough to warrant a full-fledged Enterprise Architecture. Bioss (formerly the Brunel Institute of Organisation and Social Studies), which has carried out more than 40 years of research based on the work of Elliott Jaques, has coined the following labels to epitomize these levels (McMorland, 2005; Connor and Mackenzie-Smith, 2003):

I.   *Quality*: excellence of task.
II. *Service*: effective coordination, continuous improvement, efficiency.
III. *Practice*: work practices and systems, productivity.
IV. *Strategic Development*: innovation, change and continuity.
V.   *Strategic Intent*: direction, profit, long-term viability.

The approach to and descriptions of the Enterprise Architecture should be in line with the degree of business change that the architecture is purported to support. Figure 3 illustrates how Enterprise Architecture and enterprise engineering are manifested at different levels. At the lowest level, the focus is on IT design and development, whereas the higher levels are increasingly oriented towards business, stratum V being about design and development of the business model of the organization.

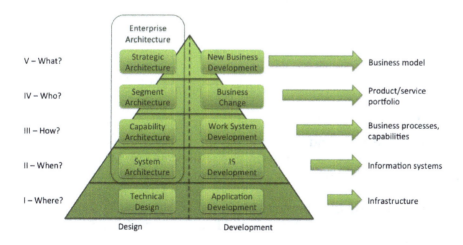

Figure 3. Increasing levers of change call for progressively sophisticated views on EA.

As the problem space faced at each requisite stratum is more complex than at the previous levels, each successive work level also calls for a progressively sophisticated level of cognitive sense-making. Table 1 outlines the cognitive logic that is required at each work level as well as some paradigmatic roles at those levels. The table also exhibits the types of architecture and typical governance vehicles characteristic to each level. The work levels are described in more detail in the sections below.

Table 1. Cognitive logics pertaining to different work levels.

Work Level	Type of Architecture	Governance Vehicles	Paradigmatic Role	Requisite Cognitive Logic
V – Strategic Intent	Strategic Architecture	Norms, relationships, vision	Enterprise Architect	Holistic, dialectical, multi-systemic
IV – Strategic Development	Segment Architecture	Rules, processes, strategic systems	Business Architect	Conscious, deductive, conceptual
III – Practice	Capability Architecture	Policies, structures	Solution Architect	Generalizing, abstracting, analytical
II – Service	System Architecture	Practices, standards	IT System Architect	Conjunctive, coordinative, inductive
I – Quality	Technical Design	Activities	IT System Engineer	Disjunctive, declarative, concrete, factual

I – Quality

The output of design and implementation work at this lowest level is clearly *prescribed* (cf. Rowbottom and Billis, 1987) by specifications, requirements, quality standards and acceptance criteria. Work is concrete and geared towards completely specified goals in the most efficient way within defined means, technology and method (Hoebeke, 1994). The IT system engineer designs and develops IT artifacts such as program code towards goals and criteria specified at higher levels.

This work level addresses the question of "where". The focus is on static aspects of the system. In the context of Enterprise Architecture, this level embraces the application and technology infrastructure: COTS applications, operating systems, infrastructure services, data stores, devices, etc. Technical Design at this level "prepares an implementation area for construction and installation. The key tasks are structured to produce a system and database that meet the user's acceptance criteria and are technically sound" (TOGAF 9). These designs will be implemented physically, e.g. through application development. Test cases represent requirements of the highest specificity: discrete, testable units of software behavior.

At this level, real governance does not exist, but idiosyncratic activities are guided by fixed target standards for performance.

At this level, human information processing has a disjunctive, declarative quality (Jaques and Cason, 1994): a number of separate actions are carried out, without connections with each other. Mental operations are concrete and factual. When things go wrong and the obstacles cannot be overcome based on previously learned methods, outside help is sought from the next higher stratum (Jaques, 1998). This type of work can be readily outsourced and offshored.

II – Service

At this level, the response to each case of work is *situational* (cf. Rowbottom and Billis, 1987) and depends on judgment and interpretation. Specific requirements of Stratum I direct action tasks are molded into minimal critical specifications regarding the output, the procedures, the tools and the input (Hoebeke, 1994). The work of the IT system architect at this level involves assessment of and adjustment to the varying requirements within specified limits.

EA work at this level has emphasis on processes, work practices and quality standards: architectural support of implementation projects, development guidelines, change management practices, etc. It supports reliable business-IT alignment and focuses on changes in the information systems landscape. Information systems are developed and integrated upon the technology and application infrastructure to support higher-level business solutions. System Architecture is "a means for describing the elements and interactions of a complete system including its hardware elements and its software elements" (TOGAF 9). Requirements specifications, such as scenarios, at this level must address the question of "when": time constraints and explicit sequence of activities. Typical specification artifacts include logical level sequence diagrams and activity diagrams.

Governance relies on vertical lines of command and standardization for coordination. It aims at optimizing work practices and quality standards and managing deviations from the acceptable limits of performance. Teams are endowed discretion to differentiate services to different customer groups.

Human information processing at this level has a pulled-together, conjunctive quality (Jaques and Cason, 1994): a number of separate ideas or actions are connected to make sense together. Work can no longer be completely specified by a prescribed pathway, but it requires interpretation and reflection on what is occurring to diagnose potential problems and obstacles, and initiate actions to prevent or overcome those (Jaques, 1998). The person must be able to construct a series of events; classify, group and compare things, and comprehend cause-and-effect relationships. The focus is on concrete, visible aspects of reality that are empirically tested. Reasoning is inductive and based on concrete experience (Fowler et al., 2004).

III – Practice

Work at this level is conceptualized as a system that accommodates to the varying needs of today as well as those of tomorrow. Rowbottom and Billis (1987) refer to this abstraction as *systematic provision*. The solution architect must be able to construct new, systemic resource assemblies towards ends that have been predefined in functional requirements. He or she needs to address not only the tried-and-true but also the conceivable future contingencies.

The practice level deals with operating and developing socio-technical work systems that use information, technology, and other resources to produce products and services. These activities are supported by Capability Architecture – "a highly detailed description of the architectural approach to realize a particular solution or solution aspect" (TOGAF 9). Architecture addresses the question of "how": how to align the organization and assemble resources to implement the chosen business models. EA work begins to emphasize effectiveness. The importance of inter-domain relationships is heightened. Reusable architecture building blocks enable expeditious reassembly of business processes and solution architecture practice facilitates capability improvement. From the development point of view, higher-level functional requirements are typically specified in use cases that describe how the work system behaves, or should behave.

This level is the watershed between analytical reasoning and dialectical inquiry, between the certainty of the present and the contingency of the future. Up to this point, the problem space has been relatively simple: cause and effect relationships are generally linear, repeatable, predictable, empirical in nature, and not open to dispute (Kurtz and Snowden, 2003). Beyond this level, however, problems become increasingly complicated: cause and effect relationships are separated over time and space in chains that may not be fully known or are understood only by a limited group of experts (ibid.).

Governance at this level is about connecting multiple teams across functions to rethink work systems and processes within an operational domain. Key mechanisms include structural means such as formal roles, committees and councils. Whereas Stratum II specifies a framework for prescribed-output activity at Stratum I, Stratum III is about setting policies to govern open-ended, discretionary decision-making at Stratum II and to ensure systematic work.

Mental processing at Stratum III is serial and based on conditional thinking: a line of thought or action is constructed of a sequence of ideas that are chained together. The work is not only direct judgment and diagnostic accumulation, but also about constructing alternative pathways to a goal, proceeding serially one of the pathways and switching to an alternative route of action, if necessary (Jaques, 1998). At this level, the person must be able to construct hypothetical entities, simple theories and generalizations; think beyond the present moment and imagine possibilities; and make deductions from observable results (Fowler et al., 2004). This logic entails abstract thought and operations – multiple views, permutations and careful comparison between pairs of items (Cook-Greuter, 2005) – but there is usually no second-order reflection on thought itself (Fowler et al., 2004).

IV – Strategic Development

Work at this level entails *comprehensive provision* (Rowbottom and Billis, 1987), where the means and ends of underlying work systems are adjusted to reshape profitability within the overall business purpose. Work at this level requires intuitive judgment to detect gaps in services and to compare known systems with one another, but not to develop yet unknown systems (Gould, 1986). The business architect must be able to translate high-level business requirements to conceptual functional requirements that specify the solutions.

At this level, the organization is divided to functions and the key question word is "who": who is responsible for what in producing a product or providing a service, either in the current situation or in the predicted future. Business change happens through pairwise comparisons of the as-is solution with related to-be alternatives (cf. Jaques, 1986), leaning on Segment Architecture – "a detailed, formal description of areas within an enterprise, used at the program or portfolio level to organize and align change activity" (TOGAF 9). The to-be work system is conceptually specified in terms of its functional requirements. EA at this level embraces Business Architecture, linking enterprise assets and capabilities with Business Architecture elements such as products, services, organizational goals, core competencies and strategic change programs.

Governance at this level is about coordinating functions and projects beyond operational domains to set goals and to devise new systems and structures. This is typically attained through organization-wide programs and strategic systems (e.g. balanced scorecard, critical success factor analysis, service-level agreements, performance management, profit sharing schemes, etc.). Rules are established to govern policy-making.

Mental processing is parallel and based on bi-conditional thinking: a number of alternative ideas or actions, each arrived at by conditional thinking, is investigated, processed in parallel, and coordinated. Trade-offs between tasks must be made in order to maintain progress along the composite route to the goal. (Jaques, 1998). Work at this level requires an ability to construct systems, to analyze multi-dimensional problems and to be aware of contradictions and inconsistencies, alternatives and contingencies. Thought processes are systematic and reflective on thought itself. The person at this level shall appreciate inherent conceptual complexity; be capable of rigorous hypothesis testing, assessment and reorientation towards new goals; and logically justify worldviews. He or she is concerned about consequences and priorities and intentional about actions (Fowler et al., 2004; Cook-Greuter, 2005).

V – Strategic Intent

At this level, the scope extends to a framework that specifies a general field of need (cf. Rowbottom and Billis, 1987). Changes at this level pertain to entire ranges of products and services, involve long-term strategies and entail social, political and financial considerations. The (lead) enterprise architect, operating at this level, must be able to holistically understand the enterprise system in its entirety within the larger context.

Accordingly, EA must enable continuous transformative change at the business level and ensure sustained resilience. It addresses the question of "what": what is the business model, what are the organization's distinctive competencies, what is its scope? Strategic Architecture at this level is "a summary formal description of the enterprise, providing an organizing framework for operational and change activity, and an executive-level, long-term view for direction setting" (TOGAF 9). It may include elements such as goals, core competencies, success factors, and operational environment of the organization. In the extended enterprise setting, the larger context of external environment variables is of particular importance. Strategic Architecture assists new business development in devising creative strategies that seek optimal congruence with the environment. These strategies are translated to business requirements that then drive business change at the next level down.

Governance at this level is collaborative in nature and integrates organizational functions to a coherent business entity to reshape the business model and establish respective norms. It requires relational capabilities: informal collaborative relationships, value-based practices and normative controls. Vision guides the establishment of governance rules.

Work at this level requires an ability to understand phenomena in all their complexity, to coordinate several aspects of multiple abstractions simultaneously from different perspectives, and to recognize the relativity of all positions (Fowler et al., 2004). The logic aims at holistic understanding of things. The tendency to define system boundaries gives way to a more "open systems" approach. Paradoxes and contradictions are embraced, not explained away or resolved towards a closure around a preconceived system (Cook-Greuter, 2005).

Towards Agile Governance

The traditional predict-and-control paradigm of governance is applicable only to operational organizational subsystems (Strata I–III). Top-down-planned governance frameworks are primarily geared to address the "agency problem": the behavior of self-interested managers is reined in through control and compliance frameworks to protect shareholders' interests. Rigid internal controls and conformance measures resist the natural, self-organizing dynamics in the organization and stifle emergent strategies. The one-dimensional utilitarian logic of minimizing costs and maximizing profits inherently results in control-oriented behavior that emphasizes short-term efficiency. This view is conceptually blind to use-values beyond the modern economic view and fails to recognize the long-term viability of the organization and its ecology.

In today's complex and dynamic environments, a clear sense of direction and just-enough coordination is better than a precise plan and tight control. Governance must facilitate proactive exploration of new ideas and behaviors and enable full system-adaptive transformation. This calls for a holistic and systemic governance practice that is distributed and based on collaboration of competencies. Governance conceptualizations of this kind, such as *sociocracy* (Endenburg, 1988), are often based on consent-based decision-making that aims at unity rather than unanimity. This is achieved with a circle organization that is created by superimposing an overlay of interlinked circles on the existing administrative hierarchy (Romme,

1996). A circle is a unit of people with a common work objective and authority over its policy domain. The circles formulate and update their objectives; perform the three functions of operating, measuring, and directing; and maintain the quality of their resources. Whereas policy decisions are made by consent, other decision methods can be applied in the implementation of the policies within the circles, as long as this is agreed upon by consent. To take into account the perspectives of the higher-level circle and lower-level circles, each circle is always *double-linked* to the overlapping circle via at least two people who belong to and take part in the decision making of both circles. One of these links is appointed from the higher-level circle and is the person with overall accountability for the lower-level circle's results, and the other is a representative elected from within the lower level circle. The principles of circle organization and double linking are illustrated in Figure 4.

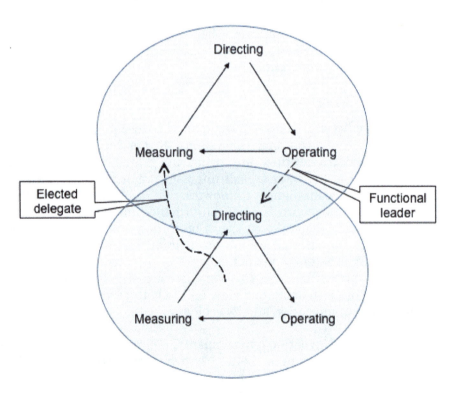

Figure 4. Circle organization and double-linking.

Optimally, the underlying managerial accountability hierarchy reflects Requisite Organization (Jaques, 1998), where each organizational stratum has its distinct type of decision-making. As the decision-making rights are distributed to the maximum degree to the self-organizing circles with just-enough coordination, the people closest to any given problem use requisite discretion within their authority to respond to arising contingencies. Rather than contributing to a tug-of-war between individuals and their personal wants, this distributed yet coordinated decision-making focuses effectively on what is best for the whole. Expectations that people hold to each other are defined in the form of roles, accountabilities and decision-making rights, setting the framework of mutual understanding within which the daily business can run smoothly and decisions can be readily made. The circle organization brings together the best of authoritarian and participative systems. It facilitates self-organized and proactive maneuvers while keeping reins on the participative system in the form of vertical authority and accountability.

Figure 5 outlines, in a simplified fashion, how circular governance could be applied to Enterprise Architecture and IT Governance. Abstract policy domains of the metastructure at the intersections of different levels and horizontal dimensions can be instantiated with pertinent governance bodies that are linked to each other with vertical double-links (Endenburg, 1988; Romme, 1996) and lateral coordination mechanisms, such as liaison roles, formal groups and managerial team arrangements (Peterson 2004).

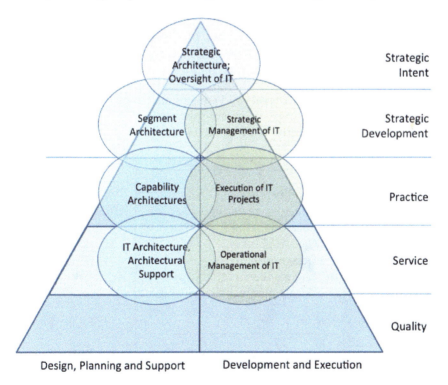

Figure 5. Circular governance applied to Enterprise Architecture.

By having both the vertical control structure and horizontal collaboration structure in place, the organization can flexibly adjust its IT-related behavior to varying business priorities and find an appropriate balance between IT efficiency and effectiveness. Such governance arrangements can compensate for the rigidity of organizational structure and help organizations to achieve seemingly conflicting objectives: "[R]ather than restructuring each time priorities shift, new governance mechanisms can force new behaviors without requiring reorganization. Governance mechanisms can provide organizational stability by demanding disciplined processes." (Weill and Ross 2005).

Shift Happens

Increasingly complex business environments require and result in progressively sophisticated sense-making and behavior at all scales. To allow respectively larger and more agile business change, the mechanistic conceptualizations of organizations as technically rational machines have been challenged by more adaptive and organic views that emphasize endogenous self-organization and resilient renewal.

As depicted in Table 2, the increase in work complexity denotes a paradigm change in focus from present day efficiency and reliability to future-aware effectiveness and validity and from top-down-driven control and planning-oriented functional view to bottom-up-emergent view facilitated by intentionally designed organizational and governance structures.

Table 2. Work levels and paradigm change.

Work Level	Paradigmatic Features
V	• Validity focus • Effectiveness • Future-looking
IV	• Constructional • Design-oriented • Endogenous; bottom–up • "IT enables business"
III	• Reliability focus

II	• Efficiency • Present day perspective • Functional • Control-oriented
I	• Exogenous; top down • "IT follows business"

Enterprise Architecture can no longer be conceived as embracing mere IT architecture, functionally subservient to "business". Rather, it shall be viewed as a more encompassing aspect-system integrally intertwined with the overall enterprise design, wherein IT essentially enables business, transcending the "IT follows business" mindset. Accordingly, Enterprise Architecture Governance shall be conceptualized as a cross-sectional overlay that distributes pertinent EA-related decision-making rights in the organization to a maximum degree, making space to endogenous emergence of new ideas and behaviors as well as to agile self-organization within the co-evolving business ecosystem.

About the Author

Janne J. Korhonen is an independent consultant and researcher, specializing in enterprise architecture governance. Mr. Korhonen has over ten years of consulting experience as an architect, consultant, team leader and developer in a variety of extensive, mission-critical and international IT projects. Along the customer engagements, he has done rigorous academic research in the area of enterprise architecture and participated in a number of global and corporate-level architecture development endeavors.

References

Connor, R. and Mackenzie, P. (2003). "The leadership jigsaw – finding the missing piece," *Business Strategy Review*, 14 (1), pp. 59–66.

Cook-Greuter, S. (2005). "Ego Development: Nine Levels of Increasing Embrace".

Endenburg, G. (1988). *Sociocracy: The Organization of Decision-Making*, Rotterdam, Sociocratic Center.

Hoebeke, L. (1994). *Making Work Systems Better: A Practitioner's Reflections*. John Wiley & Sons.

Hoogervorst, J. A. P. (2009). *Enterprise Governance and Enterprise Engineering*, Springer.

Fowler, J.W., Streib, H. and Keller, B. (Eds.) (2004). *Manual for Faith Development Research*. 3rd edition.

Gould, D. P. (1986) "Stratified systems theory in the design of organization-wide information systems," *International Journal of Information Management*, 6 (1), pp. 5–15.

Jaques, E. (1986). "The development of intellectual capability: A discussion of stratified systems theory," *The Journal of Applied Behavioral Science*, 22 (4), pp. 361–383.

Jaques, E. (1998). Requisite Organization: A Total System for Effective Managerial Organization and Managerial Leadership for the 21st Century, Revised second ed. Cason Hall & Co. Publishers, Baltimore, MD.

Jaques, E. and Cason, K. (1994). *Human Capability: A Study of Individual Potential and Its Application*, Cason Hall & Co Publishers Ltd, Falls Church, VA.

Korhonen, J.J., Hiekkanen, K. and Lähteenmäki, J. (2009). "EA and IT governance – a systemic approach," in: Politis, J. (Ed.), *5th European Conference on Management Leadership and Governance*. Academic Publishing Limited, Reading, UK, pp. 66–74.

Kurtz, C.F. and Snowden, D.J. 2003. "The new dynamics of strategy: Sense-making in a complex and complicated world," IBM Systems Journal, 42(3), pp. 462-483.

McMorland, J. (2005). "Are you big enough for your job? Is your job big enough for you? Exploring Levels of Work in organisations," *University of Auckland Business Review*, 7 (2), pp. 75–83.

Peterson, R. (2004). "Crafting Information Technology Governance," *EDPACS: The EDP Audit, Control & Security Newsletter*, 32 (6), pp. 1–24.

Romme, G. (1996). "Making Organizational Learning Work: Consent and Double Linking between Circles," *European Management Journal*, 14 (1), pp. 69–75.

Rowbottom, R. and Billis, D. (1987). Organisational Design: The Work-Levels Approach. Gower, Aldershot, UK.

TOGAF 9 (2009). The Open Group Architecture Framework (TOGAF), Version 9. The Open Group.

Weill, P. and Ross, J. (2005). "A Matrixed Approach to Designing IT Governance," *MIT Sloan Management Review*, 46 (2), pp. 26–34.

Enterprise Architecture in Enterprise Engineering

J.A.P. Hoogervorst and J.L.G. Dietz

Abstract

Originating from quite different fields of theory and practice, the terms "Enterprise Ontology" and "Enterprise Architecture" currently belong to the standard vocabulary of those professionals who are concerned with (re) designing and (re) engineering enterprises, thereby exploiting modern information and communication technologies for innovating products and services as well as for optimizing operational performance. The statement, put forward in this chapter, that the current notion of Enterprise Architecture does not offer satisfactory help and thus need to evolve into an effective conceptual tool, is clarified in a historical context. In order to let Enterprise Architecture become a sensible, effective notion, complementary to Enterprise Ontology, it is proposed to define it conceptually as normative restriction of design freedom, and operationally as a coherent and consistent set of design principles. The new, evolved notion of Enterprise Architecture is clarified and illustrated using a case example.

Keywords

Enterprise Engineering, Enterprise Design, Systems, Enterprise Architecture, Enterprise Ontology

Introduction[1]

The traditional organizational sciences fall increasingly short in helping enterprises to implement strategies effectively, and in a controlled way.

---

[1] This chapter was originally published as: Enterprise Architecture in Enterprise Engineering, International Journal of Enterprise Modelling and Information Systems Architecture, Vol. 3, No. 1, July 2008, pp. 3-13. Reprinted with permission.

Between 70% and 90% of the strategic initiatives appear to fail, meaning that enterprises are unable to derive success from their strategy (Mintzberg 1994, Kaplan et al 2004). These high failure rates are reported from various domains: total quality management (Oakland et al 1994), business process reengineering (Burlton 2001, Smith et al 2003), six sigma (Eckes 2001), e-business (Kalakota et al 1999), customer relationship management (Kirby 2001), and mergers and acquisitions (Woolridge et al 2002). Whereas all too often, unforeseen or uncontrollable events are presented, for convenience sake, as the causes of failure, research has shown that strategic failure is mostly the avoidable result of inadequate strategy implementation. Rarely is it the inevitable consequence of a poor strategy (Kaplan et al 2004). A plethora of literature indicates that the key reason for strategic failures is the lack of coherence and consistency, collectively also called congruence, among the various components of an enterprise (Miles et al 1984, Beer et al 1990, Kaufman 1992, Kotter 1995, Hoogervorst 1998, Galliers et al 1998, Pettigrew 1998). At the same time, the need to operate as an integrated whole is becoming increasingly important. Globalization, the removal of trade barriers, deregulation, etc., have led to networks of cooperating enterprises on a large scale, enabled by the enormous possibilities of modern information and communication technology. Future enterprises will therefore have to operate in an even more dynamic and global environment than the current ones. They need to be more agile, more adaptive, and more transparent. Moreover, they will be held more publicly accountable for every effect they produce.

Said problems are traditionally addressed with *black-box* thinking based knowledge, i.e., knowledge concerning the function and the behavior of enterprises. Such knowledge is definitely sufficient for managing an enterprise within the current range of control. However, it is totally inadequate for meeting performance goals that are outside the current range of control, thus for changing an enterprise. In order to bring about changes in a systematic and controlled way, *white-box* based knowledge is needed, i.e., knowledge concerning the construction and the operation of enterprises. Developing and applying such knowledge requires no less than a *paradigm shift* in our thinking about enterprises, since the traditional organizational sciences are not able to ensure that enterprises are coherently and consistently integrated wholes. The needed new point of view is that enterprises are purposefully designed, engineered, and implemented systems. The needed new skill is to (re) design, (re) engineer, and (re) implement an enterprise in a comprehensive, coherent and consistent way (such that it operates as an integrated whole), and to be able to do this whenever it is needed.

The current situation in the organizational sciences resembles very much the one that existed in the information systems sciences around 1970. At that time, a revolution took place in the way people conceived information technology and its applications (Dijkstra 1976, Langefors 1977). Since then, people are aware of the distinction between the form and the content of information. This revolution marks the transition from the era of data systems engineering to the era of information systems engineering. The comparison we draw with the information sciences is not an arbitrary one. On the one hand, the key enabling technology for shaping future enterprises is the modern information (and communication) technology (IT). On the other hand, there is a growing insight in the information sciences that the central notion for understanding profoundly the relationship between organization and IT is the entering into and complying with commitments between social individuals (Goldkuhl et al 1982, Winograd et al 1986, Dietz 2006). These commitments are raised in communication, through the so-called intention of communicative acts. Examples of intentions are requesting, promising, stating, and accepting. Therefore, like the content of communication was put on top of its form in the 1970's, the intention of communication is now put on top of its content. It explains and clarifies the organizational notions of collaboration and cooperation, as well as notions like authority and responsibility. This current revolution in the information systems sciences marks the transition from the era of information systems engineering to the era of enterprise engineering. At the same time it enables it to converge with the traditional organizational sciences, as illustrated in Figure 1.

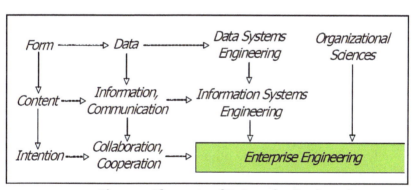

Figure 1. The roots of Enterprise Engineering

As said before, the basic premise of enterprise engineering is that an enterprise is a designed system. In order to ensure that the designing of a system is performed coherently and consistently, such that the resulting system is a truly integrated whole, two core notions are crucial: ontology and architecture. The *ontology* of a system is theoretically defined as the understanding of its construction and operation in a fully implementation independent way. Practically, it is the highest-level constructional model of a system, the implementation model being the lowest one. Compared to its implementation model, the ontological model of an enterprise offers a reduction of complexity of over 90% (Dietz 2006). The notion of Enterprise Ontology is discussed in (Dietz and Hoogervorst 2008). *Architecture* is theoretically defined as the normative restriction of design freedom. Practically, it is a coherent and consistent set of principles that guide the design of a system. Any strategic initiative of an enterprise can only be made operational through applying the notion of architecture, namely, by expressing it in principles that guide the designing of the 'new' enterprise. Only by applying these notions of ontology and architecture strategic changes of enterprises can be made intellectually manageable. Before elaborating on Enterprise Architecture as the second conceptual pillar of Enterprise Engineering, we will briefly resume some essential notions about systems and architecture in general. Subsequently, Enterprise Architecture will be discussed. The major findings from the discussions in are drawn in the last section.

Systems and Architecture

There exist many system definitions. Maier en Rechtin define a system as "a set of different elements so connected or related as to perform a unique function not performable by the elements alone" (2002, p. 6). Others speak of "a set of elements standing in interrelation among themselves and with the environment" (Bertalanffy 1969, p. 252). Essentially, the central notion regards a set of elements having certain relationships with each other and with the environment in view of the realization of one or more goals. In view of the above, an enterprise is evidently a system.

According to one of the founding fathers of the General System Theory, a core problem facing modern science is developing a theory about 'organizing', otherwise said, a theory about 'organized complexity' (Bertalanffy 1969). Based on the level of complexity, Weinberg identifies three areas (2001). The first area regards (relative) low complexity, identified by Weinberg as "organized simplicity", such as exemplified by machines en mechanisms. This type of complexity can be addressed through analytical methods. At the other end of the spectrum lies the area "unorganized complexity". Here the variety is so large that complexity can be addressed through statistical methods (such as with gas molecules in a closed space, or with certain aspects of traffic). The large area between these extremes is that of "organized complexity": too complex for analytical methods and too organized for statistical methods. According to Weinberg, this area – in which enterprises are positioned – is preeminently suitable for, and in definite need of, the system approach. Therefore, the system approach offers a formal methodology to address the enterprise as a whole, while considering its constituent parts and their mutual relationships, in order to safeguard a unified and integrated system. Many authors submit that the system approach is the only meaningful way to address aforementioned core problem of modern science, hence to study and develop enterprises (Bertalanffy 1969, Bunge 1980, Gharajedaghi 1999, Rechtin 2001). Ackoff argues therefore that the failing strategic initiatives mentioned earlier are due to the fact that the initiatives are fundamentally "anti-systemic" (1999).

As indicated, unity and integration, hence coherence and consistence between various enterprise aspects, is crucial for the success of the enterprise as a *whole*. There will be little debate about the conviction that unity and integration is not brought about spontaneously but has to be *designed* intentionally. Said intentional design aspect lies at the heart of the not 'accidental' but intentional character of the enterprise as a system, whereby realization of the enterprise function and construction should understandably not depend on chance but, as mentioned earlier, must be purposefully established. This begs the inescapable question of *how* the enterprise, in view of its goals and the required unity and integration, must be designed. The answer to this design question will be discussed later. For now we like to emphasize that any answer is essentially *normative*. We agree with Jackson arguing that the normative aspect of system design must be made explicit (2003). Architecture, in our opinion, offers the formal answer to this necessity.

The emphasized normative character of the answer to the question how the enterprise should be designed implies that the answer guides the design process, hence limits design freedom. Herein lies the essence of architecture: conceptually it regards the normative restriction of design freedom. From a general system perspective, architecture is practically defined *as a coherent and consistent set of principles that guides system design*. The set must be coherent, meaning that it must form a unified totality, but also consistent, since principles should not be mutually conflicting.

Noticeably, architecture is often viewed as a 'blueprint' or a schematic depiction of the essential components of a design and their relationships. Apparently, the concept is used in a *descriptive* manner. Sometimes both viewpoints are used in one definition. For example the IEEE standard 1471 reads (Maier et al 2001): *Architecture is the fundamental organization of a system embodied in its components, their relationships to each other and to the environment, and the principles guiding its design and evolution.* To our view, this definition is equivocal, it tries to accommodate two very different points of view, something that should be avoided in any definition. Similar remarks can be made about the definition of architecture provided by the Open Group (TOGAF 2003). Obviously, within the formal approach to architecture presented in this paper, architecture must be considered as a *prescriptive* concept, that – through design principles – *dictates* ex ante how a system must *become*, rather than a *descriptive* concept that *describes* ex post how a system *is*. We feel the descriptive use of the architecture concept is of little value form a design perspective, since the descriptive notion is essentially passive, hence – based on *after* the fact description – cannot provide *prior* active guidance in the design process. These views can be related to two philosophical characteristics about conducting science formulated by Windelband, and identified as the nomothetic and idiographic character of science [In: Nagel 1961]. Within the nomothetic view, science is about generally applicable knowledge and the search for laws that generally hold. The nomothetic approach to science is thus, in the literal meaning of the word, 'law giving'. On the other hand, within the idiographic perspective, science is about understanding and describing phenomena that are considered unique, and not guided by underlying general principals. One might argue, that the normative, prescriptive view on architecture fits the nomothetic perspective on conducting science. In light of the high failure rate of strategic enterprise initiatives mentioned earlier, and the underlying causes, the nomothetic perspective is very relevant for – to quote Kuhn (1970) – establishing the 'normal' science regarding the design of enterprises: enterprise engineering, with enterprise architecture as the essential guiding concept. Thereby, attention is not primarily given to case studies (ideographic perspective) but to generally applicable design knowledge and design principles.

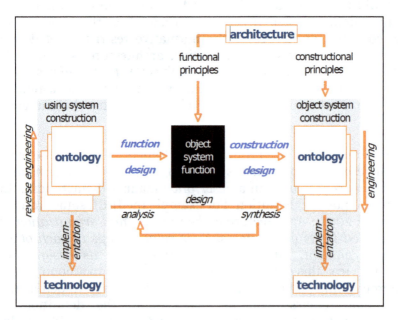

Figure 2. The Generic System Development Process

In view of the above, architecture is essentially linked to the system concept. First, design guidance is evidently crucial for establishing system unity and integration. Second, system design must satisfy various requirements. These requirements do not only regard the system function, but also regard objectives pertinent to certain areas of concern. For a technical system, these concerns might be reliability, maintainability, or safety. Through architecture these areas of concern are addressed, hence requirements are operationalized. Further, architecture ensures that areas of concern and their associated – possibly conflicting – requirements are addressed explicitly, and in a balanced manner. Figure 2 schematically shows the role of architecture in the generic system development process (Dietz and Hoogervorst 2008).

The essential aspects of the generic system development process have been outlined in (Dietz and Hoogervorst 2008). After having designed a system at the ontological level, it has to be further engineered through detailed design, such that the system can be implemented. Detailed design basically regards producing a coherent and consistent ordered set of white-box models of the system. The 'lowest' one is commonly called the implementation model. This model can straightforwardly be implemented on the available technological platform. For example, the implementation model of an information system is the source code in some programming language. Likewise, the implementation model of an enterprise consists of the functions or task packages that can be assigned to human beings on the basis of their competencies. The 'highest' model is called the ontological model or ontology of the system. This model is fully independent of the implementation; it only shows the essential features of the system.

Applying a design principle satisfies one or more requirements regarding the global design (referred to as "design" in figure 2) as well as the detailed design (referred to as "engineering" in figure 2) of a system. In line with the distinction between function and construction, we distinguish between *functional principles* or function architecture, and *constructional principles* or construction architecture. An example of a product that exhibits 'good' function architecture is the Apple MacOS; an example of a product that exhibits 'bad' function architecture is the (first) video recorder. An example of a product that exhibits 'good' construction architecture is the modern PC, whereas 'bad' construction architecture is exhibited by unstructured ('spaghetti') computer programs.

Understandably, the nature of a specific architecture is contingent upon the system category. Several system categories exist, such as mechanical, chemical, electronic, IT or socio-technical systems (Bunge 1979). In our view, the concept of architecture becomes more useful if architecture does not apply for the design of one system, but holds for all systems of a particular type, within some category. Put differently, architecture holds for a certain *class* of systems. Hence, architecture (a coherent and consistent set of principles en standards) defines how a class of systems must be designed. So, for example, IT architecture for data warehouses or applications is not only intended for one specific data warehouse or application, but intended for the class of data warehouses and applications respectively. IT architecture thus regards the normative design guidance for the class of IT systems. Likewise, enterprise architecture refers to the class of enterprises. Defining architecture can appropriately be labeled as *architecturing*, for which system design domains and areas of concern serve as the guiding context. This activity must be clearly distinguished from designing. This follows from the notion that architecture provides design guidance, hence must logically precede design. Moreover, architecturing is an autonomous activity that can be performed rather independently from design projects. It seems plausible to call the architecturing person an *architect*. Designing thus concerns the realization of a specific system within a certain system class, using architecture as a normative guidance. Summing up, the result of architecturing is architecture, the result of designing is a design. Figure 3 schematically shows the difference between architecturing and designing.

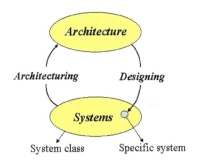

Figure 3. The difference between architecturing and designing.

The Notion of Enterprise Architecture

The Essence

The second tool for mastering the complexity of contemporary enterprises, next to Enterprise Ontology, is Enterprise Architecture. Contrary to Enterprise Ontology, it is abundantly discussed already in the literature about managing organizational change. Unfortunately, the term "Enterprise Architecture" has got many meanings also, meanings that are quire divers and sometimes even contradictory. Similarly, also the term "Enterprise Architect" is used in many different ways. To quote Thomas Kuhn, the current application of the concept of enterprise architecture does not yet show the characteristics of a 'normal science' (Kuhn 1970). In addition, the acceptance and application of Enterprise Architecture differs largely. Gartner reports (Dobrik 2000): *"People talk about enterprise architecture as if it is easily understood by technology and business professionals alike. In reality, technology professionals have a wide-ranging view of enterprise architecture...In contrast, business professionals tend to ignore the term as an IT-only issue"*.

The interpretation of enterprise architecture given in this article aims to clarify this theme in view of the general notion of architecture outlined in section 2. Subsequently, we will us the case of the Educational Administration, introduced when discussing Enterprise Ontology (Dietz en Hoogervorst 2008), for illustrating Enterprise Architecture

Goal-oriented, coordinated activities of human endeavor are identified through various labels: a business, company, organization or institution. In this article we use the, also frequently used, term 'enterprise'. Various entities that carry out commercial, non-profit or governmental activities are thus identified as enterprises. As we have mentioned in Section 1, the success rate of strategic initiatives is poor. Lack of coherence and consistency between the various aspects of an enterprise was identified as a primary cause for failures. According to the congruence theorem, enterprises will operate more effectively and perform better the higher the degree of unity and integration, hence the degree of coherence and consistency among its constituent parts. (Nadler et al 1997). These observations are likewise valid – if not even more so – if technology is part of strategic initiatives. Research about the effectiveness of technology deployment teaches us that effectiveness can only be obtained if the enterprise context in which technology operates matches and integrates with the technology and vice versa (Scott Morton 1991). Said condition is patently manifest regarding the impact of IT. Rather remarkable is the outcome of research conducted over a number of years showing no relationship between IT investments and measurable improvements in enterprise performance (Pisello et al 2003).

In our opinion, the underlying cause for this observation has to do with the suboptimal utilization of technology. Excellent performing enterprises, however, use technology in such a way that consistency and coherence is created between technology and the context in which it operates. This perspective is supported by earlier MIT research regarding the influence of IT on enterprise productivity. Only enterprises that in conjunction with the introduction of IT also changed the complementary enterprise context – hence realized an integrated enterprise design – achieved considerable gain in productivity (Brynjolfsson et al 1996). Comparable results are reported pertinent to the introduction of IT in the area of Customer

Relationship Management (Marcus 2001, Knox et al 2003). Enterprise performance therefore does not primarily depend on the use of modern technology, but depends on the overall quality of the enterprise design, of which technology is an important aspect. Herein lies the essential role of Enterprise Architecture: providing design guidance for establishing coherent and consistent enterprise design. Further, Enterprise Architecture determines how the implementation-independent design on the ontological level can be practically operationalized on the level of implementation. Noticeably, it is through enterprise architecture that the design becomes manifest. Otherwise said, identical enterprises at the ontological level (similar basic function) can only be implemented differently (and experienced by customers as differently) through different architecture. The well-known distinction between 'mechanistic' and 'organismic' ways of organizing manifests fundamentally different sets of architecture (Burns 1963).

In line with the general definition of architecture given in Section 2, we define Enterprise Architecture *as a coherent and consistent set of principles that guide how the enterprise must be designed.*

The ability to realize coherence and consistency in enterprise design will become more and more important. Progress in IT is, and will continue to be, a considerable driver in this respect. Said progress has led for example to the emergence of 'virtual' enterprises, and networks of enterprises ('extended' enterprise) where business partners and suppliers cooperate. Through various interfaces employees and customers are interacting and collaborating within and with these networks. This situation confronts enterprises with an enormous *integration* problem. Our observations about failing enterprise initiatives suggest that integration is more than establishing IT system 'interoperability'. We contend that addressing aforementioned integration problem without the concept of enterprise architecture will continue the astonishing high strategic failure rate mentioned before. Rightly so, various governments emphasize the importance of enterprise architecture for realizing governmental operation in a unified and integrated manner (USA 2003, Denmark 2003).

Enterprise architecturing

As indicated, architecture guides system design – hence applies to one or more design domains – and addresses requirements following from the system function and areas of concern. This similarly holds for systems like enterprises. Areas of concern have to do with strategic intentions and goals. Otherwise said, through strategy development insight emerges about important areas of concern, such as flexibility, customer satisfaction, time to market of new products and services, costs, or compliance to regulatory requirements. Congruent with the general system perspective, we might say that the areas of concern identify topics that necessitate certain (possibly yet to be specified) enterprise behavior. Figure 4 shows some typical areas of concern relevant for enterprises.

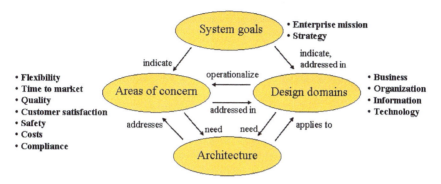

Figure 4. Reference framework for architecturing.

The normative guidance of the design process through architecture will be effectuated within a number of design domains. From the perspective of the enterprise as a whole, four main design domains can be identified:

Business. This domain regards the primary enterprise *function*, and has to do with the teleological (black-box) system perspective mentioned in Section 1. Aspects such as products and services, delivery channels, customers, the economic model, as well as general relationships with the environment (market, competitors, stakeholders) are typical areas of attention within the business design domain. In view of our overall notion of architecture, the *business architecture* is defined as a coherent and consistent set of principles that prescribes how a certain domain of goal oriented activities must be exploited and explored.   Recalling our observations in Section 2, the business architecture can be regarded as the function architecture of the enterprise.

Organization. Given a certain primary enterprise function, various degrees of freedom exist regarding the question how the production for bringing about the products and services is actually organized. The organizational design domain deals with the internal arrangements of the enterprise, having for example to do with processes, employee behavior, organizational culture, management practices, human resource management, and various provisions, such as pertinent to financial, accounting, or reward structures. The *organization architecture* can be defined as a coherent and consistent set of principles that prescribes how the enterprise must be arranged.

Information. Within both the business and organizational design domain, information is a crucial factor. Various facets play a role, like the structure and quality of information (syntax, semantics, security), the management of information (acquisition, storage and distribution), as well as the utilization of information (presentation, exploitation en exploration). Comparatively, *information architecture* is defined as a coherent and consistent set of principles that prescribes how information must be handled.

Technology. Evidently, technology is essential for current business, organizational and informational support, as well as for future developments in these domains. Specific technology entails specific associated architecture for providing the normative guidance regarding design activities for the technology in question. Taking information technology (IT) as an example, we have *IT architecture*, defined as a coherent and consistent set of principles that prescribe how IT systems must be designed.

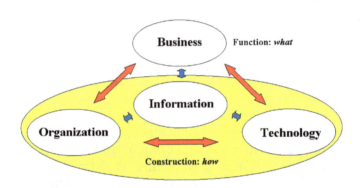

Figure 5. Main enterprise design domains.

An important distinction mentioned in Section 1 is that between the system *function* and the system *construction*. As identified in the above, the business domain regards the function of the enterprise: *what* products and services are delivered. The other three main design domains – organization, information and technology – concern the construction of the enterprise: *how* products and services are brought about. Hence, the organization, information and technology architectures constitute the construction architecture. Said distinction is schematically depicted in Figure 5.

Lack of unity and integration has been identified in the above as a core reason for failing enterprise (strategic) initiatives. Avoiding these failures requires coherence and consistency within and between the main design areas. This must be safeguarded through coherent and consistent enterprise architecture, comprised of business, organization, information and technology architectures. Overall coherence and consistence implies that important mutual relationships exist between the main design domains, like Figure 5 indicates.

As said, the specific character and description of a design domain depends on the system type and the level of perception. The perception can be directed to the total system or only part of it, such as a subsystem. So for a car, the design domains engine, chassis, interior, wheels, brakes, lamps, windows, etc., are necessary and sufficient design domains by observing the car as a whole. When observing a design domain in more detail also more detailed design domains play a role. For example, within the design domain 'engine' design domains like 'piston' and 'crankshaft' are relevant. So, from the perception of the car as a whole the design domain 'engine' suffices, but for designing the engine, more detailed design domains have to be defined. This process continues until a level is reached whereby further breakdown is not warranted. Evidently, the same notion holds for enterprise design domains.

As the illustration shows, there is specialization of design domains associated with more detailed observations. Such specialization thus creates a certain order whereby a more detailed design domain is subordinated under the next higher design domain, like 'engine' is subordinated under the overall design domain 'car', and 'piston' in turn is subordinated under the domain 'engine'. Since architecture pertains to one or more design domains, aforementioned order likewise holds for architecture. That is to say that a principle or standard a_j may not be in conflict with principle or standard a_i if $D_j \subset D_i$. Noticeably, this is an important condition for safeguarding coherence and consistency, which has been emphasized before as an important objective of defining architecture. Establishing unity and integration does not only require that architecture forms a coherent and consistent set, but also requires that the set of design domains pertinent to a chosen perception is *complete*: necessary and sufficient in view of the system purpose (function) and the objectives associated with the areas of concern. For complex systems, such as enterprise, establishing completeness is far from easy. Nonetheless, in all cases the total set of design domains within a certain perspective must be complete. Otherwise said, the set of design domains for a certain perspective must be necessary and sufficient for addressing relevant design activities pertinent to the given perspective. For the enterprise as a whole, we feel the four main design domains are necessary and sufficient. More specific design domains are obviously relevant within the four main design domains in order to carry out particular and definitive design activities (higher level of detail). For example, the design domain 'processes' can be seen a more specific design domain within the main design domain 'organization'. Process architecture is thus a subset of the organization architecture. Examples of specific enterprise design domains have been discussed elsewhere (Hoogervorst 2004). Verifying that the set of design domains is complete for a given perception is not always easy, specifically for an enterprise. Nonetheless, the completeness requirement holds and must be satisfied for every perception.

Enterprise Architecture for the Educational Administration

The first remark to be made regarding the application of the notion of Enterprise Architecture in practice is that it is just emerging. Companies that have adopted it are still in the phase of understanding what it means: they are pioneers. Yet the potentials are enormous (Hoogervorst 2004). In fact, as argued previously, it seems to be the only feasible way of 'translating' high-level statements and areas of concern, as can be found in mission and strategy documents, into operationally useful principles for design.

It is possible that an area of concern directly identifies a design domain where the concern is addressed. Generally however, this is not the case. For example, it appears not immediately clear how concerns about customer satisfaction, flexibility or societal responsible business conduct are actually operationalized, and which design domains are involved. Hence, pertinent to the main enterprise design domains, the enterprise architect must identify subsequent design domains that enable addressing the concerns through design principles. Defining the relevant design domains requires broad, design-oriented knowledge regarding business, organization, information and technology. Following example for the Educational Administration might serve as an illustration.

Suppose the process of (University) strategy development has (among other ones) identified 'student satisfaction', 'flexibility' and 'compliance' as areas of concern. The first concern has to do with the ability to attract and retain students, whereas the second concern addresses the University's ability to quickly adapt to changing internal and external conditions. Further, the area of concern 'compliance' has to do with satisfying regulatory requirements. Subsequent analysis by enterprise architects concludes that the concern 'student satisfaction' will be addressed through three design domains: 'products' (part of main business design domain), human resource management (part of main organization design domain), 'processes' (part of the main organization design domain) and 'information exploitation' (part of main information design domain). Further analysis reveals that the drive for student satisfaction necessitates easy access of students to the University network. An additional concern 'security' is thereby identified, and addressed through the design domains 'information quality' (part of the main information design domain), and 'IT security' (part of the main technology design domain). The concern

82

'flexibility' is addressed through the design domains 'processes' and 'human resource management'. Finally, within the design domain 'processes' the concern for compliance will be taken into account. Ultimately, architecture pertinent to the design domains mentioned, determines how the concerns are addressed in the actual design. Examples of architecture principles are shown in Table 1 below. As the table shows, an architecture principle can address more than one area of concern.

Area of concern	Design domain	Architecture principle
Student satisfaction	Business (products)	Products and services must allow personalization by students
	Organization (HRM)	Management must enable employee self-management
	Organization (processes)	Student administration must be locally present, under unified, central governance
	Information (exploitation)	Complete and up-to-date student information must be available at all student contact points
Security	Information (quality)	Student information must be available from one unified source
	Technology (IT security)	Network access must be based on authentication and role-based authorization
Flexibility	Organization (processes)	Process flow control logic must be separated from process execution logic
		Student administration must be locally present, under unified, central governance
	Organization (HRM)	Employee decision making must take place at the lowest possible level
Compliance	Organization (processes)	Admission rules must be in accordance with the Bologna treaty

Table 1. Examples of architecture principles.

Defining detailed design domains within the four main enterprise design domains, and more specifically, defining the appropriate architecture pertinent to areas of concern, is not a simple analytical or algorithmic process. Experience plays an important role. Architecture principles are thus (also) based on experience, best-practices and insights that can be generalized into architecture. Architecturing is thus for a considerable part a *heuristic* process (Maier and Rechtin 2002). As said earlier, enterprise design affects various stakeholders: customers, employees, suppliers, etc. Orchestrating the role and input of stakeholders within the process of architecturing implies that next to the heuristic character, architecturing also has a *participative* character (Maier and Rechtin 2002).

Architecture Frameworks

The core aspects regarding architecture and architecturing define the elements of a so-called 'architecture framework'. These elements are: (1) the system type S, the design domains D, and (3) the areas of concern A. An architecture framework can be shortly identified as <S,D,A> (Dietz 2004).

As indicated, specific design domains depend on the perception chosen. Hence, for a given system, multiple (related) architecture frameworks are possible. An architecture framework can be defined as *a conceptual structure pertinent to a certain system type, consisting of areas of concern and a necessary and sufficient set of design domains pertinent to a chosen perception.*

All too often, architecture frameworks do not satisfy the definition given before. It can be noticed that the label 'enterprise architecture' is used in cases that merely regard IT architecture for the whole enterprise. Despite the label 'enterprise' this appears not to be the system type of concern. This seems to be the case with the TOGAF architecture framework (TOGAF 2003). Frequently design domains 'business' and 'process' are added to a set of IT system design domains (like 'data and 'application') in view of the fact that IT systems support business processes. For example, the architecture framework provided by Tapscott and Caston speaks of business architecture, process architecture, application architecture, information architecture and technology architecture (1993). Comparatively, the TOGAF architecture framework identifies business, application, data, and technology architectures (2003). Ignoring the somewhat illusive use of the term 'business' in these frameworks, we notice that from an IT system design perspective the set of design domains is incomplete, since more design domains are relevant than merely 'application' and 'data'. Apart from this incompleteness, it seems clear that the design domains 'business' and 'process' cannot be part of an IT system, hence, do not fit within an IT architecture framework. One might alternatively consider the frameworks mentioned as enterprise architecture frameworks. However, in that case considerably more design domains are relevant than only 'business' and 'process'. All in all, it is often rather unclear to which system type an architecture framework pertains, while for a given (or assumed) system type, the set of design domains is all too often incomplete. In fact, the very notion of design domains and the

84

necessity for completeness appears to be absent in the architecture frameworks mentioned. These observations also hold for Zachman's architecture framework (1997).

More fundamentally, one might observe that many architecture frameworks (like the ones mentioned) do not use the normative notion of architecture. The absence of a formal, normative approach consequently also implies the absence of formal design guidance. Important objectives that the normative, prescriptive approach tries to establish are thus not addressed. This is detrimental for the design process itself, but also for professionalizing the architecture function and the architect's profession.

Finally, also development, implementation and project related (planning) issues are frequently part of architecture frameworks, such as in the TOGAF and Zachman architecture frameworks. Evidently, these aspects have to be addressed professionally, but fall outside the scope of architecture and architecturing, hence should not be part of an architecture framework. Much of what is positioned as an architecture framework is in fact a concealed development and implementation framework. Development and implementation aspects are important areas of attention within an overall enterprise governance competence, within which also the enterprise architecture competence is positioned. Reflecting on enterprise governance is however outside our current scope of discussion.

The use of a architecture framework of the type $<S,D,A>$ is important for a number of reasons. A framework structures the process of architecturing by making explicit formal attention to: (1) the system type for which architecture must be defined, (2) the areas of concern that must be addressed, and (3) the necessary and sufficient set of design domains where architecture must be applied. Next to structuring the architecturing process, another key purpose of an architecture framework is the following. The importance of coherence and consistency of design principles and standards has been emphasized. These are essential condition for a unified and integrated system operation. The explicit structure of the architecture framework enables safeguarding and assessing the coherence and consistency of architecture within, and between design domains, as well as between different frameworks. For an enterprise this regards coherence and consistency between business architecture, organization architecture , information architecture, and technology architecture. Safeguarding coherence and consistency is no sinecure, specifically for complex systems. This is definitely the case with enterprises. Knowledge and experience of the architect play a crucial role, as well as the ability to assess consequences of design principles and standards for a given design domain, for other domains. A participative, multi-disciplinary approach is also here relevant.

Conclusions

The notions of ontology and architecture, particularly the notions of Enterprise Ontology and Enterprise Architecture, can be very powerful conceptual instruments, provided they are conceived appropriately. The current state-of-the-art unfortunately shows a large variety of definitions, which are often contradictory. Most importantly, however, they suffer from being ill defined and not rigorously founded in an all-encompassing theory. As a consequence, they are often not appropriate and therefore do not offer effective help to the professionals whose task it is to (re) design enterprises.

The first step towards defining the terms such that they constitute an effective and complementary pair has been the presentation and discussion of the Generic System Design Process (Section 2). From this framework the clear and unavoidable conclusion can be drawn that two notions are crucial for conceptually managing the development of systems of any kind. One is the notion of understanding the construction and the operation of a system in a way that is fully independent of its implementation, while exhibiting comprehensibly, coherently, consistently, and concisely the essence of the system. The other one is the notion that unified and integrated design is crucial for the performance of the enterprise as a whole and crucial for addressing mission and strategy related initiatives and areas of concern that are valid at some point in time.

The discussion of the notions of Enterprise Ontology and of Enterprise Architecture in Sections 3 and 4 respectively, has demonstrated that without them the complexity the said professionals are faced with cannot be mastered. We have also shown that both notions can be defined very precisely and very consistently. At the same time, we have noticed that the practical application of Enterprise Architecture, as proposed in this paper, is still in its infancy. However, its future looks bright. There has a lot of research has to be undertaken yet, but it is the only feasible way to arrive at a practically effective notion of architecture, as effective as Enterprise Ontology.

Enterprise Ontology and Enterprise Architecture are taken as the basic elements of the new discipline of Enterprise Engineering, that is currently emerging from the convergence of the traditional organizational sciences and the information sciences. The word "Engineering" has to be taken in a broad sense, like it is used e.g., in Mechanical Engineering and in Industrial Engineering. The most important premise in the notion of Enterprise Engineering is that an enterprise is a designed system instead of an organically growing entity. We hope that this paper contributes to evoking the necessary awareness among the professionals and scholars who are currently dealing with organizational change that the engineering approach we have presented is the right one for coping with today's and tomorrow's complexity.

About the Authors

Jan Hoogervorst is Associate Professor at the Lisbon Technical University, and teaches in Master programs of several other universities. He also works as a management consultant at Sogeti Netherlands.

Jan Dietz is professor at Delft University of Technology, spiritual father of DEMO, and co-founder of the Enterprise Engineering Institute (www.ee-institute.com), and the CIAO! Network (www.ciaonetwork.org).

References

Ackoff, R.L., Ackoff's Best: His Classic Writings on Management, New York, Wiley 1999

Beer, M., Eisenbach, R.A., Spector, B., Why Change Programs Don't Produce Change, Harvard Business Review, November/December 1990, pp. 158-166

Bertalanffy, L. von, *General Systems Theory*, New York, George Braziller 1969

Brynjolfsson, E, Hitt, L., Paradox Lost? Firm Level Evidence on the Returns to Information System Spending, *Management Science*, Vol, 42, No. 4, 1996, pp. 541-558

Bunge, M.A.: *Treatise on Basic Philosophy, vol.4, A World of Systems* (D. Reidel Publishing Company, Dordrecht, The Netherlands 1979)

Burlton, R.T., *Business Process Management*, Indianapolis, Sams Publishing 2001

Burns, T., Mechanistic versus Organismic Structures (1963), In: Pugh, D.S., *Organizational Theory*, London, Penguin Books 1990

Denmark, *White Paper on Enterprise Architecture*, Copenhagen, Ministry of Science, Technology and Innovation, 2003

Denning, P., Medina-Mora, R., Completing the loops, in: *ORSA/TIMS Interfaces,* Vol. 25, No. 3 May-June 1995, pp 42-57

Dietz, J.L.G., *The Extensible Architecture Framework (xAF)*, Version 2, Delft University of Technology 2004 (http://www.naf.nl/content/bestanden/xaf-1.1_fe.pdf)

Dietz, J.L.G., *Enterprise Ontology – theory and methodology*, Springer-Verlag Heidelberg, Berlin, New York 2006.

Dietz, J.L.G., Hoogervorst, J.A.P., Enterprise Ontology in Enterprise Engineering, *Proceedings of the ACM SAC*, 2008

Dijkstra, E.W., *A Discipline of Programming*, Prentice-Hall series in Automatic Computation, New Jersey, 1976

Drobik, A., *Enterprise Architecture: The Business Issues and Drivers*, http://www.gartner.com/DisplayDocument?id=366199

Eckes, G., *The Six-Sigma Revolution*, New York, Wiley 2001

Galliers, R,D., Baets, W.R., *Information Technology and Organizational Transformation*, Chichester, Wiley 1998

Gharajedaghi, J., *Systems Thinking*, Boston, Butterworth Heinemann 1999

Goldkuhl, G., Lyytinen, K., A language action view of information systems, in Ginzberg, M., Ross, C.A. (Eds.), *Proceedings of the 3rd international conference on information systems, TIMS/SMIS/ACM*, 1982

Hoogervorst, J.A.P., *Quality and Customer Oriented Behavior. Towards a Coherent Approach for Improvement*, Delft, Eburon 1998

Hoogervorst, J.A.P., Enterprise Architecture: Enabling integration, Agility and Change, *Journal of Cooperative InformationSystems*, Vol. 13, No. 3, 2004, pp. 213 233

Jackson, M.C., *Systems Thinking*, Chichester, Wiley 2003

Kalakota, R., Robinson, M., *E-Business. Roadmap for Success*, Reading MA, Addison-Wesley 1999

Kaplan, R.S., Norton, D.P., *Strategy Maps*, Boston, Harvard Business School Press 2004

Kaufman, R.S., Why Operations Improvement Programs fail: Four managerial Contradictions, *Sloan Management Review*, Vol. 34, No. 1, 1992, pp. 83-93

Kirby, J., Implementing CRM: Business Change Program, Not Project, *Gartner Research*, July 2001

Knox, S., Maklan, S., Payne, A., Peppard, J., Ryals, L., *Customer Relationship Management*, Oxford, Butterworth Heinemann 2003

Kotter, J.P., Leading Change: Why transformation Efforts Fail, *Harvard Business Review*, Vol. 71, No. 2, 1995, pp. 59-67

Kuhn, T., *The Structure of Scientific Revolutions*, Chicago, Chicago University press 1970

Langefors, B.: Information System Theory. *Information Systems* 2, 207–219 (1977)

Marcus, C., CRM Deployment Can Focus on Most Valued Customers, *Gartner Research*, July 2001

Maier, M.W. Emery, D. Hilliard, R., Software Architecture: Introducing IEEE Standard 1471, *IEEE Computer*, April 2001, Vol. 34-4, pp 107-109

Maier, M.W., Rechtin, E., *The Art of Systems Architecting*, Boca Raton, CRC Press 2002

Miles, R.E., Snow, C.C., Fit, Failure and the Hall of Fame, *California Management Review*, Vol. 26, No. 3, 1984, pp. 128-145

Mintzberg, H., *The Rise and Fall of Strategic Planning*, New York, The Free Press 1994

Nadler, D.A., Tushman, M.L., *Competing by Design: The Power of Organizational Architecture*, New York, Oxford University Press 1997

Nagel, E., *The Structure of Science: Problems in the Logic of Scientific Explanation*, Londen, Routledge & Kegan Paul 1961

Oakland, J.S., Porter, L.J., *Cases in Total Quality Management*, Oxford, Butterworth-Heinemann 1994

Pettigrew, A., Success and Failure in Corporate Transformation Initiatives, In: Galliers, R.D., Baets, W.R.J., *Information Technology and Organizational Transformation*, Chichester, Wiley 1998

Pisselo, T., Strassmann, P., *IT Value Chain Management – Maximizing the Value from IT Investments*, New Canaan, The Information Economics Press 2003

Rechtin, E. *Systems Architecting of Organizations*, Boca Raton, CRC Press 2000

Scott Morton, M.S., *The Corporation of the 1990s*, New York, Oxford University Press 1991

Smith, H., Fingar, P., *Business Process Management: The Third Wave*, Tampa Fl., Meghan-Kiffer Press 2003

Tapscott, D., Caston, A., *Paradigm Shift – The New Promise of Information Technology*, New York, McGraw-Hill 1993

TOGAF - *The Open Group Architecture Framework* (2003) http://www.opengroup.org/bookstore/catalog/g051.htm

USA, *A Framework for Improving Enterprise Architecture Management*, Version 1.1, US General Accounting Office, Washington D.C., April 2003

Weinberg, G.M., *An introduction to General Systems Thinking*, New York, Dorset House Publishing 2001

Winograd, T, F. Flores, 1986. *Understanding Computers and Cognition: A New Foundation for Design,* Ablex, Norwood NJ.

Woolridge, L., Hayden, F., How to get value from mergers, acquisitions and divestments, *CSC Research Journal*, November 2002

Zachman,J., *Concepts of the Framework for Enterprise Architecture*, Zachman International Inc. 1997

Systems Thinking as the Foundation for Architecting the Sustainable Enterprise

Leo Laverdure and Alex Conn

Abstract

Enterprise Architecture (EA) is a key tool to help businesses transform themselves to meet changing business challenges. To do so, however, architectural methods must themselves be adapted to focus less on technology per se and more on how these technologies enable the business to survive and thrive over the long term—to be sustainable—in the shifting, uncertain business context. We call this shift to Sustainable Enterprise Architecture (SEA) a "SEA change". The practice of SEA differs from the usual practice of EA in a number of ways. First, it is based on systems thinking to highlight the complex interactions among the many systems—formal and informal—both within and surrounding the Enterprise. It is continuous, iterative, and adaptive; and calls for integrated strategic planning, architecting, governance, and learning. It considers sustainability the primary system quality and organizes other system qualities in support of sustainability. The enterprise's approach to sustainability is recorded in a formal sustainability architecture, which describes the threats to sustainability in the business context and defines sustainability goals, models, principles, policies, and standards to address them. It recognizes that sustainable architecting is a cultural change, and provides a set of essential checklists to guide that change.

Keywords

Business sustainability, business context, risk management, disruptive change, systems thinking, system qualities, sustainable enterprise architecture, architecture methods, strategy, governance, lifecycle

Introduction: Why Systems Thinking in Enterprise Architecture?[2]

Like all human beings, Enterprise Architects use models to understand our world and inform our actions. Einstein emphasized that effective models must be as simple as possible—but no simpler. There can be little doubt that the modern, global enterprise is best modeled as a complex, multi-minded, adaptive system inhabiting an uncertain, dynamic, richly populated—and richly interconnected—business environment. Anything else is too simple.

Once we admit complexity into our enterprise models, we need tools able to deal with the complexity. The most basic need is for clear thinking about complex systems and environments, and that is where systems thinking comes in. It has been honed over the last half century to deal with complex, nearly intractable, global problems, with much success.

But systems thinking is no panacea. We want to architect enterprises that can be controlled, yet systems thinking says that control is not possible—the best that we can hope for is to influence parties in the business ecosystem. We want to engineer stable, nearly independent systems. However, systems thinking tells us that while independence is an important goal, we should not expect to fully realize it, since "nearly independent" means "dependent" in some ways. In fact, these dependencies ultimately connect everything to everything else, at least indirectly. It is hard enough to understand the connections, not to mention the behavior that results from the interactions. The uncertainty does not go away.

These apparent limitations, however, are not shortcomings in systems thinking; rather, they are inherent in the reality of business today. So it is crucial that systems thinking emphasize these and related dilemmas. Systems thinking also provides us with a number of ways to look at systems, including insights into what constitutes a system and the impossibility of drawing just one system boundary. It also offers heuristics for addressing many commonly encountered system "traps," thus allowing us to set an informed path forward.

Enterprise architects, of course, must help the enterprise achieve its mission, vision, and strategy, whether or not these are well articulated. We need to answer specific questions about any proposed systems: What are

---

[2] Parts of this chapter were published by Leo Laverdure and Alex Conn under the title "SEA Change: How Sustainable EA enables business success in times of disruptive change" in Journal of Enterprise Architecture, February 2012. Reprinted with permission.

the enterprise's goals for these systems? What capabilities do they enable? Where is the enterprise headed, and how might this change over time? How might the business environment change? What pressures will these changes exert on the systems? What are the cost-benefit tradeoffs of building flexibility into the systems so that they can adapt effectively, efficiently, and quickly?

There are even more questions at the heart of defining and scoping systems: What is the role of the system in its environment? How does the system provide benefits to and otherwise impact a variety of stakeholders, either intentionally or unintentionally? What are the concerns of these stakeholders, and what is the systems context for each of these concerns?

One of the most fundamental aspects of any system is its stability, that is, its ability to persist over time, even in the face of significant change, both external and internal. For a purposeful system like an enterprise, persistence requires that it provide useful and valued contributions to society, although the specifics of the contributions are likely to change as society changes. How does an enterprise evolve its contributions effectively and efficiently? Are there fundamental limits to the resources that the enterprise can rely on for the development, operation, evolution—and retirement—of its systems?

Systems thinking also helps with some of the thorniest problems facing society and the enterprise's role in addressing them. A fundamental issue is what organizations can and should do to help society prosper over the long term, in other words, to improve our common sustainability. Seeing the big picture and balancing across many dimensions is key to improving sustainability. Focusing too narrowly on the natural environment (environmentalism) has proven limited in its ability to improve our situation, because people and corporations reject the narrow focus as impractical. And most people don't prioritize the environment ahead of their needs and lifestyle.

Focusing on improving enterprise sustainability over the long term, however, is a practical way to improve the sustainability not only of the enterprise, but also of society, the natural environment, and the broader economy, as well. Can an enterprise truly expect to prosper over the long term while ignoring or even abusing their natural, social, and economic cnvironments?

As complex, multi-minded, adaptive systems, enterprises have many component systems, including people, automated systems, buildings, and equipment, that are richly interconnected through dynamic processes, information flows, and causal structures featuring feedback loops and delays. The components are in many locations and work together to form capabilities that transform inputs into products and services for customers.

Multi-mindedness, the condition of having a number of stakeholders with both common and competing interests and ideas about directions and decisions, is one of the greatest challenges organizations face. In our increasingly information-rich and hyper-connected world, it is becoming easy for any motivated stakeholder to learn about and track how the enterprise is operating. To be effective, the enterprise must be aware of the concerns of all stakeholders, include them in the ongoing strategic conversation, and ensure that a balanced approach to addressing competing concerns gets the support of most stakeholders and eliminates any strong opposition.

Enterprise systems do not stand alone; they depend upon resources, suppliers, channels, collaborators, and other parties in the enterprise's business ecosystem. Corporate leaders understand most of these dependencies, as well as the potential impact of competitors, some of whom may also be collaborators in bounded situations. However, it is the external factors, which are fundamental but often little noticed and poorly understood, that can both enable and/or profoundly constrain the enterprise. Changes in economic, societal, and natural environmental systems, which may be large and abrupt, can disrupt the "business as usual" operation of the enterprise, presenting it with both threats and opportunities.

Getting disruptions right is almost certainly the most important factor for the long-term success of an enterprise; it merits hyper-vigilance and rapid, accurate adaptation to changing conditions. Systems thinking helps us to understand not only the complex operation of an enterprise but also the actual and potential disruptions in the business ecosystem and the broader surrounding contexts of an enterprise. And it helps us discover ways to address these disruptions. As such, systems thinking is truly the "foundation for architecting the sustainable enterprise."

The remainder of this chapter makes the case for a "SEA Change," that is, transforming traditional EA methods into Sustainable Enterprise Architecture (SEA) methods. The chapter shows why this is crucial for business success and how systems thinking, including the system environment and disruptions, is the core underpinning of SEA.

Pervasive, Unrelenting, Disruptive Change

In today's rapidly shifting business context, organizations face major challenges, including economic instability, energy and resource uncertainty, growing populations and new entrants to the global middle class, social and political unrest, climate change, and disruptive technologies. A seemingly isolated event half the world away can send shockwaves across the global economy and supply chains, severely testing a business's resilience. Worse, some disruptions signal long-term shifts rather than temporary fluctuations and require strategic changes of direction. Whole industries may be impacted.

Enterprise Architects have a long history of dealing with disruptive technologies. Indeed, one of the key skills of the architect is to recognize which emerging technologies are likely to yield business benefits and when it is time to embrace them. Architects also understand how business events, such as mergers, acquisitions, and divestitures, can drive new architecture development. What is less familiar, however, is the importance of using Enterprise Architecture as a tool to address general business context risks.

This is starting to change. The SABSA (Sherwood Applied Business Security Architecture) Institute and The Open Group recently announced the publication of a joint White Paper recommending the integration of TOGAF and SABSA as a best practice to secure Enterprise Architectures (The Open Group and SABSA Institute 2011). The paper stresses the primacy of addressing business risks. Also, the SABSA Institute's Enterprise Security Architecture (Sherwood et al. 2009) provides a useful set of Business Profile Attributes for defining business risk elements that must be managed. It correctly points out that risk management includes an opportunity side as well as threats.

Nearly all enterprises have a business continuity solution in place to assure continued operations in the face of a range of disruptive events. A basic need is to keep communications and information systems operational, while recognizing that business resilience ultimately depends upon management discipline rather than simply technology (Owens 2004).

What is common to security and business continuity/resilience arrangements is the assumption of a relatively short-term disruption, after which the business returns to more-or-less normal operations, often referred to as "Business As Usual" (BAU). But what if the business context shifts to a significantly different landscape—a "new normal" from which return to the previous conditions is infeasible? Enterprises must adapt. And the imperative for Enterprise Architects is to help them adapt effectively, efficiently, and often very rapidly. How can architects do this? There is no silver bullet, but successful architects will work with business leaders to:

- Redefine goals and directions to make clear that the fundamental goal is sustaining the business in uncertain, disruptive times
- Shift thinking to a new level, with a greater focus on understanding long-term contextual shifts and systems interactions
- Craft Sustainable Enterprise Architectures (SEAs) with capabilities, platforms, and system qualities that help to define and enable strategic agility
- Improve adaptive capacity, turning it into a core competency

The remainder of this article outlines how to accomplish these.

The Fundamental Goal: Business Sustainability

All organizations understand that they exist to provide products and services valued by their customers; for many organizations, making a profit for shareholders and/or providing jobs are also basic goals. And, there is wide and growing realization that addressing a broader set of stakeholders' concerns is good for business. This often finds expression as corporate social contribution and/or stewardship of the natural environment ("doing well by doing good").

But businesses, like most people, are also pragmatic—what matters most to them is their own prosperity. Accordingly, we define a sustainable business (or enterprise) as one that survives and thrives over the long term by balancing economic, social, and environmental considerations and by managing risks and seizing opportunities associated with disruptions.

SEA is about the architecture of a sustainable enterprise.

Understanding Systems, Contexts, and Risks

A useful heuristic in systems architecting is that the three most important things are scope, scope, and scope (Rechtin & Maier 1997). In other words, it is critical to understand the boundaries between systems and their environments.

We tend to jump quickly to system solutions because we assume that we understand the system environment. But, in a time of disruptive change, that is a dangerous assumption, akin to building in an earthquake zone without adequate understanding of fault lines, soils, and the full historical record of local seismic events. We also generally assume that the system environment is, by definition, beyond our control. Most of it is, but a large part of the environment with which we interact, while uncontrollable, is influenceable (Gharajedaghi 2006). We call this interaction environment the Business Ecosystem, depicted in Figure 1. Also depicted are Your Business, its inputs and outputs (coming from and going to other parties, not shown, in your business ecosystem), and two key internal aspects: your core Business Idea (the overall differentiating quality of the enterprise, similar to mission/vision; van der Heijden 2005) and Capabilities (abstractions of a business's offerings and competencies).

Figure 1: Your Business and Its Environment

The environment—both the multiple Surrounding Contexts and the Business Ecosystem—is the source of most disruptions, which change the competitive landscape and business models, forcing the enterprise to adapt its business idea and capabilities. (We find that viewing the environment as multiple contexts makes it easier to think about the different kinds of disruptive forces that might impact the enterprise.) Figure 2 shows one way to categorize these disruptive forces, and suggests that most, but not all, of the influence is directed from the environment to the business. In some cases, however, a business can influence one or more of these forces; e.g., with a major technical or business innovation that becomes a new de facto standard.

A number of organizations provide valuable information about the risks of potential business disruptions, ranging from government organizations to trade groups and individual companies. Each looks at the risks from a different perspective. Government organizations include the US National Academy of Sciences, the Intergovernmental Panel on Climate Change (IPCC), and the International Energy Agency (IEA). Additional sources include the UN Millennium Project, which tracks and forecasts key global indicators, and insurance companies, such as Swiss Re, who are starting to increase premiums for unsustainable corporate policies. Two especially relevant reports are Strategy under Uncertainty (McKinsey 2000) and the Shell Energy Scenarios to 2050 (Royal Dutch Shell 2008).

Figure 2: Kinds of Disruptive Change

The World Economic Forum, which publishes an annual Global Risks report (WEF 2011), is a particularly useful source that outlines some three dozen risks by perceived impact and likelihood. Figure 3 shows those risks deemed most impactful and most likely. (Technology risks were also covered in the report, but none made the top six.)

A prudent business must take reasonable steps to manage these and other macro risks, especially those that are directly relevant to its operation. But because risks are interconnected, the business must also consider indirect risks.

For example, according to the Texas state climatologist (Nielsen-Gammon 2011), increasing global warming combined with natural weather variation in Texas during the summer of 2011 caused record droughts (over 100 days of 100+ degrees Fahrenheit). This, in turn, caused not only widespread wildfires and multi-billion-dollar agricultural losses, but also a six-fold increase in the cost of electricity in spot markets as air conditioners struggled to keep indoor temperatures out of the danger zone. Even local businesses not directly impacted by the heat, drought, and fires nonetheless found themselves indirectly impacted by power brownouts and high utility bills.

Recent events have had clear impacts on the IT industry. As a result of the Fukushima earthquake, tsunami, and nuclear meltdown, there was a major disruption in Apple's supply of batteries for portable devices. At that time, a Japanese company called Kureha had 70% of the global market for a

98

resin that is a critical binder for lithium ion batteries. The only Kureha factory to make the resin is in Fukushima Prefecture and stopped production because it suffered damage and could not get raw materials. In the words of Kevin Tynan, an automotive analyst for Bloomberg Industries in New York: "in many cases companies weren't even aware of their exposure; they know their suppliers, but not their suppliers' suppliers, or the suppliers of those suppliers" (Coy 2011).

**Figure 3: World Economic Forum Top Risks
(Adapted from WEF 2011)**

Another example from the fall of 2011: according to research firm IHS iSuppli: "the devastating floods in Thailand will cause a 28% quarter-on-quarter drop in hard disk drive (HDD) production, potentially affecting notebook production in early 2012" (Ribeiro 2011). This, in turn, has dramatically affected drive delivery dates and prices, and impacted sales and/or delayed product launches of other devices, including computers, solid state disks, and cameras. In addition to lost revenue, other negative impacts of this kind of disruption include increased production costs and customer base attrition. As disruptions increase, a deep knowledge of the business environment, risks, and their interconnections is becoming fundamental to strategy formation and the development and operation of business capabilities. Architects must understand this context and its risks as a necessary precondition to crafting systems that address them effectively.

A Critical Tool for Architects: Systems Thinking

The business context today is complex and richly interconnected. Seemingly unrelated events can be linked through chains of interactions, often difficult to see. The result can be unintuitive—sometimes even counter-intuitive—behavior of the systems we encounter. This leads to policy resistance (our solutions don't work) and unintended consequences (even if they do solve the targeted problem). Systems thinking is a discipline to help us deal with this complexity to arrive at better understanding, decisions, and systems architectures.

Mental models are "deeply ingrained assumptions, generalizations, or even pictures or images that influence how we understand the world and how we take action" (Senge 1990). Systems thinking explains why we are surprised whenever the mental models we use to make decisions do not match the actual circumstances that we encounter. The problem is that our models are too simple. For example, we often assume that systems have a single, well-defined boundary, when in fact, because everything is connected, each stakeholder concern can require a different system boundary for effective analysis (Meadows 2008). For example, we think of a car as a system, but closely related systems include: (car + driver), (car + driver + road), (car + driver + road + signage + on-board-navigation + GPS), (car + fuel), (car + fuel + atmosphere), etc.

Other sources of systems complexity arise because systems are: constantly adapting and evolving; governed by feedback, with delays; exhibit non-linear/exponential responses to changing input conditions; self-organize, with emergent behavior; and are characterized by tradeoffs (Sterman 2006).

An example of a common oversimplification is to imagine that something as complex as a market can be governed by a single variable—price. A more accurate model is one that treats the market as an interacting set of variables that describe key stocks (how much there is of something) and flows (how rapidly it can move between parties or states), including: supply, demand, replenishment rates (for renewable resources), regulations, and even such intangibles as trust and confidence about the future.

A key prescription of systems thinking is to be continuously aware of how we are making sense of our world. The iceberg model (see Figure 4) differentiates five levels of understanding. The top level is concrete and directly visible, with each lower level becoming more abstract and harder to see. Lower levels are increasingly broader in scope. Solutions generated at lower levels tend to be more innovative and have a more substantial impact—and be more difficult to implement (Ambler 2006).

Starting from the top, the events level deals with what is happening. Because it is the most concrete and directly visible, it is shown as being above the "waterline". Next comes the patterns level, which deals with how the events are changing, or not, over time (i.e., trends). It is only partly visible because it takes time and close attention to spot some trends.

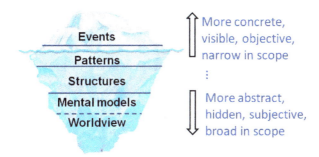

Figure 4: Systems Thinking "Iceberg" Model of Layers of Understanding (Adapted from Ambler 2006 and others)

The structures level of the iceberg describes the conditions that generate the patterns. It is modeled as a set of inter-related causal factors. This causal structure emphasizes feedback loops (direct or indirect connections back to the same component) and associated delays, which together help us understand why a system behaves in a particular—often unintuitive— way. System traps are common ways in which systems get stuck in a problematic structure (producing unintended consequences), while leverage points are general strategies for exiting the traps (Meadows 2008).

The mental models level represents the beliefs and ways of thinking that cause the structure to be the way it is. These models exist in the minds of the structure's stakeholders—the people who set up the structure and/or play a role in the way it operates. Shared mental models allow stakeholders to act quickly and in concert. It is difficult to examine mental models because we are usually unaware of them and often uncomfortable exploring them. But, in times of disruptive change, unexamined mental models (and especially worldviews) may lock us into outmoded, ineffective ways of understanding our situation. Developing more effective mental models, and corresponding language, that facilitate reasoning about long-term, disruptive change is a pre-requisite for architecting more sustainable businesses.

The worldview level is the deepest set of mental models; the framework of thoughts and beliefs (and related emotions) that shapes and constrains all our mental models. This layer is particularly relevant for sustainability considerations because these often challenge our worldviews. For example, people who believe deeply that growth is the answer to macroeconomic problems are likely to strongly resist "limits to growth" mental models.

Crafting Sustainable Enterprise Architectures

The enterprise's approach to sustainability is best recorded in a formal Sustainability Architecture, which describes the threats to sustainability in the business environment and how to address them. In turn, the Sustainability Architecture guides the transformation of the overall EA into a Sustainable EA (SEA). Because sustainability is such a fundamental concept, architects must address not only the sustainability of the enterprise they are architecting, but also the process and methods used to do the architecting. Indeed, even the way we think about the enterprise and architecting needs to change.

Architecting must be Continuous, Iterative, and Adaptive

One of the central insights of systems thinking is that the complexity of our systems and their environment is dynamic; that is, it arises due to changes over time. Worse, many changes are unforeseeable. Yet the building-architecture metaphor often used for information systems architecture suggests that nearly all of the architecting is done once at the front end of projects. A better metaphor for SEA is the architecting of urban planning and renewal, which implies that enterprise architecting needs to be continuous.

Most of the detailed architecting is done as a series of projects, including renewal initiatives, so it is iterative. (Many projects, of course, will be under way in parallel.) And conditions change after some original overall vision is established, so the architecting must be adaptive in the presence of disruptive change and resource limits.

The Sustainable Business Cycle

An important implication of the need for continuous, iterative, and adaptive architecting is that the Plan-Design-Implement-Manage (PDIM) lifecycle commonly used for systems development needs some revision. Specifically, it needs to be:

1. Front-ended with a phase to sense and interpret changes occurring in the business environment, paying particular attention to potential disruptions
2. Back-ended with a phase to monitor and adapt to significant changes in the context

In addition, there must be a continuous effort to improve sustainability-related mental models and use them across the entire extended enterprise. The resulting Sustainable Business Cycle is shown in Figure 5.

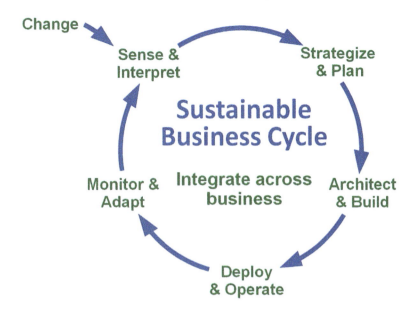

Figure 5: The Sustainable Business Cycle

To be effective, architects must participate actively in all of these phases. This interaction ensures that the architecture will continuously track and inform the evolving strategy and plans. In practice, there will be architectural activities for different enterprise systems and subsystems simultaneously in progress in all of the phases.

Before examining the activities of each phase in more detail, we next consider the structural model of a sustainable enterprise.

The Sustainable, Adaptive Business Model: The Enterprise in Context

The Sustainable Business Cycle is a process model. Adaptive architecting also requires that structural models of the enterprise make it clear how the enterprise can adapt to changes in the business environment. We have found that the overall enterprise—and its context—are effectively modeled as a sustainable, adaptive business, at multiple levels of detail. Figure 6 shows the highest-level model. For more-detailed levels of this model, see our White Paper (SBSA Partners 2010).

We developed this model by adding sustainability considerations to a commonly used model of the organization as an adaptive system (Rummler & Brache 1995).

Even in this high-level model, you can see small but important changes:

- The addition of Waste with a recycle loop

- The usual "shareholders" is generalized to Stakeholders
- The usual "competition" adds Collaboration

In addition, the Strategic Business Factors include the full range of potential disruptions over all meaningful timescales (not shown).

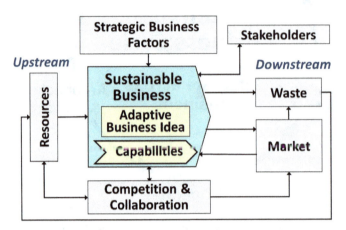

Figure 6: Sustainable, Adaptive Business Model (Generic, High-Level)

The architecture team creates the Sustainable Adaptive Business Model, at multiple levels of detail, as part of the initial Sustainability Architecture. The team then continuously refines and adjusts it with each iteration of the Sustainable Business Cycle. For example, as Sense & Interpret activities uncover relevant changes in the Strategic Business Factors, including Resource shifts, the team updates the model to reflect these new conditions.

Sense & Interpret: Tracking Strategic Business Factors, Including Resources

Understanding strategic business factors is a crucial precursor to strategy formation. In the Sustainable Business Cycle, this is formally part of the Sense & Interpret phase, but, like architecting, is really a continuous activity.

One of the biggest risks to any enterprise is a disruption in its resources supply chain. This can be sudden as in the case of a storm, earthquake, or other natural disaster or infrastructure failure. Or it may be gradual, as in the case of resource depletion. It may range from relatively short-lived to permanent, partial to complete. In our global economy with lean supply chains and volatile but generally rising energy and commodity prices, the risk of resource disruption is a primary strategic factor.

As previously discussed, a sustainable enterprise needs to pay attention to societal and natural environment considerations as well as economic ones. We have found it helpful to cross these three domains (Society, Economy, Environment) with a full range of Resource risks to create a general model for analyzing potential risks and how they might cascade to other resources, producing impacts in any or all of the three domains. We call this matrix a SEER chart, an example of which is shown in Figure 7. The entries in the cells are disruptive risk factors and impacts (color-coded for severity). Arrows show how some of the disruptions can flow from cell to cell.

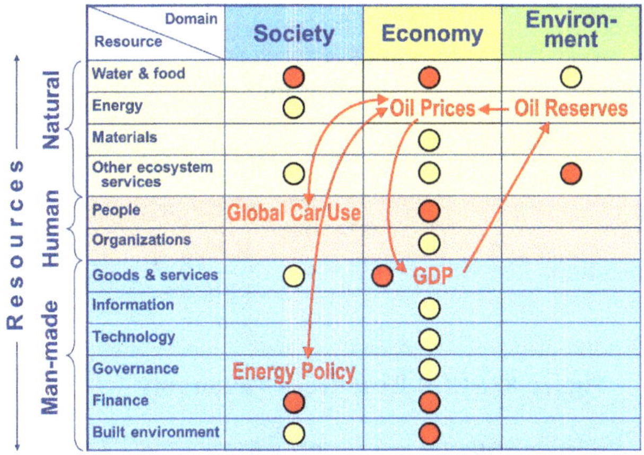

Figure 7: SEER Chart for Analyzing Cascading Resource Risks (Example) (light and dark circles indicate moderate and large impacts, respectively.)

In this simplified example, the ongoing depletion of Oil Reserves, along with a rapidly increasing demand from developing countries, is triggering the economic risk of higher, volatile Oil Prices. These prices impact, and are impacted by, Global Car Use. Governmental Energy Policy, including taxes, subsidies, leases, drilling oversight, strategic reserves, etc., is a key co-factor in the disruptive threat. The cells with red circles are the most impacted by the threat; for example, the overall output of Goods & Services (GDP) of our Economy is directly tied to Oil Prices. In turn, the rate of depletion of the Oil Reserves is directly impacted by the GDP, completing a causal loop.

Each cell has a broad set of information about the risks associated with the cell, including description, magnitude, likelihood, scope, and relevance of impacts; upstream and downstream linkages; timeframes; information sources and uncertainties; and opportunities, strategies, and actions.

We have found that by adopting a broad understanding of resources, we can model all disruptions as resource related risks (see Figure 8). Thus, the SEER chart becomes a broadly useful risk management tool.

An important reason for architects to participate in the Sense & Interpret phase is to better understand which potential disruptions require architectural flex points (aspects that can be readily changed to accommodate likely needs; for example, re-usable services and configuration parameters).

- **Natural**
  - Water & food
  - Energy
  - Materials
  - Other ecosystem services
- **Human**
  - People
  - Organizations

- **Man-made/Cultural**
  - Manufactured/harvested goods & services
  - Built environment/ infrastructure
  - Information/knowledge
  - Technology
  - Governance
  - Finance

Figure 8: SEER Resources Taxonomy

Strategize & Plan: Sustainable Strategic Planning

Given the large degree of uncertainty across a wide range of interconnected risks, how does the architect make choices that enhance the enterprise's adaptive capacity? The simple answer: by participating in the strategic conversation (a continuous senior-management dialog about directions and key decisions) that is an integral part of the Strategize & Plan phase.

Many practitioners of EA take the view that strategy formulation is not part of the architect's job description. Strategy, however, is concerned with the fit of the business with the emerging business context. The organization must evolve its unique competencies and capabilities to remain competitive. Architects define capabilities, and hence their participation in the strategic conversation is imperative.

We believe that the scenario-based planning approach, championed by Royal Dutch Shell (van der Heijden 2005), amongst others, provides especially powerful insights to guide the strategic planning process. In this approach, senior management adopts a small number of potential scenarios that cover the full landscape of possible future conditions. The scenarios, however, are strictly limited to plausible futures only; that is, future states—including the status quo—that can't be ruled out because reaching them, or staying in them, would take "too many miracles".

The process also divides future conditions into those that are "locked-in" and those that are truly uncertain. Locked-in change refers to conditions that are already inferable from present conditions; e.g., future school populations are predetermined by current birth rates; downstream flooding is predictable from upstream water levels. Strategic planners must incorporate locked-in changes into any future directions.

Figure 9 shows the high-level process strategic planners can use to adapt the enterprise's fundamental Business Idea to be sustainable; that is, to accommodate locked-in future change as well as each scenario. Of course, the enterprise's future capabilities must also be viable under each of the plausible futures.

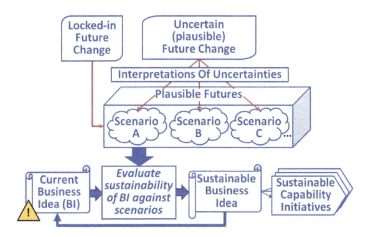

Figure 9: Process for Developing Sustainable Business Idea and Capabilities

Enterprise Architects use this information about future conditions, Sustainable Business Idea, and Sustainable Capabilities to build the needed capabilities and flexibility into the enterprise's future-state architecture.

Architect & Build: Sustainable Architecting

As previously mentioned, the first stage of creating a Sustainable Enterprise Architecture is to define a Sustainability Architecture for the business, which is then used to guide the transition to a full SEA over time. Figure 10 shows the high-level process that is used during each iteration of the cycle to improve the sustainability of the EA, starting with the outputs from the Sense & Interpret and Strategize & Plan phases.

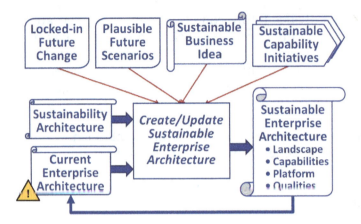

Figure 10: Process for Developing Sustainable Enterprise Architecture

The Landscape component of the Sustainable Enterprise Architecture (lower right in Figure 10) describes how the architecture is guided and constrained by the SEER information and the Sustainable Strategy.

The next section provides an overview of the Capabilities and Platforms components of the SEA; it is followed by a discussion of the sustainability-related qualities of the architecture.

Sustainable Capabilities and Platforms

Business capabilities and platforms are central to Enterprise Architecture.

Businesses sustain themselves by providing a range of attractive capabilities to their customers. Business capabilities constitute the top-level services of the business architecture. They are provided by the business's systems, and include or make use of people, processes, technology (including automated systems), information, and other resources (physical plant, materials, energy, working capital, business agreements, etc.).

A business capability can be as simple as a physical product or service. However, even simple offerings require delivery channels and support. Many of today's products involve whole ecosystems of related products and services that must function together as a cohesive capability.

A business platform is a set of lower-level capabilities upon which the top-level business capabilities are built and operated. The platform may be offered to clients and other parties (e.g., as "cloud" services), or it may be restricted to use by the enterprise itself and perhaps its business partners. By providing a common, stable base, the platform facilitates the creation, operation, and evolution of an integrated set of business capabilities. An effective platform enables strategic agility (Ross et al. 2006).

Important principles that architects can adopt to improve the sustainability of the enterprise's business capabilities include:

- Radical efficiency: Revise mental models and rearchitect to deliver products and services with radically more efficient use of resources. See, for example, the work of the Rocky Mountain Institute (RMI 2010; Lovins 2010).
- Zero waste: Eliminate product and service waste and emissions using Life-Cycle Assessment (EPA 2011) and Zero Waste strategies (Langenwalter 2006; ZWA 2011).
- JIT-JIC balance: Balance Just-In-Time lean supply chains with Just-In-Case alternatives that reduce the impact of disruptions.
- Build for change: This preserves overall system value by effective modularity and configurability, accommodating different lifetimes for different subsystems and components, and reducing the costs of technology refresh.
- Virtual and local: Increase virtual and local operations to reduce the need for travel and transportation.

Effective platforms follow these same principles. In addition, they provide leverage by propagating the benefits to all capabilities built on the platforms, at low or no additional cost to each capability. Of note in all of these strategies is that they not only improve enterprise sustainability, but also save costs.

An important aspect of the platform is its ability to disseminate information in real time to all people and enterprise systems that need to know, including management and operation center dashboards. Delta Airlines developed such a "digital nervous system" using a service and event-based architecture (Weill 1998, Ross et al 2006).

A number of sustainability dashboards have appeared, providing quick access to sustainability-related metrics. These range from global and national sustainable development indicators (CGSDI 2011) to a "comprehensive view of economic, ecological, and social aspects" of data center and cloud computing (Bash et al. 2011).

There are also a number of recent commercial products in the business sustainability dashboard space, many with a focus on energy and water use and carbon emissions.

As dashboards evolve, we anticipate that they will begin to provide insight on strategic, long-term disruptive risks, including risks originating outside the enterprise. As such, they will likely become integral to the practice of SEA.

Sustainability as the Prime System Quality

The most fundamental need for a business is to stay in business, surviving and ideally thriving in the face of even significant disruptions. Accordingly, business sustainability is the prime system quality that the architecture for the business capabilities and the platform must ensure.

To be sustainable, a business needs not only to address supply chain security and disruptions to business operations, but also to look beyond them. The entire landscape within which the business provides value could be greatly altered. Sustainability thus requires that the enterprise continuously adapt to provide goods and services that:

- Fit the customers' purposes (address their evolving needs and concerns)
- Maintain a high degree of Usability with minimal requirements for customer adaptation
- Remain Safe within the evolving operational context
- Continue to be Economical as the landscape changes

Figure 11 illustrates these four essential supporting qualities with the FUSE acronym. These four, in turn, must be supported at the next layer by a variety of additional system qualities.

Figure 11: Hierarchy of System Qualities

For example:

- Fitness-for-purpose/utility requires situational awareness to meet the rapidly evolving needs and concerns of the business and other stakeholders, including scaling (up or down) as well as responding to disruptions.
- Usability requires not only manageability and customizability, but also graceful evolvability (adaptability over the long term) and business continuity/resilience for shorter-term disruptions.
- Safety broadly includes not only potential physical damage but also the security, privacy, reliability, etc. of information communication and storage.
- Continuing to be economical within a landscape of increasing resource costs may require the enterprise to adopt a strategy of radical efficiency in its operations while remaining socially responsible and environmentally sound by internalizing true lifecycle costs.

A good way to ensure that your Enterprise Architecture addresses sustainability considerations effectively is to include a Sustainability Architecture as part of your overall EA. Over time, you can use the Sustainability Architecture to guide broader integration of sustainability concepts throughout the entire EA, transforming it into an SEA. This is similar to the way most EAs use a security architecture to ensure that the entire EA addresses security appropriately.

Architect & Build: Sustainable Building

The Architect & Build phase addresses how sustainability is realized in the capabilities and platform. In the Build sub-phase, the architect actively engages in helping to interpret the sustainability architecture. The architect and developers, working together, respond to unforeseen problems and thus learn by doing. As new sustainability approaches to architecting and building become better understood, they are incorporated into a growing body of knowledge of sustainable practices, which over time become standard practices.

Deploy & Operate: Getting Sustainability into your Business Operations

The benefits of sustainable architecting are, of course, only realized once the sustainability-based improvements to systems are placed into operation. These improvements include retrofits, reconfiguration, and upgrades of existing systems to achieve efficiency and long-term viability. It is critical for architects to be actively involved in this phase to ensure that the sustainability benefits are actually being achieved in practice.

Change management is a critical success factor when modifying people-related systems, and this means minimizing user disruptions. We introduce the principle of "progressive transition" to emphasize designs that facilitate user acceptance of changes.

Monitor & Adapt: Recognizing Key Signals and Responding Effectively

While all enterprises monitor operations on a day-to-day basis, many are not equipped to recognize trends that are potentially disruptive over a longer term. In addition, while they may be focusing on certain performance measures, they may be overlooking other critical indicators, especially those external to the enterprise. The analyses carried out in the Sense & Interpret and Strategize & Plan phases depend upon assumptions about uncertain conditions. These analyses may also identify events that would signal the timing of locked-in changes or the likelihood of one scenario over others. Sustainability monitoring looks for these signal events and triggers re-examination of relevant strategic business factors, allowing the organization to react, and potentially change direction, in a timely fashion. With a clear understanding of the flexibility incorporated into the deployed systems, the architect helps the organization respond rapidly and effectively.

Growing Adaptive Capacity into a Core Competency

While it is possible to anticipate some disruptions and make relevant preparations, there will always remain considerable, irreducible uncertainty about what will happen, when, and with what impacts. Accordingly, successful organizations must not only prepare for what is foreseeable, but also grow their ability to deal effectively with uncertain and unforeseen disruptions. Recent research has identified three traits common to companies that significantly outperformed comparison companies, over a period of at least 15 years, in a highly disruptive business environment: fanatic discipline, empirical creativity, and productive paranoia (Collins & Hansen 2011). These are characteristics of the entire business, to which the practice of SEA could make a large contribution by focusing on: planning for the long term, support for limited deployments of new capabilities before scaling up, and tracking a broad range of disruptive risks and building in alternatives for addressing them.

Sustainable Business Methods

Successful businesses would do well to formalize these SEA contributions as part of a set of Sustainable Business Methods, which would also cover sustainable business strategy (already discussed in Strategize & Plan: Sustainable Strategic Planning) and sustainable governance (discussed in Sustainable Governance and Learning). Together, the methods help you define disruption-resistant directions and initiatives, evolve business capabilities, and manage change. You will also need methods to manage disruptive risks, including procedures for maintaining and using your SEER information and for handling signals associated with disruptive events.

For TOGAF® practitioners, the Preliminary phase would be extended to include a more complete examination of the business environment and its disruptive factors. These would be retained in the repository and updated as the situation changes, possibly triggering changes to the requirements and/or rework in any of the phases. The sustainable business methods can be introduced and improved over time using a sustainable business capability maturity model (a formal way to assess the development level of an organization's sustainability practices).

Sustainable Business Checklists

An effective means for introducing sustainable business practices and methods is the adoption of Sustainable Business Checklists, which help you get the important things right. Rather than providing an exhaustive list of things to do, these checklists focus on the essentials that together "solve the problem", change the culture to focus on the right problem, and include only what are necessary and sufficient additions to common practice. They incorporate many of the insights used in the medical field to address significant problems that have resisted technology-based solutions (Gawande 2010). We have developed prototypical checklists for each phase of the Sustainable Business Cycle (Figure 5). Before any checklist can be put into operation, it must be tailored to each organization by those who will be using it.

Example checklist items for the Strategize & Plan phase include:

- Are all key stakeholders involved in the strategic conversation, including Enterprise Architects?
- Is there a mechanism to ensure that participants challenge BAU assumptions? Is there a catalog of strategic resource risks to be considered?
- Is there a robust process for scenario selection, including recording of what was rejected and why?
- Are your Sustainable Business Idea and Capabilities regularly analyzed for viability under identified locked-in-change conditions and all plausible future scenarios?

Example checklist items for the Architect & Build phase include:

- Do you have a Sustainability Architecture as part of your EA? Is it used in architectures at all levels (enterprise through solution)? Does it address long and short-term trade-offs, helping you find immediate benefits for working toward long-term goals?
- Does your architecture identify and describe flex points and how they are intended to help you adapt to a range of disruptions? Are the flex points designed to be stable over the long term?
- Are you using sustainable, adaptive systems thinking for dealing with complexity and uncertainty? Have you identified a comprehensive range of stakeholder issues and appropriate systems boundaries for addressing each?
- Have you architected in the flexibility to make real-time adjustments between just-in-time and just-in case operations based upon resource supply-chain threats and disruptions?

Sustainable Governance and Learning

Improving sustainability requires that businesses measure sustainability and integrate sustainability considerations into everyday practices. This includes the continuous monitoring and evaluation of both internal and external events, making decisions, and taking timely action to adapt and revise strategies and operations. Because a disruptive environment necessitates much on-the-job learning, it is best to integrate learning, doing, and governance (Gharajedaghi 2006). In particular, it is important to record the reasoning behind each significant decision so that a future review of the decision can maximize learning. More fundamentally, future parties can use this information to understand why a decision was made and "unmake" it or know how to revise it if the circumstances have changed.

Making decisions about funding proposed initiatives is a basic part of governance. Accordingly, a critical skill for sustainable Enterprise Architects is the ability to create strong business cases for projects that have relatively long timeframes for return on investment. Two general strategies are possible:

- Develop financial models for the cost of avoided disruptions
- Rethink the project to include more short-term returns along with the longer-term benefits

While this article does not attempt to quantify the benefits of making a SEA Change, many authors do discuss costs and savings associated with efficient/sustainable design and operations. The referenced works offer rather different but helpful perspectives (Bash et al. 2011; Esty & Simmons 2011; Lamb 2009; Lovins 2010; McKinsey 2012).

Summary and Practice Recommendations

Today's business landscape is characterized by pervasive, unrelenting, and disruptive change. Businesses that thrive in this business climate will exhibit:

- Fanatic discipline: They will pursue with intensity clear, long-term goals with steady, measured progress, maintaining deep reservoirs of resources and agile capabilities and platforms to take advantage quickly of favorable conditions presented by disruptive change.
- Empirical creativity: They will sense the business environment, test innovative and efficient offerings until they are certain of their merits, scale them rapidly but judiciously, and then repeat.
- Productive paranoia: They will pay obsessive attention to the myriad things that can go wrong and find effective trade-offs between efficiency and safety, innovation and continuity, the short and the long term, and across societal, economic, environmental, and resource challenges.

To succeed, architects must work with business leaders and sustainability experts to:

- Redefine goals and directions to make clear that the fundamental goal is sustaining the business in uncertain, disruptive times
- Shift thinking to a deeper level, with a greater focus on understanding long-term contextual shifts and systems interactions
- Craft Sustainable Enterprise Architectures (SEAs) with capabilities, platforms, and system qualities that help define and enable strategic agility
- Improve adaptive capacity, turning it into a core competency

Immediate steps that architects can take are to:

- Learn more about business sustainability and the management of disruptive risks across all SEER (Society, Economy, Environment, and Resources) dimensions.
- Participate actively in your company's strategic conversation. Seek first to understand the dynamic business context and its implications for the practice of SEA, and then to convince others of the beneficial role SEA can play in helping the company to meet its challenges.
- Start crafting your Sustainability Architecture.
- Share SEA ideas with other SEA practitioners to increase our common body of knowledge. Use these ideas in your practice, and grow your competency.

About the Authors

Leo Laverdure (leo.laverdure@sbsapartners.com) is a managing partner of SBSA Partners, LLC. He has led a number of Enterprise and Solution Architecture programs at HP and other companies, serving as lead architect for HP's Adaptive Enterprise and heading up their Architect profession. Leo holds a BA from Harvard University. He is a member of the Sustainability Commission for the town of Groton, Massachusetts.

Dr. Alex Paul Conn (alex.conn@sbsapartners.com) is a managing partner of SBSA Partners, LLC. He has extensive experience as both a practitioner and professor in computer systems architecture and engineering, concentrating on the early business-critical development phases. His focus on system qualities stresses the importance of minimizing the disruptions introduced by changes in systems architectures and associated policies and governance. Alex received his PhD from University of California, Berkeley.

References

Ambler, G.: Systems Thinking as a Leadership Practice (2006)

Bash, C., Cader, T., Chen, Y., Gmach, D., Kaufman, R., Milojicic, D., Shah, A., Sharma, P.: Cloud Sustainability Dashboard, Dynamically Assessing Sustainability of Data Centers and Clouds, HP Laboratories, HPL-2011-148 (2011); available at: www.hpl.hp.com/techreports/2011/HPL-2011-148.pdf

CGSDI, Consultative Group on Sustainable Development Indicators: Dashboard of Sustainability (2011); available at: www.iisd.org/cgsdi/dashboard.asp.

Collins, J., Hansen, M.: Great By Choice: Uncertainty Chaos, and Luck—Why Some Thrive Despite Them All, HarperCollins Publishers, New York (2011).

Coy, P.: Japan: Economic Aftershocks, Bloomberg Businessweek (March 30, 2011); available at: www.businessweek.com/magazine/content/11_15/b4223012614574.htm.

EPA, Environmental Protection Agency: Life Cycle Assessment Research website (2011); available at: www.epa.gov/nrmrl/std/lca/lca.html.

Esty, D., Simmons, P.J.: The Green to Gold Business Playbook: How to Implement Sustainability Practices for Bottom-Line Results in Every Business Function, Wiley, Hoboken, NJ (2011).

Gawande, A.: The Checklist Manifesto: How to Get Things Right, Metropolitan Books, New York (2010).

Gharajedaghi, J.: Systems Thinking: Managing Chaos and Complexity: A Platform for Designing Business Architecture, Second Edition, Elsevier, Butterworth-Heinemann (2006).

Lamb, J.: The Greening of IT: How Companies Can Make a Difference for the Environment, IBM Press/Pearson plc, Upper Saddle River, NJ (2009).

Langenwalter, G.: "Life" is Our Ultimate Customer: From Lean to Sustainability, Target Magazine, Volume 22 No. 1, Association for Manufacturing Excellence (2006); available at: www.zerowaste.org/publications/Lean_to_Sustainability.pdf.

Lovins, A.: Profitable Solutions to Climate, Oil, and Proliferation, Royal Swedish Academy of Sciences, Springer (2010); available at: www.rmi.org/cms/Download.aspx?id=4953&file=2010-18_ProfitableSolutionsClimateOil.pdf&title=Profitable+Solutions+to+Climate%2c+Oil%2c+and+Proliferation.

McKinsey & Company: Strategy Under Uncertainty, McKinsey Quarterly (2000); available at: www.mckinsey.com/insights/managing_in_uncertainty/strategy_under_uncertainty.

McKinsey & Company: Resource Revolution: Meeting the world's energy, materials, food, and water needs (2012); available at: www.mckinsey.com/insights/energy_resources_materials/resource_revolution.

Meadows, Donella: Thinking in Systems: A Primer, Chelsea Green, White River Junction, VT (2008).

Nielsen-Gammon, J.: Texas Drought and Global Warming (2011); available at: blog.chron.com/climateabyss/2011/09/texas-drought-and-global-warming/.

Owens, C.: Fostering Business Resilience (2004), available at: www.interisle.net/sub/Business_Resilience.pdf.

Rechtin, E., Maier, M.: The Art of Systems Architecting, Second Edition, CRC Press, p. 234 (1997).

Ribeiro, J.: Thailand Floods Hit Hard Drive Production, Macworld website (2011); available at: www.macworld.com.au/news/thailand-floods-hit-hard-drive-production-39511/.

RMI, Rocky Mountain Institute: Factor Ten Engineering Design Principles (2010); available at: www.rmi.org/10xE+Principles.

Ross, J.W., Weill, P., Robertson, D.C.: Enterprise Architecture as Strategy: Creating a Foundation for Business Execution, Harvard Business School Press, Boston (2006)

Royal Dutch Shell: Shell Energy Scenarios to 2050 (2008); available at: s01.static-shell.com/content/dam/shell/static/investor/downloads/presentations/2008/bentham-csfb-june2008.pdf.

Rummler, G., Brache, A.: Improving Performance: How to Manage the White Space on the Organization Chart, Second Edition, John Wiley & Sons, Inc., Hoboken, NJ, pp.10, 82 (1995).

SBSA Partners: Improving Business Sustainability, pp.15-16 (2010); available at: www.sbsapartners.com/SBSA/ideas/Improving-Business-Sustainability-4dnld.pdf.

Senge, P.: The Fifth Discipline: The Art and Practice of the Learning Organization, Doubleday/Currency, New York (1990).

Sherwood, J., Clark, A., Lynas, D.: Enterprise Security Architecture White Paper (2009); available at: www.sabsa-institute.com/members/sites/ default/inline-files/SABSA_White_Paper.pdf.

Sterman, J.: Sustaining Sustainability: Creating a Systems Science in a Fragmented Academy and Polarized World; available at: jsterman.scripts.mit.edu/docs/Sterman%20Sustaining%20Sustainability%20 6-19.pdf.

The Open Group and SABSA Institute: TOGAF® and SABSA Integration: How SABSA and TOGAF complement each other to create better architectures (2011); available at: www.opengroup.org/bookstore/catalog/w117.htm.

van der Heijden, K.: Scenarios: The Art of Strategic Conversation, John Wiley & Sons, Ltd., Chichester, England (2005).

WEF, World Economic Forum: Global Risks, Sixth Edition (2011); available at: reports.weforum.org/wp-content/blogs.dir/1/mp/uploads/pages/files/global-risks-2011.pdf.

Weill, P. (1998) Leveraging the New Infrastructure: How Market Leaders Capitalize on Information Technology, Harvard Business Review Press

ZWA, Zero Waste Alliance: Publications and Case Studies (2011); available at: www.zerowaste.org/publications.htm.

Embedding Systemic Thinking into Enterprise Architecture

Mesbah Khan

Abstract

Enterprise Architecture (EA), a discipline that emerged from IT with the aim to link 'strategy to design' provides various frameworks, taxonomies and languages for articulating organizational design. However, it lacks an appreciation of the dynamic relationship between technology and organization and the complex process of strategy. Systems Thinking (ST), a multidisciplinary science of praxis that evolved through the fusion of social systems theory and second order cybernetics, provides a holistic and reflexive approach for intervening in complex systems. Similar to EA, it has a number of concepts and methods for describing and diagnosing organization as systems. However, it lacks precise and rigorous modeling approaches for describing technology solutions. This article explores the process and possibility of embedding systemic thinking into enterprise architecture and the practice of organization design by combining theoretical research with practical inquiry in a particular oil and gas independent.

Keywords

Systems Thinking, Enterprise Architecture, Viable Systems Model, VSM

Introduction

Petroleum has evolved into an important determinant of modern political economy over the past century. It has been likened to the rivers of the ancient riparian civilizations (Davis, 2006) because like rivers with their uncertain, territorial and fluid nature it shapes the economic and political history of those that depend on it. The oil industry has been the source of many intrigues in the 20th century because of its vital role in determining the fates of nations (Yergin, 1993). As such the 'oil system' comprises a complex network of techno-political forms of organization that are competing yet collaborating around the oil 'streams'.

Ever since the Tehran-Tripoli agreements in 1971 when OPEC assumed control of international crude prices, the industry has witnessed major structural changes through mergers and emergence of many new independents. These upheavals also included a reevaluation of the 'vertical integration' business model by the 'majors' due to nationalization and the new dynamics created by the futures markets, which gave producers a new level of commercial flexibility.

This new environment spawned a number of upstream explorers who would invest in new oil provinces, make discoveries and divest at a profit prior to entering the field development stage. Alternatively, some companies continued through the development stage but managed their transaction costs through the market rather than internal hierarchy by outsourcing the Engineering, Procurement and Construction (EPC) (Davis, 2006).

Oil and gas field development involves complex multi-billion dollar capital projects to deliver wells, production facilities and export infrastructure. Field development is the second major stage of value realization in the oil and gas value chain (see Figure 1). The figure also highlights the change in investment, risk and timescales.

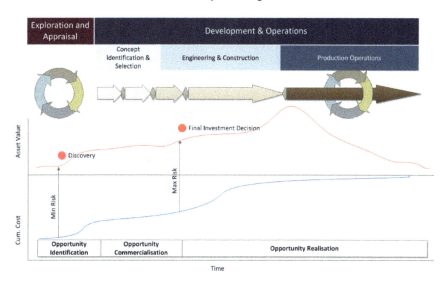

Figure 1 Typical Oil and Gas value chain and cumulative cost, NPV profiles. Risk is shown in terms of asset value and overall capital expenditure.

This article explores the question of organizational design in the context of the nascent Development and Operations (D&O) organization of an upstream oil and gas independent. The D&O organization was as formed in late 2009 in response to the company's recent success with delivering a major field development through the outsourcing model. The success and resultant growth created the drivers for the board to invest in expanding the company's field development and production operations capability. In early 2010 the organization formed its vision of achieving 'sustainable and world class project delivery capability', embedded project services teams into the on-going projects and established a core project management and controls team in the center to provide support and advice to the business units.

During mid-2010 the company was reorganized from being a functional to a region-based matrix structure. The functional structure was deemed inappropriate by senior management because field development and production activities require a longer-term commitment to a region and a context specific strategy. However, Exploration and Appraisal (E&A) activities are intrinsically linked with identifying geological structures that span geographic boundaries and even continents. E&A therefore would prefer to operate on a functional model to maintain their focus on geology. Furthermore, E&A requires a flexible, agile and entrepreneurial organizational style because decisions need to be made quickly when new exploration opportunities arise - whereas a more rigorous engineering and project management discipline is required for executing development projects due to the complex techno-commercial nature of such projects.

The situation presents organizational design problems around balancing agility and standardization, autonomy and cohesion and achieving interoperability across complex contracting environments. The challenge lies in translating an abstract business strategy (e.g. 'we need to acquire project delivery capability') into concrete design principles that can be used to develop clear and effective organizational models. It is therefore a systemic and architectural problem. This situation presents a unique opportunity for exploring how Systems Thinking and Enterprise Architecture could provide techniques and tools for solving these specific organizational design problems.

This situation exposes a site for integrating concepts and practices from Enterprise Architecture (EA) and Systems Thinking (ST) to address design issues in a specific organizational context. The author undertook Participatory Action Research (PAR) (Barton, Stephens & Haslett, 2009a) as the intervention approach and then applied a combination of EA and ST concepts for diagnostic and therapeutic ends.

EA and ST have an integration potential because of the number of overlapping concepts used in the two disciplines, including that of system, boundary, modeling and multiple perspectives/views. Additionally, ST and EA are both methodologically better equipped for solving detailed organizational design problems compared to other theories of organization that are more explanatory and analytical such as Actor Network Theory (Latour, 1986), Weick's theory of sense-making (Weick, 2000), and transactional cost economics (Coase, 1937).

Organization, System and Architecture

Organizational theory emerged as a specialized branch of sociology by problematizing the process of organization and functioning of organizations. Primarily dominated by structural functionalism (G. Burrell & Morgan, 1985), it generated a body of research and concepts around various social and technical aspects of organizations. However, these abstract sociological concepts are difficult to render into context specific designs. In this respect, Enterprise Architecture (EA) and Systems Thinking (ST) are two domains of practice that have a shared interest in and a range of concepts for solving the organizational design problem.

Enterprise Architecture (EA) is defined by The Open Group (The Open Group, 2011) as:

> 'The description of a system and the structure of components, their interrelationship and principles and guidelines governing their design'.

It is the science and art of linking strategy to design (Aier & Winter, 2008). The science involves building design principles and design instructions (models) for each domain (e.g. structure, process and information and technology) (Gharajedaghi, 2011). The art involves critically reflecting on purpose, goals and strategy based on implications of the design (Bean, 2010). However, architecture practices (e.g. definition of organizational structure, process and technology requirements) pervade organizational life, even where the EA function has not been institutionalized, making it difficult to govern and organize them.

Systems Thinking (ST) is a set of approaches that revolve around the concept of 'purposeful systems' that are emergent wholes and greater than the sum of their interacting parts. It provides methodologies and modeling tools for intervention into and appreciation of complex socio-technical situations (Reynolds & Holwell, 2010). With a legacy in both social and natural sciences, including social systems theory and cybernetics, it has strong theoretical foundations primarily rooted in structural functionalism (G. Burrell & Morgan, 1985) and control theory. More recently, with the incorporation of second order cybernetics and critical theory, systems approaches have moved towards reflexivity and self-critique (Ison, 2010).

A large body of EA and ST literature has emerged over the past 20 years that indicates a growing interest in both domains. There have also been a few initiatives by members of the EA community to incorporate ST into the EA (e.g. (Graves, 2010), (Gharajedaghi, 2011)), but largely the two domains have continued to grow independently of each other.

Architecting the Enterprise

EA emerged in the 1980s in response to the widening gap between organizational vision and technology strategy. The first architecture framework (Zachman, 1987) used the 'building' metaphor and was a matrix of views (e.g. owner, designer, and builder) and domains (e.g. data, process, and network and later evolved to include people, time and motivation). It was an IT-focused taxonomy for organizing architectural artifacts (e.g. business requirements, design documents and models) and contained limited methodological guidelines. Subsequently, process oriented frameworks evolved such as The Open Group's Architecture Development Methodology (ADM) that provided templates for 'architecting' the enterprise (Sessions, 2008). With a heritage in IT, EA theory and practice has evolved rigorous formal languages, modeling tools and deployment templates. By applying these tools and methodologies, a large body of architectural artifacts (principles, designs and models) can be created in organizations but also significantly increasing the CIO's budget and head-count.

However, a large number of EA projects have failed because they created yet another organizational silo filled with architects who were isolated from both the IT and the business communities (Cardwell, 2008). This failure can be attributed to the mechanistic and instrumentalist paradigm of the current EA frameworks. A static hierarchy of entities coordinating work processes is inadequate in accounting for the complexity of organizational phenomenon because it ignores social and interpersonal dynamics involved (Seidl & Becker, 2005) as well as the way real world processes are actually structured. In response to this inadequacy, there is a growing interest in organization theory, complexity and systems thinking within the EA community (Bean, 2010).

Organization as System

Organization theorists have used various mechanistic, organic and cultural metaphors (Morgan, 1996) to conceptualize organization. Burrell & Morgan (1979) suggest that organization theory can be categorized into functionalist, interpretivist, radical humanist and radical structuralist paradigms. These paradigms have evolved from shifting positions on ontology, epistemology, human nature and methodology (Figure 2). For instance, the debate on epistemology has moved from Parson's analysis of stable constructs based on equilibrium to process-based assumptions emphasizing subjectivity and sense-making and more recently to a focus on recursivity, complexity, emergence and adaptation (Bakken & Herenes, 2003).

Social Systems theory was developed in the 1950s as a popular means for social analysis by social theorists of the structural functionalist school. It aimed to explain the three areas of Radcliff-Brown's inquiry, namely sociological morphology (structure), physiology (function) and morphogenesis (development). Social systems theories used the concept of a system as the organizing principle in society. At around the same time, General System Theory (GST) was being introduced as an integrative discipline for the sciences. A system was defined by von Bertalanffy as 'a complex of elements standing in interaction'. Bertalanffy's application of the systems concept was intended to unite all science by 'cutting across substantive differences in sciences, because they are all a study of systems or complex interacting elements' (Bertalanffy, 2003).

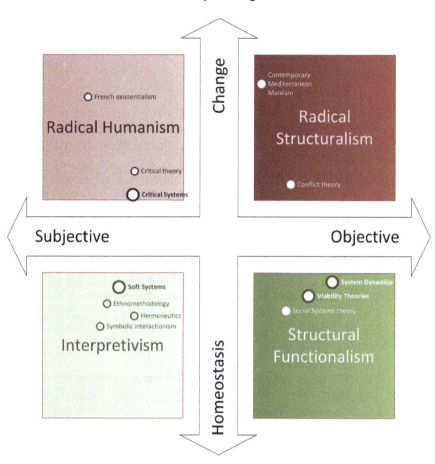

Figure 2. Sociological Paradigm Map (adapted from Morgan and Burrell, 1979). Four systems thinking approaches (Soft Systems, Critical Systems Thinking, Viability Theories and System Dynamics) have been overlaid based on the author's understanding of the paradigms.

Initially social systems theories were more focused on morphology and physiology using the mechanistic and organismic metaphor to describe organizations. With the introduction of the cybernetics (Schwaninger, 2004), systems theory moved towards a more generalized concept of organization based on goal seeking behavior not tied to any specific mechanical or organismic analogy (G. Burrell & Morgan, 1985).

In the next 40 years, systems theory had branched off into numerous schools and approaches including Soft Systems Methodology (SSM) (Checkland & Scholes, 1993b) and Critical Systems Thinking (R. L. Flood, 1990). These schools stressed the plurality of perspectives and the partiality of knowledge, moving systems approaches towards self-critique, reflexivity and second order analysis. Other systems approaches have adopted a number of structural functionalist themes such as interrelatedness (Morecroft, 2010), (Schwaninger, 2006), openness (Emery, 2000) and viability.

Viable Systems

From systems approaches based on viability, the two most notable are Beer's Viable Systems Model (VSM) (Beer, 1994) and Miller's Living Systems Theory (LST) (Miller, 1978). The difference between the two is that VSM is cybernetics focused (managing complexity through variety engineering) and constructivist (purpose is constructed by people) whereas LST is more closely aligned to General Systems Theory (openness, inputs and outputs) and takes a positivist standpoint (Schwaninger, 2006).

Beer's VSM is the more popular of two and derives the model of viability from a generalization of the functional systems of the human brain and their interconnectivity. The notion of functional systemization of viability has its roots in Parson's "four functional imperatives to be fulfilled for a system, by its sub-systems, if that system is to continue to exist". These imperatives are adaptation, goal-attainment, integration and latency (pattern maintenance) (Parsons, 1967).

Beer's model incorporates Ashby's concept of variety into the Parsonian schema and modeling communication across system boundaries as a variety modifying operation. Secondly, Beer introduces recursion to the model by arguing that viable systems are composed of a self-similar structure composed of five subsystems at every level of recursion. The VSM is intended to be a heuristic device for diagnosing social systems for cybernetic gaps against a normative functional structure. It is also an approach for identifying the necessary variety equations across various communication channels necessary for maintaining viability. It is an attempt to address the inadequacy of the linear hierarchy structure typically used to define control and governance in organizations. However, it is still based on stable constructs of goal attainment and functional imperatives.

Process and Structure

Whereas viability theories apply the goal/means schema to conceptualize organizations, certain sociological systems theories seek to replace goal seeking rationality with a systems rationality (Seidl & Becker, 2005). For instance, Niklas Luhmann (1995) reoriented the Parsonian action frame of reference to a model of social systems based on communication. Luhmann's model of the organization is based on Maturana and Varela's theory of autopoiesis combined with Spencer-Brown's calculus of distinctions and indications (Mingers, 2002). *Poiesis* means 'dynamic production', and *auto* means autonomous, independent or self-referential. Autopoiesis theory was developed (Maturana & Varela, 1987) to determine the essential difference between living and non-living systems and how living systems manage to persist despite changes in structure, internal components and external environment (Lawrence & Botes, 2011).

Communications for Luhmann is conceptualized as events as opposed to the standard transmission model in information theory that is based on what he calls the 'thing schema'. Communication events in society are selective and based on a double contingency because both utterance and understanding are subject to the selectivity of the 'meaning systems' that form the background of social communication. Luhmann's theory radically re-constructs organizations as communicating systems that are autopoietic, operationally closed but structurally coupled to the function systems (institutions) and psychic systems (individuals) that are present in the organization's environment. The organization for Luhmann is a decision processing system containing a network of positions interacting with a hierarchy of previous decisions and decision premises (where decision premises are programs (plans), personnel and communication paths (structure)) (Mingers, 2003). These decisions communicate, i.e. are selections which involve making distinctions between what is selected and what is excluded. An interesting aspect of Luhmann's theory of social systems is the notion of interpenetration of the society and individual (what he refers to as psychic systems). This means that the individual and society are ontologically distinct entities that participate in the each other though structurally coupling (Mingers, 2003) just like distinct functional systems (e.g. the blood circulation system and respiratory system).

In EA terms Luhmann's model can be visualized as a dynamic event architecture that is constantly evolving. The application of Luhmannian concepts to organizational theory has been limited, especially in the US and UK, due its obscurity and difference in style of sociology (bottom up vs. top down) (Jokisch, 2010), however, a growing body of research reveals its possible pragmatic value for organizational analysis (Bakken & Herenes, 2003; Seidl & Becker, 2005; Jensen, 2010).

Luhmann's theory can be classed as a process theory of the organization where the organization is not a "thing made" but a process "in the making" (Langley & Tsoukas, 2010). Process theories (e.g. Latour's actor network theory (Latour, 1986), Weick's sense-making theory and Giddens' structuration theory) all shift focus from paradigmatic to narrative thinking, stressing the importance of kairological time (the here and now of improvisation) over chronological time (the punctuated calendar based planner's view) and process over substance (Langley & Tsoukas, 2010). The application of process theories to EA may provide an opportunity to rethinking the model of organization as *structuration* rather than structure.

However, whereas process theories do possess a broad explanatory power and can be classed as 'grand theories', their usability in their current state for design purposes is somewhat limited. Attempts at operationalizing Luhmann's theories (Brier, Baecker & Thyssen, 2011) for instance, are still formative and therefore of little relevance to the task at hand. Looking outside of systems traditions, very little literature was found on Weick's sense-making theory and EA, with some exceptions (e.g. (Graves, 2010) and (Jensen, 2010)). Similarly, searching on ANT and EA delivered sparse results, with exceptions that prove the rule (e.g. an explanation of EA institutionalization using ANT concepts (Iyamu, 2011)).

Models as Observation

Both EA and ST emphasize the development of models, maps and diagrams. However, they differ on epistemological, methodological and ethical positions on models and model building.

EA models are system descriptions articulated in languages that have formal denotational, operational, axiomatic and action semantics (Lankhorst, 2005). However, these languages are IT focused and lack the expressiveness of natural languages which has led to recent developments in semantic process modeling approaches (Thomas & Fellmann M.A., 2009). Frameworks to evaluate the expressiveness and domain appropriateness of these languages have evolved over the past decade (Wand and Weber's ontology based representation theory (Wand & Weber, 1990), the workflow patterns framework (van der Aalst, Kiepuszewski, Barros & Dogac, 2003) and Lindland's quality framework (Lindland, 1994) to evaluate semantic suitability for technical actor and social actor interpretation.

Recent developments in ontology have taken a closer look at the fundamental paradigms underlying information systems modeling to explain the gap between organizational reality and its implementation in information technologies. Dietz's Enterprise Ontology (Dietz, 2006) focuses on modeling commitments and differentiating facts and acts. Partridge's BORO methodology is based on a 4D Ontology (Partridge, 2005). BORO uses concepts from modern analytical philosophy and set theory to provide a method for building foundational models for exposing the underlying structure processes, events, relations and things relevant to the organization. 4D ontology has already made headway in the oil and gas space through the introduction of ISO 15926 (ISO) because it seeks to provide a data foundation for supporting interoperability across functional boundaries and complex supply chains typical to the oil industry.

There is a variety of views in ST on the question of what a model is. Usually the model is considered a construct of the observer that has an iconic, symbolic or analogous relation with what is being modeled and a boundary judgment determining what to include in the model (Robert L. Flood & Carson, 1993). Others treat models to be more than just representation and include 'working models' (Beer, 1995) i.e. they retain the structure and function of the thing being modeled. Modeling approaches range from loosely defined pictographic representations of the context and situation (e.g. in Rich Pictures) to more specific notations for describing and predicting system behavior and dynamics (e.g. systems dynamics and iThink (Gharajedaghi, 2011)).

Modeling as a process of observation and hence selection has also been explored extensively in systems traditions. Von Forester's observing systems (Müller, 2010), Luhmann's concepts of form and distinction (Luhmann, 1995) and more recently the theory of cybersemiotics (Brier, 2006). These concepts explore the semiotics of models and more broadly how meaning systems operate in society (e.g. how authority and expertise are reified through a model) (Ison, 2010). These aspects of semiotics and power are now also emerging in EA literature as well (Fez-Barringten, 2009).

A bridge between the explanatory models of ST and the analytical modeling in EA is yet to be built such that both can be used introduce the balance of rigor and relevance in organizational and information systems design.

Systemically Thinking Enterprise Architecture

Recent EA literature reveals that practitioners have been able to demonstrate improvements to organizational design and EA practices by applying systemic approaches to emphasize the importance of balancing socio-cultural, holistic, operational and design thinking (Gharajedaghi, 2011).

For instance the Viable Systems Model (VSM) (Leonard, 2009) was used for designing viable virtual enterprises (Assimakopoulos & Dimitriou, 2006), strategic planning processes (Stephens & Haslett, 2011), and creating 'reflective organizations' (Nolte, 2011). Similarly, System Dynamics has provided more deterministic and predictive models to assess architecture adoption and diffusion (Choi, Nazareth & Jain, 2010).

A review of literature from both discipline exposes a number of overlapping themes that can be plotted on a Venn diagram (see Figure 3). The diagram also highlights certain key differences of perspective between the two domains. Some examples are:

- ST construes systems as emergent wholes comprised of complex interacting elements whereas EA deconstructs systems as complexes composed of simple functionally decomposable parts.
- ST posits that models and knowledge are socially constructed, whereas EA models are based on objectivist assumptions.

Analyzing the overlapping concepts reveals differing positions on basic questions such as is a system a material construction of the world or just a mental construct of an observer. More fundamentally the thing vs. process distinction is problematic as it is based on long established habits of thought, that are not accurate at describing reality. Similarly, there is a bias towards either ontic (what exists) or epistemic (what we can know) facts, which leads to inconsistencies in various systems and EA schools. Any serious integration project will therefore have to scrutinize the underlying semantics of shared terms between EA and ST, such as system, boundary, people, and technology. Furthermore, a consistent theory of practice is required that can work alongside these concepts such that interventions into particular organizational situations can be designed as an organic and self-organizing process.

Engagement and Intervention

A key dimension of model building is the process of stakeholder engagement, alignment and agreement. EA uses requirements gathering and stakeholder management concepts and tools derived from information systems analysis and design traditions. ST approaches also have preferred engagement and intervention methodologies such as action research (Reason & Bradbury, 2008), Participative Design Workshops (Emery, 2000), and cognitive mapping (Fran Ackermann & Colin Eden, 2005).

From the current engagement methodologies, action research has gained significant support in systems thinking circles (Peters, 1984) and has seen a shift from focus on delivery of outputs to analyzing dynamics of the research process (e.g. Triple Task Method (Bell & Morse, 2010) and the multiple modalities involved in research (determinative to normative) (e.g. Multi Modal Method (Britto, 2011)). A further consideration for selecting methodologies is how well they can assist in double loop learning (Barton, Stephens & Haslett, 2009b) and how those learning systems can be sustainably embedded into practice.

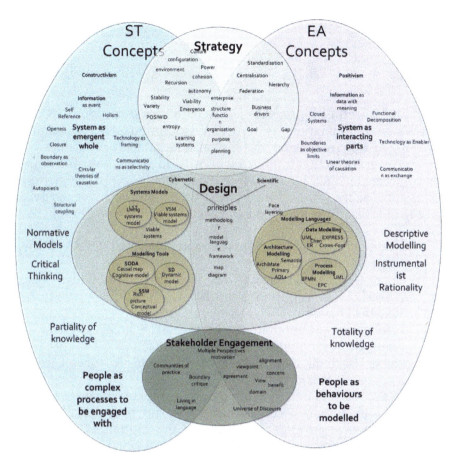

Figure 3: EA and ST Concept map showing overlapping and differentiating concepts

Research Design

In the context of the situation of interest, the following question was posed to problematize the integration of EA and ST:

How can an EA practice be *systemically* established within the D&O in order to enable stakeholders to continuously reflect on and modify organizational design based on a shared vision?

Due to its contextual nature the question does not provide an objective definition of success that can be quantitatively evaluated. This lack of generalizability and verifiability is somewhat inherent in the case based nature of the research and the complex social dynamics of organizational situations (Harvey, 2009). This research aim may be construed as 'experimental' but it is in fact the opposite. An experiment aims to arrive at a general statement about a process through predicated outcomes whereas in a case, both outcomes and process are equally important (Mjøset, 2009).

Sample Space

The criteria for selecting approaches is based on how successful they are in achieving a shared understanding and consensus amongst the stakeholders both in terms of a shared vision and organizational design to achieve that vision. Since every selection implies exclusion and given the rich history of systems approaches that have evolved over the past 60 years, only a handful of approaches were selected based on the author's familiarity and relevance to organizational design as follows:

1. Strategic Options Development and Analysis (SODA) (Shaw, F Ackermann & C Eden, 2003)
2. Open Systems Theory (OST) and the Participative Design Workshop (PDW) (Emery, 2000)
3. Systems Dynamics (SD) (Morecroft, 2010),
4. Soft Systems Methodology (Checkland & Scholes, 1993b),
5. Viable Systems Model (VSM) (Beer, 1994)
6. Critical Systems Heuristics (CSH) (Reynolds & Holwell, 2010)

Each of these approaches was used for specific contexts. For instance, SSM tools such as Rich Pictures, conceptual maps and root definitions was employed to co-evolve an understanding and description of the context. Similarly, the VSM was used to develop an overall organizational model that could indicate systemic and communication gaps in terms of viability. The stakeholders that were interviewed/observed during the projects were analyzed using the CSH. The boundary critique of CSH revealed the sources influence clearly as well as an appreciation of the author's own selectivity towards the situation. In order to gather the broadest range of views, the inquiry included representatives from both beneficiaries, and witnesses (the affected, including potential victims) in the observation process.

Data Generation and Collection

The following tools were used for data generation and gathering:

Active Interviews

Opinions were gathered and formed through semi-structured interviews using the active interviewing approach (Atkinson & Coffey, 2003) which involves creating structured conversations where both interviewer and interviewee can discuss their concepts in order to co-create knowledge. This approach provided the opportunity to introduce systems concepts to the interviewees in order to assist the articulation of issues and concerns.

Email Surveys

Systems models were constructed and presented to individuals for comments and to answer basic questions around utility of the model in a diagnostic and therapeutic capacity.

Participant Observations

Participant observations were recorded during meetings and informal conversations where the researcher was actively engaged in debates around the themes of interest.

Textual Analysis of Official Communications

Certain key documents and communications around the subject of architecture were reviewed to extract key themes and concerns relevant to architecture practice.

Analysis & Findings

Concerns

Concerns have a specific meaning in EA that can be described as "an interest of a stakeholder with regards to the architecture description of some system, resulting from the stakeholder's goals, and the present or future role played by the system in relation to these goals" (Lankhorst, 2005). Therefore the first aspect of the analysis was to understand organizational concerns from various stakeholder perspectives. In this respect the results from the semi structured interviews and official communications were ranked by frequency in a mind map (see Figure 4).

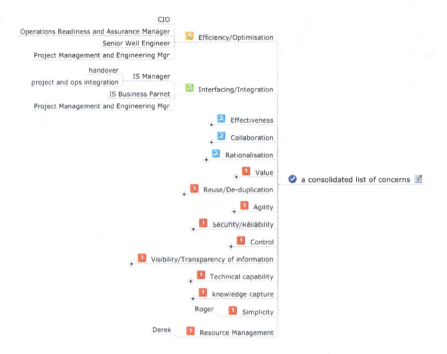

Figure 4. Ranked list of concerns recorded in MindManager®.

The numbers indicate the number of stakeholders who share the concern. The top two concerns have been expanded to show the role of the stakeholders involved.

These concerns typify the dichotomies and issues faced by managers in an organization that is growing into new areas of capability but wishes to sustain its flexible and nimble approach, which delivered its earlier success (e.g. agility vs efficiency, visibility vs security).

Stakeholders and Viewpoints

In EA, a key practice is the definition viewpoints and views for addressing specific concern. A view in EA parlance is 'the representation of a system from the perspective of a related set of concerns' (Lankhorst, 2005). However, conventional EA takes an instrumentalist position when selecting the views that matter, in that it uses the building metaphor to define the views (owner, builder, planner etc.) and is not very specific on which viewpoints matter and how to be sensitive to those views that are unvoiced. In this respect the CSH taxonomy was applied for the selection and critique of the stakeholder list and boundary of the research.

The use of the CSH taxonomy was tested in various organizational settings to integrate with existing EA language (e.g. the concepts of 'stake' similar to 'concerns' from EA terminology). The concept of boundary critique supplemented the standard EA stakeholder management and benefits realization processes by providing an alternative approach for appreciating *sources of influence and motivation* and introduced a moral and ethical dimension to the problem.

Therefore the process of selecting specific decision makers and nominating the right experts as well as the consultation of *witnesses* was all evaluated as boundary decisions that needed to be explicitly appreciated as selective and by that account exclusive. The result was that the stakeholder group that was initially limited to D&O became broader and encompassed the E&A and other corporate functional groups (e.g. finance and supply chain).

Context

A Rich Picture (RP) (a context mapping technique from SSM) (Checkland & Scholes, 1993a) was developed based on the interviews and researcher's knowledge of the context (Figure 5). It was circulated via an email survey to all the interviewees with very positive outcomes. Subsequently a few of the senior managers, including the Group D&O Manager, were presented the RP and interviewed for their views on both diagnostic and descriptive utility. The comments from the email survey were around what was missing, and that the picture should be made richer. The discussion with the D&O Manager brought forth a number of answers to the 'so what, we know this already?' question. These were 'first time we can see it all on an A3', 'this can help diagnose and negotiate our organizational structural design decisions', 'this can be used to explain what we do to other functions and the emphasis on the need for working together.

Subsequently, a number interviewees requested similar detailed RPs to be drawn for their areas of the business in, which constitutes a positive change in terms of embedding awareness of architecture practices and their benefits into the business.

It was also presented in a few meetings alongside some EA models for comparison (process maps in BPMN and conceptual data models in Crow's Foot Notation). The EA models were perceived as too complex and perhaps constraining. However, when the RP was presented, it was met with interest and suggestions for expanding the scope to the Exploration and Appraisal (E&A) part of the business.

The use of consistent notations on the RP is unusual and it may be argued that it was depicting more information than usually expected in SSM.

Furthermore, it was also pointed out that it was highlighting the technical aspects of the situation as opposed to the contractual and relational aspects. This inherent lack of overall structure to the RP process creates the risk of missing the blind spots. Therefore, one can manage to draw a RP that everyone accepts and agrees with, yet it might be hiding or overemphasizing aspects of the situation based on the modeler's own knowledge and capacity. Therefore, the research revealed two possible uses for the RP; firstly as a tool for engaging with the stakeholders and their perspectives to explore the situation at a high level, and secondly, as a tool for presenting the outcomes of some modeling exercises in order to communicate the essential features to various stakeholders.

Purpose

Root definitions (a concept from SSM (Checkland & Scholes, 1993a)) were developed to define purpose for a number of D&O disciplines. This provided a useful high-level map of each function, and how it could be connected to the overall architecture in terms of inputs, outputs and services to develop a top-level process definition. An example of the process definition diagram for the Cost Engineering discipline alongside its root definition is shown in Figure 6.

The Figure shows how Archimate notation can be used alongside SSM Root Definition format (i.e. 'a system to do x using y in order to achieve z'). It was noted that the Archimate could also be used for representing outcomes of the SSM CATWOE (Customers, Actors, Transformation Process, Worldviews, Owners, Environment) identification process by using the 'actor' notation for Customers and Actors, the 'meaning' notation for Worldviews.

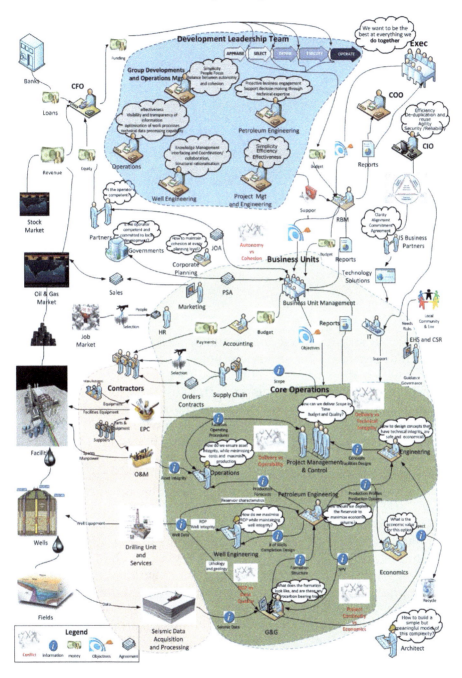

Figure 5 Initial Rich Picture showing the context of the D&O organization and its environment

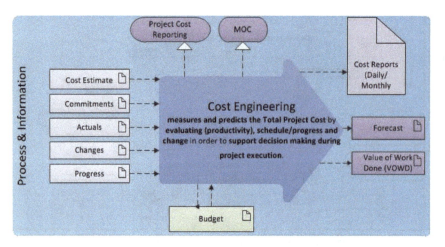

Figure 6. Example of the Cost Engineering process overview from the solution blueprint

Viability

The VSM was first introduced to the stakeholders during the interviews and then made part of the interview notes/minutes. Subsequently, the VSM was used by the author to build possible organizational models and then consulted with the stakeholders. Initially the model was built by using the organization's regional model as the recursion criteria (i.e. the recursion levels were region, country, business function). However, when the model was compared to the actual operations it was soon realized that despite the new region based organizational structure, operatively there were two quasi-viable systems at the second level of recursion, namely a stable and well-established E&A function and the newly formed D&O function. This provided a new way of approaching the problem of maintaining the autonomy of E&A and D&O. The new model represented the regional aspects as part of the environment and highlighted the relationship between D&O and E&A as the key area to be modeled. This paralleled with Beer's description of VSM interventions in an insurance company, where a very similar reorganization on matrix structure was facing governance challenges between functions and regions (Beer, 1994). The insurance company model was similar in terms of the relationship between marketing and investment and the 'asset balancer' that needed to be designed between them. This new version of VSM (see Figure 7) based on functions was then presented to 3 stakeholders for review and comments.

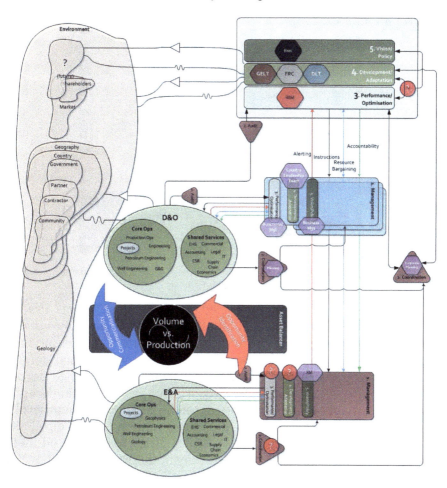

Figure 7 VSM with functional recursion

The Group D&O Manager, found it very 'thought provoking' and needing more analysis to a) find out if all the areas at each level are covering all subsystems, b) design right signals to prevent 'Rome from burning while we play fiddles'. A critical comment was that the 'jargon' (e.g. managing variety attenuation, transduction) should be replaced with more 'manager friendly' words (e.g. designing value equations).

The detailed model was then developed in VSMod®, a java based modeling tool that can facilitate the overall visual presentation and navigation for the modeler. An example VSMod® screen capture is shown in Figure 8. The model of the 'asset balancer' remains to be constructed, however, the fact that it was agreed to be the core focus for the organization reflects the power of the VSM approach in collectively locating points of interest for viability analysis.

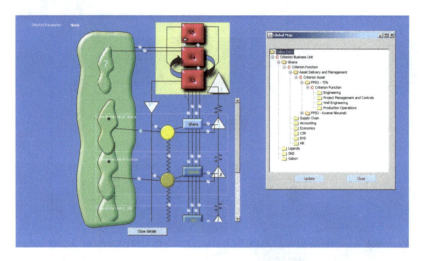

Figure 8 VSMod® screenshot showing the model view and the recursive hierarchy (right).

Given the reception of the RP developed earlier, the VSM was used to structure the RP for each level of recursion. In effect creating RPs for each level was a good way to enrich the VSM with a more business friendly presentation layer. These recursive RPs that were developed for the organizational context and were also connected with a few detailed process and data models to demonstrate its utility as a multi-domain landscaping map. In order to present VSM concepts at the higher management level, a Venn diagram type map called the Capability Framework was developed that translated key VSM concepts into familiar terms (e.g. replaced meta-system with leadership). The overall hierarchy of these models is shown in Figure 9.

The outstanding issue with VSM modeling was the absence of an expressive modeling language for developing the variety equations in a rigorous and unambiguous fashion. Furthermore, the knowledge of individual operations was necessary to understand the variety of the system and environment clearly.

It was noted VSM lacked a clear ontological grounding for the intentionally constructed subsystems that are supposed to exist in viable systems and therefore requires a reference ontology that can be used to identify and model both structure and dynamics of real world objects. This creates a possible integration site between the VSM and ontological modeling frameworks like the BORO (Partridge,2005) and merits further exploration.

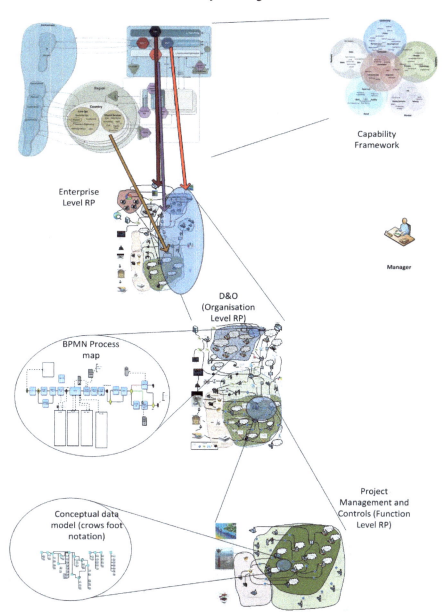

Capability
Framework

Enterprise
Level RP

Manager

D&O
(Organisation
Level RP)

BPMN Process
map

Conceptual data
model (crows foot
notation)

Project
Management and
Controls (Function
Level RP)

Figure 9. Recursive VSM to Rich Picture to Capability Framework Mapping

Structure and Collaboration

The OST design principles (Emery, 2000), namely the redundancy of parts (DP1) and redundancy of functions (DP2) were communicated to the interviewees during the active interviews whenever the subject of structure was broached. It provided a useful schema to explain organizational structure design in general. However, these did not provide any extended benefits beyond being a descriptive concept. This is because it relates more to the detailed design of task environments which was not in scope of the research.

However, the OST Participative Design Workshop (PDW) (Emery, 2000) (also based on DP2) was organized to bring various stakeholders in the projects community together to design the project planning processes and data structures. The workshop participants included people from various levels, business units and across disciplines as shown in the Figure 10.

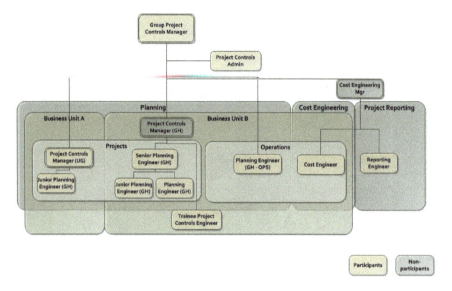

Figure 10. Planning workshop design

The approach was very successful in achieving the following:

1. First time that the planning community engaged face to face to discuss issues, thus sowing the seeds for an internal community of practice.
2. Multi-level participation meant that managers and staff were discussing and solving common issues
3. Empowerment of staff to voice concerns
4. Communication across disciplines (e.g. cost engineering) to understand how integration can be achieved

Motivation

Cognitive mapping (Shaw, F Ackermann & C Eden, 2003) was used in the PDW mentioned above to identify issues, and emergent goals. It was a useful tool to determine which aspects of the design needed immediate attention. The group was divided into 3 teams and Postit® notes were used for gathering issues and undertaking 30 minute options analysis based on the prioritized issues list. The author facilitated the sessions by encouraging the participants to think about dynamics and interdependences between issues, goals and options. Commonalities and interrelations between issues were then discussed and agreed, and final outcomes captured on a mindmap. The relationship between options, issues, and goals was first mapped manually. It was mapped more formally using the ArchiMate® 2.0 motivation extensions which has recently to describe hierarchies of requirements, goals, assessments and drivers. This development originating from the EA community is an example of areas where EA languages can be used for ST approaches. The output of the options analysis in ArchiMate is shown in Figure 11.

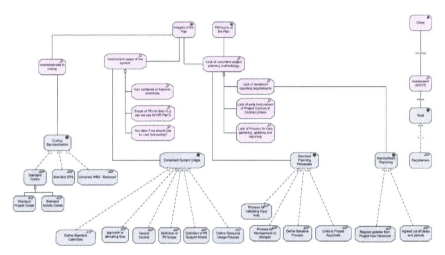

Figure 11. Archimate 2.0 motivation extension concepts used for developing a SODA causal map

Reflections

There have been many attempts to link the Euclidian space of management with the swampy space of operations (Ciborra, 2001). In trying to establish this link, one needs to be aware that such models reify the simplistic structures used to build them and take focus away from the complexity of human action and communication (Jensen, 2010). Therefore the models were assessed for what they leave out, how they evolve and what reification processes are underway alongside the modeling activities.

As an example, the evolution of the Rich Pictures within the organization can be analyzed to explain the diffusion of models within the organisation. From a Luhmannian perspective, every model can be construed as a condensed set of decisions/selections. The RPs therefore acted as decision premises for further decisions (e.g. around the role and position of a business function). In Luhmann's lens, the RP was not transmitting a particular meaning from one system to another. Meaning was reconstructed at every interaction by the participants with the model. The discursive formation that revolved around the RP continued to grow because, the RP was contributing towards answering the question of 'what is it that we do?' in a post reorganization social reality.

From an Actor Network Theory perspective, the RP's proliferation in the organization can be construed as going through the stages of problematization, interessment, enrolment and mobilization (Latour, 1986). The RP has now created a network of interested actors (D&O, HR, Supply Chain, Finance) who have gone through enrolment and mobilization. The ANT lens also reveals how the RP and architectural artifacts in general can be construed as actors that have their own dynamics, that they have agency and they are active in mobilizing others through their meaning generating potential.

The intervention process has opened up a number of discourses on both what the organization is and should be doing. However, what remains to be seen is how those discourses will evolve and how system theory can guide architecture practice both in terms of designing and orchestrating change. Here 'orchestration' is taken both as improvisation/performance and composition/coordination and this is where art and science need to collaborate.

Conclusions and Future Research

In essence organizational reality presents various brands of challenges, one relates to knowing what is going on and the other relates to propagating that knowledge and another relates to creating a platform for change based on that knowledge. Technically these problems have ontological as well as epistemological dimensions and socio-politically they relate to the issues of change and reasons for action. These dimensions are entangled. Any approach to solutions therefore requires both ontologically robust theories of society and technology and grounded theory of practice.

The integration of selected concepts from ST and EA offers a possible search space for such a set of theories. When applying ST it was found that it

1)   Provides a context sensitive approach to modeling the situation of interest
2)   Shifts focus away from individual components to whole systems and their emergent function and behavior

3) Provides normative guides to assess if a particular designs can lead to viability

4) Makes possible the co-creation of knowledge though active engagement with multiple perspectives at different levels in the organisation

5) Raises awareness of the ethical dimensions of interventions and the underlying biases in every selective activity

However, ST modeling tools lack the rigor required for articulating detailed design specifications that can be used for building information systems. EA tools and concepts offer the complimentary logical and ontological grounding required for specification level modeling. The issue is to discover which of the brand of EA on offer can provide for that requirement.

Figure 12 shows a possible way of situating ST within the EA space by mapping the EA concepts evaluated so far onto the Zachman Framework. This mapping reveals the sites where ST approaches can possibly complement and/or replace the EA models.

Figure 12. ST and the Zachman Framework mapping to ST approaches

There is also a number of areas where ST approaches need to be integrated internally in order reduce the fragmentation within the ST space. Some

145

example areas of particular interest to the ST approaches explored in this article are:

1. The introduction of SD to describe homeostasis and other dynamical relations operating across the VSM channels.
2. Complementing the lack of elaboration in the VSM around metasystemic subsystems with LST's 20 subsystems (Nechansky, 2010).
3. Grounding the concepts of system, boundary and channel by highlighting the ontological assumptions that each ST school makes when using these terms. This should be tested at the case/instance level to see how the same reality can be interpreted by different systems approaches under different ontological assumptions.

About the Author

Mesbah Khan is a Group Projects Solution Architect at Tullow Oil Plc.

References

van der Aalst, W.M.P., Kiepuszewski, B, Barros, A P and Dogac, Asuman (2003) 'Workflow Patterns', Distributed and Parallel Databases, pp. 5-51.

Ackermann, Fran and Eden, Colin (2005) 'Using Causal Mapping with Group Support Systems to Elicit an Understanding of Failure in Complex Projects: Some Implications for Organizational Research', Group Decision and Negotiation, 14(5), pp. 355-376, [online] Available from: http://www.springerlink.com/index/10.1007/s10726-005-8917-6.

Aier, Stephan and Winter, Robert (2008) 'Virtual Decoupling for IT/Business Alignment – Conceptual Foundations, Architecture Design and Implementation Example', Business & Information Systems Engineering, 1(2), pp. 150-163, [online] Available from: http://www.springerlink.com/index/10.1007/s12599-008-0010-7 (Accessed 5 August 2011).

Anon (2011) The Open Group TOGAF 9.1, The Open Group.

Assimakopoulos, Nikitas and Dimitriou, Nikolaos (2006) 'A cybernetic framework for viable virtual enterprises: The use of VSM and PSM systemic methodologies', Kybernetes, 35(5), pp. 653-667, [online] Available from: http://www.emeraldinsight.com/10.1108/03684920610664681 (Accessed 22 December 2011).

Atkinson, Paul and Coffey, Amanda (2003) 'Revisiting the Relationship Between Participant Observation and Interviewing. Postmodern Interviewing.', In Gubrium, J. F. and Holstein, J. A. (eds.), Postmodern Interviewing, Thousand Oaks, SAGE Publications, Inc.

Bakken, Tore and Herenes, Tore (2003) 'Introduction: Niklas Luhmann's autopoietic theory and organization studies - A space of connections', In Bakken, T. and Hernes, T. (eds.), Autopoietic Organisation Theory, Copenhagen, Copenhagen Business School Press, pp. 9-22.

Barton, John, Stephens, John and Haslett, Tim (2009a) 'Action Research: Its Foundations in Open Systems Thinking and Relationship to the Scientific Method', Systemic Practice and Action Research, 22(6), pp. 475-488, [online] Available from: http://www.springerlink.com/index/10.1007/s11213-009-9148-6 (Accessed 11 September 2011).

Barton, John, Stephens, John and Haslett, Tim (2009b) 'Action Research: Its Foundations in Open Systems Thinking and Relationship to the Scientific Method', Systemic Practice and Action Research, 22(6), pp. 475-488.

Bean, Sally (2010) 'Re-thinking Enterprise Architecture using Systems and Complexity Approaches', Journal of Enterprise Architecture, 6(4), pp. 7-13.

Beer, Stanford (1994) The Heart of Enterprise, Chichester, John Wiley & Sons.

Beer, Stafford (1995) *Brain of the Firm*, Wiley.

Bell, Simon and Morse, Stephen (2010) 'Triple Task Method: Systemic, Reflective Action Research', Systemic Practice and Action Research, 23(6), pp. 443-452,

Bertalanffy, Ludwig Von (2003) General System Theory: Foundations, Development, Applications, George Braziller Inc.

Brier, Søren (2006) 'The cybersemiotic model of communication: An evolutionary model of the threshold between semiosis and informational exchange', Semiotica, 2006(158), pp. 255-296, [online] Available from: http://www.reference-global.com/doi/abs/10.1515/SEM.2006.008.

Brier, Søren, Baecker, Dirk and Thyssen, Ole (2011) 'Foreword : Luhmann Applied — For What ?', Cybernetics and Human Knowing, 14(c), pp. 5-10.

Britto, Christian Maciel (2011) 'Sustainable Community Development: A Brief Introduction to the Multi-Modal Systems Method', Systemic Practice and Action Research, 24(6), pp. 533-544, [online] Available from: http://www.springerlink.com/index/10.1007/s11213-011-9206-8 (Accessed 22 December 2011).

Burrell, G. and Morgan, Gareth (1985) Sociological Paradigms and Organisational Analysis, Gower Publishing Ltd.

Burrell, Gibson and Morgan, Gareth (1979) Sociological paradigms and organisational analysis : elements of the sociology of corporate life, Sociology The Journal Of The British Sociological Association, Heinemann, [online] Available from: http://sonify.psych.gatech.edu/~ben/references/burrell_sociological_paradigms_and_organisational_analysis.pdf.

Cardwell, Geoff (2008) 'The influence of Enterprise Architecture and process hierarchies on company success', Total Quality Management & Business Excellence, 19(1-2), pp. 47-55, [online] Available from: http://www.tandfonline.com/doi/abs/10.1080/14783360701601959 (Accessed 7 July 2011).

Checkland, Peter and Scholes, Jim (1993a) Soft Systems Methodology in Action, New York, John Wiley & Sons Ltd.

147

Checkland, Peter and Scholes, Jim (1993b) Soft systems methodology: a 30-year retrospective, John Wiley & Sons Ltd, [online] Available from: http://books.google.com/books?id=R2dQAAAAMAAJ&pgis=1.

Choi, Jae, Nazareth, Derek L. and Jain, Hemant K. (2010) 'Implementing Service-Oriented Architecture in Organizations', Journal of Management Information Systems, 26(4), pp. 253-286, [online] Available from: http://mesharpe.metapress.com/openurl.asp?genre=article&id=doi:10.2753/MIS0742-1222260409 (Accessed 1 September 2011).

Ciborra, Claudio U. (2001) From Control to Drift: The Dynamics of Corporate Information Infrastructures, OUP Oxford, [online] Available from: http://www.amazon.co.uk/Control-Drift-Corporate-Information-Infrastructures/dp/0199246637.

Coase, R. H. (1937) 'The Nature of the Firm', Economica, New Series, 4(16), pp. 386 - 405.

Dietz, Jan L.G. Enterprise Ontology: Theory and Methodology, Springer

Davis, Jerome D. (2006) '"And then there were four.." A Thumbnail History of Oil Industry Restructuring, 1971-2005', In Davis, J. D. (ed.), The Changing World of Oil: An Analysis of Corporate Change and Adaptation, Hampshire, Ashgate Publishing Limited, pp. 1-12.

Emery, Merrelyn (2000) 'The Current Version of Emery ' s Open Systems Theory', Systemic Practice and Action Research, 13(5), pp. 623-643.

Fez-Barringten, Barie (2009) 'Metaphor as an Inference from Sign', Journal of Enterprise Architecture, 5(4).

Flood, R. L. (1990) 'Liberating Systems Theory: Toward Critical Systems Thinking', Human Relations, 43(1), pp. 49-75, [online] Available from: http://hum.sagepub.com/cgi/doi/10.1177/001872679004300104 (Accessed 5 October 2011).

Flood, Robert L. and Carson, Ewart R. (1993) Dealing with Complexity: An Introduction to the Theory and Application of Systems Science, New York, Plenum Press.

Gharajedaghi, Jamshid (2011) Systems Thinking: Managing Chaos and Complexity: A Platform for Designing Business Architecture, Morgan Kaufmann.

Graves, Tom (2010) Everyday Enterprise-Architecture: Sensemaking, Strategy, Structures and Solutions, Colchester, Tetradian Books.

Harvey, David L. (2009) 'Complexity and Case', In Byrne, D. and Ragin, C. C. (eds.), The SAGE Handbook of Case-Based Methods, Oxford, England, Sage Publications, Inc.

Ison, Ray (2010) Systems Practice: How to Act in a Climate-Change World, Media, Springer, The Open University.

Iyamu, Tiko (2011) 'Institutionalisation of the Enterprise Architecture', International Journal of Actor-Network Theory and Technological Innovation, 3(1), pp. 27-38.

Jensen, Anders Østergaard (2010) 'Government Enterprise Architecture Adoption: A Systemic-Discursive Critique and Reconceptualisation', Copenhagen Business School.

Jokisch, Rodrigo (2010) 'Why Did Luhmann's Social Systems Theory Find So Little Resonance in the United States of America?', Addressing Modernity: Social Theory and U.S. Cultures, not publis, pp. 240-271.

Langley, Ann and Tsoukas, Haridimos (2010) 'Introducing " Perspectives on Process Organization Studies "', In Hernes, T. and Maitlis, S. (eds.), Process, Sensemaking, and Organizing, Oxford, England, OUP Oxford, pp. 1-26.

Lankhorst, Marc (2005) Enterprise Architecture at Work: Modelling, Communication and Analysis [Hardcover], Berlin, Springer.

Latour, Bruno (1986) '"The Powers of Association". Power, Action and Belief. A new sociology of knowledge', 32nd ed. In Law, J. (ed.), Sociological Review Monograph, London, Routledge & Kegan Paul, pp. 264-280.

Lawrence, Stewart and Botes, Vida (2011) 'ACCOUNTING AND ORGANIZATIONAL CHANGE : AN AUTOPOIETIC VIEW', Journal of Global Business and Technology, 7(1), pp. 74-86.

Leonard, Allenna (2009) 'The Viable System Model and Its Application to Complex Organizations', Systemic Practice and Action Research, 22(4), pp. 223-233, [online] Available from: http://www.springerlink.com/index/10.1007/s11213-009-9126-z (Accessed 2 September 2011).

Lindland, Ivar (1994) 'Understanding Quality in Conceptual Modeling', IEEE Software, 11(2), pp. 42-49.

Luhmann, Niklas (1995) Social systems, Stanford, Standford University Press, [online] Available from: http://books.google.com/books?hl=en&lr=&id=zVZQW4gxXk4C&pgis=1.

Maturana, Humberto R. and Varela, Francisco (1987) Tree of Knowledge, Boston, Massachusetts, Shambhala.

Miller, James Grier (1978) Living Systems, McGraw Hill Higher Education.

Mingers, John (2002) 'Can social systems be autopoietic ? Assessing Luhmann ' s social theory', Review Literature And Arts Of The Americas.

Mingers, John (2003) 'Observing organizations: An evalaution of Luhmann's organisation theory', In Bakken, T. and Hernes, T. (eds.), Autopoietic Organisation Theory, Copenhagen, Copenhagen Business School Press.

Mjøset, Lars (2009) The Contextualist Approach to Social Science Methodology, Byrne, D. and Ragin, C. C. (eds.), Social Science, Oxford, England, SAGE Publications, Inc.

Morecroft, John (2010) 'System Dynamics', In Reynolds, M. and Holwell, S. (eds.), Systems Approaches to Managing Change: A Practicle Guuide, London, Springer, The Open University, pp. 25-86.

Morgan, Gareth (1996) Images of Organization, Sage Publications, Inc, [online] Available from: citculike-article-id:3955293.

Müller, Karl H (2010) 'The Radical Constructivist Movement and Its Network Formations', Constructivist Foundations, 6(1).

Nechansky, Helmut (2010) 'The Relationship Between : Miller ' s Living Systems Theory and Beer ' s Viable Systems Theory', Systems Research and Behavioral Science, 112(December 2008), pp. 97-113.

Nolte, Heike (2011) 'Reflective Organization', Cybernetics and Human Knowing, 17(c), pp. 77-91.

Parsons, Talcott (1967) Structure of Social Action: 001, New York, Free Press.

Partridge, Chris (2005) Business Objects: Re-engineering for Re-use, The BORO Centre

Peters, M. (1984) 'The Origins and Status of Action Research', The Journal of Applied Behavioral Science, 20(2), pp. 113-124, [online] Available from: http://jab.sagepub.com/cgi/doi/10.1177/002188638402000203.

Ragin, Charles C. (2007) 'Comparative Methods', In Outhwaite, W. and Turner, S. P. (eds.), The SAGE Handbook of Social Science Methodology, London, Sage Publications Ltd.

Reason, Peter and Bradbury, Hilary (2008) The SAGE Handbook of Action Research, 2nd ed. Reason, P. and Bradbury, H. (eds.), London, Sage Publications Ltd.

Reynolds, Martin and Holwell, Sue (2010) Systems Approaches to Managing Change: A Practical Guide, London, Springer, The Open University.

Schwaninger, Markus (2006) 'ResearchArticle Theories of Viability : a Comparison', Systems Research and Behavioral Science, 347, pp. 337-348.

Schwaninger, Markus (2004) 'What can cybernetics contribute to the conscious evolution of organizations and society?', Systems Research and Behavioral Science, 21(5), pp. 515-527, [online] Available from: http://doi.wiley.com/10.1002/sres.636.

Seidl, David and Becke, Kai Helge (2005) Niklas Luhmann and Organization Studies, Copenhagen, Copenhagen Business School Press.

Sessions, Roger (2008) Simple Architectures For Complex Enterprises, Washington, Microsoft Press.

Shaw, D, Ackermann, F and Eden, C (2003) 'Approaches to sharing knowledge in group problem structuring', Journal of the Operational Research Society, 54(9), pp. 936-948, [online] Available from: http://www.palgrave-journals.com/doifinder/10.1057/palgrave.jors.2601581 (Accessed 5 August 2010).

Stephens, John and Haslett, Tim (2011) 'A Set of Conventions, a Model: An Application of Stafford Beer's Viable Systems Model to the Strategic Planning Process', Systemic Practice and Action Research, 24(5), pp. 429-452, [online] Available from: http://www.springerlink.com/index/10.1007/s11213-011-9194-8 (Accessed 6 October 2011).

Thomas, Oliver and Fellmann M.A., Michael (2009) 'Semantic Process Modeling – Design and Implementation of an Ontology-based Representation of Business Processes', Business & Information Systems Engineering, 1(6), pp. 438-451, [online] Available from: http://www.springerlink.com/index/10.1007/s12599-009-0078-8 (Accessed 10 August 2011).

Wand, Y and Weber, R (1990) 'An Ontological Model of an Information System', IEEE Transactions on Software Engineering, Los Alamitos, CA, USA, IEEE Computer Society, 16, pp. 1282-1292.

Weick, Karl E. (2000) Making Sense of the Organization (KeyWorks in Cultural Studies), Wiley-Blackwell.

Yergin, Daniel (1993) The Prize: The Epic Quest for Oil, Money, & Power, Free Press.

Zachman, J. a. (1987) 'A framework for information systems architecture', IBM Systems Journal, 26(3), pp. 276-292, [online] Available from: http://ieeexplore.ieee.org/lpdocs/epic03/wrapper.htm?arnumber=5387671.

Part 2

The Brain and the Heart of the Enterprise

Why Business Should Take Enterprise Architecture Seriously

Patrick Hoverstadt

Abstract

This chapter discusses why business leaders should take EA more seriously as a truly strategic discipline. The author argues that to manage a complex enterprise you must understand how it functions, and to understand it an adequate model designed for the purpose is needed. Also, you must have the right information on which to base decisions, and for the organization to provide that information reliably, an adequate model of the organization as a system is necessary to make any sensible judgment about the informational needs of strategic decision making.

Keywords

Enterprise Architecture, Complexity, Conant-Ashby, Conway's Law, McCulloch's Redundancy of Potential Command Principle, Viable Systems Model, VSM

The Credibility Problem

Traditionally, EA has shared the fate of many other business disciplines that aspire to be taken seriously and listened to by those "leading" the enterprise that sit on the exec team. And the question of whether EA deserves to be taken seriously by the rest of the business is not either a flippant one, or indeed a trivial one - well not if you happen to be an enterprise architect anyway. In case this is interpreted as a whinge by some disappointed and disillusioned techie frustrated that their voice isn't heard in the corridors of power, let me start by pointing out that I don't count myself as an "Enterprise Architect" although my business is the design of organizations.

The traditional view of the strategic role of EA rests on a view of its relationship to strategy that itself sits within a traditional model of the strategic process and the nature of organizational change. This tends to start with formulating the organization's strategy. Typically the execution of the strategy will involve some sort of organizational change and very often the change will have an aspect of change to IT and EA may be engaged to: plan that change, integrate it into the overall structure of IT in the organization and to reconfigure the model of the organization's IT. All this is quite valid and clearly EA can have a useful, some would argue even an essential role in the execution of strategy.

However, if this is the limited view that both corporate boards and even the EA community have of EA, then it's not surprising if the discipline has an extremely limited significance for exec teams and strategic decision makers. In this model, the legitimate role that EA could or should have for the strategic decision process (as opposed to the process of carrying out strategy) is advising on opportunities that new technologies or information sources might offer and on the limitations to adoption and risks of change. Again, this is a legitimate role as an informational input to strategic decision making, but a very limited one.

To some extent, the limitation of ambition here is in line with EA's history as a discipline which is often perceived - and indeed practiced – as a glorified IT requirements capture exercise. If however we look at it from a management science and specifically a systems perspective, then a very different picture emerges about its potential systemic role and there are two important and distinct arguments that can be advanced for taking EA much more seriously as a truly strategic discipline.

Coping with Complexity: Conant-Ashby – We Can Only Manage What We Can Understand

One of the core tenets of management science is Conant-Ashby Theorem. This states that "every good regulator of a system must contain a model of that system". Translated into plain English this means that our ability to manage any organization or business situation depends directly on our understanding of the organization or situation and that in turn depends on how good and relevant our mental models are. We can't manage what we don't understand - except by luck. Once upon a time, it was possible for an individual at the head of an organization to be confident that they really did understand the business. As organizations become more complex, as business practice becomes more complex, and as the length of time that individuals tend to spend in the same business decreases, so the validity of relying on such tacit models becomes increasingly problematic. It is now very common to find organizations where as soon as you scratch the surface you discover that nobody really understands how the whole business works. Talking to a business architect in a large multi-national I asked "so who apart from you has an understanding of how the whole business works?" "nobody" was the reply "some individual directors understand some of their areas, but nobody, not even the CEO, understands the whole picture." How then can they manage the whole organization? How can they understand the risks that activities in one area of business may pose for other areas, or the potential synergies or opportunities that are available?

The lessons of Conant-Ashby are simple and to some extent obvious, but rarely taken seriously. In the recent credit crisis it became clear that we were reliant on a financial system that nobody had designed, nobody understood and nobody was managing. Most of the individual components making up the system had been designed, most were understood – in their own terms – and most were managed – in isolation, but the system as a whole had evolved without design, understanding or management. The system as a whole had become so large and complex that nobody could see the effects in one area of changes or instability in another part of the system. The most shocking realization is that the drive has been to recreate the system whilst still not addressing the need to build a model of how this works as a system that would allow regulation to stand a chance of working.

How then does this relate to EA and its potential as a genuinely strategic service for the organization? Well, if exec teams need a model of the organization they are trying to manage if they are to manage it successfully, then the question of how and by whom such a model could be built and maintained is not currently clear. Nor is the nature of the model that is necessary. Clearly it is far from being just a model of the IT. What is needed is a genuine architecture of the enterprise – what it does, processes, people, structures, finances, values, performance, decision making, communications, information flows, markets, change, risks, relationships and technology. This may seem like a tall order, but actually is relatively straight forward and eminently do-able provided it is structured around a core model of the organization. Currently, no business function provides decision makers with such a model. The informational vacuum is usually filled by purely financial models which try to reduce the complexity of the enterprise to a set of accounts – accounts which have been designed for quite a different purpose.

So, does it matter? This is a reasonable question. After all, businesses have managed without such multi-faceted models of organizations up to now, so what's the problem? Well apart from the theoretical argument posed by Conant-Ashby which, even if it does have considerable face validity and read as basic common sense is nevertheless still just a theory, I would argue that there are compelling and brutally practical reasons for taking the need for a model of the organization seriously. Organizations are going out of business at an alarming and increasing rate and this includes the largest and most successful businesses. Of the original S&P 500 – the list of the top 500 companies in the US, only 15% survive. Over the past 40 odd years, 85% have gone out of business. Of the 1000 largest companies in the world, half suffered a 20% drop in capital value within a one month period at some point in the decade before the 2009 credit crunch. That's half of the ones that survived such a dramatic drop in value. Overwhelmingly, these are organizations that were subjected to changes in their business that they had not foreseen. In organizations that went out of business because of strategic threats, 35% were hit by threats that came from directions that they had never even thought to look in.

For these organizations, their model of the enterprise was not just deficient, but fatally deficient. They simply did not understand their business and how it sat in its operating environment until it was far too late. Someone, some business discipline needs to provide adequate models of how the enterprise works that can assist decision makers to understand the working of their organizations as systems to manage them more effectively and whatever the current role and practice of EA, what is needed is a genuine architecture of the enterprise. This is a truly strategic role.

The implication is that EA models must be understandable by the business, not just IT and preferably should be constructed with the business, not just IT. If you want business leaders to take EA seriously, then it follows that Enterprise Architects should take business leaders seriously and engage with them on that basis. This isn't a battle that is likely to be won overnight and the development of trust, credibility and a shared language will need some work.

There are however considerable grounds for optimism. EA could be pushing at an open door because there is evidence that not only is dealing with complexity a serious business problem that puts organisations out of business, but also that this is recognized by exec teams as a serious issue. In a 2005 survey of 1,400 Global CEOs, 77% said that dealing with complexity was a high priority for them, 91% believed it needed special tools, only 5% believed they had those tools. So at board level, the problem posed by Conant-Ashby of needing models to help us deal with complexity, is already understood as urgent and important. These CEOs know it's a problem and they need new tools to deal with it. All EA needs to do is step up to the challenge.

Does Strategy Drive EA, or EA Drive Strategy?

The second argument for taking EA seriously as a strategic partner to decision makers is related to the Conant-Ashby argument and also to both Conway's Law and McCulloch's "Redundancy of Potential Command Principle". Conway's law states that: "organizations which design systems are constrained to produce designs which are copies of the communication structures of these organizations". Conway was referring to the design of IT systems, but the same principle also applies to the formulation of strategy by organizations – strategy will mirror the structures that produced it. McCulloch's Redundancy of Potential Command Principle states that "in any complex decision network the ability to act effectively depends on an adequate concatenation of information". In other words, we need the right information to take effective decisions. This is in one sense obvious, but its implications are profound. The corollary I draw from this is that the "concatenation of information" confers the ability to act effectively.

The argument here is quite simple, but disconcertingly radical. The decisions that organizations take tend to depend on the information available. This means that strategic decisions are often driven by the structure of information – which is very clearly in the domain of EA. Management science laws and theorems aside, the argument has good common sense underpinning it. Any strategy worthy of the name has to be built from information available to the decision makers. If it isn't, is it any more than a fantasy?

And of course, the information available to the decision makers is a function of the structure of the information system (in its broadest sense) and of the structure of the organization. Organizations are structured to take in, process, understand and store particular types of information and

159

not others. Organizations can only hear what they are structured to hear and learn what they are structured to learn. If you doubt this, then try complaining to a company that doesn't have a complaints process and structured resources to deal with it. You very soon become aware that whilst the individual listening (or pretending to listen) to your complaint may hear what you are saying, there is nowhere for that information to go and it is dissipated through the organizational system. The individual may hear it, but the organization as a system cannot hear it unless it has been structured to do so. The structure determines what information the organization can hear and specifically what information is available to strategists.

According to this view then, the design of information systems (part of EA's domain) is a driver of strategy and can determine the strategic options that decision makers are capable of seeing. In practice this can be clearly seen despite the fact that it can be both very subtle – almost insidious and is often invisible to the organization itself. By definition, our blind spots are often blind to us. The scale of the distortion of strategy, purpose and values and its impact can be truly chilling.

An analysis of the use of business intelligence in decision making for commissioning in the UK National Health Service is a good example. The role of commissioning was to analyze health needs in the community and then commission a set of health providers to deliver services to meet those needs. At the time, the bodies charged with fulfilling this critical role were Primary Care Trusts – PCTs. This was an explicit attempt by the government to build a mechanism for breaking the cycle of year on year contracting of the same health services that existing providers were already providing irrespective of need and to ensure that services were provided that did actually cover the full range of needs in the community.

This is a classic strategic decision making process in which the organization was supposed to recognize and address the strategic gap - the gap between what the organization is capable of doing now and what it needs to be doing to fulfill health needs, both existing and future, in the environment. And fulfilling this strategic role for the NHS was precisely the reason for setting up PCTs. It is also a role that is of fundamental importance – this isn't simply a question about which drug should be used to treat a particular illness, it is about whether certain illnesses get treated or not, it's about whether we carry on relying on treating diabetes, or switch resources instead to prevent it. It is about taking real strategic decisions which for some are literally a matter of life and death.

The information needs are clear and as with most strategic decisions, fall into two broad classes of information: information which we can generically refer to as "performance measurement" – information which tells us about the internal capability of the system in question to deliver what it currently does - and information which tells us about need outside, both current and future. The two sorts of information come from two different directions, are about completely different things and are quite different in quality and analysis. Information about future health needs is necessarily more speculative and qualitative than performance management information about how many hip operations were done last year needs to be. Given the two sorts of information, the strategy process – or in this case the commissioning process is "simply" one of comparing current capability against expected future demand and taking some admittedly difficult and uncomfortable decisions about how best to deploy limited resources to address those needs – how many hip operations versus how many heart by-passes.

That's the theory. The practice was very far from this. In practice what we found, when we looked at this situation, was a massive imbalance in information provision. Performance management information was in plentiful supply, so the principal providers of acute care –hospital trusts had copious information on levels of activity and even sometimes on the quality of outcomes. The data quality of this information and the interpretation of it were both highly questionable – as one director of commissioning said "for over 80% of services we contract, we don't understand them well enough to even know what questions we should be asking to find out if they're any good". Nevertheless, there was information of sorts and lots of it available to commissioners. On the other side of the equation, in the information to understand health needs, information was very scarce, extremely patchy, had to be sought and specifically sourced, and the data quality was extremely poor, so the information wasn't trustworthy.

The result was entirely predictable. Commissioners took the decisions that they had the information to take and these were to do with using performance management data to try to control hospital services in increasing levels of detail. They started to try to micro-manage service delivery. At an operational level of course this meant by-passing hospital management to try to dictate directly to clinicians what they should be doing, and when and how they should be doing it. The by-passing of hospital management reduced the ability of hospitals to manage themselves effectively and exacerbated the problem of control of clinicians which is one of the problems that PCTs had been set up to address. Because of course, the PCTs were too far removed from service teams in hospitals both geographically and in time to be able to exercise any responsible managerial control of operations – in systems terminology, they lacked requisite variety.

Much more serious was the strategic deficit. PCTs largely failed to break the cycle of year on year contracting. So the central problem they were set up to solve – assessing health needs and commissioning services to match those needs – was largely ignored. In fact of course the reverse happened, existing services became more entrenched as the focus of PCTs fell on managing the relationship with them more and more tightly.

The reality then was that the strategic direction for health provision had switched from that intended – creating new services to address known health needs - to managing existing services more efficiently. This strategy shift was driven and determined by the availability of information. The architecture of the system was dictating the strategy. This wasn't a single example remember, this was replicated across all the PCTs investigated.

It was also invisible. Those taking these decisions were aware that they were supposed to be taking cycle breaking decisions and changing provision, but they pushed this to the back of their minds and got on with the job they could do, rather than worrying about the job they couldn't. The problem was largely undiscussable. The psychological trap for those engaged in decision making was difficult for them to see and of course was extremely uncomfortable when it was made visible. Not just the strategy itself was being dominated by the availability of information which was in turn determined by the enterprise architecture, but even the thinking processes of the strategists. At a more mundane level, the clarity that there were two types of information necessary for effective decision making – external information on health needs and internal information on performance – was lost. Information was just information, numbers were just numbers and their meaning and significance of people requiring healthcare were largely lost.

Looking from the outside in this case, the outcome seems perverse – organizations set up with huge budgets to do a fairly specific strategic job, not only do not do so, but also manage to create a situation where they can remain largely unaware that they are not doing it. And yet it is hard to see what else the outcome could have been. With a highly unbalanced information system, decision makers took the only decisions they were able to take given the information available. The strategy was determined by the architecture. The NHS isn't an isolated example; the same effect can be seen in all sorts of organization, public sector, private sector, large and small.

In this view then, Enterprise Architecture can be seen as not merely a tool of strategy, as something deployed to help execute strategy, but as a "meta-discipline" something that needs to be done right for the strategy formulation process to function reliably. The story that the design of information systems may determine the thinking of strategists may not be as attractive to exec teams as the argument about the ability to manage complexity, but is critically important. As a value proposition for EA, this can be framed as "we design the information systems that provide you with the information you need to take more effective decisions".

Towards Business Led EA

So, this begs the question of what sort of EA approach is needed to address this sort of meta-strategic need? The need for an architectural model that provides business leaders with a model of the enterprise that they can genuinely use to understand how it operates – the Conant-Ashby requirement and an architecture that has the capability to ensure that the information strategic decision makers need is actually made available to them (or at the very least information shortfalls known and identified rather than genuine blind spots).

One option is to use Stafford Beer's Viable System Model (VSM) as a core structural model of the enterprise on which to hang a variety of information generated by specific disciplines: financial, HR, IT, operations, marketing etc.

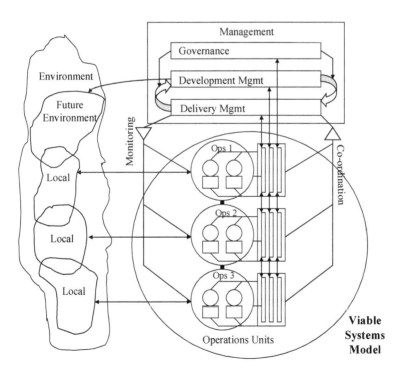

The VSM has a number of key features which make it almost uniquely suited for this role. Firstly it has a fractal structure which means that a relatively simple rule set can be used to model enterprises of any size or complexity in as much or little detail as necessary. It is applicable to any type of organization in any sector and of any size. It models both operational activities and management functions and shows the systemic role of different management disciplines. So for example, not only can it be used to model financial flows in an organization – where revenue and profits are generated, but also where financial management functions sit in relation to other activities such as operations. Critically in view of the arguments made above, it provides a way of modeling the structure of decision making throughout the organization, the information needed to make those decisions, where that needs to come from and how it needs to be integrated in decision making. And of course from a more traditional EA perspective, it provides a blueprint of the organization and its information sources and needs that can be used to plan IT. From a technical point of view, VSM ticks a number of critical boxes.

Then there are the issues of accessibility and utility.

One other advantage of VSM in particular and organizational models in general is that they provide a very different way for EA to do its business and to engage with the organization. In a study of a small number of classic business issues that EA might be expected to engage with and the tools that might be employed to deal with these, organizational models (particularly VSM) came out top in terms of the number of problem topics to which they were applicable. That's hardly surprising as any significant change will involve the organization (whereas not all will touch the process architecture, the information architecture, the technical architecture etc.)

There are two consequences of this. First is that if we build EA practice using organizational models as the "spine" and building other approaches as the ribs off that, the spinal organizational model can help to integrate other tools and provide continuity of language and approach – it simplifies modeling for both EA and the organization. Second is that it provides EA with a much more business friendly interface. The interface with the organization is a model of ... the organization.

This provides a very different set of opportunities to engage with the business. If the interface EA presents is recognizable by the business, then it becomes easy and natural for the business to pick it up and use it for solving their own problems. Our experience is that if these models are presented in the right way, exec teams in multi-nationals are not just capable of picking them up and using them, but are eager to do so, and can do so very quickly, taking less than an hour to move from problem to action plans for complex business issues. Since they solve the CEO's problem of understanding complexity, why would they not?

Conclusions

Looked at from a systems and management science perspective, there are at least two arguments that can be advanced for why business leaders should take EA much more seriously as a truly strategic discipline. Comfortingly both these arguments have the ring of common sense about them. How can you hope to manage a complex enterprise if you don't understand how it functions and how could you understand it without an adequate model designed for the purpose? And how can you take strategic decisions if you don't have the right information on which to base those decisions and how will the organization provide that information reliably if it isn't designed to do that? Of course the two arguments are mutually supporting because it is only with an adequate model of the organization as a system that we can make any sensible judgment about the informational needs of strategic decision making.

There is then a credible claim that can be made on behalf of EA for it to be taken seriously as critically important at a strategic or meta-strategic level by business leaders. However, this requires EA to start to take this sort of role seriously and to raise its own sights from that of playing an IT centered role to a truly enterprise level role.

About the Author

Patrick Hoverstadt is a leading writer and practitioner of systems approaches to organization. He has worked as consultant for 19 years, is a research fellow at Cranfield School of Management and guest lecturer at several business schools in the UK and Europe. He has developed a number of innovative approaches to common organizational problems.

References

Ashby, W. R. (1957). An Introduction To Cybernetics. London: Chapman & Hall.

Beer, S. (1979). The Heart of Enterprise, John Wiley, London and New York

Beer, S. (1981). Brain of the firm. Wiley.

Conant, R. C. & Ashby W.R. (1970) Every good regulator of a system must be a model of that system Int. J. Systems Sci. vol. 1, No. 2, 89-97

Conway, M. E. (1968), "How do Committees Invent?", Datamation14: 28–31

Hoverstadt, P. (2008). The Fractal Organization : Creating Sustainable Organizations with the Viable Systems Model. Chichester, West Sussex: John Wiley & Sons.

Mculloch W. (1965) Embodiments of Mind. MIT Press

PWC (2005) 9th annual Global CEO Survey

Diagnosing the Enterprise Architecture with the Viable System Model

Adrian RG Campbell

Abstract

This chapter presents Stafford Beer's Viable System Model as an important aid to understanding how an enterprise is organized into systems (Business Capabilities) and an important addition to the techniques within the Enterprise Architecture discipline. It provide that extra dimension to designing not just the structural components of the enterprise but also the interactions between them that are needed to keep the enterprise healthy, flexible and viable in the face of an every changing business environment.

Keywords

Viable Systems Model, VSM, Enterprise Architecture, Capabilities

Introduction to Viable System Model (VSM)

The Viable System Model was developed by Anthony Stafford Beer who was inspired by the way the human body works. Beer saw the human body as composed of interacting systems such as the brain, nervous system, organs, muscles, bones etc. that together react effectively with the external environment. He saw that the human body has numerous positive and negative control feedbacks loops and time delays that control the interactions between all its parts. Beer started to apply the same theory and thinking to his research in Operational Research and the study of regulatory systems known as Cybernetics, and wrote a series of books about his Viable System Model and how it applied to the design and management of organizations.

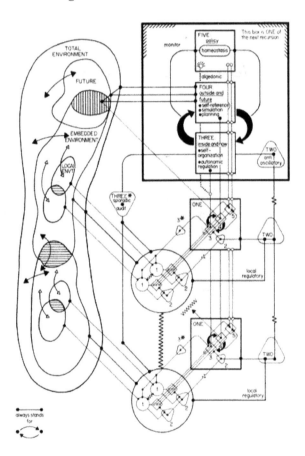

Figure 1. The Viable System. Beer (1972)

This diagram (Figure 1) looks complex doesn't it? At the most basic level it is a model of the operations (the systems that do the work), the Management (the systems that ensure that the operations systems work together) and the external Environment. The interactions between these

168

elements are a bi-directional value exchange with a feedback that can both amplified and attenuate the interactions.

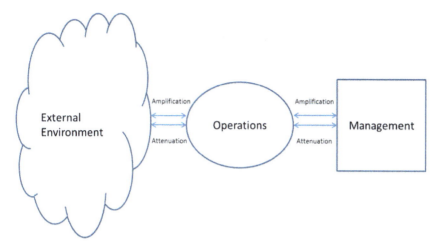

Figure 2. VSM: Operation, Management, Environment.

Viable Systems are in balance with the environment in which they operate when they have the ability to continuously adapt and change to react with changes in the external environment.

A Viable system can maintain stability according to Ashby's Law of Requisite Variety. This states that 'If a system is to be stable the number of states of its control mechanism must be greater than or equal to the number of states in the system being controlled'. Variety is the total number of distinct states of a system.

Accordingly, for an organization to remain viable it must respond when the external environment changes. For an organization, the external environment is the market in which it operates, it's customers, prospects, suppliers, partners, competitors, regulators, government, shareholders, unions, media etc. all of which will have both a direct and indirect, positive or negative impact on the organization.

VSM principles

The Viable System Model uses the following principles:

Principle	
Autonomy/ Independence	Each system in a VSM can potentially exist independently of other systems that a it communicates with.
Recursion	The VSM is a recursive system of systems. At each level of recursion, the same 5 types of system will exist.
Feedback	All relationships (flows etc.) between the systems are bi-directional with a built in feedback relationship
Requisite variety	In a VSM, the controlling systems must have as many states (Variety) as the system (or external environment) being controlled, to ensure balance.
Viability	Viability is the ability of a system to maintain itself or recover its capabilities in the event of change.
6 types of systems	VSM has 6 types of system for handling Operations, Coordination, Control, Monitoring, Research and Policy

Table 1. VSM Principles.

System types

A viable enterprise is a system that is an aggregation of autonomous systems – a system of systems.

The Viable System Model is a recursive model that consists of six types of systems that occur at each level of recursion. The word 'System' here does not mean an IT system or an information system but has the more generic meaning of the word 'System'. The viability and cohesion of an enterprise depend upon these 6 types of systems being recursively present at all levels of the enterprise. Those six systems are concerned with the following purposes:

System	Purpose	Description
5	• Policy • Ultimate authority • Identity • Consciousness • Concepts • Governance	• These systems provide the strategy and business direction via promises. • Sends messages to System 4 and system 3, balancing the interaction between them. • Contextualizing the organization in the business environment. • Managing the relationships between system 3, 4 & 5. • Taking things up a level of recursion.
4	• Strategic Development • Adaptation • Forward planning • Intelligence • Outside and future • Memory • Learning • Research	• These systems are those that look forward to the future and the external business environment. It's easy to see that the enterprise architecture function is a system 4 system. • Provides reports to System 5. • Manages the relationships with regulators, governance and compliance functions. • Builds awareness and manages strategic change.
3	• Control • Internal regulation • Optimization • Synergy • Inside and now	• These systems are concerned with managing operations and those that provide the audit and operational control functions. • Management of delivery of new and updated capabilities. • Optimizes the allocation of resources to System 1. • Provides reports to System 4. • Establishing overall optimum among systems, e.g. via resource bargain
3*	• Monitoring • Sporadic Audit • Senses and inhibits	• These systems provide a random and sporadic audit of every activity of the System 1 systems, for example a quality check. Different audits may be done for each key measure or core value. The audit is not performed on the System 1 systems at the same level, but on the next level of recursion down. This provides an independent assessment of the management of system 1 systems by the System 3 system. • (System 3* is a subtype of System 3). • Investigation and validation of information via auditing/ monitoring activities. This is a sense and inhibit function.
2	• Coordination • Conflict resolution • Stability • Anti-oscillatory	These systems provide the coordination functions between multiple System 1 systems. They coordinate system 1 activities via information and communication relationships. This includes facilitation and mediation functions that attenuate and amplify as needed to damp down oscillations.
1	• Operations • Production • Value creation	These systems within an organization are those that actually make products, deliver business services, perform the core activities and create value.

Table 2. Purposes of Systems

Although the Viable System Model is recursive so that the same five systems appear at all levels within an organization, but it is easy to see equivalent VSM systems at various levels in an organization.

At the top level it is possible to see that the Executive Board is a level 5 system, the general management are mainly level 3 systems, the system 2's are the program managers, project managers and solution architects. The system 1's are the operational service delivery units and project teams.

Where does that leave Enterprise Architects? Well the Enterprise Architect function is essentially a system 4 system with its focus on strategic planning for the long term view and creation of roadmaps of strategic initiatives. It can also be seen as a combination of System 4 and System 3 with the system 3 focuses on Audit/control/governance.

The strategic Enterprise Architects (system 4) with their long term, external and strategic focus work in co-operation with the Solution Architects (system 3) with their immediate operational, internal, lean, design and delivery focus. It is clear to see with our Viable System Model lens that solution architects and enterprise architects are not doing the same job but a completely different job.

External and Future

Unlike Lean manufacturing which only focuses on operational efficiencies in the lowest level System 1, System 2 and System 3 systems within an organization, the Viable System Model looks at the whole enterprise from a recursive perspective which is more sound and holistic.

In some ways it is surprising that it hasn't yet reached a tipping point within organizations or their enterprise architects. Maybe this is because everyone is too focused on the day-to-day need for operational efficiency and approaches such as Lean Manufacturing and forgets about planning for the future. This is the difference between being reactive and proactive.

The next time you are challenged on the purpose and value of Enterprise Architecture, then answer that it's the difference between the external and future oriented perspective of the VSM system 4 as opposed to the inside and now, operational efficiency perspective of system 3 and service delivery perspectives of system 1 and 2.

As a system 4 system, the enterprise architecture function focuses on:

- Supporting the business strategy developed by system 5
- Analyzing strategic change initiatives

- Planning and creating strategic road-maps
- Scenario analysis
- Assessment of future risk, agility and viability of the enterprise
- Coordinating with system 3 systems (i.e. portfolio and program management, project management and solutions architecture)
- Governing the realization of those strategic changes and development of new business capabilities.

VSM as a Reference Architecture

The Viable System Model is an example of a generic reference architecture, i.e. what TOGAF9 calls a Foundation Architecture, and is a thus a key architecture pattern to reuse when designing organization specific target enterprise architecture models. The following is an exploration of how this powerful viable systems approach could be used as a basis for modeling an organization using the Archimate enterprise architecture modeling language.

The effect of using the VSM is an increased focus on the underlying dynamic interactions between systems rather than simply on their static structure.

The following table shows the mapping between VSM concepts and ArchiMate. ArchiMate is much more detailed and specific about its concepts, whereas VSM is more abstract so VSM concepts can be mapped to many different ArchiMate concepts depending on context. For example, VSM seems to be quite flexible about what a 'System' actually is. I have indicated the strongest mapping.

VSM Concept	ArchiMate Concept
System	**Business Function**, Actor, Business Role
Function	**Business Process**, Business Interaction, Business Function, *Behavior*
Environment	**Business Role**, Actor
Variety	**Business Event**, Product, Business Service

Table 3. VSM and ArchiMate Concepts.

The following table illustrates the use of Business Roles to represent the different types of VSM systems.

Business Roles

Recursion level							
System type	Focus	Outcomes	1 Corporate	2 BU / Division	3 Group / Workstream	4 Project	5 Indi-vidual
5	Direction	Strategy	Executive / Director	Head of Business Unit	Head of work group	Project Sponsor	
4	Intelligence	Knowledge	Enterprise Architect	Domain Architect	Program Architect	Solution Architect	
3	Governance / Control	Decisions	Governance board	Steering group	Quality manager	Project steering group	
3*	Audit	Assessment	Auditor / Regulator	Design Authority	Program management Office	Business Systems Analyst	Tester
2	Coordination	Plan	Planning / PMO	BU manager	Program Manager	Project manager	
1	Operations	Activities	Enterprise	Business Unit	Program	Project Team	Worker

Table 4. Business Roles.

The following table illustrates the use of Business Functions to represent the different types of VSM systems.

Business Functions

Recursion level							
Sys-tem type	Focus	Outcomes	1 Corporate	2 BU / Division	3 Group / Workstream	4 Project	5 Indivi-dual
5	Direction	Strategy	Strategic Planning / Strategic Change	BU Strategy	Program Strategy	Project Mandate	
4	Intelligence	Knowledge	EA development (TOGAF ADM)		Program Design	Solution Design	
3	Governance / Control	Decisions	Compliance planning / Governance & Control functions (COBIT)				
3*	Audit	Assessment	Business intelligence / Management Information				

2	Coordina-tion	Plan	Corporate Planning	BU manage-ment	Program management (MSP)	Project manage-ment (Prince 2)	Operations manage-ment (ITIL)
1	Operations	Activities	Performance analysis	Business as Usual	Program delivery	Develop-ment (RUP)	Service Support

Table 5. Business Functions.

System = a Business Capability

Within an Enterprise Architecture model, a (VSM) System is closely associated with a Business Capability or an Architecture Building Block in TOGAF9.

The concept of a Business Capability has yet to be included in ArchiMate but I think that it is one that would be good to include. TOGAF9 does already include the concept of a Business Capability but is not yet clear about it. MODAF also includes the concept of a Capability.

A Business Capability would be the best match for representing a System in VSM.

When using ArchiMate I frequently overload the Business Function concept to use it to represent a Business Capability. A Business Capability is defined as the ability to do something in terms of expertise and capacity. A Business Capability is therefore a grouping concept that can group all other ArchiMate objects including actors, business functions, business processes, business services, application services, application components, infrastructure services, infrastructure components, business objects, data objects, artifacts etc.

The illustration below illustrates a System (System A) that is represented by a Business Function together with associated Actors, Business Roles, Business Processes, supporting a number of Business Events and producing outcomes defined in terms of Products and Business Services. All of these concepts would form part of a Business Capability (= System A).

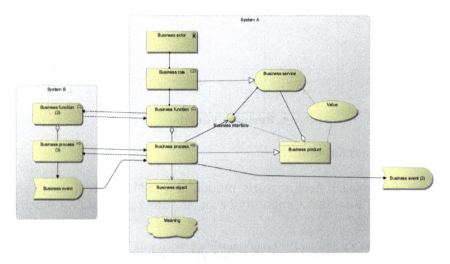

Figure 3. System Representation.

Viable Enterprise Architecture

The diagram below illustrates a macro view of views that have been developed to explore an enterprise architecture model based on the VSM.

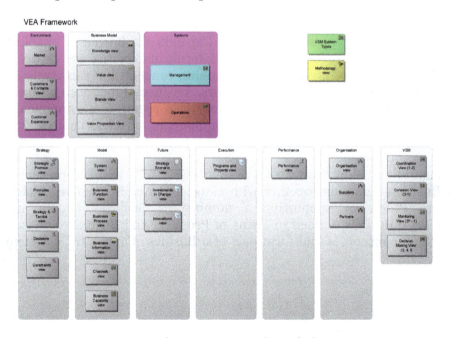

Figure 4. Macro View of Views.

The following diagrams illustrate the way ArchiMate can be used to show the following views:

- Interaction between the 6 different types of VSM systems
- Monitoring view (interaction between System 3*'s and System 1's)
- Cohesion View (Interaction between system 3's and System 1's)
- Coordination View (interaction between System 1's and System 2's)
- Intelligence View (interaction between System4's and the business environment)
- Decision making view (interaction between System 5, System 4 and System 3)

Interactions between Systems

This diagram illustrates the interaction between the 6 different types of VSM systems and the business environment. The Business Environment is represented for simplicity as a generic Business Role but would aggregate specific Business Roles and Actors in detail. Such specific Business Roles would therefore represent customer or market segments and specific customers, contacts, third parties etc. as well as more specific Business Roles (for example Regulators) or Actors (for example HMRC).

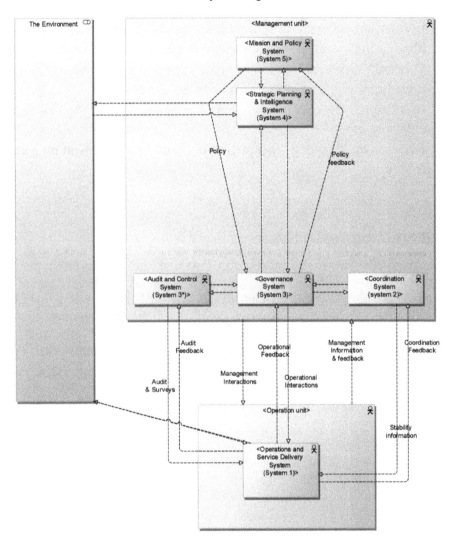

Figure 5. System-Environment Interactions.

Monitoring View

This diagram illustrates the interaction between the System 3* systems and the System 1's at the next level of recursion down. System 3* deliberately skip a level of recursion in order to bypass the management at the same level and provide an independent audit of the operational activities.

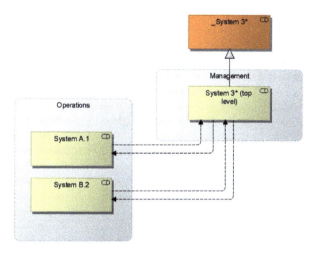

Figure 6. System 3* Interactions.

Cohesion View

This diagram illustrates the interaction between System 2 systems and the System 1 systems that they coordinate.

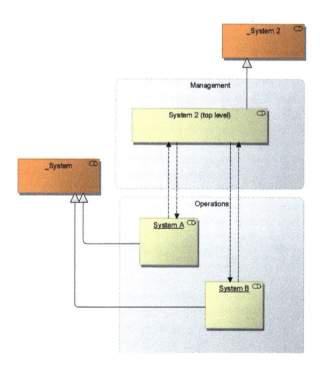

Figure 7. System 2 Interactions.

Coordination View

This diagram illustrates the interaction of System 2 systems with the management systems of system 1's that they coordinate.

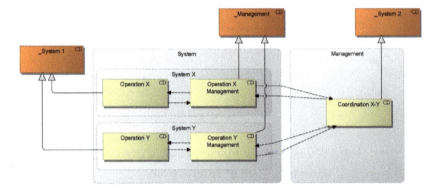

Figure 8. System Coordination View.

Intelligence View

This diagram illustrates the System 4 system interacting with the Business Environment which is represented by Business Roles. The Business Environment includes Customers segments, Market segments, competitors, regulators, government, partners etc. The interactions with the external business environment will contain similar detail to that shown in a Porter's Five Forces diagram.

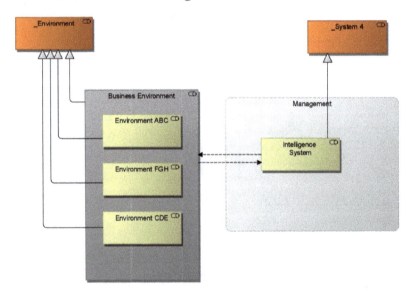

Figure 9. Intelligence View.

Decision Making View

This diagram illustrates the interaction between the Management systems i.e. System 5's, System 4's, and System 3's. System 3*'s can also be included here. This interaction represents the overall decision making and strategic planning functions.

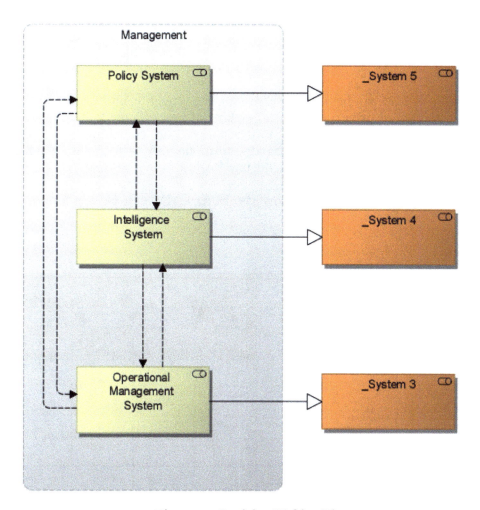

Figure 10. Decision Making View.

EA Assessment Model

In the previous section, the focus has been on the modeling of a VSM system with an Enterprise Architecture language, ArchiMate. In this section the focus is on how to use VSM to assess the Enterprise Architecture.

The recommended approach is to use the SCiO Organisational Maturity Model (OMM) that has been developed by SCiO to assess the structural integrity of an organization based on the Viable System Model. Read more about the model on http://www.scio.org.uk/organisational-maturity-model.

The SCiO OMM can be used for assessing the strengths and weaknesses of the current enterprise architecture, looking at how efficiently it is working today, and for designing the future target and transition enterprise architecture models to ensure the long term viability of your enterprise in the face of changing external market and business environment.

The following table looks at how the SCiO OMM can be supported by objects in an Enterprise Architecture model.

	Viable System Model			Enterprise Architecture			
#	Aspect (system type)	SCiO OMM Question		Business Archi-tecture	Infor-mation Archi-tecture	Application Archi-tecture	Infra-structure Architecture
1	Operations (System 1)	Within your organization, to what extent do you have enough resources to meet the needs of your customers?	Within your organization, do you have the people, equipment and funding to provide the services and / or products to your customers that they need?	Actor, Business Role, Product, Business Service	Funding	Application Components	Equipment
2		To what extent does your organization have ways, or routes, for two-way communication with both your customers and with your suppliers?	Does your organization have mechanisms and processes to communicate effectively enough with your customers for receiving orders precisely and with enough information, and for receiving feedback from customers? Does your organization also have mechanisms and processes for dealing with your suppliers - for	Business Process, Business Interface (Channel), Actors, Business Role (Suppliers)	Business Object (Order, Information, Feedback, Quality, cost, Revenue), Business Event	Application Service, Application collaboration, Application Interface	Infrastructure Service, Infrastructure Interface, Communication Path

			ensuring that they deliver the right products and / or services to the right quality, cost and in a timely manner?				
3		To what extent can your organization meet the needs of your customers to their satisfaction?	Are you able to deliver the full service that your customer(s) require within your target market?	Business Role (*Target Market, Customers, Prospects Contacts*), Business Process (*Value Stream, Business Scenarios*)	Business Object (*Satisfaction, Key Performance Indicators, Critical Success Factors*)	Application Service	
4		To what extent do operations share an up to date understanding of how they deliver their products or services, and how well they deliver them?	How well do your operational staff understand what is important about their roles and in particular, the key features of the services and / or products from the customers' perspective and from your business' perspective?	Business Role, Actor (*Organization Unit*), Product, Business Service	Business Object (*Customer Journey, Customer experience*)	Application Components, (*Service Levels*)	Nodes, Devices, Networks
5	Co-ordination (system 2)	To what extent do your operations and partners have operating between them the necessary standards, IT support tools, common plans, schedules, agreements, knowledge or other ways to ensure a smooth flow of delivery?	Do you have mechanisms to ensure that your organization works smoothly within itself and when working with partners, whether working as part of a bigger process or a supply chain, or collaborating to provide a shared service?	Actors, Business Roles (*Partners*), Business Process (*Value Chain, Supply Chain*)	Business Objects (*Standards, Plan, Schedule, Agreement, Knowledge*) Meaning, Value	Application Components (*IT Support Tools, B2B system interface*), Application Service (*shared Services*)	Infrastructure (*CMDB*), Infrastructure Interface (*B2B gateway*)
6		To what extent are all your operations and partners using these ways of coordinating?	Do the other organizations that your organization interacts with, co-operate with you in coordinating the areas of overlap and interaction in resource, work, processes and so forth?	Actors, Business Roles, Business Collaboration		Application Collaboration	Communication path
7		To what extent is your organization free from unreasonable disturbance caused by lack of coordination within your operations?	In day-to-day operations, is your organization able to get on with its work without unreasonable disturbance by other organizations? Equally, do you provide the support to other organizations that they could reasonably expect from shared requirements? Does this effectively	Business Process, Business Service	Meaning, Value,		

			ensure that work bottlenecks and work "feasts and famines" are avoided?				
8		To what extent do you understand the potential conflicts that could occur within your operations and does your organization have ways of addressing these?	Are you aware of the areas where conflicts for resource, materials etc. could arise within your organization or between your organization and other organizations that you work alongside?	Actor, Business Role (*Organization, organization units*)	Business Object (*Resources*)		Artifact (*Resources, materials*)
9	Resource and Performance Delivery (system 3)	To what extent are there processes in your organization for deciding the levels of resourcing and performance required of your operations?	Are there processes in your organization for taking decisions about resourcing? Are they linked to and based on the performance of operations? Are there processes for measuring performance and rational processes for allocating resource?	Business Process	Business Object (*Resources*), Meaning, Value (*service levels, KPI's, CSF's*) Contract (*Service level Agreements*)		
10		To what extent do your operations managers input into the resource and performance decision process ensure that the resources are adequate to enable them to meet their performance obligations?	Do you take input into - or do you consult about - the resource and performance decisions for your organization, so that your organization is appropriately resourced and measured?	Business Process	Values (*Balanced Scorecard, metrics, measures, Performance*)		
11		To what extent are you able to take decisions about resources and performance so that your organization is able to deliver to meet users' needs?	Do Operations Managers get a fair hearing when they make requests for resource or report on performance? Are their requests taken seriously by your organization and acted on when appropriate, or do they think it seems like going through the motions? Do external factors override the right decisions?	Business Process	Business Objects (*Performance, Factors*), Meaning (*Decision*)		
12		To what extent are the potential	Is there enough understanding in your organization of how the units within	Business Collaboration, Business		Application interaction,	

		synergies within your operations in your organization realized?	the operations do – might – work together to deliver synergy?	Interaction		Application Collaboration	
13	Monitoring (system 3*)	To what extent do you allocate time and have a process to understand how things work within the operations of your organization?	Do you ever go to find out what is going on in operations? Are you able to understand your managers' operational issues?	Business process (Governance, Compliance, Audit, Design Assurance)	Risks, Issues, Assumptions, Dependencies		
14		To what extent do you directly observe, over a period of time, the workings of every operation in your organization?	Do you make a point of routinely (but not too regularly or too frequently) talking to the staff in operations to see what goes on and how well things are running?	Business Event, Business process (*Scenarios, Value Streams*)	Business Object (*Performance metrics*), Value (*Performance measures*)		
15		To what extent do you refrain from micro-management to enable operations managers to get on with running the business?	Are you involved (perhaps unhelpfully) in the day to day running of your organization? Are you "interested but hands off" or is it inappropriate, perhaps verging on micro-management?	Actor, Business Role, Business Process, Business Interaction, Business Collaboration			
16		To what extent is the need for directors to understand operational processes recognized?	Do your managers (and other directors) understand the need to understand what your people do and how this knowledge can help you in your own role?		Meaning, Value		
17	Development (system 4)	To what extent does your organization have resources to understand its external operational environment, predict future opportunities and risks, and plan change?	Does your organization dedicate resource to understanding what is going on outside it, looking at new developments and how they may affect it; identifying both opportunities and threats?	Business Role (*Enterprise Architecture team, customers, contacts, suppliers, vendors etc.*), Business Function (*Enterprise Architecture function*), Business Event	Meaning (*Opportunities, threats, assumptions*), Value (*Risks, Issues*)		
18		To what extent does your organization access information on all the key	Does your organization have clear processes for looking at new developments, within your business / organization and outside it, and	Business Process, Business Event	Meaning (*Opportunities, threats, assumptions*), Value (*Risks,*		

185

		features of its external operational environment?	mechanisms for reporting on them and reacting to them?		*Issues)*		
19		To what extent can your organization implement responsive changes rapidly enough to meet changes within its external operational environment?	Can your organization change quickly enough to match changes in the world outside, in technology, in your customer group and in the wider organization?	Business Process, Business Event	Meaning *(Opportunities, threats, assumptions,* Value *(Risks, Issues)*		
20		To what extent is there a process to identify key future risks to the relationships your organization has with its external operational environment and to what extent does it have plans that can be deployed for its survival if these risks occur?	Is your organization aware of the importance of changes in the outside world that impact both within your business and outside it, impacting its future success and even survival?	Business Process, Business Event, Business Interaction, Business Collaboration	Meaning *(Opportunities, threats, assumptions,* Value *(Risks, Issues)*		
21	Managing Strategy (system 5)	To what extent is your organization clear on how it fits with changes in its external operational environment?	Does your organization understand its role with respect to the external organizations and individuals that it works with?		Meaning *(Goals),* Value *(Objectives)*		
22		To what extent does your organization have a way to reconcile the needs of the future to its external operational environment with the capabilities it has today?	Does your organization have a strategy for delivering services or products over the longer term?	Product, Business Service	Meaning *(Strategy),* Value *(Objectives)*		
23		To what extent can your organization develop strategies that are both practicable and appropriate for the future demands of its external operational	Does your organization have a way of balancing the always present needs of the delivery of operational services or products with a longer term view?	Product, Business Service	Meaning *(Strategy),* Value *(Objectives)*		

		environment?					
24		To what extent does your strategy create a purpose for your organization that is consistent with the purposes of units within your operations and is referred to by them?	Does your organization have an up-to-date strategy that is meaningful to your staff, referred to by them and is consistent with that of the organization as a whole?		Meaning *(Guidelines, Policy, Principle, Standard),* Value		

Table 6. VSM, SCiO OMM and Enterprise Architecture.

Summary

It is clear that the Viable System Model is an important aid to understanding how an enterprise is organized into systems (Business Capabilities) and an important addition to the techniques within the Enterprise Architecture discipline. It provide that extra dimension to designing not just the structural components of the enterprise but also the interactions between them that are needed to keep the enterprise healthy, flexible and viable in the face of an every changing business environment.

The more one looks at the Viable System Model, the more it looks like the unifying theory behind Enterprise Architecture.

About the Author

Adrian Campbell is a consultant and enterprise architect in England.

References

Beer, S. (1972) Brain of the Firm - The Managerial Cybernetics of Organization, London: Allen Lane and Penguin Press.

Beer, S. (1994) The Heart of Enterprise, Chichester, John Wiley & Sons.

Enterprise Architecture and the Viable Systems Model

Mikkel Stokbro Holst

Abstract

The Enterprise Architecture discipline is moving away from being a discipline primarily rooted in information technology theory and practice towards a more business-centric discipline. This increases the complexity of the overall discipline and to be able to handle this greater degree of complexity, new thoughts and tools are required within Enterprise Architecture. This chapter explores how Enterprise Architecture can use Systems Theory and the Viable Systems Model as a tool and mind-set for organizational analysis in order to comprehend and manage the increased complexity involved in moving focus from IT to the business and strategic aspects of the modern enterprise.

Keywords

Enterprise Architecture, Viable Systems Model, Systems Thinking, Systems Theory, Enterprise Architecture Value

The Enterprise Architecture Discipline Today

The Enterprise Architecture (EA) discipline came into existence due to a rising complexity of information systems as a consequence of technological development and increased adaption to World Wide Web solutions by organizations. In this connection EA was seen as a discipline that could assist management in coordinating IT development and systems architecture (Zachman 1987). Simultaneously with this technological development, the way organizations manage and structure themselves changed causing an increased decentralization and diversification of the organizations, again resulting in decision makers facing an ever increasingly complex task of managing these organizations (Doucet, et al. 2009). The fact that organizations have become more dependent on information technology as a tool for coordinating and structuring the organization has resulted in the need for a discipline that can bridge business and IT. The EA discipline has emerged as one of the tools that organizations and their management can turn towards to handle complexity and help improve coordination and transformation across the whole of the Enterprise (Gravesen 2010).

EA is no new concept (Doucet, et al. 2009). If one looks at the organization, there is and always will be an architecture of the enterprise. The major difference is whether or not the architecture is formalized and structured. EA can be defined as the architecture that describes a functioning organization (Doucet, et al. 2009), a definition which illustrates that EA is now characterized as all the words and pictures that together describe the enterprise and not only the technical architecture and infrastructure of the origin of the discipline. In addition to the technology aspect, EA has also started to focus on the more strategic and business oriented dimensions of overall enterprise management. EA can therefore increasingly be characterized as a meta discipline, aiming to provide infrastructure that furthers the understanding of the relationship between management practices used by the organization, e.g. Governance, Strategic Planning etc. EA has been described as a discipline that permits the design and redesign of both private and public sector organizations allowing them to compete in the new dynamic environments partly created by the technological development (Doucet, et al. 2009).

However, at present it is difficult for decision makers to define a single purpose for EA (Bean 2010). One can observe a series of distinct theoretical perspectives within the EA discipline – all with a different understanding of the value that EA should add to the organization:

- **An IT oriented EA perspective**

  In the IT oriented EA perspective the EA purpose is to deliver effective IT (Nielsen and Krogh 2010) and to help simplify IT transformation so that the organization can compete more effectively in the market. This IT centric perspective is embodied in Ross, Weill and Robertson's book, Enterprise Architecture as Strategy (Ross, Weill and Robertson 2006) and Sogeti's concept of Dynamic Enterprise Architecture (Wagter, et al. 2005).

- **A business and IT oriented EA perspective**

  The business and IT oriented perspective is a more holistic view represented by Scott Bernard and his concept of EA supplying information about the entire organization (Tamm, et al. 2011). According to this perspective, EA concerns and considers strategy, business, and technology within the organization. This is exemplified in Bernard's framework, the EA3 Cube (Bernard 2005), leading to faster decisions, improved performance and lower costs (Tamm, et al. 2011).

- **A culturally oriented EA perspective**

  The culturally oriented perspective is a human resource oriented approach to EA and the purpose is to create an EA mind-set. The value of EA arises through the way the employees think and because EA becomes embedded in the culture of the organization. This is illustrated by the concept of Embedded Architecture in the book Coherency Management, in which architecture is a natural part of all day-to-day processes and human resource artifacts (Doucet, et al. 2009). The cultural orientation is also seen in the concept of design thinking in Gartner's Hybrid Thinking, putting human experience at the center and human factors such as culture, religion and history are essential. (Gall, et al. 2010).

- **A market oriented EA perspective**

  The last EA perspective is a market oriented style of EA value creation, clearly seen in the work of the English management strategist Chris Potts. In this case the EA discipline has to consider the market outside the organization, both customers and suppliers; if EA leaves the market out of the picture the organizations will perish (Potts 2008). The value of EA comes from improving the structural performance of the organization, resulting in longer-term value for the enterprise and improved performance in the market (Potts 2010A).

All EA initiatives in organizations are deliberate and accidental variations of these perspectives, but the IT oriented perspective as well as the business and IT oriented perspective are the most commonly seen (Allega and Burton 2011). Up until recently EA was mostly developed and practiced within IT-related fields and has therefore been regarded by many organizations as a very technical discipline inaccessible for non-technicians. This has by many been seen as one of the discipline's biggest disadvantages. The American consulting firm Gartner describes this as an invisible wall between business and IT within the different EA efforts in organizations (Gartner 2010B).

Gartner considers the EA discipline to be at the tipping point of moving away from the IT oriented perspective (Burton and Allega 2011) in the direction of the three more business focused EA perspectives. The invisible wall between business and IT mentioned earlier is dissolving, and according to Gartner EA is the bridge that can successfully integrate business and IT (Gartner 2010B). Philip Allega, research vice president at Gartner, points out the movement of the EA discipline in this quote:

"EA's original promise was its ability to provide future safe guidance given the desires and vision of an organization's senior leadership team. As IT roles shift away from technology management to enterprise management, EA is suited to bring clarity to these blurred boundaries, and, by 2015, increased adoption of EA processes and uses by business will further IT's alignment with the organization's culture, future-state vision and delivery of business value outcomes." (Gartner 2010B)

In 2010 the EA discipline received its first Hype Cycle from Gartner (Gartner 2010A), which can be seen as a sign of the growing maturity of EA as a discipline. The Hype Cycle depicts how new technologies usually experience an initial hype and subsequently move into disappointment, also known as "Trough of Disillusionment". While some technologies end up failing, others continue through the cycle becoming widely accepted. Gartner calls this the "Slope of Enlightenment" which finally ends in the "Plateau of Productivity" (Gartner 2011C). The EA Hype Cycle shows that the EA discipline is moving away from "Trough of Disillusionment" and going up the "Slope of Enlightenment" towards, according to Gartner, becoming a recognized management practice. Gartner argues that there are two important reasons why the EA discipline will move away from the "Trough of Disillusionment". The first is that a greater number of organizations will begin to endorse a more business oriented EA approach and if the EA discipline has to survive, it has to move out of the domain of IT and instead start focusing on both business and IT issues. The second reason Gartner identifies is an emerging number of new practices and disciplines that will support and help the evolution and maturity of the general EA discipline (Gartner 2010B).

It is important to point out that EA in its embrace of business must not forget its IT origin, transform completely into a business discipline and move away from its ability to manage IT almost entirely. An example of this could be Potts and his perspective on EA, in which IT is no longer central to the discipline (Potts 2010B). By completely separating the IT focus from the EA discipline, there will be a risk that EA loses its unique value and ability to build bridges between technology and business - which is also Gartner's point (Allega and Burton 2011).The EA discipline should embrace its move towards a more business focused discipline, but retain the knowledge of information technology. This EA approach is illustrated by Bernard in the business and IT oriented EA perspective.

The move towards becoming a meta discipline and the adaptation of a more holistic view, must logically result in an increase of the complexity that the EA discipline has to handle. This increased complexity requires a new set of tools to help break down the complexity into manageable pieces for the organization and EA practitioners. One of these tools could be the Viable Systems Model.

The Viable Systems Model

The Viable Systems Model (VSM) was originally developed by Stafford Beer in his book Brain of the Firm (Beer 1972). The purpose of VSM is to produce a viable organization which translates into structuring the organization in such a way that it is able to meet and adapt appropriately to the demands of the ever changing environment (Hoverstadt 2008). Beer's VSM has emerged from the Management Cybernetics and the Systems Theory disciplines, both of which are not very well established and defined and beyond the scope of this chapter. However, Beer has encapsulated a large part of the above mentioned disciplines' teachings into the VSM. One of the most important cybernetic influences on the VSM is W. R. Ashby's Law of Requisite Variety (Ashby 1956) that simply states: "Only variety can absorb variety". Another thing to note about the VSM is the concept of Systems Thinking. Systems Thinking can be described as the mind-set behind all System Theory. In Systems Thinking the world is viewed as a long array of systems that are all connected as a complex whole within an overall environment. Systems Thinking believes that in the process of analyzing and solving a problem, you need to understand how the problem plays its part within the overall system to which it belongs. System Thinking hence rejects any idea of simple linear cause and effect as the focus of problem solving and instead adopts a cyclical approach to explaining and unraveling problems.

The VSM has been used by Patrick Hoverstadt in his book *The Fractal Organization* (Hoverstadt 2008). Hoverstadt's book is an attempt to solve what he identifies as today's crisis of management. The old models of management have not progressed in the same rate as the complexity of the organizations and these are struggling to cope with environmental complexity such as new customer demands. Hoverstadt exemplifies this in his Balancing the Complexity Equation based on the above mentioned Ashby's Law. In this equation, the complexity is balanced by the concept of attenuators and amplifiers. Management can amplify the organizational variety by increasing the autonomy of business units and attenuate by grouping complex tasks into departments and divisions. Another important rule to consider with regards to the Balancing the Complexity Equation is a statement from cybernetics embedded in the VSM, called the Conant Ashby Theorem. This theorem states that management needs an up-to-date and effective model of the system they are managing. All of these concepts have been put into Hoverstadt's answer to the management crisis, the Fractal Organization. The VSM developed by Beer is Hoverstadt's overall answer to organizing and in his book he sees VSM as being superior to the traditional bureaucratic and hierarchical models which are no longer sustainable organizing models in the information age (Hoverstadt 2008).

The VSM consists of an environment and a system. The system again consists of 5 sub-systems: operations, coordination, delivery, development and policy. All of the 5 sub-systems and the relationship between them – which include both observing the market outside the organization, operations and development internally in the organization as well as adapting automatically to the identified market changes – is what makes the system viable. It is important to note that the viable systems are called recursive in Beer's work and fractal by Hoverstadt, meaning that a viable system contains one or more viable systems which again contain viable systems similar to a Russian Doll. What in cybernetics is described as lower and higher-level systems in a containment hierarchy is called cybernetic isomorphism by Beer (Beer 1972). In other words, the VSM is a powerful model that can be used to show the structures of the organization and the relationship between these structures. The VSM can for example provide an overview of the communication and information flows between management and the primary activities of the organization. Showing the relationship of the structures of the organization is also an essential goal of EA, therefore the VSM must be able to support EA or the other way around.

The Viable Systems Model applied in an EA context

Systems Theory and EA have a common mind-set regarding the need for a higher degree of understanding of organizations. Hoverstadt states how it is necessary to change the organizational models from being tacit to being explicit and shared, enabling decision makers to manage and change the organizations (Hoverstadt 2008). Similarly EA has come to the realization that the world is becoming so complex that one needs to model this reality and expose all dependencies in order to reach one's goals. EA and Systems Theory share the notion of modeling as a way to comprehend the complexity of the organization in order to obtain a basis of knowledge for decision making.

In the context of EA, VSM can first of all be used as a tool for analysis, and the goal of the VSM should be to help the EA team to manage and create an overview of the organization. However the organization can also view the VSM as something more than only a tool for analysis. The VSM can become the mind-set of the organization and in this case the model, through its systems thinking and recommendations, would become part of the culture of the entire organization. In this way the VSM is in fact used for designing or redesigning the organization.

When placing the VSM into Bernard's framework, the EA3 Cube (Bernard 2005), the VSM models the two top layers of the EA3 Cube: the Strategic Initiatives and the Business Processes layers. In the VSM the first three systems, system 1, 2 and 3 (operations, coordination and delivery), are placed in the Business Processes layer as these are focused on running the day-to-day operations of the organization. The last two systems in the VSM, system 4 and 5 (development and policy), concentrate on the environment, the future and the overall strategy of the organization and are hence placed in the Strategy Initiatives layer of Bernard's EA3 Cube. The choice not to place the VSM in the three bottom, more technical layers of the EA3 Cube is due to the fact that the VSM suffers from certain limitations when it comes to analyzing and understanding an organization in detail. For instance it does not properly model the details of the primary activities, i.e. how tasks and activities are carried out and performed. Here the use of a tool like BPMN or other process modeling tools seems more appropriate. The same limitations apply to the VSM's ability to model technology and infrastructure.

However certain relevant qualities are added when applying the VSM within the field of EA. The first quality to pinpoint when discussing the VSM in an EA context is that the model with its focus not only on the internal side of the organization, but also on the external environment, brings an external dimension into EA that normally does not exist in the EA discipline (Bean 2010). EA almost always focuses on the internal side of the organization with the exception of the market oriented EA perspective represented by Potts. The VSM can consequently help an organization and its EA team to respond and understand changes in the market and more importantly direct how the organization reacts when changes occur, creating a more agile and responsive organization.

The second aspect to discuss when applying the VSM as a tool in an EA process is the model's evident ability to help identify structural errors in the construction of the organization. The VSM can show how different lines of business work together, thus assisting management to achieve a higher understanding of how the organization works. The VSM can for example identify organizational silos and help management deal with any sub-optimization caused by the recognized silo structure. The information provided by the VSM can then be addressed by the EA team together with the management and create a more coherent organization. Coherency is about linking the various parts of the enterprise in such a way that they appear logical, orderly and consistent (Doucet, et al. 2009). A coherent organisation is able to adapt to changes in the market quickly, cheaper and more successfully than an incoherent organization (Wagter, et al. 2005). A coherent organization is necessary in today's market because of increased competition demanding that organizations constantly seek new opportunities in order to gain a competitive advantage (Wagter, et al. 2005).

It appears that Hoverstadt is aware of the previously mentioned limitations of the VSM which is why he developed the so called Complexity Drivers with the purpose of breaking down the primary activities into more manageable clusters. However just as the VSM, the Complexity Drivers are mainly focused on the structure of the organization and the relationship between the structures and they do not identify for example information flows between the tasks of the operations. Nevertheless this lack of going into detail is not a reason to disregard the VSM as a tool for organizational analysis.

As described earlier the VSM can be used as something more than a tool. If the management of the organization commits itself to the philosophy and thinking behind systems theory, the VSM can also be used for designing new organizational units or the redesign of existing organizational units. Using the VSM as a culture and belief system for the organization, the VSM can also function as a reference model for the organizing and structuring of an organization's EA process. In this way the VSM becomes a reference point around which both the EA framework and EA process can be developed. Furthermore the overall EA governance, procedures and standards could be built in a way that they comply with the five sub-systems of the VSM.

Another interesting usage of the VSM can be as a guide to measure structural performance of the EA influence. To determine the value of an EA process is seen as a challenge both in EA theory and EA practice (Tamm, et al. 2011). An article by Potts in the Journal of Enterprise Architecture argues how most formalized EA processes fail because they are unable to show value to the executive team. Potts reasons that most EA initiatives are measured by operational measurements and not structural measurement, the latter being far more important for guiding and monitoring the architectural interventions made by the EA process (Potts 2010A). When implementing Potts' structural performance measurement instead of operational capital based measurement, the VSM could become a powerful tool to define structural indicators for overall EA value measurement, improving the possibilities for EA teams to show their success.

As EA moves away from the IT focus of its roots, supporting organizational adaptability to change only within IT, EA is on its way to becoming a discipline that supports both innovation and adaptability to the changes internally in the organization as well as in the external environment. This change will increase EA's ability to improve the organization's capability to execute its normal business procedures. In this context the VSM can function as one of the tools the EA teams could use to handle the new increased complexity emerging due to the enlarged scope of the EA discipline.

About the Author

At the time of writing Mikkel Stokbro Holst was a master student at the IT University of Copenhagen attending John Gøtze's Enterprise Architecture Program. Today Mikkel Stokbro Holst works as an IT Strategist and Program Manager at Falck, a global public safety company. Mikkel also is a board member of the Danish chapter of the Association of Enterprise Architects. Mikkel holds a bachelor in business studies from Roskilde University and a MSc in Business and IT from the IT University of Copenhagen.

References

Allega, Philip, and Betsy Burton. Enterprise Architecture in Organizations Beyond the Tipping Point. Stamford: Gartner, 2011.

Ashby, Willam Ross. An Introduction to Cybernetics. London: Chapman & Hall, 1956.

Bean, Sally. "Re-thinking Enterprise Arcjitecture using Systems and Complexity Approaches." a|EA journal, November 2010: 7-13.

Beer, Stafford. Brain of the Firm. London: The Penguin Press, 1972.

Bernard, Scott A. An Introduction to Enterprise Architecture EA3. Linking Business and Technology. 2nd edition. AuthorHouse, 2005.

Burton, Betsy, and Philip Allega. Beyond the Tipping Point: EA Is Strategic. Stamford: Gartner, 2011.

Doucet, Gary, John Gøtze, Scott Bernard, and Palab Saha. Coherency Management : Architecting the Enterprise for Alignment, Agility, and Assurance. AuthorHouse, 2009.

Gall, Nicholas, David Newman, Philip Allega, Anne Lapkin, and Robert A. Handler. Introducing Hybrid Thinking for Transformation, Innovation and Strategy. Gartner, 2010.

Gartner. "Enterprise Architecture Hype Cycle." Technology Research & Business Leader Insight | Gartner. Juli 2010A. http://www.gartner.com/hc/images/201646_0001.gif (accessed Oktober 26, 2010).

— Gartner's Enterprise Architecture Hype Cycle Reveals Two Generations of Enterprise Architecture. 5 August 2010B. http://www.gartner.com/it/page.jsp?id=1417513 (accessed December 14, 2010).

—. Gartner's Hype Cycle. 2 Maj 2011C. http://www.gartner.com/technology/research/methodologies/hype-cycle.jsp (accessed Maj 2, 2011).

Gravesen, Jan. Enterprise Architecture – Effektiv ressourceudnyttelse som en tværorganisatorisk kompetence. København: Børsen, 2010.

Hoverstadt, Patrick. The Fractal Organization : Creating Sustainable Organizations with the Viable Systems Model. Chichester, West Sussex: John Wiley & Sons, 2008.

Nielsen, Tomas Hannibal, and Jean Krogh. IT Håndbogen Enterprise Arkitektur. København: Børsens Ledelseshåndbøger, 2010.

Potts, Chris. "Using Structural Performance Ratios to Guide Investments in Enterprise Architecture." a|EA journal, November 2010A: 14-18.

Potts, Chris. "Enterprise Architecture Driving Business Innovation - Time to Break Out of IT." GEAO Journal of Enterprise Architecture Extract, no. 3 (1) (Marts 2008).

—. RecrEAtion. Bradley Beach: Technics Publications, 2010B.

Ross, J. W., P. Weill, and D. C. Robertson. Enterprise Architecture As Strategy. Harvard Business Press, 2006.

Tamm, Thomas, Peter B Seddon, Graeme Shanks, and Peter Reynolds. "How Does Enterprise Architecture Add Value to Organisations?" Communication of the Association for Information Systems, marts 2011: 141-168.

Wagter, Roel, Martin van den Berg, Joost Luijpers, and Marlies van Steenbergen. Dynamic Enterprise Architecture. John Wiley and Sons, 2005.

Zachman, John A. "A framework for information system architecture." IBM Systems Journal, 1987: 276-292.

Enterprise Controllability and Viability

Olusola O. Oduntan and Namkyu Park

Abstract

There is significant evidence that high environmental complexity and turbulence will continue to affect many markets for many years to come, and pose an extreme challenge to the practice of enterprise management. To thrive in today's markets enterprises must be able to adapt efficiently and quickly. Enterprise architecture (EA) is a practice that enables enterprises to manage their transformations effectively. An enterprise's Management Control System (MCS) is critical to its ability to sense and respond to changes in its environment. In spite of this, many enterprise architecture frameworks (EAFs) do not provide comprehensive support for modeling management control systems. The Enterprise Viability Model (EVM) was developed to fill this gap in the modeling, analysis and design of management control systems. The EVM was developed as a practical application of Stafford Beer's Viable System Model (VSM), and it integrates viability farsightedness into the MCS of any organization to help assure its structural viability. In this chapter, we describe how the EVM can be used by any enterprise to model its business context and its MCSs to enhance its viability potential.

Keywords

Enterprise Architecture, Management Control Systems, Axiomatic Design, Viable System Model, Enterprise Viability, Enterprise Agility

Introduction

High market complexity and high turbulence are significant stressors in many markets today. There is significant evidence that these two factors will continue to affect many markets for many years to come, and pose an extreme challenge to the practice of enterprise management. To thrive in today's markets, enterprises must be designed to cope with the complexity in their environment, and must be able to adapt efficiently and quickly. Many companies are experiencing an increased complexity in their business environment, which has been caused by the fragmentation in many facets of their business environments. Increased variety in customer tastes and segments, types of commodities, types of technologies, types of competitors, and globalization, pose impose additional burden on all enterprise systems involved in fulfilling the customer's needs. To achieve high customer satisfaction, it is necessary that enterprise functions, ranging from marketing, product development, manufacturing, order fulfillment, sales, and service, are structured appropriately to deal with the high complexity in the market. Enterprises that are unable to match the variety in their environment face significant peril to their viability.

In addition to the increased complexity in the environment, the business environment of many companies has become very volatile. The world today is undergoing changes at a faster rate than ever before in history. Industrialization, globalization, and major changes in world politics are continuously transforming many societies and economies worldwide, and the increased pace of technology innovation, rising consumer expectations, and government deregulation is creating opportunities for new competitors to change the basic rules of the game through new products, processes, and distribution patterns. For companies operating in complex and turbulent business environments the job for management becomes a very challenging activity. Managers recognize that the survival of their companies requires a built-in capability to navigate these challenges. In surveys by leading management consulting firms like Bain and Co. and IBM, executives identified the ability to navigate their firms through change as being their most critical challenge (Rigby and Rogers 2000; Højsgaard 2011).

Viability is an important attribute if a business enterprise, or an organization, is to achieve its intended longevity. A system is viable if it is capable of responding to changes to its environment, even those changes that could not have been foreseen when the system was designed. Like the central nervous system of most living systems, the Management and Control Systems (MCS) of an enterprise is essential to its ability to adapt and respond to change in its environment. But in spite of the critical nature of the MCS to the adaptability of an enterprise, and the increased need for enterprises to be able to transform themselves to deal with the increasing turbulence in their business environments, few enterprise architecture frameworks provide effective tools for the modeling of the MCS of enterprises. Enterprises need to be designed to handle the high complexity of their markets, and be able to effectively and rapidly transform themselves to meet the needs of their business environment. Enterprise architecture is the practice of informing the business decision making process through an understanding of the structure, functions, and technologies required to manage and support change in complex organizations (Bailey 2006). Enterprise architectures facilitate the development of a "proactive, aware enterprise which is able to act in a real-time adaptive mode, responsively to customer needs in a global way, and to be resilient to changes in the technological, economic, and social environment" (Theodore J. Williams et al. 1994).

In this chapter, the Enterprise Viability Model (EVM), is presented as an extension to enterprise architecture frameworks for managing change in organizations operations under conditions of turbulence. The aim of the EVM is to support the modeling and analysis of an enterprise's management control system (Oduntan 2008). The EVM was developed by integrating the Viable System Model (VSM) (Espejo and Gill 1997) and Axiomatic design (Suh, Bell, and Gossard 1978). The EVM has been applied in the development of a model for sustainable manufacturing (Park, et al. 2007), and in development of an agent-based simulation test-bed for enterprise viability analysis (Oduntan 2008; Oduntan and Park 2009; Park and Oduntan 2009; Kondabolu, et al. 2011; Oduntan and Park 2012).

Theoretical Background

Environmental Complexity

Environmental complexity is measure of the number of components in an organization's environment (Anonymous 2011). Complexity can be conceptualized as the number components and factors in a decision environment, and the amount heterogeneity between them (Duncan 1972; Tung 1979; Cannon and St. John 2007). An increase in environmental complexity makes it more difficult for management to grasp and understand the relationships between the environmental factors. Environmental complexity can be conceptualized as having the following three dimensions (Tung 1979):

- Number of components and factors to be considered
- Relative differentiation and variety of the components and factors
- Interdependency between the components and factors being considered

High environmental complexity increases the difficulty of decision makers in the organization to grasp and understand the patterns of behavior in the environment, and increases the variety needed by the enterprise to influence desired behavior in the environment.

Business Turbulence

Turbulence is a word that is increasingly being used to describe the business environment in which a lot of companies operate today. In spite of the awareness of academics and managers about the importance of turbulence for over three decades, there is no universally accepted method of measuring turbulence. One approach that has been used by a number of researchers (Child 1972; Wholey and Brittain 1989) isolates the measure of turbulence into three components:

- Frequency: The frequency of the change in the level of the resource
- Amplitude: The degree of difference in the level of the resource
- Predictability (uncertainty): Degree of irregularity in the overall pattern of change

One common issue with most published methods of measuring turbulence is the objective nature of the measures, which measures the turbulence independently of the ability of the organizations experiencing them to regulate their influence. Thus, these measures of turbulence do not provide any information regarding the amount of stress the turbulence causes the enterprise under its influence.

Enterprise Architecture Frameworks

Enterprise Architecture Frameworks are a modeling approach for organizing and systematizing the bag of tools used for designing and managing change in all the various aspects of an enterprise throughout the entire life-cycle of the enterprise (Bernus, Nemes, and Schmidt 2003). However, few enterprise architecture frameworks provide effective tools for the modeling of the MCS of enterprises. Table 1 summarizes how each of the major EA models the management control system of an enterprise.

Enterprise Architectural Framework	Level of Support for Management Control System View
Zachman	The MCS is not represented in the Zachman architecture. Components of an MCS can be modeled separately in the Enterprise, System, and Technology sub-models of the Zachman framework
CIMOSA	The MCS is not represented in CIMOSA. However, some processes underlying the MCS can be modeled using existing

	CIMOSA modeling constructs.
GRAI/GIM	Compared to other frameworks that tend to have an information processing modeling focus the GRAI/GIM places the most emphasis, and most explicitly represents the management and control view (Noran 2003). The GRAI Grid is capable of modeling the decision-making architecture of an organization. The GRAI Net is used to model the activities, resources, inputs and outputs within the decision centers.
ISO15704/GERAM and PERA	CS is explicitly represented in the PERA
CEN TS 14818	Like the GRAI/GIM from which it was developed, the CEN TS 14818, supports the modeling of the MCS by focuses on the definition of an integrated decision making structure that enables consistent decisions to be made enterprise-wide.
ARIS	Although it has a control/process view that can be used to analyze relationships between the objects of the data, organization, and functions, ARIS has no tools for effectively modeling MCS.
TOGAF	The TOGAF has no support for modeling MCS.
FEAF	The FEAF has no support for modeling MCS.
DODAF	The DoDAF has no support for modeling the MCS.

Table 1: Support for Management Control System View

Viable System Model (VSM)

Cybernetics is a study of how systems use information, models, and control actions to steer toward and maintain their goals, in the presence of various internal and external disturbances (Heylighen and Joslyn 2001). Cybernetics provides a theoretical framework that enables the laws governing the control system of an organization to be studied. The Viable System Model (VSM) is one of the most significant contributions of cybernetics to management science (Jackson 2000, 156). The VSM was developed to provide a basis for understanding the structure and behavior affecting the viability of complex adaptive systems. The VSM is a cybernetic model of the organization of complex and adaptive systems, and it is based on a comprehensive model of the structure and behavior of autonomous systems, such as organizations, that need to adaptively interact with their environments in order to survive. The VSM is a model of the organizational characteristics of any viable system (Jackson 2000, 157). The VSM depicts how a system consisting of multiple interconnected checks and balances, distributed decision-making, problem-solving and implementation processes can produce a cohesive system with the capacity to deal with high environmental complexity (Beer 1979, 406).

The VSM identifies five subsystems that are necessary and sufficient to ensure the viability of any system (Beer 1979, 263). A representation of the VSM is shown in Illustration 1. Each of these subsystems contributes in a unique way to system viability. The purpose of these systems, starting from System 1 to 5, can be labeled as: implementation, coordination, control, development, and policy (Jackson 2000, 158). In addition to defining these subsystems, the VSM also defines rules that govern the relationships and interactions of these subsystems. In addition, it defines the attributes of the information channels that connect the different functions within the system and its environment.

Turning over the VSM unto its side highlights the similarities and dissimilarities between the VSM and the classical feedback control system (Table 2, Illustration 2) (Herring and Kaplan 2001) .

Similarities
The controller of the feedback control system is represented in the VSM by the SYSTEM FIVE-FOUR-THREE, which are responsible for making sure the system achieves its goals
The actuator in the feedback control system is represented in the VSM by SYSTEM TWO-ONE, which are the operations doing the work
Like the classical feedback control system the VSM has channels for sending information within subsystems of the control system, and between itself and its environment.
Dissimilarities
VSM is able to represent multifunctional control systems that are present in complex systems.
VSM is able to represent hierarchical and recursive organization of decision making units.
VSM is able represent the decentralization of decision making in the control system.
VSM uses cybernetic concepts, such as, requisite variety and homeostasis to determine stability.

Table 2: Similarities in Classical Feedback Control and Viable System Model

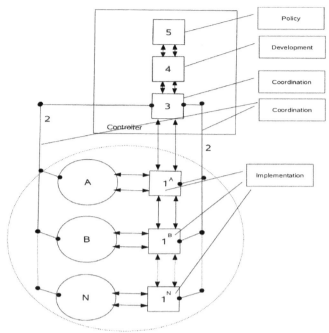

Illustration 1: Viable System Model

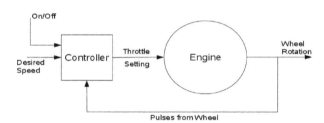

Traditional Feedback Control System

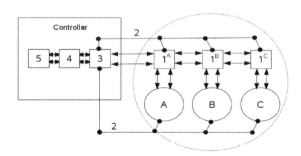

Viable System Model

**Illustration 2: Comparison of VSM to Classical Feedback Control System
(adapted from Herring and Kaplan 2001)**

Part of the strength of the VSM comes from its fractal and recursive architecture which enables the different hierarchical levels of management achieve the autonomy they each require to cope with highly complex and turbulent environments (Espinosa, Harnden, and Walker 2007; Hoverstadt 2008, chap. 4). In spite of its many successful applications, the VSM is not widely known in management circles (Espejo and Gill 1997). Hindering its wider adoption is the fact that many ideas behind the model are not easy to grasp, and that the model embodies non-conventional thinking about organizations (Espejo and Gill 1997).

Axiomatic Design

Axiomatic Design Theory was developed to provide a scientific foundation for creating designs of products, processes, and systems (Suh, Bell, and Gossard 1978). In Axiomatic Design, the design process is defined as the generation of synthesized solutions that satisfy different needs through the mapping of Functional Requirements (FRs) in the functional domain to Design Parameters (DPs) in the physical domain (Trewn and Yang 2000). This is achieved through the rational selection of DPs that satisfy the FRs, while conforming to Constraints (Cs), which place bounds on acceptable values and characteristics of the FRs or DPs. The Design Constraints are conceptualized as restrictions on allowable design choices during the selection of Functional Requirements, Design Parameters, and Process Variables.

According to axiomatic design theory, good designs must satisfy the following axioms (Suh 1984):

> *Axiom 1: The independence axiom*
>
> Maintain the independence of functional requirements.
>
> *Axiom 2: The information axiom*
>
> Minimize the information content

Axiom 1 states that the functional independence defined in the problem statement should be carried through the definition of the minimum independent set of FRs and design of the solution (Suh 1984). Axiom 2 states that the design with the minimum information content is the best design (Suh 1984),(S. J. Kim, Suh, and S.K. Kim 1991). After FRs are defined, they are mapped to DPs, which are the attributes of the system that will be manipulated to achieve the FRs. If the design is not detailed enough to be implemented, both the DP and its corresponding FR must be decomposed to define more specific FRs and DPs (Gebala and Suh 1992).

The Development of the Enterprise Viability Modeling Framework

Enterprise Viability

Enterprise viability is defined as the capacity of an enterprise to survive in its business environment until the needs of all its current and future stakeholders are met (Oduntan 2008; Oduntan and Park 2012). Due to its forward looking and uncertain nature, viability is measured using a probabilistic measure, which is called the viability potential (Oduntan 2008). Viability potential is defined as the probability that the enterprise will survive until the time the needs of its current and future stakeholders are met. Once viability is viewed from this perspective it becomes apparent and clear that maintaining and increasing the viability potential of the enterprise should be the ultimate strategic goal of corporate leaders, and all other goals should become subordinate to it.

The Development of Enterprise Viability Model

To design a high quality system a methodology must be used to systematically relate the desired design outcomes to the design principles and design parameters used to achieve the desired results (Cochran and Reynal 1996). The role of AD in EVM is therefore to establish a relationship between our desired outcome, enterprise viability, and the design principles and system parameters for achieving this result. AD is utilized in the EVM to identify the functions that are core to the viability of an enterprise. In AD, the design of the enterprise begins with the definition of the Customer Needs (CNs), which express the requirements of the stakeholders of the enterprise. In the EVM the CNs of the stakeholders of the viable enterprise are defined as:

CN1: An economic system that creates value for the purpose of fulfilling specific material needs of its diverse community of stakeholders throughout the duration of time during which those specific needs of its stakeholders exist.

Enterprises survive only as long at its constituent agents or stakeholders are willing to participate in the exchange relationships facilitated through the enterprise. When the needs of one of more groups of stakeholders can no longer be satisfied through the exchange relationships those stakeholders will no longer participate, and as a consequence the enterprise will suffer the loss of their contribution, resulting in diminished economic activity. If the loss of participation of the stakeholder group continues unabated, eventually all activities in the enterprise ceases, and the very existence of the enterprise will be threatened. The demise of the enterprise means that for those stakeholders that still have needs that were fulfilled by the enterprise, they will need to proceed elsewhere to meet those needs. For this reason, it is important that the enterprise is able to fulfill the needs of all its stakeholders for the entire duration of time that one or more of its group of stakeholders has a need to be fulfilled. This intended lifespan of an enterprise can range in duration from the time it takes to complete single project, which is the case in such industries like film production, to multiple product life cycles lasting many years, such as is the case with many consumer products companies.

After the customer needs are established, the next step in the AD process is the definition of the highest level functional requirements of the viable enterprise. Functional requirements (FRs) represent how the customer needs will be accomplished in the functional domain. The selection of the correct FRs is critical to the quality of the final design (Cochran and Reynal 1996; Suh, Cochran, and Lima 1998). According to Theorem 18 of AD theory (Suh 1998), for an engineered system to accomplish its intended objectives in the most effective manner, the topmost functional requirements must be correctly selected due to the fact that wrong choices made at the highest level of the functional requirements cannot be corrected lower in the design hierarchy. Thus, it is necessary that the topmost functional requirements for the design of a viable enterprise, or guidelines for their selection, are prescribed in the EVM to ensure that the correct FRs are selected in the design process. From the definition of viability potential, the most viable enterprise is the one that has the highest probability of surviving through its desired lifespan. Thus, from this argument the first FR of the viable enterprise is proposed as:

FR1: Maximize the viability potential of the enterprise

FR1 states that the first objective in viable enterprise design should be to ensure that the internal and external relationships that define the enterprise, give the enterprise the highest probability of surviving through its expected lifespan. As stated previously, the selection of FR1 as the top-level FR is critical to the quality of the final design, and it is necessary that we eliminate the probability of a incorrect choice of FR1. Enterprise architecture principles used in the EVM to guide the selection of the FRs and DPs during the application of AD. Enterprise architecture principles are general, enduring, and seldom amended rules that guide the design, development, and evaluation of enterprise architectures (Stelzer 2009; Anon.). Thus, the choice of FR1 is the first architectural principle of the EVM (Table 3).

Statement
The primary functional requirement (FR1) of the viable enterprise design is to maximize the viability potential of the enterprise
Rationale
This principle supports the long-term stakeholders needs of the viable enterprise design which is defined as CN1.
Implications
Without this principle, it is possible to design an enterprise to fulfill primarily the short-term needs of its stakeholders

Table 3: Principle 1: Selection of FR1

After its primary the top-level FR is defined, the next step is to map the FR to the physical domain in order to identify design parameters that will fulfill the FR. According to AD theory, in the design of manufacturing organizations, the design parameters can be programs, offices, machines, layouts of machines, or the arrangements or the design of manufacturing elements (Gebala and Suh 1992; Suh 1997). However, in order select the proper design parameter to fulfill FR1, it necessary to consider the nature of enterprises as "large flexible systems" (Suh 1997). A system is classified as a large flexible system if the total number of functional requirements that the system must satisfy during its lifetime is large, and, if at different times, the system is required to fulfill different subsets of functional requirements (Suh 1997). The functional requirements of an enterprise change over time because of changes in the environment and the needs of its stakeholders. As a large flexible system, the enterprise has a large set of functional requirements, of which at any point in time, the enterprise is only required to fulfill a subset of the requirements. From Theorem 20 of AD theory on the design of large flexible systems (Suh 1997), when the complete set of functional requirements is not known, as is the case under turbulent business environments, there is no guarantee that one specific design will always have the minimum information content for all possible subsets of functional requirements, which means that there is no guarantee that the same design will always be the best.

If all the functional requirements are not known ahead of time, the strategy for designing a system that can fulfill the changing functional requirements is to provide the system with intelligence so that it can select the right set of design parameters according to the Independence Axiom (Suh 1997). Applying this principle to the design of the enterprise means that the enterprise must be designed with the intelligence that will enable it to adapt itself to changes in the environment. The ability to recognize changes to its functional requirements and select a new set of design parameters means that the enterprise must have intelligence, which can be defined as the capacity to make structural adjustment in response to environmental disturbances within the context of a set of overarching goals. So, in order to remain viable at all times during its lifetime, the enterprise should be capable of identifying the correct set of functional requirements necessary for its existence , selecting the corresponding design parameters that will be required to satisfy it, and then reconfiguring itself to provide the required set of design parameters. In many man-made systems, the ability to adapt to disturbances in the environment while steering a system towards its objective is embodied in their feedback control systems, and for complex adaptive systems, this capability is embodied in their VSM. Thus, the design parameter DP1 required to fulfill FR1 is the VSM of the enterprise.

DP1: Enterprise VSM

The Enterprise VSM is the conceptual VSM of the enterprise that defines how the various control systems and processes in the enterprise must be integrated to ensure viability. The VSM of an enterprise is an sufficient design parameter for fulfilling FR1 for the following reasons:

- It identifies the systems and processes necessary to maximize viability in an environment.
- It is general enough to be applied for modeling the management and control systems of any organization.
- It identifies, in general terms, the systems necessary to manage current and future business requirements of any enterprise.

The selection of the Enterprise VSM as DP1 is critical in the EVM because it constrains the design parameters that can be selected, later in the AD decomposition process, to subsystems, processes, or attributes of the Enterprise VSM (DP1). Thus, the selection of DP1 is the second enterprise architecture principle Table 4.

Statement
The design parameter selected to fulfill FR1 is the VSM of the enterprise
Rationale
The enterprise VSM enables the enterprise to maintain its viability in a complex and changing environment, which fulfills FR1
Implications
Every design parameter obtained from decomposing DP1 must be an element of the enterprise VSM

Table 4: Selection of DP1

In order to complete the design of DP1, axiomatic decomposition is applied to both FR1 and DP1. The decomposition of FR1 involves a further decomposition of the Enterprise VSM to obtain the details necessary to implement the management control system of the enterprise. From the above discussion, it has been shown that to maximize its viability potential an enterprise must be able to satisfy the needs of all current and future stakeholders. In a changing environment in which the needs of the stakeholders are changing, the functional requirements that made the enterprise capable of satisfying current stakeholders might not be able to satisfy future stakeholders. The functional requirements that enable us to fulfill the needs of the current and future stakeholders of the enterprise, and thus achieve FR1 are:

FR11: Maximize fulfillment of current stakeholder's needs

FR12: Maximize adaptability of enterprise to the future environment

These two functional requirements state that to maximize its viability, every enterprise must be able to fulfill the needs of its current stakeholders, and be positioned such that is will be able to fulfill the needs its future stakeholders. The selection of FR11 and FR12 are next two architectural principles of the EVM (Table 5).

Statement
To maximize the viability potential of the enterprise (FR1), the enterprise must maximize the fulfillment of its current stakeholder needs (FR11) and maximize the adaptability of the enterprise to the future environment (FR12)
Rationale
The fulfillment of current and future stakeholder needs will enable the customer to maintain its stakeholders through its intended lifespan and maximize its viability
Implications
The design of enterprise VSM will be focused around two objectives, managing the ability of the enterprise to fulfill current stakeholder needs, and managing the positioning of the enterprise to fulfill future stakeholder needs

Table 5: Principle 3 - Selection of FR11 and FR12

The selection of DPs that will satisfy FR11 and FR12 are defined in the VSM model of the enterprise. According to the VSM, the DPs that will enable the satisfaction of the current stakeholders of the enterprise (F11) are System Three-Two-One of the VSM, which are the systems responsible for the Implementation, Coordination, and Control (Espejo and Gill 1997) of the current operations of the enterprise.

DP11: Systems Three-Two-One

The systems that enable the adaptability, and thus the satisfaction of the needs of future stakeholders, of the enterprise (FR12) are System Four-Five, which are the systems responsible for the Intelligence (Development) and Policy (Espejo and Gill 1997) of the enterprise. By intelligence we mean, the ability of the enterprise to obtain information about the future trajectory of the environment, and develop plans based on internal capabilities to adapt to the future. The ability of a viable system to develop feasible plans towards the future is highly dependent on a good understanding of the current operational context by the Intelligence of the viable system. The system with the best understanding of the current operational context is the Control (System Three), but since it is already defined in DP11, it cannot be defined a second time in DP12. To resolve this conflict the decoupling principle from Axiomatic Design ((Suh 1998)) is applied, and fulfillment of FR12 is achieved by combining the use of DP11 and DP12:

FR12 = f(DP11, DP12)

Where,

DP12: System Four-Five

f(DP11, DP12) represents the interaction of System-Four-Five (Intelligence and Policy) with System-Three (Control) from DP11 to develop feasible plans for the future of the enterprise. The selection of DP11 and DP12 as a a coupled set of design parameters to achieve the enterprise VSM are Principle 5 and Principle 6 of the EVM (Table 6, Table 7).

$$\begin{pmatrix} FR11 \\ FR12 \end{pmatrix} = \begin{bmatrix} X & 0 \\ X & X \end{bmatrix} \begin{pmatrix} DP11 \\ DP12 \end{pmatrix}$$

| **Statement** |
| The design parameter selected to fulfill current stakeholder requirements (FR11) is System Three-Two-One, which is responsible for managing the current operations of the enterprise |
| **Rationale** |
| According to the VSM, System Three-Two-One are responsible for ensuring that the operations of a system fulfills its current goals. |
| **Implications** |
| The decomposition of FR11, to further define the systems for maximizing the stakeholder's current needs, will be constrained to systems responsible for managing the implementation, coordination, and control of the operations of the enterprise. |

Table 6: Principle 4: Selection of DP11

| **Statement** |
| The design parameter selected to adapt the enterprise for the future is DP12 (the intelligence and policy), and it interacts with the control from DP11 to ensure that feasible plans for the future are developed. |
| **Rationale** |
| According to the VSM, System Five-Four-Three are responsible for ensuring that the enterprise adapts to fulfill its future goals. |
| **Implications** |
| The decomposition of FR12, to further define the systems for adapting the enterprise, will be constrained to systems responsible for intelligence and policy of the enterprise. |

Table 7: Principle 5: Selection of DP12

This concludes the extent of axiomatic design decomposition required for the specification of the EVM framework. To ensure the universality of the EVM framework, it is necessary for Eq 1, and the architectural principles it embodies, to be generic. The design matrix in Eq.1 should be used as a skeleton to begin the architectural design of the management control systems of the enterprise.

Modeling and Measuring Environment Complexity and Turbulence

The business environment of enterprises contains many resources which are utilized by the enterprise to conduct its activities. These resources, include customer, procured materials, labor, capital markets, technologies, and natural resources. The number of different customer segments of an enterprise, and the number of different types of commodities utilized as raw material by an enterprise are examples of the components of an environmental resource. In the example of the customer resource, the higher the number of customer segments, or the more heterogeneous the customer segment are, the higher the variety of products that will need to be developed and produced, as well as, factors that will have to be taken into consideration in making decisions about managing the customers' satisfaction. In the EVM, the complexity in each environmental resource is measured by using the number of categories, with distinct management requirements, of each resource of the environment. The distinct management requirements of each component of each resource must be accounted for during the definition of the MCS of the enterprise. In the EVM, the need to manage separately the unique requirements of each component (of each environmental resource) is addressed in Principle 6 (Table 8).

- Statement
  If a functional requirement is defined to manage an aspect of an environmental resource, each component of the resource must be defined with its own functional requirement.
- Rationale
  This ensures that components of the environmental resources that have independent requirements can be managed independent of one another, and are not coupled together.
- Implications
  Multiple DPs and FRs will need to be defined to manage aspects of environmental resources with multiple components.

Table 8: Principle 6: Functional Requirements of Components of Environmental Resources

Environmental Turbulence

The probability that a design parameter will satisfy a functional requirement, given the uncertainty due to turbulence, can be represented by a probability distribution, such as the one shown in Illustration 3 (Suh, 1997). For simplicity purposes only, the probability distribution of the design parameter is shown as a Normal distribution.

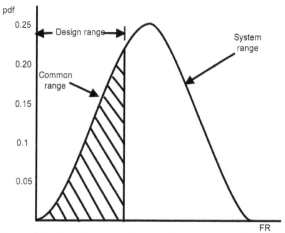

Illustration 3: Design Range, System Range and Common Range

The probability a design parameter will be able to successfully satisfy its functional requirement can be calculated from the area under the design range of the FR, and its overlap with the area under the system range of the DP. The overlap of the design range and the system range is the only region where the functional requirements are satisfied. The probability that the design parameter will satisfy the functional requirement can be calculated by the area of the common range divided by the area under the system range:

$$P\left(\frac{FR}{DP}\right) = \frac{common range}{system range}$$

Turbulence in the environment influences the ability of a design parameter to fulfill its functional requirements by influencing the spread (variance) of the system range, which reduces the overlap between the probability distribution under the system range and the design range. Reduction in the probability of design parameters to fulfill their intended functional requirements reduces the overall quality of the design of the viable enterprise, and as consequence, its viability potential. Using Axiom 2 of the axiomatic design (Suh 1998) the probabilities of the DPs can be converted to the information of the design, which can be used to measure design quality. Although this approach is theoretically possible, in a viable enterprise design with many functional requirement and design parameters, computing the information content might be impractical, if not unfeasible. For this reason we have developed a simple approach to measure the impact of the turbulence on the enterprise. Our observation has been that the conceptualization and treatment of turbulence in management practice is often impeded due to a lack of practical techniques for characterizing its behavior and effect. The EVM utilizes a new measure of turbulence that can be readily operationalized (Oduntan 2008; Oduntan and Park 2012). The EVM approach adopts an existing multidimensional approach (Child 1972; Dess and Beard 1984; Wholey and Brittain 1989) which breaks turbulence in to its component parts: amplitude, frequency, and uncertainty. Each dimension of turbulence is divided into three regions of varying turbulence, using a normative scale to delineate each region Table 9.

Level of Disturbance	Magnitude (Amplitude)	Uncertainty (Predictability)	Frequency
1 (Low)	The disturbance and its regulation is localized to one functional unit in the enterprise.	The future is quite clear and it is possible to define point forecasts that are "close enough".	Rare occurrence of the disturbance over the life-cycle of the enterprise.
2 (Moderate)	The disturbance is distributed and affects more than one functional unit in the enterprise. Its regulation exceeds the variety handling capacity of one functional unit but is within the variety capacity of the overall system.	Future outcomes are not known, but possible outcomes can be defined as a set of scenarios.	Occasional or repeated occurrence of the disturbance over one or several operations management cycle.
3 (High)	The disturbance is system-wide and its regulation exceeds the variety currently available in the enterprise.	The future is so "cloudy" that is not possible to define even a range of possible outcomes or scenarios.	Occurrence of the disturbance is likely or highly likely to be encountered during day-to-day transactions.

Table 9: Levels of Turbulence (Oduntan, 2008)

Every enterprise depends on the availability of resources in its environment for its survival (Dess and Beard 1984), (Aldrich 1979). These resources include the sources of customer demand, procured materials, natural resources, skilled labor, technology, financing, favorable government regulations, and mother nature. At its very core, turbulence is about volatility of resources. Once turbulence is viewed from the perspective of its influence on an enterprise's resources, it stops being a nebulous abstract concept that we are powerless to work under, but instead becomes a condition that is easier to identify, assess, and design for. To aggregate the measure across all three dimensions, a numerical measure was associated to each of the three dimensions of turbulence by using a scale from 1 to 3 with: 1 representing low magnitude, uncertainty or frequency; 2 representing moderate magnitude, uncertainty or frequency; and 3 representing high magnitude, uncertainty or frequency (Oduntan 2008). The product of the measures across all three dimensions represents the cumulative level of experience experienced by the enterprise for that resource, and results in a score ranging from 1 to 27. With this numerical scale, the overall level of turbulence for all resources in the environment can be characterized as low turbulence (1– 2), moderate turbulence (3 – 8), high turbulence (9 -27) Table 10.

Cumulative Turbulence Score	Cumulative Turbulence Ranking	Nature of Disturbance
1 to 2	Low	Low level of disturbance on two or more of the dimensions of turbulence.
3 to 8	Moderate	Moderate level of disturbance on at least 2 dimensions.
9 to 27	High	High level of disturbance on at least two dimensions, or a high level on one dimension with moderate levels on the remaining two dimensions.

Table 10: Classification of Turbulence Level According to Cumulative Across all Dimensions

A list of some common sources of turbulence is shown in Table 11 (Oduntan 2008).

Sources of Turbulence	Description
Customer turbulence	Demand of types of products and services as a result of changing customer taste and needs.
Sourcing turbulence	Availability or price of raw materials
Financial turbulence	Availability or cost of financial capital or in currency rates
Technology turbulence	Direction and pace of technology development
Labour turbulence	Availability or cost of human resources
Governmental & regulatory turbulence	Governmental rules and regulations
Environmental (mother nature) turbulence	Environmental and natural conditions

Table 11: Sources of Business Turbulence

Illustration of the EVM in the Definition of The MCS of an Academic Department

The following example illustrates the application of the EVM in defining the management control system of a viable organization. The organization in this example is the academic department of a university, and although the context of an academic department is not the same as a enterprise, the EVM is equally applicable, and its application is consistent across both contexts. The purpose of this illustration is not to provide a comprehensive design of the MCS of an academic department, but to demonstrate how the EVM can be utilized in defining the contextual requirements of the department's management control system, as well as, the major components of the management control system of the department.

Analyzing Complexity in the Environment of the Academic Department

The first step in analyzing the complexity of the environment of the academic department is to identify all the resources required by the academic department to perform its activities. After that, each resource is then analyzed to identify the different components constituting the resource. The environmental resources and their components are shown in Table 12. As stated previously, the management of each component is distinct from the other.

Resource	Components
Prospective students	Undergraduate
	Graduate
Budgetary funds	College
Faculty recruiting pool	Fresh PhD graduates
	Experienced faculty
Research funds	Private corporation
	Government grants

Table 12: Environmental Resources of an Academic Department and their Components

Analyzing the Turbulence in the Environment of the Academic Department

For the purpose of simplifying the turbulent analysis, the turbulence of each component of each resource was not analyzed, but instead each resource was analyzed in aggregate. The turbulence analysis of the environment of the academic department is shown in Table 13. In the prospective student resource, the amplitude, uncertainty, and frequency was estimated as low because:

- Fluctuation in volume could be managed entirely by the department
- Uncertainty new student volume was reduced due to information obtained from the number of applications
- Fairly stable historical acceptance rates
- Student enrollment frequency was annually, which was very low

Conversely, the turbulence of the research pool was very high due to:

- High fluctuation in research funding, which has the potential of resulting in the closure of some laboratories
- No predictability regarding prospects of new research funding
- Occasional changes in the research funding during each planning period.

	Magnitude	Uncertainty	Frequency	Cumulative Score
Prospective students	1	1	1	2
Budgetary funds	3	2	1	6
Faculty recruiting pool	1	1	1	1
Research funds	3	3	2	18

Table 13: Turbulence in Environmental Resources of an Academic Department

Enterprise Viability Modeling of Academic Department

It is necessary to decompose DP11 (System Three-Two-One) and DP12 (System Five-Four) to identify the FRs and DPs necessary for the viability of the academic department. System Three-Two-One, which is responsible for managing the current operations of the department is decomposed as shown in Table 14. The decomposition of System Five-Four which is responsible for developing future plans for the department is shown in Table 15.

X	Functional Requirement (FR11x)	Design Parameter (DP11x)	VSM Component
1	Deliver quality undergraduate education	Undergraduate programs management system	Management system of the undergraduate programs viable system
2	Deliver quality graduate education	Graduate programs management system	Management system of the graduate programs viable system
3	Perform quality government sponsored research	Government research program management system	Management system of the government research programs viable system
4	Perform quality private sector sponsored research	Private sector research program management system	Management system of the private sector research programs viable system
5	Perform quality service	Community service management system	Management system of a community service viable system
6	Maintain high quality faculty pool	Human resource management system	System-Three of the department
7	Achieve goals set by college	Administrative management system	System-Three of the department

Table 14: Decomposition of System Three-Two-One of the Department

X	Functional Requirement (FR12x)	Design Parameter (DP12x)	VSM Component
1	Gather information about future state of environment	Faculty research into future of field	Channel between System-Four and the environment
2	Develop strategic plans for the department	Department's planning committee	System-Five-Four

Table 15: Design of System Five-Four of Academic Department

From the design of *DP11 and DP12* it is possible to construct the highest level VSM of the department Illustration 4. It is necessary that each of the design parameters in the designs of *System Three-Two-One* and *Systems Five-Four* be decomposed further in order to define the details necessary to implement the MCS of the department.

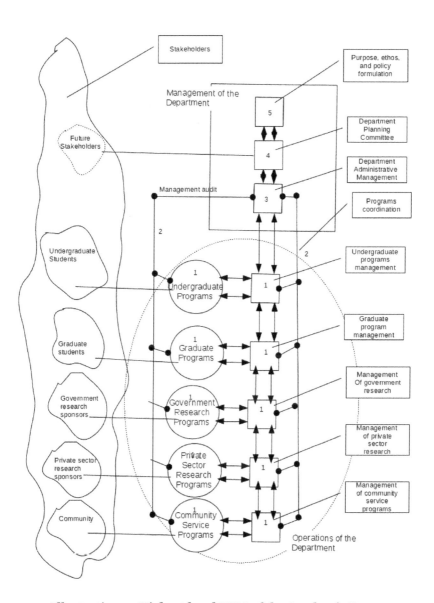

Illustration 4: Highest level VSM of the Academic Department

The decomposition of the management system of the undergraduate academic program is performed to illustrate some of the additional decomposition.

X	Functional Requirement (FR111x)	Design Parameter (DP111x)	VSM Component
1	Develop high quality curriculum	Curriculum committee	System-Four of undergraduate academic program
2	Deliver quality internal instruction	Faculty management system	Management system of child VSM (faculty staff)
3	Deliver quality external instruction	Institutional assessment system	System-two of undergraduate academic program
4	Provide academic advise to students	Academic advising system	Management system of child VSM (Advising staff)
5	Manage the quality of the undergraduate program	Undergraduate program management system	System-Three of undergraduate academic program

Table 16: Design of the Management System of the Undergraduate Academic Program

The design of the management system of the undergraduate academic program (Table 16) shows the design of the different function that need to be managed, and their management system, in order to deliver quality education. Although the structure of the management and control system of the academic department is beginning to take shape, further decomposition of all the system components will be required to construct the VSM of all the programs and their components.

Conclusion

The Enterprise Viability Model (EVM) was presented in this paper as a modeling framework for analyzing and enhancing the viability of enterprises. From our review of existing enterprise architecture frameworks, we identified the lack of emphasis of the management control view by most of the enterprise architecture frameworks. The MCS was presented as a critical design parameter for the adaptability and viability of an enterprise under turbulence. The EVM was presented as a framework for defining the architecture, and model of an enterprise's MCS. The EVM was shown to provide a systematic methodology for identifying the VSM of an organization, the functions of the VSM, and interactions between all components of the VSM. Another benefit of the EVM is its ability to identify the performance metrics that should be monitored to ensure that the organization is viable. This is due to the clear definition of the functional requirements of the organization, the ability to easily assign metrics to those functional requirements, and the assignment of each functional requirement to specific components of the management control system of the organization.

About the Authors

Olusola Oduntan is currently a part-time lecturer at Wayne State University. Olusola has over nineteen years of experience in system integration, business process transformation, and organizational change management. He earned his Ph.D. in Industrial and Systems Engineering at Wayne State University.

Namkyu Park is Associate Professor in the Department of Industrial and Systems Engineering at Ohio University. He received his PhD in Industrial Engineering from Seoul National University in Seoul, Korea (1994). His current research interests include applied optimization, viability and sustainability modeling in socio economic systems, and strategic technology management.

References

Aldrich, Howard. 1979. Organizations and environments. Englewood Cliffs, N.J: Prentice-Hall.

Anon. TOGAF.

Anonymous. 2011. What is Environmental Complexity? Accounting for Management. http://www.accountingformanagement.com/index.htm.

Bailey, Ian. 2006. A Simple Guide to Enterprise Architecture. URL: http://www.modelfutures.com/file_download/4/SimpleGuideToEA.pdf.

Beer, S. 1979. The Heart of Enterprise. J. Wiley, West Sussex, England

Bernus, P., L. Nemes, and G. Schmidt. 2003. Handbook on Enterprise Architecture, Springer Verlag, West Berlin, Germany

Cannon, A. R., and C. H. St. John. 2007. "Measuring Environmental Complexity: A Theoretical and Empirical Assessment." Organizational Research Methods 10 (2): 296-321.

Child, J. 1972. "Organizational structure, environment and performance: The role of strategic choice." Sociology 6: 2–21.

Cochran, D.S., and V. A. Reynal. 1996. Axiomatic Design of Manufacturing Systems, The Lean Aircraft Initiative. Cambridge, MA: The Lean Aircraft Initiative, Center of Technology and Industrial Development, MIT.

Dess, G.G., and D.W. Beard. 1984. "Dimensions of Organizational Task Environments." Administrative Science Quarterly 29 (1): 52–73.

Duncan, R. 1972. "Characteristics of Organizational Environments and Perceived Environmental Uncertainty." Administrative Science Quarterly 17 (3): 313-327.

Espejo, R., and A. Gill. 1997. The Viable System Model as a Framework for Understanding Organisations. 1997. Phrontis Limited & SYNCHO Limited. www.phrontis.com/vsm.

Espinosa, A., R. Harnden, and J. Walker. 2007. "Beyond hierarchy: a complexitymanagement perspective." Kybernetes 36 (3/4): 333-347.

Gebala, D.A., and N.P. Suh. 1992. "An application of axiomatic design." Research in Engineering Design 3 (3): 149–162.

Herring, C., and S. Kaplan. 2001. The Viable System Architecture.

Heylighen, Francis, and Cliff Joslyn. 2001. Cybernetics and Second-OrderCybernetics. In Encyclopedia of Physical Science & Technology, ed. R.A Meyers, 155-170. 3rd ed. New York: Academic Press.

Højsgaard, Hjalte. 2011. "Market-Driven Enterprise Architecture." Journal of Enterprise Architecture 7 (1) (February): 28-38.

Hoverstadt, Patrick. 2008. The Fractal Organization: Creating sustainable organizations with the Viable System Model. John Wiley & Sons Inc., West Sussex, UK

Jackson, M.C. 2000. Systems approaches to management. Kluwer Academic/Plenum Publishers.

Kim, S. J., N.P. Suh, and S.K. Kim. 1991. "Design of Software Systems Based on Axiomatic Design." Robotics & Computer-Integrated Manufacturing 8 (4): 243–255.

Kondabolu, V., O. Oduntan, and N Park. 2010. An analysis of the effectiveness of supplier innovation as a competitive strategy for an enterprise under conditions of high-turbulence. In TIIM 2011 Conference Proceedings. Oulu, Finland

Noran, O. 2003. A mapping of individual architecture frameworks (GRAI, Pera, C4ISR, CIMOSA, Zachman, ARIS) onto GERAM. In Handbook of Enterprise Architecture, ed. P. Bernus, 65–210. Springer Verlag, West Berlin, Germany

Oduntan, O. 2008. A systematic Approach for the Design of Viable Enterprises Under Conditions of Business Turbulence. PhD. Dissertation, Wayne State University.

Oduntan O. and Park, N. EVAT: A Platform for Enterprise Viability Analysis and Prediction, 2009 INFORMS annual meeting, San Diego, Oct. 11-14, 2009

Oduntan, O., and Park, N. 2012. Enterprise Viability Model: Extending Enterprise Architecture Frameworks for Modeling and Analyzing Viability under Turbulence, IIE Journal of Enterprise Transformation, Vol.2 , Issue 1, 2012, pp 1-25

Park, N., and Oduntan, O. 2009. An Operational Ecology Model for Enhancing the Sustainability of the US Health Care Industry, 2009 INFORMS annual meeting, San Diego, Oct. 11-14, 2009

Park, N., and Oduntan, O. 2010. Distributed Innovation as an Enabler of Long-Term Customer Satisfaction and Sustained Competitiveness under Turbulence. In TIIM 2010 Conference Proceedings. Pattaya, Thailand.

Park, N., Oduntan, O., and Mejabi, O. 2007. An operational ecology model for viability in a complex business ecosystem. In INFORMS Annual Meeting, Seattle, WA, Nov. 2007.

Rigby, D., and P. Rogers. 2000. Winning in turbulence-strategies for success in turbulent times European Business Journal. UK.

Stelzer, Dirk. 2009. Enterprise Architecture Principles: Literature Review and Research Directions. In ICSOC/ServiceWave 2009, LNCS 6275, 12-21. November 23.

Suh, N.P. 1984. "Development of the science base for the manufacturing field through the axiomatic approach." Robotics and Computer Integrated Manufacturing 1 (3/4): 397–415.

Suh, N.P. 1997. "Design of systems." ANNALS-CIRP 46: 75–80.

Suh N.P. 1998. "Axiomatic Design Theory for Systems." Research in Engineering Design 10 (4): 189–209.

Suh, N.P., A.C. Bell, and D.C. Gossard. 1978. "On an axiomatic approach to manufacturing and manufacturing systems." Journal of Engineering for Industry 100 (2): 127–130.

Suh, N.P., D.S. Cochran, and P.C. Lima. 1998. "Manufacturing System Design." ANNALS-CIRP 47: 627–640.

Trewn, J., and K. Yang. 2000. A treatise on system reliability and design complexity. In Proceedings of ICAD2000, First International Conference on Axiomatic Design, Cambridge, MA, 162--168.

Tung, R. 1979. "Dimensions of Organizational Environments: An Exploratory Study of Their Impact on Organization Structure." Academy of Management Journal 22 (4): 672-693.

Wholey, D.R., and J. Brittain. 1989. "Characterizing environmental variation." Academy of Management Journal 32 (4): 867–882.

Williams, T.J., Bernus, P., Brosvic, J., Chen, D., Doumeingts, G., Nemes, L., Nevins, J.L., Vallespir, B., Vlietstra, J., Zoetekouw, D. (1994) Architectures for Integrating Manufacturing Activities and Enterprises. Computers in Industry 24 (2-3), Special Issue on CIM. pp111-140.

Enterprise as Story, Enterprise as System

Tom Graves

Keywords

Enterprise Architecture, business transformation, systems thinking, viable systems, Viable Systems Model, Zachman framework, Business Model Canvas, Enterprise Canvas

An Aversion to Abstracts

As an enterprise architect, much of my world is abstract, 'big picture', about structure and strategy, about working with the uncertainties of the future. It's a world of concepts and models and frameworks: TOGAF, MoDAF, VSM, VPEC-T, eTOM, SCOR, TRAK, ITIL, CoBIT, BPMN and all of those other seemingly-impenetrable acronyms.

It's a world I'm very much used to. But it isn't the world that most of my business colleagues live in – or want to live in. Their world is one that's full of complex, chaotic, concrete detail: transactions, servers, real buildings, real parcels and trucks and conveyor-belts that jam and components that don't fit and all the myriad complications created by all of those clients –

human and otherwise. Not much space – or time – for any abstractions there.

Given the gap between those worlds, it can be difficult to engage 'regular business-folk' in the unavoidable abstractions in disciplines such as enterprise architecture and systems thinking. It's easy to become frustrated, dismiss the others as 'idiots' with an inbuilt aversion to the abstract, and then retreat back to the strange certainties of our own ivory tower. Which, of course, doesn't help anyone at all.

Yet what does work, to bridge this gulf of misunderstanding, is something very simple indeed: we tell a story.

Our team learnt this lesson the hard way. We were doing a typical enterprise architecture task, proposing a restructure of the relationship between half a dozen major projects to create greater synergy at lower cost. We had to present our proposal to the executive: and the centerpiece of that presentation was a BPMN (Business Process Modeling Notation) diagram, showing everything as nice, clean, clear abstract entities – the 'boxes and lines' beloved by every architect. *Big* mistake... But we were at least allowed to start again: and when, at the next meeting, we showed a new version of the same diagram, but this time populated with pictures of trucks and conveyor belts and storefronts and real people doing real tasks, everyone was very happy indeed. We were given the go-ahead for our restructure of the projects, *because the story made sense to everyone.*

And that's the point. It isn't actually about the abstract versus the concrete, or visual versus verbal or the like, but about whether there's a story that makes sense, that helps to create *shared* understanding. And that's important whether we're working at the 'big-picture' level of strategy and business-purpose, or right down in the detail of a single system or service. Whatever we're working on, and whomever we're working with, we *co-create* a story with them, about some aspect of the enterprise. A story that is *also* always about the enterprise as a whole – because everything in the enterprise ultimately connects with everything else, as an interdependent system.

The Enterprise as Story

One way that we've found to make this 'sensemaking via story' to work is by building the story around the common notions of service, and services (Graves, 2009; Graves, 2010).

In this view, *everything* is regarded as a service. (In this sense, a product is also a kind of proto-service, in that it enables 'self-delivery' of a service.) As a service, everything is a kind of 'black box' of functions and activities

228

resources, all with its own specific business-purpose, and its own relations and transactions and interactions other services within its broader context - the 'enterprise' that it shares with those other services.

If everything is a service, this implies that it should be possible to describe everything in much the same way, regardless of role or scope or level of granularity. And this approach also provides a means to link enterprise architectures – about structures and purpose – with systems and systems thinking – about interdependencies and relationships across the enterprise 'ecosystem'. Yet the key point here is that all of this arises from a kind of story – a story about the enterprise in which those services exist, and which provide those services their reason to exist.

It's not just a story *about* the enterprise: in a very real sense, the enterprise *is* a story, told on many different levels, and in many different ways. For enterprise architectures, it's usually seen as a story about change, about the tension between the 'why' and the 'how' of the enterprise, the tension between desired-ends – what is aimed for – and realised-ends – what has actually been achieved. We could present this kind of story through a simple 'back-of-the-napkin' sketch-diagram (Figure 1).

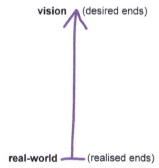

Figure 1: Tension between desired ends and realised ends

The desired-ends are typically described via terms such as *vision* or *Cause* (Ghosh, 2011). Whatever label we use for this, what it describes must always be in the future, and must always be larger in scope than the service itself. The tension of this 'story' then provides the motivation for action and for change.

At the whole-enterprise scope, this vision must represent an idealized yet *unattainable* future, so as to maintain the tension indefinitely between 'desired' and 'real'. The vision at this level will typically consist of a very brief phrase – usually no more than four or five words, with a distinctive three-part content and structure:

- A noun that identifies the 'things' or context that are the main focus for everyone in the enterprise;
- A verb summarizing the main activity on those 'things' or context that concerns everyone in the enterprise;
- An adjective or qualifier that validates and bridges between content and action, and that summarizes people's engagement in those 'things' and activities, and that provides the driving 'why' for the shared-enterprise.

These components may occur in any order, but all of them need to be present in a vision-descriptor. For example, take the vision for the TED conferences, "ideas worth spreading". It's clear, succinct and emotive – and it conforms exactly to that structure above: 'ideas' [content], 'worth' [qualifier], 'spreading' [action].

Note too that none of these items describe the organization as such – but do describe the focus, the area of action, and the key value-metrics that define the meaning of 'success' for the overall enterprise.

Linking the above components together, what vision is common to all stakeholders in the enterprise? What single phrase describes the overall enterprise, beyond the organization itself? That's what we look for at this topmost layer.

At lower layers, addressing a single domain closer to the real-time world, we might use some kind of descriptor for a desired 'future state' as our working vision here – yet in each case, that changeable 'future state' needs to be anchored in the unchanging whole-enterprise vision.

This then brings us back to that assertion that everything in the enterprise is a service. Whatever it is that we're looking at in the enterprise delivers some kind of service – and in doing so, it serves the enterprise vision. It *adds value* in some way to the overall enterprise through the activities and processes of its service. And each service forms part of one or more *value-flows* that move around the overall enterprise – delivering on the promise of the vision (Figure 2).

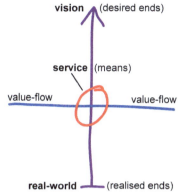

Figure 2: Each service connects the value-web to the vision

In effect, the vision represents the aim or purpose of the overall the enterprise story; each value-flow is or represents another story within that greater story. To make sense of the enterprise, we describe it through *stories* of exchange and flow of value and added value.

One common way we might depict these stories of value-flow is by describing the characters that play their parts in each of these value-flow stories. For example, each service has its *suppliers* – other services in a 'service provider' role relative to this service. And each service has its *customers* – other services in a 'service consumer' role relative to this service. We could then summarize each of these roles on our 'back-of-the-napkin' sketch (Figure 3). Note that 'supplier' and 'customer' represent only the service-roles here, not any kind of absolute relationship: for example, in many types of supply-chain relationships, one organization may well be both a supplier *and* a customer for another.

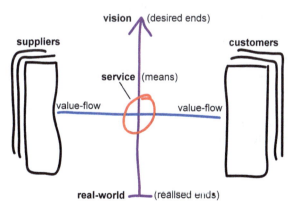

Figure 3: Service, suppliers and customers

An alternate approach to this kind of story is to concentrate on the nature of the flows between services, rather than the nominal roles in which services act on those flows. We might, for example, explore the values, policies, events, and content that make up and guide each of the flows, leading to greater trust across the overall enterprise – the *VPEC-T* framework (Green and Bate, 2007).

So there are at least two ways we can frame the enterprise-story here: as flows of value that are acted on by services, or as actors linked together by flows and relationships. Or, in our back-of-the-napkin sketch, summarized as the boxes and lines so typical of any kind of architecture – except that in this case the abstract entities provide anchors for a real, concrete, *human* story.

Whichever way one may choose to describe this, the point here is that both the boxes and the lines – the services and the flows – are necessary if we are to describe how and why the enterprise works. Each type is essential, yet neither is sufficient on its own. Together, they help to describe the enterprise as a whole, *the enterprise as a system.*

We can also note that the same principle applies at *every* scale, from detail-level code services, to application-layer 'business services', to the relationships between whole organizations within the shared enterprise. We can use the same kind of story, in much the same way, anywhere within the overall system that is the enterprise.

There are plenty of standard modeling-techniques and notations to describe these 'boxes and lines', the flows and the activities on and interactions with those flows. BPMN (Business Process Model Notation) and UML Activity Diagrams are two well-known examples of this. But the catch is that often these are too detailed and too abstract to make much sense to an ordinary business-audience; and, paradoxically, they're also often not detailed enough, in that they frequently exclude anything that is not part of the 'main process flow', and in some cases anything not directly linked to IT. The result is that many of the conventional notations provide an illusion of certainty that can be dangerously incomplete.

To make things worse, most 'business process' software is written only for 'Easily Repeatable Processes' with predictable flows and predictable paths; whereas in knowledge-work especially, unpredictable 'Barely Repeatable Processes' are much more common in practice (Rinde, 2007). There is a real danger in assuming that all process flows in scope are predictable – and often the only way in which we can find out that they are *not* predictable is by getting someone from the frontline to tell the story of each flow or service, using this simple 'Enterprise Canvas'.

One other catch is that often the conventional 'process model' story only describes the most visible flow, encompassing only the activities of the main transaction. What it usually does not tell us is all the flows and interactions that need to happen not merely *during* that main-transaction, but *before* it and *after* it (Figure 4). In a commercial business, for example, the processes of payment from the customer, and onward to the supplier, may typically take place after the main transaction – but they need to be linked to that main transaction, as part of the same story. And likewise for everything that sets up the conditions for that transaction, in marketing, standards and protocols, governance and so on: they're all part of the same story of relationship between services. And we do need to be able to describe all of this in a consistent way, in order to reinforce the sense of enterprise as system – the enterprise as a unified whole.

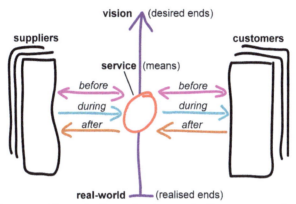

Figure 4: Flows before, during and after transactions

Another way to look at this – particularly at the whole-organization level, for business-architecture and the like – is to describe this in terms of a 'market cycle' (Figure 5). Before the transaction can take place, we need to have established the other service's attention in some way. Before that can happen, we need to have established some kind of relationship with that other service; and before that, or in parallel with that, there needs to be some way to establish trust, a notion that the relationship itself would be mutually beneficial to both services. Going the other way, we need to establish completions after the transaction itself: not just completion of process itself, or completion of payment, but also reaffirmation of trust – which is what keeps the cycle going. And note too that some of these 'before' or 'after' flows may be with different services: for example, the person who is the customer for something, and the person who pays for it, may both be different from the person who enacts the actual transaction.

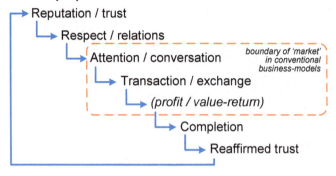

Figure 5: The market cycle

This again applies at all levels, with all types of services. The cycle is usually self-evident – if only by its incompleteness – at the business-transaction layer. But it also applies right down at the code-level: we establish an initial connection, with an identified protocol and appropriate credentials, to gain the metaphoric trust of the other service; get the attention of the other service, using the agreed signals of that protocol, to set up and prepare for a transaction; enact the transaction itself; and then signal that the transaction is complete, again using the signals and messages of the respective protocol. It's the same kind of story: the services and flows are different, but the principles of what we use to elicit that story are much the same.

We can also partition the activities of the service itself in much the same way (Figure 6). There are activities that deal with the 'before' of the service itself – for example, identifying the service's own 'value-proposition' to the overall enterprise. There are activities that enact the 'now', that apply the service's own value – its 'value creation'. And there are activities that follow on afterward, to keep it on-track to its intended path – its 'value governance'. Each service is symmetrical, in that it is both a provider of services and a consumer of services: and these too have their 'before' – building relations with a supplier or customer; their 'during' – inbound and outbound channels for transactions; and their 'after' – monitoring and enacting the 'back-channel' of value returned from customers, and value outlay to suppliers.

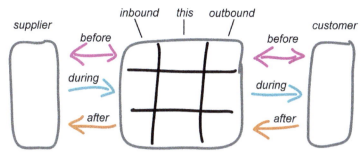

Figure 6: Service, suppliers, customers and flows

In some ways this resembles the Business Model Canvas (Osterwalder and Pigneur, 2009), a popular framework for business architecture and the like. In fact, it is possible to map directly from the Business Model Canvas to this 'Enterprise Canvas' – though not always the other way, in part due to an important asymmetry in the Business Model Canvas (Appendix B in Graves, 2010). The other key concern, and limitation, is that, as its name implies, the Business Model Canvas is optimized for business architecture, and in practice is not well-suited for use outside of that scope – a point we will return to later.

Expanding the Story

Each of these partitioned sets of activities within the service in focus is itself composed of one or more services, each with its own flows and 'child'-services. In other words, the story of the service becomes recursive, in both directions – a classic characteristic of complex systems.

This recursion and overall consistency also allows us to weave some other facets of systems theory into the service's story. For example, we can make the story much richer by incorporating links to the Viable System Model (henceforth abbreviated as VSM) (Beer, 1972), particularly if those principles from VSM are explicitly adapted to the 'services' context (Graves, 2008; Graves, 2009). For those familiar with VSM, the service itself becomes the entity's 'System 1', or *delivery service*. To make up a 'viable system', this needs to be linked to other services that provide overall direction (VSM 'System-3', 'System-4' and 'System-5'), coordination with other services (VSM 'System-2') and anchoring into and validation against the enterprise values (an expansion of VSM 'System-3*'). The links to each of these 'guidance services' would each have their own flows between them and the main 'delivery service' in focus for the story – expanding the overall story of the service. We denote them on our back-of-the-napkin sketch via simple geometric symbols derived from the VSM notation, linked to the overall service (Figure 7) – but the key point is that each of these is simply a placeholder for a *story* of connection and shared purpose.

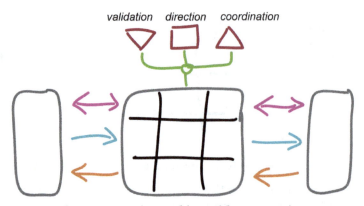

Figure 7: Service and its guidance-services

We could also do much the same with the service's relationships to its investors and beneficiaries. These are much like suppliers and customers, except that the main flows of value go the opposite way (Figure 8). We use the back-of-the-napkin sketch to help build the story of those relationships. One of the common dangers, for example, is that investors and beneficiaries may not be the same people: the community and the employees may invest a great deal of commitment and energy into a company, for example, but only the shareholders are acknowledged as 'owners' of the company, entitled to extract value from its operations. Serious systemic problems can arise if these relationships are not in balance – which in the business world at present, they often are not.

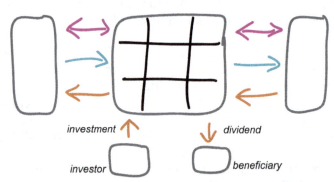

Figure 8: Service investors and beneficiaries

We can add all of these components to our back-of-the-napkin sketch of the selected service (Figure 9), although in practice it's best to build it slowly, link by link and story by story.

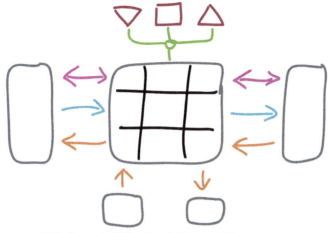

Figure 9: 'Kitchen sink' back-of-the-napkin Canvas (service)

A hand-drawn back-of-the-napkin sketch is probably the best style for use in eliciting stories about the service – its activities and flows, its suppliers and customers, its 'child'-services, and its relationships with the other parts of the enterprise-as-system. As we start to move towards detailed implementation, though, we may need a more formal-style of presentation (Figure 10) – even if the resultant core-diagram does bear an unfortunate resemblance to some strange kind of robot chicken...

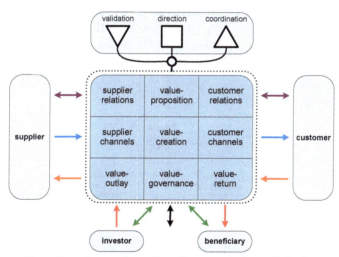

Figure 10: Complete formal version: investors, beneficiaries, guidance

Translation into high-level enterprise-architecture notations such as Archimate is relatively straightforward, because we have started from the premise that everything is a service – a key entity within Archimate. Each service has interfaces, includes functions and processes, and so on – a direct mapping to Archimate entities.

Before we delve into the detail of that, though, it's useful to re-anchor all of this into another type of system-story, about cycles within cycles, and transitions within those cycles.

Cycles and Transitions

To make this link, we need to move back into the abstract for a moment. In much the same way as we can assert that everything in the enterprise is a service, we could also assert that everything that happens is a project, or part of some project, that aims to support the enterprise vision. Every purchase-transaction is a kind of project, with a beginning, a middle and an end; the same is true of every conversation, every interaction. Projects contain other projects, which contain and intersect with other projects: *everything* is a project.

Also, projects have their own distinct lifecycle. A classic description of this – one that is well known in the business world – is the Group Dynamics sequence: forming, storming, norming, performing and adjourning or 'mourning' (Tuckman, 1965). If we take a systemic view, the cycle is recursive; yet different people and different parts of the business will emphasize different phases – especially at the larger scale within the organization. Hence strategy people focus more on the 'forming' phase, or *Purpose*; the HR department and organizational development department will tackle the 'storming' of the myriad of *People* issues; planners deal with the 'norming' of *Preparation*; production do the 'performing' of *Process*; whilst in the 'adjourning' phase, analysts and record-keepers look back to assess *Performance* – which should, we hope, always link back to Purpose (Figure 11).

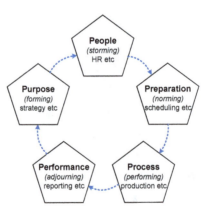

Figure 11: Five Elements: five phases in the continuing lifecycle

We can also view this cycle in terms of their respective emphases on strategy, tactics and operations (Figure 12). Serious systemic problem can arise if these phases are not in balance – for example, if the organization clings too much to the 'quick-profit' short-cut from Performance back to

Preparation, trying to use short-term tactics as a substitute for strategy, and eventually losing any connection with Purpose or People.

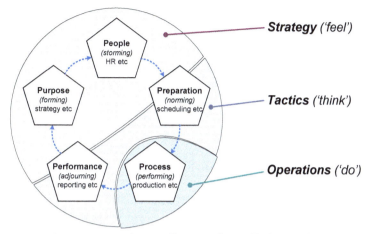

Figure 12: Strategy, tactics, and operations: links to Five Elements

Once again, each of these phases or 'Elements' represents a specific set of services – and hence, in turn, flows that link those services, in ways that support that cycle. We would typically use frameworks such as VPEC-T to assess the nature and content and timings of each of those flows, as summarized earlier; yet we can also use an adaptation of the VPEC-T concepts to summaries the emphases of each of those flows both as transitions between the phases, and as in-organization analogues of the market-cycle (Graves, 2011). The result is a lifecycle-model that can be applied to any part of the organization or enterprise, in which the primary phases represent clusters of related services, and the adapted VPEC-T concepts represent both the respective emphases of the content of each of those flows, and the signal for transition between phases in the cycle (Figure 13).

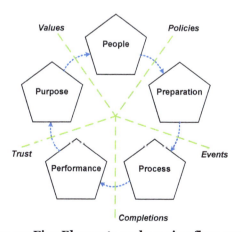

Figure 13: Five Elements and service-flow content

Each phase and flow in this cycle also requires its own distinct form of leadership, to guide activities *within* each phase, and to initiate and lead the transition *between* phases. For example, we need clarity on values and the like to engage people in purpose; we need leadership to act on events, to stop us *thinking* about what we'll do (Preparation) and get us *doing* it instead (Process). There's also a further form of leadership, to 'hold the center', to keep the balance between all the phases and flows in this overall system: in principle – though sadly often not in practice – this would be a key role of the Managing Director or CEO. If *no one* holds the balance, serious problems can arise – which is exactly what happens, all too often, in real-world practice. This type of systems-view helps us to explain what will go wrong, *why* it will go wrong, and what we can do to prevent or recover from that type of systemic failure.

We can also see this balance between phases and flows as a back-and-forth across the Enterprise Canvas, seen in a somewhat different perspective as 'inside-facing' versus 'outside-facing' (Figure 14). Each of the phases represents a cluster of related activities; each of the flows represents how and why (and, typically, when) we would connect those activities with the 'outside world'. The enterprise-vision acts the center-point around which the whole cycle revolves. The overall thrust of the sequence moves 'downward' on the Enterprise Canvas, from an emphasis on future (value proposition) to present (value creation) to past (value governance). Crucially, *trust*, and reaffirmation of trust, is what keeps the cycle rolling.

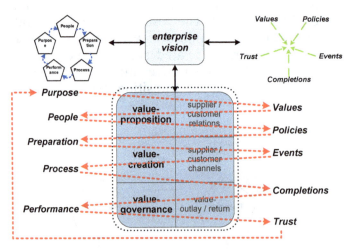

Figure 14: Enterprise Canvas and continuous lifecycle

We need to remember, though, that this structure of phases and transitions is also fully recursive – just like the services themselves. Services contain services, and intersect and interoperate with other services; projects contain projects, each interweaving with other projects; services are enacted by projects that call on other services that likewise are enacted through other projects, at every scale within the story of the enterprise. Abstract services and portfolios or programs of change projects expand downward into detailed business services and projects, and downward again into web services and data-services and individual human tasks, acquiring more and more detail as each gets closer to real-world implementation and action.

The practical problem, in most organizations, is that the sheer scale and complexity of all of these relationships and interdependencies soon becomes almost impossible to comprehend. It becomes all too easy to lose track of the story, of how anything fits in with everything else in the overall system, what part each item plays in the overall story, or even why it exists at all. The 'service oriented' view of the Enterprise Canvas does help to make sense of the complexity, yet we also need something that will again provide a means to elicit the stories associated with all of that detail, consistent across every aspect of the enterprise, and at every level of abstraction – linking strategy to execution. We'll explore some examples of what has worked for this in practice in the last part of this paper.

From Strategy to Execution

One of *the* classic models in enterprise-architecture is the Zachman Framework (Zachman, 2003). This consists of a simple two-dimensional matrix: a set of five or six rows, from context-layer to detailed implementation, and six columns, consisting of the interrogatives What, How, Where, Who, When and Why. It's a useful taxonomy, but in practice it tends to be used in a strongly IT-centric way – with data as the only acknowledged form of What, for example – which greatly limits its usefulness outside of that narrow scope. There is also an unfortunate tendency for architects and analysts to try to populate the framework with every possible entity – 'in excruciating detail', as Zachman himself is alleged to insist – yet without much attention to the *meaning* of those entities, or the use of the overall categorization. To make matters worse – as we'll see shortly – there is an entire dimension missing from the framework, without which it can easily become so misleading as to be worse than useless. Which is a real problem for enterprise architects.

Yet if we start from the story-oriented view of the Enterprise Canvas, there's a way in which we can re-use the Zachman concepts in a way that enables us to elicit information about all of the detail, yet without drowning in the detail itself. The key is that we split the framework into two parts: the vertical axis, remaining much the same as in the original; and the horizontal axis, reworked somewhat, and with a missing dimension of *asset-types* and/or *decision-types* added to the mix.

The vertical axis consists of seven distinct layers, labeled from 0 to 6, to retain compatibility with the original 1-5 row numbering (Figure 15). In essence these are much the same as in Zachman, whose rows 1-5 represent both layers of abstraction (from most-abstract to most-concrete) and distance from 'the Now' (with row-1 being furthest in the future, and row-5 immediately prior to execution). The added row-0 represents the unattainable and indefinite future of the enterprise-vision – the 'desired ends' – whilst the new row-6 represents the unchangeable past, on the far side of 'the Now' – the 'realized ends'. Between these two extremes lie the spaces where we have choices for change. Linking across the layers in this way gives us a consistent means to describe the transitions from strategy to execution.

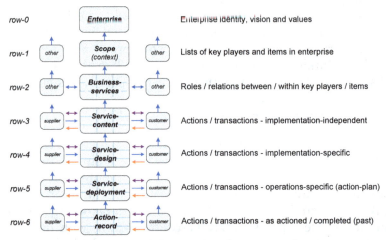

Figure 15: Layers of abstraction for Enterprise Canvas

Different model-types tend to describe only a subset of this spectrum. The Business Model Canvas, for example, typically describes only a region that straddles somewhat uncomfortably across the row-2 to row-3 boundary, from a general description of business services to a fairly generic summary of the content of the respective business model. A BPMN process model tends to straddle a region further down, more usually in row-4 but sometimes up to row-3 or down to row-5. The practical problem is that it's often unclear as to what the respective model actually describes – or as to how, architecturally, the model's elements could be re-used or re-structured into another form. What this rework of the Zachman layers provides is a consistent means to identify what each model should describe at each layer:

- Row-0 'Enterprise': enterprise identity, vision and values only; in principle, should never change – otherwise it ceases to be the same enterprise

- Row-1 *'Context'*: lists of key players and items in the enterprise; usually *generic name only*, without content, relationships, implementation-detail or anything else
- Row-2 *'Business-services'*: includes roles and relationships between those key players and/or items
- Row-3 *'Service-content'*: includes *implementation-independent* descriptions of actions, transactions etc. (see the 'Service-content' frame below)
- Row-4 *'Service-design'*: includes *implementation-specific* descriptions of those same actions, transactions etc. – e.g. type of server or software, type of skills required, machine model
- Row-5 *'Service-deployment'*: includes individual *instances* of each item, the details of the intended configuration for run-time – e.g. software license, server-ID, network address, building location, machine serial-number, staff-roster
- Row-6 *'Action-record'*: the *actual* configuration as applied in a specific (past) run-time

We can also run this backward: to tell us which layer is in scope in any discussion or story. For example, if the story includes specific *items* – rather than generic ones of a specific or general *type* – then it cannot be above row-5; if it includes a specific type of anything, it can't be above row-4; if it includes attributes, it's row-3 or lower, and so on. If it can change, it can't be in row-0; and row-1 consists *only* of lists, without relationships or attributes other than the name itself.

This separation is important because, at first, most stories contain a muddled mixture of each. By tearing apart the layers, we gain clarity on what options we have for redesign (by moving upward in the layers), or those that are real-world constraints (from further downward in the layers) that have kind of wandered into the party, and may need to be reconsidered or discarded entirely.

In effect, design and redesign is a dance of moving up and down through the layers, upward to strategy and the abstract, downward to the concrete and real-world execution. Architecture looks upward towards the vision; implementation looks downward towards the real world of the 'now' and, eventually, the unchangeable past; design maintains a dynamic balance between the two.

As we move 'downward' towards execution, the story necessarily gains more detail. In the upper layers – row-1, row-2 and much of row-3 – we can get away with Zachman's simple interrogatives: What, How, Where, Who, When, Why. (We need to remember, too, that *everything* needs to link back in some way to the core Why of the enterprise, as represented by

243

the vision.) For business model development – typically centering on row-3 – we would often cluster these into simple abstract categories such as the 'Key Activities' and 'Key Resources' of the Business Model Canvas. But as we move closer to real-world implementation, we need details that are much more descriptive and specific – for which we would rework Zachman's interrogatives into a more precisely nuanced checklist, describing the *structural content* for each of our services (Figure 16).

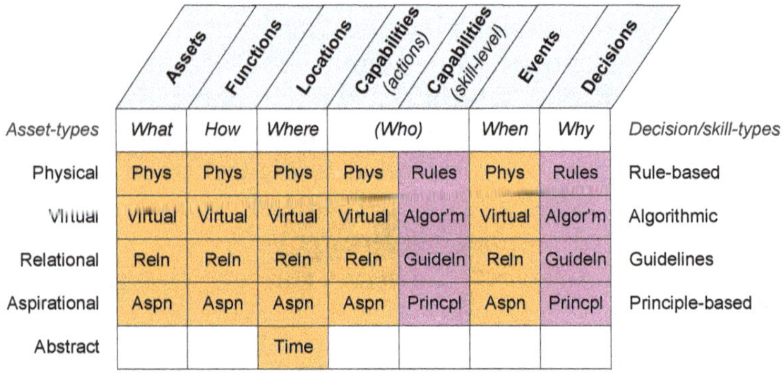

	Assets	Functions	Locations	Capabilities (actions)	Capabilities (skill-level)	Events	Decisions	
Asset-types	What	How	Where	(Who)		When	Why	Decision/skill-types
Physical	Phys	Phys	Phys	Phys	Rules	Phys	Rules	Rule-based
Virtual	Virtual	Virtual	Virtual	Virtual	Algor'm	Virtual	Algor'm	Algorithmic
Relational	Reln	Reln	Reln	Reln	Guideln	Reln	Guideln	Guidelines
Aspirational	Aspn	Aspn	Aspn	Aspn	Princpl	Aspn	Princpl	Principle-based
Abstract			Time					

Figure 16: Single-row extended-Zachman frame to model service-content

Once again, this checklist is used to guide storytelling that elicits requirements, process flows, exceptions, and other subtleties and complexities of the service that's currently in focus. In one dimension of this checklist, we rework Zachman's categories into terms that make more sense in terms of implementation: hence assets, functions, location, capabilities, events and decisions, reasons or 'business rules'. In the other dimension, we identify the *type* of entity involved:

- *Physical* or 'alienable': a physical 'thing', location, or event, or a function, capability or business rule that acts on or applies to physical things
- *Virtual* or 'non-alienable': data, a virtual location such as an IP-address, URL or phone-number, a data-driven event, or a function, capability or business rule that acts on or applies to virtual things
- *Relational*, particularly a link between real people: a 'relational asset' (such as implied in a CRM system), relational location (such as in a reporting hierarchy), relational events, or a function, capability or business rule that acts on or applies to relational links
- *Aspirational*, typically a relation between a real person and an abstract entity: brand, values, vision, relationships between these 'things', and events, functions, capabilities and business rules that act on or apply to such relationships

Many real-world entities are combinations or *composites* of these types: for example, a book is both a physical 'thing' and contains virtual information; a server will have a location that is both virtual (IP address etc.) and physical (position in a server-rack). The point here is that such composites need to be managed in accordance with *all* of their implied types: a book must be managed as a physical object – hence storage, inventory, stock-take, environmental conditions and so on – *and* as a virtual object – hence metadata, copyright, peer-review and the like. Each of these contextual conditions implies other services to implement them – taking the story deeper and deeper into the detail that's needed to make *this* service work in the real world.

To keep the story simple, we usually conflate this with what is actually yet another dimension, about the *repeatability* or complexity-type, which in turn also implies a required level of skill to enact it. This particularly applies to decision-types and the skills-component of capabilities:

- Simple or *rule-based*: context is assumed to be exactly repeatable – best suited to machines and IT-systems, and for the fine-detail parts of skilled work
- Complicated or *algorithmic*: context is repeatable but has many factors with complications such as delayed-feedback, attenuation etc. – best suited to IT-systems and 'knowledge-workers'
- Complex or *guideline-based*: context shows partial repetition through patterns – usually requires true skill, though pattern-matching IT may be able to do some types of decision-making here
- Chaotic or *principle-based*: context includes elements that are always unique and non-repeatable – suitable only for skilled human decision-making

Down at the row-5 level, everything must be an 'architecturally-complete' composite across all of the content-model columns. We could summaries this 'completeness' as "with *Asset* do *Function* using *Capability* at *Location* on *Event* because *Decision*". The point here is that we use 'architectural incompleteness' to enable re-use: for example, if we don't specify a location as part of a process design, we could in principle re-use that process at any location. As we move upward towards the abstract, we also loosen the bonds that enforce 'completeness'; and as we move downward towards implementation, everything must mesh together more and more. Things are usable to the extent that they architecturally complete, and *re*-usable to the extent that they're architecturally *in*complete. By playing with the story in this way – moving up and down the layers, and experimenting with other service-configurations via that service-content checklist – we create a richer understanding of the service and its role in the enterprise as a whole.

There's one more theme that's essential to explore in this architectural story of systems and services: *responsibility*. An enterprise is bounded by vision, values, and commitments, but an organization is bounded by rules, roles and responsibilities – and it's through those responsibilities that things actually happen. To identify responsibility for a service, and needs for engagement with stakeholders on any aspect of that service, we make use of the standard RACI checklist (Figure 17).

Figure 17: RACI responsibility-model

There should always be *one* person who is uniquely responsible for any item; and, equally, every item needs one person who is uniquely responsible for it at all times. So in eliciting the story of each service, we need to identify that 'one person', and the ways in which responsibility is transferred from one person to another over time. We need to check for any overlaps in responsibilities, such as may often occur in transitions between layers: for example, one person may have operational responsibility for an item, another has tactical responsibility, another the strategic responsibility. We need to search also for gaps in responsibilities, where no one has apparent responsibility or where the responsibility has been nominally assigned but not actually taken up or enacted.

Note that responsibility cannot simply be assigned to someone: to make it work, the responsibility needs to be accepted and taken on by that person as an active choice, a personal commitment. And note too that responsibility can only be held by a real person: a machine or an IT-box will assist in implementation, in the RACI sense, but is not capable of taking responsibility for anything in any legal sense of the term. Hence, especially where IT or machines are involved, it may be necessary to follow lengthy trails of non-responsibility – or evasions of responsibility – in order to identify the real person who is actually responsible for any given item.

Finally, a person can only be responsible for something if they also have the authority and competence to make the required decisions. If they don't have that authority or competence, they cannot and must not be considered responsible or accountable for the item, and hence a further search will need to be made for someone who can have both responsibility and authority. We need to be wary here, because mismatches of responsibility, authority and competence are very common, especially in dysfunctional organizations. In exploring the story of the service, we need to be clear that the service will be reliable – especially over the longer term – only if responsibility, authority and competence are in appropriate balance.

Summary

Introducing systems theory to business decision-makers is often problematic, not least because it can seem too abstract to be relevant to their real-time world. One practical solution is to focus on the notion of services. By asserting that 'everything is a service', we introduce a strong theme of consistency that can be applied at every level of the enterprise, and in every aspect of work. In particular, we elicit information and enable restructure and redesign through the medium of *story* – the enterprise-as-story, or service-as-story. A simple notation called the Enterprise Canvas provides a consistent frame for that story, assisted by structural yet story-oriented checklists derived or adapted from well-known sources such as the Viable System Model, an expanded version of the Zachman taxonomy, the Tuckman Group Dynamics project-lifecycle and the RACI responsibility-matrix. The result is a method to introduce systems theory and enterprise architecture 'by stealth', engaging stakeholders in systemic redesign without actually needing to use either of those problematic terms.

About the Author

Tom Graves has been an independent consultant for more than three decades, in business transformation, enterprise architecture and knowledge management. His clients in Europe, Australasia and the Americas cover a broad range of industries including banking, utilities, manufacturing, logistics, engineering, media, telecoms, research, defense and government. He has a special interest in architecture for non-IT-centric enterprises, and integration between IT-based and non-IT-based services.

References

Beer, A. S. 1972. *Brain Of The Firm,* London: Allen Lane, The Penguin Press.

Ghosh, G. 2011. "What's Your Cause", *Building Social Business* weblog. www.gautamblogs.com/2011/05/whats-your-cause.html

Graves, T.S. 2008. "The Viable Services Model: Service quality, service interdependence and service completeness", in *IT Service Management: Global Best Practices*, J. van Bon (ed.), Zaltbommel, NL: Van Haren, pp.511-529.

Graves, T.S. 2009. *The Service Oriented Enterprise: enterprise architecture and viable services*, Colchester, England: Tetradian.

Graves, T.S. 2010. *Mapping The Enterprise: modelling the enterprise as services with the Enterprise Canvas*, Colchester, England: Tetradian.

Graves, T.S. 2011. 'More on 'Not-quite VPEC-T'', *Tetradian* weblog, weblog.tomgraves.org/index.php/2011/04/21/more-on-not-vpect/

Green, N., and Bate, C. 2007. *Lost In Translation: A handbook for information systems for the 21st century*, New York, NY: Evolved Technologist Press.

Osterwalder, A., and Pigneur, Y. 2009. *Business Model Generation*, Self-published.

Rinde, S. 'Here's 30 megs. Now go run Germany.' http://30megs.com

Tuckman, B. 1965. Referenced in Wikipedia article, 'Tuckman's stages of group development', http://en.wikipedia.org/wiki/Forming-storming norming-performing (accessed 30 May 2011).

Zachman, J.A. 2003. *The Zachman Framework for Enterprise Architecture: Primer for Enterprise Engineering and Manufacturing*, Zachman International. E-book: www.businessrulesgroup.org/BRWG_RFI/ZachmanBookRFIextract.pdf

Part 3

Practicing Systems Thinking

An Open Socio-Technical Systems Approach to Enterprise Architecture

James Lapalme and
Donald W. de Guerre

Abstract

Despite the many available Enterprise Architecture methodologies and approaches, very few distinguish themselves from the rest in fundamental ways, especially from the perspective of beliefs and ideals. Socio-technical systems theory, a systems thinking theory which has been extensively researched for more than 50 years, has much to offer to the discipline of Enterprise Architecture. It offers a clear set of beliefs, ideals and guidelines which can serve as the basis of a new class of Enterprise Architecture methodologies that are humanistic in their beliefs and are capable of addressing the complexity of the people-technology fabric of modern organizations. In this work, we will present how socio-technical systems theory and design can contribute to the discipline of Enterprise Architecture as well as offer a comparison between current Enterprise Architecture methodologies and those that would be grounded in socio-technical systems theory.

Keywords

Enterprise Architecture, open systems, socio-technical systems, systems thinking, organizational design, open socio-technical systems, participative design

Introduction

Many associate the birth of Enterprise Architecture with the publication of John Zachman's seminal work in the IBM Systems Journal (Zachman. 1981). Others still look further back to Finkelstein's Information Engineering methodology and Chen's Entity-Relationship (E-R) models of the late 70s (Hagan. 2004). However, the trail of modern enterprise theory according to the IT world seems to stop there. Depending on one's definition of Enterprise Architecture, it is possible to push the clock back even further to the early 50s. At that time, Trist and Bamforth (1951) were doing research on the paradoxical observation that despite the introduction of state of the art technology in certain coal mines, their productivity was falling, and that despite better pay and amenities, absenteeism was also increasing. The cause of the problem was hypothesized to be the introduction of the new technology which had created the need for a bureaucratic form of organization. The intent of their work was to help organizations design better working environments that met the needs of both people and technology. They realized that organizations are both social and technical systems and that optimizing one would sub-optimize the other.

Socio-technical systems theory is a long-standing systems thinking approach to the design and understanding of modern organizations. Since the 50s, much advancement based on action-research has been achieved such as Open Systems Theory, Search Conferences and Participative Design Workshops; Integrated Organizational Renewal, Democratic Dialogue, Business Process Reengineering, and Participative Socio-Technical analysis and design to name a few (van Eijnatten. 1993; Lytle. 1996; Mumford. 1996).

In this chapter, we will explore the relationship between Enterprise Architecture and the modern form of socio-technical systems design: open socio-technical systems design. It is our belief that Enterprise Architecture is in fact open socio-technical systems design. Through this narrative, we will explain our beliefs as well as their implications for Enterprise Architecture methodologies.

In order to present our ideas, we will first propose our definition of Enterprise Architecture and its relationship to socio-technical systems. This will be followed by an explanation of open socio-technical systems design. We will then explain the key ramifications for Enterprise Architecture if we grounded it in such a design approach. We will conclude with a comparison between typical Enterprise Architecture methodologies and our approach to Enterprise Architecture.

It must be noted that our intent is not to give an exhaustive explanation of open socio-technical systems theory and design for such an endeavor would require a complete book. We would rather refer you to the many books and articles which are available. In addition, our intent is not to offer a step-by-step guide for the execution of Enterprise Architecture according to open socio-technical systems theory for again this would require a vastly more substantial text in order to be of practical use. Rather, we offer important guidelines that should serve as the grounding for Enterprise Architecture practice and execution if one wishes to take a more holistic approach that has a systems theoretical grounding with more than 50 years of supporting research.

Enterprise Architecture — A Definition

Before delving into the task of explaining how a socio-technical systems approach to Enterprise Architecture would differ from more conventional approaches, let us first define what we believe to be the objective of Enterprise Architecture.

en·ter·prise noun	*ar·chi·tec·ture* noun
1. *a project or undertaking that is especially difficult, complicated, or risky* 2. *readiness to engage in daring or difficult action* 3. 　a. *a unit of economic organization or activity; especially : a business organization* 　b. *a systematic purposeful activity*	1. *the art or science of building; specifically : the art or practice of designing and building structures and especially habitable ones* 2. 　a. *formation or construction resulting from or as if from a conscious act* 　b. *a unifying or coherent form or structure* 3. *architectural product or work* 4. *a method or style of building* 5. *the manner in which the components of a computer or computer system are organized and integrated*
or·ga·ni·za·tion noun 1. 　a. the act or process of organizing or of being organized 　b. the condition or manner of being organized	

2.	

a. association, society
  b. an administrative and
     functional structure (as a
     business or a political
     party); also : the personnel
     of such a structure	

Table 1 Merriam-Webster Definitions

The expression "Enterprise Architecture" consists of two words. Table 1 offers the definition of these two words according to the Merriam Webster dictionary. Within the context of this article, we believe that the most relevant definitions of enterprise are 3.a and 3.b because they put emphasis on an enterprise as a unit of economic organization (or activity) which is purposeful. However, the definition 3.a introduces another key word, that of "organization". The Merriam-Webster dictionary offers us several definitions which are presented in Table 1; we believe that a combination of all definitions is most appropriate, hence we will continue forward with "organization" as: a functional structure consisting of people which are organized and which can reorganize themselves. The last word that we must address, but not the least important, is "architecture". Again we propose to use a combination of definitions (see 2.b and 1 in Table 1). We propose: the art or practice of designing and constructing a unifying or coherent form or structure.

So in summary the definitions that we are retaining are the following:

- **Enterprise**: a unit of economic organization (or systematic activity) which is purposeful;
- **Organization**: functional structure consisting of people who are organized and who can reorganize themselves.
- **Architecture**: the art or practice of designing and constructing a unifying or coherent form or structure.

Given these definitions, Enterprise Architecture would be concerned with:

> *"The art or practice of designing, organizing and integrating functional structures into unified and coherent forms consisting of people that undertake purposeful systematic activities."*

The previous informal definition is the stepping stone we needed in order to offer a more formal definition. We would propose to replace "functional structures into unified and coherent forms consisting of people that undertake purposeful systematic activities" with the concept of an open socio-technical system. According to Emery (1972), an *open socio-*

technical system is a purposeful system composed of an interrelated social component (people, culture, norms, interactions, roles, etc.) and technical component (technology, tools, materials, etc.) which is embedded in a greater context, an environment, which the system is influenced by and also influences. If we accept this definition as a mere refinement, formalization of the previous informal definition then we can conclude that Enterprise Architecture is concerned with the organization and integration of open socio-technical systems (people and technology) or more simply open socio-technical systems design. For the remainder of this chapter, this is the definition that shall serve as a basis for exploring the relation between open socio-technical systems design and Enterprise Architecture.

Open Socio-Technical Systems Design

In the previous section, we developed a definition for the term open socio-technical system. Building on this definition, open socio-technical systems design is about the act of consciously designing such systems.

At the heart of open socio-technical systems design is socio-technical systems theory, a theory grounded in a number of principles but just as importantly a number of espoused values and ideals. Consequently, socio-technical systems theory is not aesthetically or value neutral. Having said this, all theories are aesthetically or value laden whether implicitly or explicitly (Popper, 1959). Furthermore, as practitioners, we have our own biases which shape the way we approach a design challenge, especially organizational design. Currently, other worldviews exist which contrast with that of socio-technical systems theory. Probably the most prominent one is mechanism which can be described as Tayloristic or technologically driven. One of the assumptions underlying this worldview is that people are unpredictable parts. That is, if they are not stopped by the system design, they will make mistakes and so, it would be best to eliminate them completely. However, since organizations cannot completely eliminate people, designs based on mechanism try to anticipate all eventualities and then program them into the machines (Cherns. 1976).

Since societal values today are changing, socio-technical systems theory expresses a set of ideals that are meta to values and therefore more stable (Emery. 1976). Table 1 is a summary of the ideals of contextualism and operational modes expressed in socio-technical systems analysis and design (Emery. 1976). Socio-technical systems theory wants to design social systems that allow the expression of the ideals of contextualism because this will allow more effective human relations at work, which in turn will allow better control of the technical system.

Table 1 Mechanism vs. Contextualism

Mechanism		Contextualism	
Ideals	*Operation*	*Ideals*	*Operation*
The Good	Literacy	Homonomy	Dialogue
Truth	Teaching abstractions	Nurturance	Learning through Perception
Plenty	Materialism	Humanity	Spirituality
Order	Hierarchy and domination	Beauty	Participative Democracy

The social system comprises the work related transactions and inter-dependencies among people. Four variables or processes must be well managed for any social system to survive (Parsons. 1951).

- Goal setting and attainment (e.g. daily or weekly goals or targets linked to long term strategic goals)
- Adaptation to the external environment (e.g. changes demanded by new regulations or new customer requirements)
- Integration of the activities of people within the system (e.g. how they resolve their differences)
- Long term development to ensure the future survival and growth of the system (e.g. through recruitment, training etc.)

In socio-technical systems theory, each of these variables is assessed with respect to a particular key variance in the technical system and, in general for each of the four most probable social system interactions, namely:

- Superior/Subordinate or vertical relationships
- Intra-group relations or horizontal relationships within the work group involved with the control and coordination of work to control key variances in the technical system
- Inter-group relations or horizontal relationships between the work group and groups they interact with to carry out their work tasks
- Organizational goals or relationships across the larger organization that contains the social system under study.

The analysis of these social system variables and their key variances with respect to the technical system can be achieved by using the GAIL analysis tool (Taylor & Felten. 1993).

The technical system comprises the system inputs, throughputs and outputs. There are three steps involved in conducting technical system analysis (Trist. 1981). They are:

- Complete a workflow analysis and identify unit operations
- Identify Key Variances and complete a key variance matrix showing how key variances affect other variance
- Complete a variance control table for each key variance to show how the social system keeps that variance in range

Socio-technical systems theory insists that optimal system design is achieved by joint optimization of the social and technical systems. In order to achieve joint optimization of the social and technical systems rather than optimizing one and sub optimizing the other, they must be analyzed and designed together (Emery. 1959).

Socio-technical systems theory complements Parsons' (1951) model by offering a set of principles that guide the design of socio-technical systems. These principles should serve as a guide but not a blueprint (Cherns. 1976).

1. **Compatibility.** The process of design must be compatible with its objectives
2. **Minimal Critical Specification.** No more should be specified than is absolutely essential.
3. **Socio-Technical Criterion.** Variances, if they cannot be eliminated, must be controlled as near to their point of origin as possible.
4. **Redundancy of Function.** Use redundancy of function rather than redundancy of parts. The intent must be to rely on a redundancy of skills (function) in each person instead of a redundancy of people (parts) as a way of dealing with flexibility needs and work design.
5. **Boundary Location.** Departmental boundaries should be drawn, usually to group people and activities on the basis of one or more of three criteria: technology, territory and time.
6. **Information Flow.** Information systems should be designed to provide information in the first place to the point where action on the basis of it will be needed.
7. **Support Congruence.** The systems of social support should be designed so as to reinforce the behaviors that the organization structure is designed to elicit.
8. **Design and Human Values.** An objective of organizational design should be to provide a high quality of work life.
9. **Incompletion.** Design is an iterative process.

Four principles that we wish to elaborate here are principles 1, 2, 8 and 9. Principle 1 basically states the process used to create a design should embody the objectives that the design tries to accomplish. Consequently, if one wishes to achieve joint optimization of the social and technical systems then it is important to address both systems in the design process. If it is important that the people who will implement the new socio-technical system understand the design, then they need to be involved in the design process.

Principle 8 states that the final design should allow for a high quality of work life. This is measured by the six psychological factors required for productive human activity. Each person should have the right amount of autonomy for making decisions so that their work provides a challenge for them; the opportunity to set learning goals and to receive feedback on their progress to achievement of goals; and the right amount of variety so that their work does not become routine and boring. The organization should provide an atmosphere or climate where there is mutual trust and respect; meaningful work so that people can see their contribution to the whole, are proud of it and see it contributing to society; and some sense of desirable future which does not necessarily mean promotion (Emery & Thorsrud. 1969).

In order to take into account principle 8 in the design process, it becomes necessary to allow the people that will be affected by the design to participate in creating their working conditions. The principle of incompletion is also relevant here. Design teams leave the design somewhat incomplete so that the people who have to live with the new system need to become involved in completing the design of the system. If we add the latter point to what was stated previously about joint optimization, it becomes clear that the design process must address both the social and technical systems and furthermore, the people that will be impacted by the design must be participants in the design process, hence participative design is necessary. The process should also be democratic in order to transfer responsibility of the design process outcome to the system because the design must be optimized according to their needs and not those of a third-party.

Open socio-technical systems design is also grounded in open systems theory. As mentioned previously an open system is a system-in-context, in it environment. The system and environment are co-implicative (Emery. 2000). An open system is not independent of its environment, as the system changes the environment is influenced to change and the opposite is also true. If we reconsider principle 1 in this light, then the design process must also address how the system which is under design is influenced by its environment and how the system can influence its environment in order to achieve coherence between both. If this is not done, one can imagine a system which is irrelevant to the needs of the environment or a system which hopes to redesign itself without addressing environmental pressures that are in contradiction with the desired vision.

Co-evolution of the system and its environment is a reality that designers need to take into account.

Enterprise Architecture as Open Socio-Technical Systems Design

We have previously proposed a number of characteristics which an open socio-technical systems design process should possess:

1. Participative and democratic;
2. Address jointly both the social and technical systems to achieve joint optimization;
3. Address system-in-context coherence and co-evolution.

The question now is "what would an Enterprise Architecture process possessing these characteristics look like?"

The first characteristic would entail that the Enterprise Architecture outcome be owned by the organization (or sub-organization) under design – for the reminder of the text, we will use the expression *system* in replacement of organization (or sub-organization) under design. Moreover, the members of the *system* would be full participants in the process co-determining the outcome by making design decisions.

The second characteristic would entail two elements. The first element is that the Enterprise Architecture process would address both the social system (people, culture, norms, interactions, roles, etc.) and the technical system (technology, tools, materials, etc.). In modern organizations, IT technologies play a key role in the technical system hence the traditional IT domains (data, application and infrastructure) must be addressed. The traditional business architecture would be separated into three portions: one in the social system (people, culture, roles, etc.), another in the technical system (process) and the last in the system-in-environment coherence (objectives, vision, competition, etc.). The second element is that current *system* boundaries (i.e. divisions, departments, sectors) might have to be redrawn in order to achieve a coherent and stable system. Consequently, all the organizational entities that are interacting with the *system* must participate in the process in order to help determine new boundary relations.

The third characteristic would require that the Enterprise Architecture process addresses a number of points: (1) determining the new boundaries of the *system* (including members), (2) learning about the environment (stakeholder needs, competition, expectations, etc.), (3) learning about the historical context of the *system* (how has the past has shaped the current state and what to drop and what to take forward), (4) determining the vision and objectives of the **system** and (5) influencing its environment in order to achieve co-evolution.

A consequence of the Enterprise Architecture outcome being owned by the **system** is that an enterprise architect can't be responsible for the outcome per se. His/hers responsibility is one of nurturing and upholding the design process itself in order to uphold the socio-technical systems principles and open socio-technical systems design process characteristics. A corollary of this latter point is that the people nurturing and upholding the design process (enterprise architects) must have a solid grounding in both how machines/technology behave as well as the way people and social groups behave. Since this double specialty is rare, an engineer-social scientist pairing is required.

Key Execution Guidelines for Enterprise Architecture

The following section offers a number of key guidelines that should be followed in order to ground Enterprise Architecture in open socio-technical systems theory. These guidelines are not intended to address the full complexity of undertaking Enterprise Architecture. A comprehensive Enterprise Architecture intervention design would require complete descriptions for elements such as: the various phases of the intervention, the task-groups, the activities of the task-groups, the member composition of the task-groups as well as the recruitment/selection methods, etc. However, the presented guidelines will offer anchor points that should guide the enterprise architect in adjusting current ways of working and designing workshops.

Facilitation & Group Dynamics. Beware of group dynamics and the importance of proper group process design and facilitation. The role of the enterprise architect is above all to develop and facilitate the design process which must be a sound group process. He/she may act as a subject matter expert in certain instances, but it is important that the members of the systems under design who will "live" with the decision make the decision.

An enterprise architect should have an understanding of how people and groups behave. Consequently, a minimum understanding of group dynamics and processes as well as a minimum level of skills in group facilitation is necessary if he plans on designing and facilitating the design process. If he/she does not have such skills or knowledge (and even if he/she does), given the organizational significance and importance of the outcome, the aid of a social scientist should strongly be considered. It is important to note that the poor performance of a working group is not indicative of the general performance of group-centric work processes (vs.

individualist) but rather indicative of the lack of knowledge and skills underlying group workshop design and facilitation.

Participative & Democratic. The members of the *system* must be the primary participants and decision makers in the process in order to get their commitment as well as insure that the final design meets their psychological and social needs. This cannot be achieved effectively if the members of the *system* are not participants in the process nor if they are not making key decisions. This is not to say that all the members of the *system* should be active participants. However an adequate recruiting approach should be used (Taylor & Felten. 1993). The Enterprise Architecture process itself could be achieved according to Emery's two-step participative organizational design process (Search Conference and Participative Design Workshops) (Emery. 1993, de Guerre et al. 1997).

Holistic. The Enterprise Architecture process must consider and redesign if necessary a number of domains which cannot be addressed in a piecemeal fashion. A divide-and-conquer approach would be inconsistent with the systemic nature of the design problem. The domains that should be addressed are the typical IT domains (applications, data, infrastructure and other automation/mechanization technologies) in addition to an extensive business architecture (strategy, education, work processes, work team design, organizational boundaries, planning, pay system, human resource policies, labor management, capital investment system, etc.). Addressing any of the IT and business architecture sub-domains separately and trying to adapt the others to it will probably produce an ineffective and unsustainable outcome. In addition to scanning the environment (opportunities, competition, industry trends etc.), it is equality important to scan the history of the organization in order to achieve shared understanding on how the current organization was shaped by past events and how the past will continue to influence the organization in the future.

Learning. It is important to remember that the most important outcome of the Enterprise Architecture process is not a perfect, elegant design (especially not according to industry dictated best practices) but rather a system, which is capable of continuous learning and adaptation. It is much more important to enable continuous learning because one can rarely predict the future hence a perfect design could easily become a dysfunctional one before it is delivered, a victim of changes within and/or outside of the organization (Mintzberg et al. 1998). The Enterprise Architecture process should be viewed as a never-ending iterative process. In addition, learning to learn is important for participants. Those organizational members that did participate in the design process not only understand and are ready to implement the new design; they also have implicitly learned design thinking and therefore are prepared to go on learning and changing the new design as necessary. Over time, this iterative process does lead to elegant solutions (de Guerre. 2000).

Shared tools. It is important that the tools used during the Enterprise Architecture process be understood by all the people that must use them. Moreover, it is important that tools used in the design process be relevant for the continuous management and improvement of the *system*. Consequently, the design process must allow the necessary time for the participants to learn, adapt and create the necessary tools for the design. In addition to the already existing tools available in current Enterprise Architecture methodologies, the following previously presented analysis tools of socio-technical systems (see Open socio-technical systems design section) should be considered: (a) workflow analysis and unit operations identification, (b) key variance matrix and control analysis, and (c) GAIL model analysis.

A Comparison with Conventional Enterprise Architecture Approaches

In order to deepen further the meaning of Enterprise Architecture as open socio-technical systems design (EAaOSSD), let us compare it with current approaches to Enterprise Architecture. Our intent is not to make side-by-side comparisons but rather to highlight and contrast some of the predominant characteristics of mainstream approaches to EAaOSSD.

Participative vs. Top-Down

In many organizations, the execution of Enterprise Architecture is often given to an elite group of senior IT specialists (sometimes management specialists), which are typically positioned in the higher levels of the organizational hierarchy. This select group has the mandate, guided most often by Enterprise Architecture methodologies rooted in strategic planning (Ansoff. 1965) and strategy design (Christensen et al. 1982) to define the desirable future state of the *system*. The members of the *system* are typically involved in only a limited capacity, usually for requirements gathering and final design validation. The Enterprise Architecture team usually solicits the members of the *system* for business requirements, future business targets and objectives as well as current irritants. In addition, the gathering of potential solutions is often avoided; it is not rare to hear requests from the EA team such as: "please give us requirements and not solutions; we will propose the solution which will take into consideration the larger picture." This separation between those with the needs and those determining the solutions usually creates misunderstanding and resistance. It is not rare to have the *system* reject (even sabotage) the solution proposed. Both the challenges with regards to gaps and acceptance are often exacerbated by the fact that the people solicited for the requirements are not those doing the work but rather the supervisors who are: (a) not always aware of the workflow details that workers have long since developed and implemented a work around, and/or (b) who have divergent views from their team on how the work should be improved. EA teams typically try to get around these challenges by using an iterative two-step design and validation process. They also develop a very keen sales aptitude in order to get their ideas across. However, currently, most EA teams do not have deep support within their organizations; according to Forrester, only 15% of EA teams are recognized (DeGennaro. 2010). This very low rate would seem to support the predicted resistance of a top-down process.

Enterprise Architecture achieved through EAaOSSD would be necessarily participative in nature. As described earlier, EAaOSSD is based on a design process that is democratic and participative. Enterprise architects in this context are guardians of the process, not the outcome. It is the *system* that owns the outcome.

Mechanist vs. Contextualist

Most Enterprise Architecture methodologies have been designed and supported by the engineering and computer science communities. These communities typically have a mechanistic view of the world. According to Pepper (1961), mechanism is a worldview that is based on the metaphor of a machine. Because of this underlying metaphor, the engineering and computer science communities often hold implicit assumptions and beliefs that an organization can be viewed as a machine which can be engineered to achieve ultimate perfection. In the extreme case, if it were possible to engineer out people that would be perfect because people are inherently unpredictable and perfect machines should be predictable. These assumptions often lead to an overemphasis on the technical system to the detriment of the social. Often the objective is to adapt or coerce the social system to fit the optimized technical system, according to "best practice". Consequently, these methodologies and their outcomes reflect these assumptions.

In contrast, EAaOSSD is grounded in explicit ideals and values, which are humanistic. It is also very much influenced by the social science research communities which have a more ecological or contextual view of the world and organizations (Pepper. 1961). EAaOSSD tries to achieve joint optimization between social and technical systems and not put overemphasis on either. The underlying objective is to achieve cohabitation between people and technology and not replace one by the other. The emphasis is on developing technologies for smart people rather than smart systems to replace people.

Task vs. Process

Many Enterprise Architecture methodologies explain in great detail the various steps and/or artifacts which should be produced. They are very focused on the outcomes, and the tasks or steps to achieve these outcomes. However, they often offer very little with regards to how to conduct the tasks in order to achieve the best outcome given that it is people that are doing the tasks. In other words, current methodology might explain clearly what steps must be done as well as describe the inputs/outcomes of these steps but they offer very little on how to get people involved in actually executing the steps, the process. It is not rare to see such preoccupation swept beneath the concept of "governance".

In contrast, EAaOSSD is firmly grounded in a theoretically sound process by applying a participative open socio-technical systems design process. The process guides both design accomplishment and group dynamic management. Moreover, the process is designed to uphold the socio-technical systems principles and process characteristics, which are key to achieving joint optimization. Consequently, equal consideration is given to task accomplishment and process management.

Piecemeal vs. Holistic

Most Enterprise Architecture methodologies that propose a process offer one that is fairly linear. Moreover, it is not rare for them to choose a starting point such as process redesign or IT ecosystem design and then, in a linear fashion, adapt the other dimensions of *system*, one at a time building on the previous decision. This linear approach complemented with an underlying mechanistic worldview goes a long way to explain why most Enterprise Architecture approaches are techno-centric and socially coercive in nature. However, what underlies these shortcomings is caused by a much deeper assumption: divide-and-conquer. Based on the problem solving tools of the engineering communities, most Enterprise Architecture methodologies assume that the design of a system can be addressed in a piecemeal, linear fashion. The strategy is to recursively divide the larger problem into independent sub-problems, solve these sub-problems and reconstitute the combined solution. At best, most mainstream Enterprise Architecture methodologies will propose iterative processes, which try to refine an optimal solution by using multiple gap-and-fix steps. It is very rare to find an Enterprise Architecture methodology, which explicitly acknowledges that the design process cannot use a linear problem solving approach, but requires rather a more holistic approach.

Most Enterprise Architecture methodologies are also piecemeal in the domain that they consider. Many dimensions such as education/training, pay system, human resource policies and important historical events are swept aside because they are judged to be unimportant to the final design. In order to achieve an optimal, coherent and stable system, all systemic dimensions must be addressed together as a whole. This holistic nature to EAaOSSD is probably one of the most challenging, but its avoidance is an avoidance or denial of the systemic nature of the problem at hand as well as the co-implicative nature of the system-in-environment relationship.

Process vs. Artifact

Most current Enterprise Architecture methodologies implicitly or explicitly use one of three stances when defining Enterprise Architecture: Enterprise Architecture as a process, Enterprise Architecture as an artifact or Enterprise Architecture as both a process and an artifact.

The stance taken by EAaOSSD is that of a process and artifact for the key outcome of the process is a redesigned open socio-technical system, which is capable of learning and influencing its environment as well as the necessary shared tools (artifacts) that are required to support the management and future evolution of the system. Two things are particular about this stance. The first is that the outcome is not a repository of artifacts or a redesigned system but rather a system, which is capable of learning, the basis for continuous active adaptation. The corollary of this is that the redesign process is never really finished but rather is embedded in the day-to-day activities of the system, which strives to better itself. The second particularity of this stance is that the tools used to guide analysis and decision-making must be adopted by the system both during the design process and after (for continuous evolution). Since the tools serve to help the participants in the process (the *system*) to make decisions, this necessarily means that the participants understand how to use the tools as well as their meaning and implications. In order to achieve this, an enterprise architect cannot merely use a pick-and-choose approach of best practice tools and sell (coerce) them to the *system*. An inquiry and learning process must be planned as well as time for tool creation, adaptation and adoption. It is important to understand that the objective is not to use the latest fad analytic or modeling tools but rather to foster learning and appropriation of system design.

In practical terms, the stance taken by EAaOSSD on modeling artifacts and tools is that that the majority of people designing and implementing the new EA must understand the design as well as be able to use the tools/artifacts to redesign as necessary. Consequently, having only a select few EA experts is neither appropriate nor desirable. In contrast, it could be said that current EA methodologies give too much importance to creating comprehensive (most often very complex) tools and artifacts which hinder conversation, consequently hindering enterprise architecture. According to EAaOSSD, conversation, teamwork and ongoing organizational learning are the key tools of enterprise architecture... the rest is secondary.

Conclusion

Modern organizations are faced with the challenge of surviving in high relevant uncertainty (Emery & Trist. 1965). Moreover, since organizations have permeable boundaries with this environment, they cannot escape the increasing turbulence within their own boundaries that mirrors the reality of their environment (Ashby.1958).

Enterprise Architecture should be a tool that allows modern organizations to cope and thrive within these turbulent times. The past decades have been plagued by two major realities. The first is the low life expectancy and high early mortality of organizations (De Geus. 2002). The second is the unresolved challenges surrounding IT project delivery (Eveleens & Verhoef. 2010). In light of these facts, one is forced to wonder if current Enterprise Architecture methodologies are adequately adapted to the current realities. Very few conventional Enterprise Architecture methodologies are based on a worldview other than mechanism. Mechanism offers many insights when coping with a world that is predictable, decomposable, cause-effect, and linear. The constant, unexpected and sometimes dramatic change that we all experience in our daily lives doesn't seem to be accounted for by the worldview of mechanism. Hence, how are tools built upon the foundations of the latter supposed to be effective in today's context?

Within this narrative, we introduced the theories of open systems and socio-technical systems in a discourse on Enterprise Architecture. We have concluded that Enterprise Architecture may be informed as open socio-technical systems design. Based on this proposed insight, our objective was to present an alternative path to conventional Enterprise Architecture methodologies; an alternative grounded in explicit theory, which is supported by many decades of fieldwork and research: open socio-technical systems theory (Mumford. 2006; Trist. 1981). We believe that the world view of contextualism underlying open socio-technical systems theory serves to provide a firm basis for new Enterprise Architecture methodologies which can better account for the inner and outer turbulence of today and tomorrow organizations.

Finally, our intent was to foster the coming together of two rich communities, which could learn from each other in order to complement one another if not join, that of socio-technical systems and Enterprise Architecture.

About the Authors

Dr. James Lapalme is a Professor at École de technologie supérieure in Montreal.. He received a Ph.D. in Computer Sciences from l'Université de Montréal in Montréal. He has been a senior enterprise architect at the National Bank Financial Group. His major areas of interest are Enterprise Architecture as system of systems design and socio-technical systems.

Dr. Donald W. de Guerre is an associate professor at Concordia University in Montreal. He received a Ph.D. in Human and Organisation Systems from The Fielding Graduate University in California. He has a distinguished international career as a consultant and manager. His major area of interest is the development of participative governance and organization and the further development of Open Systems Theory.

References

Ansoff, H.I. 1965. *Corporate Strategy,* NY: McGraw-Hill.

Ashby, W.R. 1958. "Requisite variety and its implications for the control of complex systems," *Cybernetica,* (1:2), p. 83-99.

Cherns, A.B. 1976. "Principles of Socio-technical Design," *Human Relations,* 29, pp-783-92.

Christensen, C. R., Andrews, K. R., Bower, J. L, Hamermesh, G., and Porter, M. E. 1982. *Business Policy: Text and Cases (5th ed),* Homewood, IL:Irwin.

De Geus, A. 2002. *The Living Company,* Harvard Business Press.

de Guerre, D 2000. "The codetermination of cultural change over time," *Systemic Practice and Action Research,* (13:5), pp. 645-663

de Guerre, D., M. Noon, & Salter, Sam (1997). Syncrude Canada Limited: A Canadian Success Story. Association for Quality and Participation Annual Spring Conference, Clevland, AQP.

DeGennaro, T. 2010. *The profile of corporately supported EA groups: Tactics for improving corporate management's support for EA in large firms.* Forrester, September.

Emery, F. E. 1959. *Characteristics of socio-technical systems: The emergence of a new paradigm of work,* Canberra, ANU/CCE.

Emery, F. E. 1976. *In Pursuit of Ideals,* Canberra, ANU/CCE.

Emery, F. E. and Thorsrud, E. 1969. *Form and Content in Industrial Democracy,* London, Tavistock.

Emery, F.E. 1972. "Characteristics of Socio-Technical Systems",. In *Design of Jobs,* Davis, L.E. and Taylor, J.C. (eds.), Penguin Books, pp. 157-186.

Emery, M. 1993. "Participative Design for Participative Democracy," Canberra, ANU/CCE.

Emery, M. 2000. "The Current Version of Emery's Open Systems Theory," *Systemic Practice and Action Research*, (13:5), pp 685-703.

Eveleens, J. L. and Verhoef, C. 2010. "The Rise and Fall of the Chaos Report Figures," *IEEE Software Journal*, January-Febuary, p. 30-36

Hagan, Paula J. 2004. *Guide to the (Evolving) Enterprise Architecture Body of Knowledge*. VA:The MITRE Corporation.

Lytle, W. O. 1996. *Accelerating the design of high-performance organisations*, MA: William O. Lytle & Associates

Mintzberg, H., Lampel, J. and Ahlstrand, B. 1998. *Strategy Safari: A Guided Tour Through The Wilds of Strategic Management*. Free Press.

Mumford, E. 1996. "Risky Ideas in the Risk Society," *Journal of Information Technology* 11(4).

Mumford, E. 2006. "The story of socio-technical design: reflections on its successes, failures and potential," *Information Systems Journal*, 16, pp. 317–342

Parsons, T. 1951. *The Social System*. London: Routledge and Kegan Paul.

Pepper, S. 1961. *World Hypotheses: A Study in Evidence*. CA:University of California Press.

Popper, K. 1959. *The Logic of Scientific Discovery*. London: Hutchington & Co.

Taylor, J. C. and Felten, D. F. 1993. *Performance by Design: socio-technical systems in North America*. Englewood Cliffs, Prentice Hall.

Trist, E. 1981. *The evolution of socio-technical systems: a conceptual framework and an action research program*, Ontario Quality of Working Life Center, Ontario Ministry of Labour.

Trist, E. L. and Bamforth, K. W. 1951. "Some social and psychological consequences of the longwall method of coal-getting." *Human Relations,* (4:1), pp 3-38.

van Eijnatten, F. 1993. *The Paradigm that Changed the Workplace*. Assen, van Gorcum.

Zachman, J. A. 1987. "A framework for information systems architecture," *IBM Systems Journal*, (26:3), pp 454-470.

Viewing Enterprises and their Architectures from a Unified System Perspective

Harold "Bud" Lawson

Abstract

By learning to utilize a system perspective on the structure and operation of an enterprise a unified shared vision can be achieved. This can be accomplished by developing a broad understanding of fundamental concepts and principles of systems as well as the deployment of system thinking and systems engineering. Based upon an established system perspective capability organizations and their enterprises can exploit this knowledge in organizing their analysis of problem and opportunity situations, decision-making and life cycle management of its system assets. Via a unified shared vision of life cycle management system related data and information may be collected in a uniform manner. All of these improvements can be exploited in developing and utilizing a lightweight architecture framework that is based to a large extent upon the integrated utilization of international standards.

Keywords

Enterprise Architecture, Systems Thinking, Situation Awareness, Change Management, Systems Engineering, Organizational Cybernetics, Architecture Framework, Management Systems, International Standards

Introduction

Ludwig von Bertalanffy (von Bertalanffy 1968), the Austrian biologist considered by many as the father of modern systems thinking, points to the fact that systems are everywhere. We may not always formalize our view of systems, but we certainly feel the effect of them in our personal and professional life. Our understanding of systems, particularly complex ones are at best cursory. For all but trivial systems complete understanding is virtually impossible. So, we live with the fact that our understanding lies somewhere between mystery and mastery (Flood 1998). This uncertainty often causes an uneasy feeling about systems. However, by understanding fundamental concepts and principles of systems and mental model paradigms leading to a shared vision much of the mystery can be removed and a positive step towards systems awareness and at least partial mastery can be achieved. This is the goal established by (Lawson 2010) in developing a body of knowledge concerning systems and presented as a modular journey through the systems landscape.

It is interesting to note that the one of the eight principles that demonstrates quality in (ISO 9001 2008) certification is as follows:

> *System approach to management – Identifying, understanding and managing interrelated processes as a system contributes to the organization's effectiveness and efficiency in achieving its objectives.*

Even though this principle calls for a system approach, the standard does not provide sufficient guidance of what this means in practice. Understanding what is meant by the word "system" and abiding by this principle is a challenge for organizations and their enterprises. This presentation as well as the book (Lawson 2010) provides substance to this principle.

So, what if all or most of the people in an enterprise held a shared view of the concepts, principles and meaningful mental models of systems. Further, as a result, that they learn to "think" and "act" in terms of systems by utilizing Systems Thinking, respectively Systems Engineering methodologies and tools as a central part of the enterprise culture. How would this affect communication, discussion and dialogue and most importantly decision-making within the enterprise. Could this be used as a basis for building more effective enterprise architectures? Could this be the route to abiding by the ISO 9001 quality principle? This is the hypothesis that will be supported by arguments presented in this presentation. That is, in contrast to many of the complex architectural frameworks being used to architect enterprises, a Light-Weight Architectural Framework (LAF) is proposed. Utilizing LAF for enterprise architectures is based upon identifying the system assets (at least the critical ones) of the enterprise

270

and defining the collective architectures of the assets in a unified system related manner. LAF is to a large extent based upon the implementation of international standards.

A Systems Survival Kit

The first step is establishing a basis for broad system understanding in the enterprise as described by (Lawson 2010). The survival kit is composed a limited set of concepts and principles as well as a universal mental model called the System Coupling Diagram. Russell Ackoff (Ackoff 1971) provided some pioneering observations by proposing that one should view collective concepts about systems as a System of System Concepts. While the set of concepts presented here is not the same as those presented by Ackoff, the notion of viewing a set of concepts as a system is the same.

The most fundamental concept of systems has been provided by (Boardman and Sauser 2008):

> *"We believe that the essence of a system is togetherness, the drawing together of various parts and the relationships they form in order to produce a new whole...."*

This first fundamental concept of "togetherness" permits us to recognize as von Bertalanffy postulated that systems are everywhere. Structures and behaviors are further concepts that are present in all man-made systems. The structure of a system is a static property and refers to the constituent elements of the system and their relationship to each other. The behavior is a dynamic property and refers to the effect produced by a system "in operation. "

Another fundamental concept that is attributed to systems is the concept of emergence. Emergence arises from both the predictable and unpredictable operational behavior of a system itself and/or in relationship to the environment in which the system resides. This concept is captured in the following quote by Peter Checkland (Checkland 1999):

> *"Whole entities exhibit properties which are meaningful only when attributed to the whole, not to its parts . . ."*

These four fundamental concepts of systems are complemented with the additional concepts identified in Table 1 thus forming a System of System Concepts. In this chapter, the definitions are not further elaborated, but the meaning with perhaps the exception of roles (described in more detail below) should be clear. The category Types is based upon a classification by (Checkland 1999) and the category Focus based upon contributions by (Flood and Carson 1998). The categorization of Complexity is based upon an original contribution by (Weaver 1948) as well as extensions by (Flood 1998) and your author.

Concept Categories	Concepts	Definitions
Fundamental	Togetherness	Two or more elements are related resulting in a new whole.
	Structure	The constituent elements and their static relationship.
	Behavior	The effect produced by the elements and their dynamic element relationships in operation.
	Emergence	The predictable or unpredictable behavior occurring as the result of a system in operation.
Types	Defined Physical System	Two or more physical elements are integrated together producing a new whole.
	Defined Abstract System	Two or more abstract elements are related resulting in a new whole.
	Human Activity System	Two or more elements, at least one involving a human activity are integrated resulting in a new whole.
Topologies	Hierarchy	A level-wise structure of systems and system elements that is defined recursively.
	Network	A node and links structure of system elements and their interrelationships.
Focus	Narrow System-of-Interest (NSOI)	The system upon which focus is placed in respect to a view.
	Wider System-of-Interest (WSOI)	The systems that directly affect (including enabling) the NSOI in respect to a view.
	Environment	The context that has a direct influence upon the NSOI and WSOI.
	Wider Environment	The context that has an indirect influence upon the NSOI and WSOI.
Complexity	Organized Simplicity	There are a small number of essential factors and large number of less significant and/or insignificant factors.
	Organized	The structure is organized in order to be understood and thus be amenable for describing complex behaviors.
	Disorganized	There are many variables that exhibit a high level of random behavior. Can be due to not having adequate control over the structure of heterogeneous complex systems (complexity creep).
	People Related	Perception of the system fosters a feeling of complexity. Also, rational or irrational behavior of individuals in particular situations.

Roles	Sustained System Asset	A system that is life cycle managed and when instantiated provide system services.
	Situation System	Two or more elements become related together resulting in a problem or an opportunity. Alternatively, an objective or end state that defines a desirable situation is established.
	Respondent System	A system composed of two or more elements that are assembled in order to respond to a situation.
	Thematic System	A system that is composed for the study of possible outcomes of a postulated situation system as well as one or more respondent systems ("what if").

Table 1: Concrete Concepts (Categories and Definitions)

Now we proceed to the important concepts identified in the Roles category. This is based upon a paradigm that conveys the essence of what systems are used for and how systems relate to each other as portrayed in Figure 1.

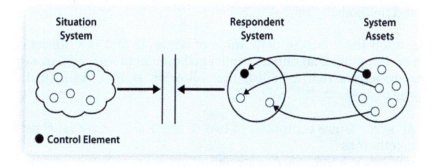

Figure 1: System Coupling Diagram

- Situation System – A problem or opportunity situation; either unplanned or planned. The situation may be the work of nature, be man-made, a combination of both or a postulated situation (Thematic System) that is to be used as a basis for deeper understanding and training (for example, business games or military exercises). Thus, the situation may be catastrophe, terrorist action, the capabilities needed for a new system, the next stage in a life cycle of a system. In all cases, in order to affect the situation a response is required.
- Respondent System – The system created to respond to the situation where the parallel bars indicate that this system interacts with the situation and transforms the situation to a new situation. A Respondent System, based upon the situation that is being

273

treated can have several names such as Project, Program, Mission, Task Force, or in a scientific context, Experiment. Note that one of the system elements of this system is a control element that directs the operation of the respondent system in its interaction with the situation. This element is based upon an instantiation of a Control System asset, for example a Command and Control System, or a control process of some form. In some cases the control element may be distributed in which case the elements interact autonomously.

- System Assets – The sustained assets of an enterprise that are to be utilized in responding to situations. System assets must be adequately life cycle managed so that when instantiated in a Respondent System will perform their function. These are the systems that are the primary objects of an Enterprise and include their value added products or services as well as their infrastructure systems. Examples of assets include concrete systems such as produced products and/or services, facilities, instruments and tools as well as abstract systems such as theories, knowledge, processes and methods.

Building upon the concrete definitions of concepts and the utilization of the System Coupling Diagram as a universal mental model, we can express concrete principles that establish the following system rules (truths to abide by):

- All systems are composed of two or more elements that constitute togetherness
- Systems are composed of structural elements or behavior elements
- Defined elements and relationships can be abstract, physical or human activities
- Systems are organized as a hierarchy or a network
- Bounding of systems in respect to views are defined by a Narrow System Of Interest, its Wider System Of Interest, their Environment and Wider Environment
- Complexity can be reduced by the identification of essential factors (concepts and principles)
- Complexity is addressed by proper organization in describing complex behaviors
- Complexity rises when systems are disorganized resulting random behavior
- People have various perceptions of complexity as well as potentially participating in a system resulting in the addition of complexity
- Situation systems result from (problems or opportunities) or from defined objectives in the form of end states

- Respondent systems are developed and utilized to handle situation systems
- Sustained system assets are instantiated and deployed in respondent systems
- One of the elements of a respondent system must provide control

The system survival kit provides a strong basis for building a shared vision of systems and as a basis for establishing an enterprise culture. The creation of guiding concepts and principles as described by (Lawson and Martin 2008) is a prerequisite for dealing with complexities of any type of system. Naturally this also applies to viewing the Enterprise as a system.

Thinking and Acting in Terms of Systems

Building further on the knowledge provided by the system survival kit, we now summarize what it means to think and act in terms of systems. A deeper explanation is given in (Lawson 2010) where several paradigms that convey essential concepts and principles and their application are provided.

Systems Thinking

In relationship to the System Coupling Diagram of Figure 1, we are interested in analyzing and building an understanding of situations be they problems or opportunities. To analyze situations, the body of knowledge from the various approaches to Systems Thinking provides very useful avenues for understanding. (Senge, et.al. 1994) have characterized systems thinking as follows:

> *"Systems thinking is a process of discovery and diagnosis – an inquiry into the governing processes underlying the problems we face and the opportunities we have."*

Note: Your author has added the opportunities aspect.

According to Senge and his colleagues, a good systems thinker, particularly in an organizational setting, is someone who can see four levels operating simultaneously: events, patterns of behavior, systems, and mental models.

Systems thinking evolved during the 20th century, via multiple contributions into a somewhat more understood discipline. Building upon the pioneering contributions of Ludwig von Bertalanffy in the 1920s, Jay Forrester, Russel Ackoff, Ross Ashby, Stafford Beer, Wes Churchman, Peter Checkland, Peter Senge, John Warfield, John Boardman and others have made important contributions to systems thinking in the latter half of the 20th century.

Peter Checkland (Checkland 1993), starting from a systems engineering perspective, successively observed the problems in applying systems engineering to the more fuzzy ill-defined problems found in the social and political arenas. Thus he introduced a distinction between hard systems and soft systems.

Hard systems of the world are characterized by the ability to define purpose, goals and missions that can be addressed via engineering methodologies in attempting to in some sense "optimize" a solution. Soft systems of the world are characterized by extremely complex, problematical and often mysterious phenomenon for which concrete goals cannot be established and which require learning in order to make improvement. Such systems are not limited to the social and political arenas and also exist within and amongst enterprises where complex, often ill-defined, patterns of behavior are observed that are limiting the enterprise ability to improve. Recognizing this important difference, Checkland points to the fact that a process of inquiry that itself can be organized into a learning system is the most appropriate approach for analyzing and learning about soft systems in which human activities exist as elements.

A number of methodologies, tools, models, languages, and techniques have been developed in relationship to systems thinking that assist in the fundamental aspects of seeing wholes, interrelationships, and patterns of change in hard systems, soft systems and mixtures of the two. This includes such descriptive approaches as the determination of root causes via the Five Why's, Loops, Links and Delay language used to express growth and limiting loops as well as Archetypes of patterns of growth and limits (Senge, et.al. 1994), Rich Pictures (Checkland 1993) and Systemigrams (Boardman and Sauser 2008). Some approaches are used for both description and simulation such as DYNAMO (Forrester 1975) as well as Stella and iThink (See www.iseesystems.com).

Situation Awareness and Action

The understanding produced by the application of systems thinking in analyzing situations, regardless of the approach is utilized to make prudent decisions about changes to the systems that are of interest for the enterprise. In (Lawson 2010) the underlying processes of situation awareness and change action are characterized by coupling together two well know loops; that is, the OODA and PDCA loops into the paradigm in Figure 2.

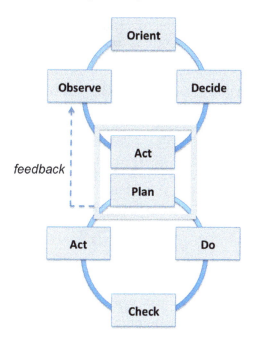

Figure 2 Integrated OODA and PDCA Loops

The OODA Loop

Col. John Boyd of the U.S. Air Force, a veteran of aircraft combat during the Korean conflict of the 1950s, set out to explain why some pilots succeeded in air combat while others, equally well trained, failed. Over the course of a lifetime, the insights that Boyd gained from studying dogfights grew into a broader description of tactical decision-making in dynamic situations (Boyd 1987). Long taught in military circles especially for command and control, Boyd's ideas gained increasing influence in business and governmental circles.

The heart of Boyd's theory is based upon the premise that a tactical decision is the result of activities in a four-step loop. Boyd called these activities Observation, Orientation, Decision and Action. The loop begins with an observation.

> Observation: Whether observation consists of the visual cues that guide a fighter pilot or the staff papers and briefings presented to a senior administrator, the decision-maker must first perceive and assimilate information about the environment as a basis for decision.

Orientation: Once the decision-maker has gained information through his/her or others observations, he/she must fit those pieces of information into a useful understanding of the situation.

Decision: The decision-maker selects a course of action.

Action: The desired course of action is executed.

OODA activities are highly related to systems thinking and decision-making and in enterprises are typically executed continuously in leadership and management functions. This "spawning" for problems and opportunities is an integral part of the establishing change actions.

The PDCA Loop

The PDCA (Plan, Do, Check, and Act) loop was first introduced by Walter Shewhart in the 1920s as the activities required to achieve successful Statistical Quality Control. The PDCA concept was later popularized by MIT professor W. Edwards Deming as one of the guiding principles of TQM (Total Quality Management). Deming had worked under the mentorship of Shewhart at Bell Telephone Laboratories.

While there are some similarities as to the general goals of OODA and PDCA in respect to identifying problems and opportunities, the latter is action based and goes deeper into actually making changes, measuring the effect of changes and taking corrective actions to achieve planned goals. The description of the detailed meaning of individual PDCA activities has varied amongst numerous authors since its popularization by Deming. Some utilize PDSA (where the S means Study). When used in conjunction with soft systems, the use of study instead of check is quite appropriate. In the description that follows the meaning is related mainly to project management and has a direct coupling to the usage of PDCA within the scope of the Project related processes as provided in the ISO/IEC 15288 standard (described below). The loop begins with the creation of a Plan.

Plan: Create a project plan for accomplishing a goal or set of goals that are related to solving a problem or pursuing an opportunity. The plan will include the definition of the processes required to achieve the changes necessary to achieve the goals.

Do: Make the change.

Check: The results of the change are checked (verified) against the goals that were established.

Act: If necessary, corrective actions are taken to adjust the project plan, perhaps renegotiate the goals and then to recycle the loop until the goals are achieved or a decision is made to terminate the project.

The application of OODA is always continuous in nature. The application of PDCA in guiding projects is discrete in nature; that is, it is typically applied for achieving specific goals within a specific time frame with provided resources after which the project is terminated.

OODA and PDCA Integration

The integration of the two loops is realized by coupling the Act activity of the OODA loop to the Plan activity of the PDCA loop. That is, the action to be performed involves the formation of a project, the first activity of which is the Plan. As a result of the execution of the project data and information concerning results, problems and opportunities are feed back for Observation in the OODA loop as portrayed in Figure 2.

The reader should keep this paradigm in mind as it relates to our mental model System Coupling Diagram. The paradigm can be used to explain most any situation related to thinking and acting in terms of systems and relates directly to Situation Systems and Respondent Systems. It is a good model for understanding important relationships between enterprises and the projects that they create and monitor in order to manage change. The connection of the OODA part to the systems thinking should be obvious. We can observe that the systems thinking methodologies are providing support for the first three activities; namely Observing, Orienting and Deciding. As noted, acting in an enterprise setting most often will involve the initiation, execution and follow-up of projects or other forms of organized activities.

Systems Engineering

The methodologies and practices of Systems Engineering provide a controlled means of Acting. Transforming needed capabilities into product or service has been the traditional goal of Systems Engineering. Several standards and best practices have evolved in this discipline. An important standard that is utilized to describe the essence of the life cycle management of systems via a limited set of processes is (ISO/IEC 15288 2002 and 2008). This standard was created in order to promote trading in system products and services and has a direct impact upon enterprise and business management as noted by (Arnold and Lawson 2004).

A detailed description of the processes provided by ISO/IEC 15288 is not within the scope of this presentation and is not permitted. See Lawson (2010) for a summary description of the set of processes. However, let us consider a paradigm illustrating the essence of systems engineering as portrayed in Figure 3 (see Pyster and Olwell (2013)). The provisioning of a System of Interest is accomplished by creating a System Breakdown Structure and then by managing the Life Cycles of the system as well as the Life Cycles of elements of the system when they are systems as well.

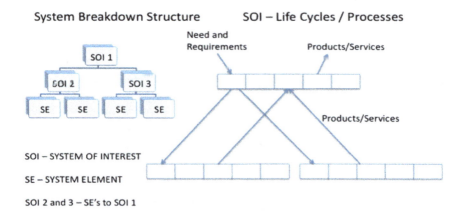

Figure 3. Fundamental Aspects of Systems Engineering

On the left hand side of the figure observe that there are three Systems of Interest identified in the form of a System Breakdown Structure. SOI 1 is decomposed into its elements that in this case are systems as well (SOI 2 and SOI 3). These two systems are composed of System Elements which are not further refined.

On the right hand side of the figure observe that each of the Systems of Interest has a corresponding Life Cycle Model composed of stages that are populated with processes that are used to define the work to be performed. Note that some of the requirements defined to meet the need are distributed in the early stages of the life cycle for SOI 1 to the life cycles of SOI 2, respectively SOI 3. This decomposition of the system illustrates the fundamental concept of Recursion as defined in the ISO/IEC 15288 standard. That is the standard is reapplied for each of the systems of interest.

Note that the system elements are integrated in SOI 2, respectively SOI 3 thus realizing a product or service that is delivered to the life cycle of SOI 1 for integration in realizing the product or service that meets the stated need.

Some examples that relate to this system need could be an embedded system (SOI 1) composed a hardware system (SOI 2) and a software system (SOI 3), a sub-assembly composed of a chases and a motor, a human resource system composed of a recruitment system and a capability management system.

In performing the process work in stages, most often Iteration between stages is required. For example, in the successive refinement of the definition of the system or in providing an update (upgrade or problem solution) of a realized and even delivered product or service.

The work performed in the processes and stages can be performed in a Concurrent manner within the life cycle of any of the systems of interest and concurrent amongst the multiple life cycles.

Life Cycle Transformations

Various work products are produced as a result of "executing" carrying out processes during the life cycle as the System of Interest evolves from need to concept and to reality in the form of products and services. To portray these transformations based upon the knowledge that has been provided thus far, consider the life-cycle structure illustrated in Figure 4.

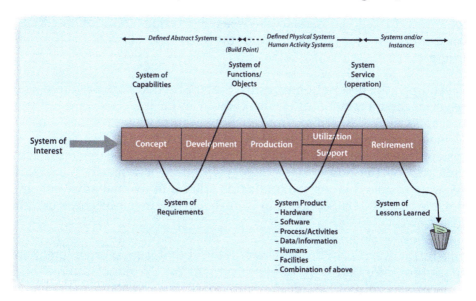

Figure 4: Life Cycle Transformations (System-of-Interest Versions)

Here we observe at the top of the figure that the System of Interest is first described as Defined Abstract Systems that are then transformed into concrete Defined Physical and/or Human Activity Systems when they become a product, that is instantiated for utilization. An eventual retirement of a System of Interest involves disposing of instances and can also involve retirement of the system definition, that is, the Defined Abstract Systems.

It is important to note the perspective portrayed in the figure in naming the various stage and process related work products as "systems". We view the various descriptions as well as the eventual product as "versions" of the System of Interest. That is from a need, the first version of the System of Interest is created as a System of Capabilities. This description meets all of the criteria for a system as defined earlier where the most fundamental aspect is "togetherness".

From this System of Capabilities, the next version of the System of Interest is created in the form of a System of Requirements reflecting both the functional as well as non-functional requirements to be placed upon the System of Interest. The next version of the System of Interest is a System of Functions or Objects that describe the basic transformations that the instantiated System Products are expected to perform when they provide their service. Typically, this involves some type of flow of energy, material, data or information.

In order to provide for orderly development, production and usage, it is important to keep consistency between the various descriptions, that is, traceability between the elements of the various versions of the System of Interest.

Based upon the description versions, System Products are produced as the result of the integration of elements that can include hardware, software, processes/activities, data/-information, humans, facilities, natural elements or combinations thereof. (Note that the early versions of the system (prototypes) may actually be realized in the Development stage as indicated by the dotted line "build point" that is typically the case for software systems) When the product is utilized in its final environment, it provides the System Service, that is the behaviors that it has been designed to achieve.

One further version of the System of Interest that is most often forgotten is to capture information about the history of the System of Interest in the form of a System of Lessons Learned based upon system conception and development as well as product instances and the services they have provided.

The reader should keep this "system perspective" on life cycle transformations in mind as we now proceed to consider other aspects of life cycle transformations.

The various system version transformations that take place during the life cycle as portrayed in Figure 4 form a basis for defining the authority and responsibility of various system actors. In order to focus the discussion of important aspects of the transformations, we introduce three fundamental transformations; namely Definition, Production and Utilization as portrayed in Figure 5. Even though a given life cycle stage structure may vary from the general format portrayed in Figure 5 these three transformations are generic for all types of man-made systems. Further, in the figure the utilization of the universal System Coupling Diagram model is provided in order to portray its applicability in the "situations" that is, the transformations that arise during the life cycle management of systems. This planned usage of the System Coupling Diagram illustrates how system assets that are required to do the work in the stage are instantiated in a Respondent System that interacts with the current situation and transforms it into a new situation.

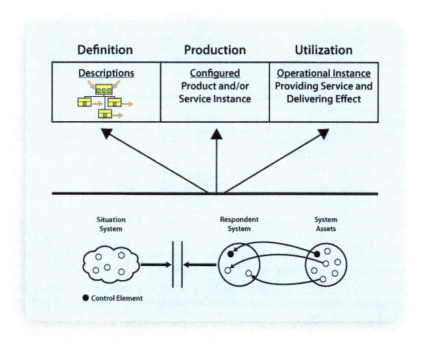

Figure 5: Fundamental Life Cycle Transformations and the System Coupling Diagram

Cybernetics and Change Management Systems

The field of cybernetics was developed in the mid to late 1940s by Warren McCulloch and Norbert Weiner as a discipline independent means of explaining complex system interrelationships with regard to control, information, measurement and logic. A generic cybernetic system composed of three system elements and their relationships is portrayed in Figure 6.

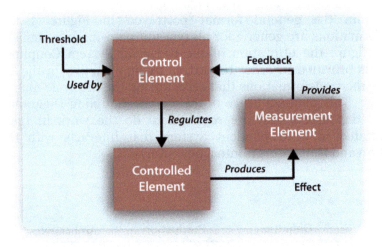

Figure 6: A Generic Cybernetic System

A Control Element regulates a Controlled Element. The Controlled Element produces Effect. A Measurement Element measures the effect and provides Feedback to the Control Element. The Control Element compares the current effect with a Threshold value that it uses in deciding upon further regulation of the Controlled Element.

Cybernetics is applied in physical systems, for example in the regulation of room temperature. In this case, physical regulation sensors are used to measure the current effect which is fed back to a Control Element where the current effect is compared with a threshold setting which can result in activating or deactivating a heating or cooling element. Such regulation operates continuously as long as the Controlled, Control and Measurement Elements are operational.

In relationship to the System Coupling Diagram in Figure 1, it is useful to note that some form of control element is necessary for Respondent Systems in which case this element controls the other elements as the Respondent System handles the Situation System. Thus, the cybernetic model is directly applicable whether we are regulating room temperatures, the progression of stages in a life cycle, or treatment of a problem or even crisis that has arisen. In fact, control elements should be viewed as system assets that are life cycle managed and instantiated as operative controllers.

While the nature of the control, controlled and measurement elements are different, the principles of cybernetics can be equally applied to non-physical systems. While many others have exploited this similarity, it is Stafford Beer that formalized the usage of organizational cybernetics in what he called a Viable System Model (VSM) (Beer 1985). The VSM stipulates rules whereby an organization is, "survival worthy"- that is, it is regulated, learns, adapts, and evolves. Such a learning organization, according to Beer, is constructed around five main management functions; namely operations, coordination, control, intelligence and policy. All of these functions are treated in a cybernetic manner in the VSM. Roughly speaking, the operations function is the Controlled Element. The control function corresponds to the Control Element, intelligence is the result of Measurement that is feedback to the Control Element, policy is used in evaluating a threshold; and finally, coordination deals with the interrelationships between concurrently operative Cybernetic Systems.

Beer also realizes that in complex organizations, several levels of VSM exist and that interrelationships can be described, as systems, via recursive decomposition. In this case Controlled Elements at one level include Control Elements at the next level.

Cybernetics forms the basis for the implementation of the Change Management Model introduced by (Lawson 2010) and presented here in Figure 7.

- Change Management functions as the Control Element. It uses Knowledge as Feedback in making decisions. Purpose, Goals, and Missions to be accomplished along with policy, rules and regulations serve as Threshold values.
- When changes are made via Projects, the Project becomes the Controlled Element. When operational parameter changes are made by a line organization, it is the Controlled Element.
- Outputs produced by the execution of ISO/IEC 15288 Technical Processes produce Effect in respect to changes in System Description and Operational Parameters.
- The Effect (outputs) produced by all of the elements on the left arc gathered as data, interpreted as relevant information and when related to other information becomes the Knowledge that is fed back and fed forward.

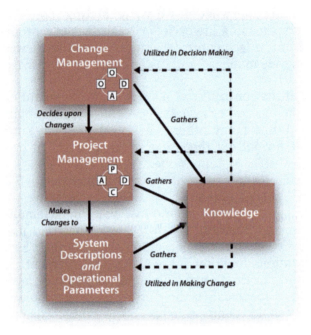

Figure 7: Change Management System

In implementing the model as a system, the Control Element operates continuously according the Observe, Orient, Decide, and Act paradigm. The Controlled Element, be it a project or a line organization operates in a discrete manner; that is, it makes the change within planned time constraints. For structural changes, the project form is most common where the project follows the Plan, Do, Check, Act paradigm. Even a line organization charged with the responsibility for a change should use the PDCA paradigm, especially for non-trivial changes to an operational environment.

All system elements of the Change Management System gather data that can then be interpreted according to information classification thus providing information. The data can also be measured according to additional relevant information classification and provide more data and information. This corresponds to the Measurement Element of Figure 7. By relating information, knowledge is obtained that can be used both as cybernetic feedback as well as fed forward in the form of "know how" capabilities for the actual change related activities.

Based upon the type of system that is being controlled, various forms of measurements are made in order to determine if the Effect produced by operation of the system meet the threshold of change requirements. The following two measures can be applied to any type of man-made system.

286

Measure of Effectiveness (MOE)

Measurement of the ability of a system to meet needs expressed as stakeholder requirements. The requirements indicate what the system should be capable of achieving. When measuring the MOE of a system element, the MOE can only be evaluated by determining how well the system element has assisted in meeting the needs of a System of Interest of which it is a part, meet the system stakeholder requirements.

MOE measurements vary in respect to the type of system involved. For defined physical systems quantitative requirement related measurements can be made. For example, that a climate conditioning system shall maintain a room temperature of no less than 18 and no more than 22 degrees Celsius. For defined abstract and human activity systems, the MOE can involve both quantitative as well as qualitative measurements. For example, an enterprise operates within the limits of an allocated budget (quantitative) as well as meets a requirement of sustaining employee satisfaction (only measurable in a qualitative manner).

Measure of Performance (MOP)

Measures the actual performance achieved due to the inherent system design. Field-testing and/or trials of systems resulting in measurements that can be assessed against some form of performance baseline can determine MOPs.

Quantitative MOP measurements can clearly be applied for defined physical systems; for example that a climate conditioning system due to its design actually sustains an average room temperature of 20 degrees ± 0.5 degree Celsius at least 95% of the time during each day of operation. In the case of defined abstract and human activity systems such as an enterprise, quantitative measurements can also be made in respect to meeting project plans within budget limits. In evaluating performance of qualitative aspects of a system property, like employee satisfaction, measurements can be made by questionnaire or interviews resulting in some form of judgment of the degree of satisfaction.

While MOE and MOP measures have traditionally been applied to physical systems, it is certainly possible to find corresponding measures for other man-made systems; both quantitative and qualitative. Both measures are essential contributions to the knowledge used as feedback to the Change Management controlling element as well as in providing feed forward guidance for actual change activities by projects or by a line organization.

Customer Satisfaction Index (CSI)

A non-technical "Effect" measurement that is of vital importance for enterprises is the degree of their customer's satisfaction. From a quality point of view, it is customer satisfaction that is the desired effect of a quality management system as stipulated in the ISO 9001 standard (ISO 9001 2008).

The Customer Satisfaction Index was developed by Professor Claes Fornell (Fornell 2001). It is used as predictor of consumer spending and corporate earnings. The CSI model is a set of causal equations that link customer expectations, perceived quality, and perceived value to customer satisfaction. These measurements are in turn linked to consequences defined by customer complaints and customer loyalty – measured by price tolerance and customer retention.

The model has been applied to a wide variety of commercial products and services. A variant of the model provides measurement of satisfaction with the services provided by governmental agencies. The index relates to an initial baseline established from the first year in which measurements where made. Thus, the index shows the successive customer satisfaction increase or decrease relative to that point. The CSI for many industries are frequently published in prominent financial newspapers since they provide an indication of the value of a vital asset, namely satisfied customers.

An important side effect of customer satisfaction that has been observed in making measurements is the degree of employee satisfaction that shows a high degree of correlation with the CSI.

Process Assessment

Another type of "Effect" measurement that can be applied in enterprises is the assessment of process capability. There are a number of Capability Maturity Models that are aimed at measuring human activity capabilities in several areas including software development, system development, acquisition, and others. Based upon the processes that are implemented, the enterprise is evaluated as to how well it executes the processes. Such measurements are based upon the actual achievement of process outputs and are graded in a scale such as the following:

- Level 1 Performed
- Level 2 Repeatable
- Level 3 Defined
- Level 4 Managed
- Level 5 Optimizing

At the initial level, processes are performed and provide basic output results, but are not necessarily repeatable, not well defined, not well managed, and certainly not optimized in order to provide for continuous enterprise improvement. At the higher levels, the enterprise provides assessment evidence that indicates process repeatability, well-defined processes, well-managed processes, and finally that enterprise is continually improving (i.e. optimizing) its processes.

In an assessment, the enterprise is scored for each process and then collectively for the set of processes that are assessed. By binding the assessment to achieved work product outcomes from process execution, the assessment measurements attempt to be quantitative. However, due to subjectivity some measurements tend to become qualitative in nature. In any event, the assessments are valuable inputs for feedback to the Change Management control element as well as feed forward knowledge related to the accomplishment of change.

Balanced Scorecards

Balanced Scorecards (BSC) is a control mechanism for enterprises or projects that promote capturing, communication and review of various activities or properties of the top-level system (the enterprise and its projects) in relation to the enterprises or project's strategy and goals. See (Kaplan and Norton 1996). A BSC present various perspectives on the enterprise, typically including:

- the financial perspective,
- the customer perspective,
- the business processes perspective,
- the innovation and learning perspective.

Further perspectives can be added where appropriate. Within each perspective, a set of measurable (or ratable) Key Performance Indicators (KPI's) is defined, which are suitable to demonstrate the current business performance in relation to target values (thresholds). The result is an overview on the strengths and weaknesses on the top level, and can guide the management's overall decision-making process to focus on the most relevant areas for improvement.

A major strength of BSCs is the holistic view on the business it provides as it shows key performance indicators of quite different domains in one overall representation. Consider as an example for an issue stretching over several domains and perspectives: Employees perceive a lack of training with a new IT system (learning and innovation perspective), resulting in sluggish, error-prone customer support services (processes perspective), thus decreasing the customer satisfaction (customer perspective) and slowly lowering sales (financial perspective). In this example, a BSC can serve as discussion basis about actions to be taken, such as further increasing training costs, further IT improvements or the like.

While Balanced Scorecards are useful in obtaining an overview on a variety of topics, subsystems, organizational qualities etc. by key performance indicators, they do not inherently show the interdependencies between these. Systems Thinking methods, as introduced earlier, such as systemigrams and archetypes are suitable to visualize these interdependencies. E.g. archetypes can be used to point out limiting loops and alternative concepts, which reduce undesirable limiting effects or add new growth loops.

In relation to BSC, Systems Thinking methods can be used to demonstrate:

- the interdependencies between key performance indicators,
- optimizations within a system, which generates a single key performance indicator,
- the relationships of a key performance indicator system to its environment.

Concerning the latter point it is notable that it can include environmental systems, which are outside the scope of the BSC. These environmental systems can be factors outside the organization (e.g. raw material prices) or within, just not captured by the currently used BSC.

Thus, in implementing a Balanced Scorecard for both the establishment of thresholds as well as a means of measurement in a cybernetic model, the need to measure individually and collectively can well lead to a hierarchy of interacting cybernetic systems. This corresponds quite well to Beer's VSM (Viable System Model).

Situation Coverage

There are no known methods of measuring the "goodness" of architectures. However, it would be useful to develop such measures and thus be able to establish thresholds. One obvious measurement that can be related to the System Coupling Diagram with respect to Respondent Systems is their degree of situation coverage. That is, how well the respondent system addresses the problems or opportunities that arise in a Situation System. Further, when system assets are taken from the Enterprise portfolio for incorporation into the Respondent System, some form of measure as to their contributions (as elements) toward assisting the Respondent System in meeting its objective of situation coverage would be useful. However, this is still an open research question.

There is an international standard (ISO/IEC 15939) that provides guidance in measurement as well as guidance in establishing measurement indicators from a systems engineering perspective. (Roedler, et. al. 2010)

In an enterprise setting, decisions are often delegated to some type of organized activity that may be in the form of a Change Control Board (CCB). Thus the Change Management element indicated in Figure 7 can be the Change Control Board. They make the decisions concerning systems at various levels of the systems that are of interest for the enterprise. For large organizations, there may exist several CCB's that have authority and responsibility for systems or even portions of systems. At the enterprise level, a CCB can well be involved in planning and following up on change activities within the enterprise as illustrated in Figure 8.

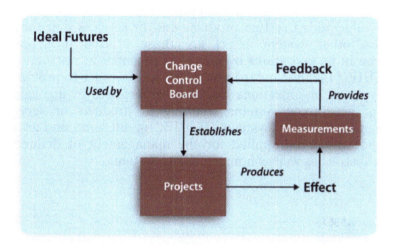

Figure 8: Change Control Board for Enterprise Planning

In this case, the CCB plans for the ideal futures of the enterprise and establishes projects in pursuing these goals. The measurement of the effect produced by projects is used by the CCB in determining how well progress is being made in achieving the ideal future threshold. Indeed the cybernetics in omnipresent in enterprises.

While there are additional aspects of learning to think and act in terms of systems, this summary has provided some of the essential aspects that should be used in building a learning organization that can establish its enterprise architecture and operate the enterprise with a unified system perspective.

Enterprise System Properties

It is imperative to understand the operational aspects of an enterprise in order to be able to establish a basis for their architecture. In this section, several operational aspects are presented that provide a background for the establishment of enterprise architectures based upon a Light-Weight Architectural Framework (LAF).

Achieving Purpose, Mission and Goals

There are a variety of planned man-made systems in operation within all types of organizations (public, private and even non-profit). These planned systems are essential to endeavors (enterprises) that work towards achieving purpose, goals and missions as portrayed in Figure 9. Thus, the enterprise as well as the organization must focus upon (institutionalize) its portfolio of system assets. The availability of, as well as the condition (that is, state) of these assets is an essential aspect of managing the organization and its enterprises. Some of the portfolio assets are the value added system products and/or services that the enterprise produces; other system assets are those utilized in supporting the enterprise in its operations by providing essential infrastructure services. The ISO/IEC 15288 standard was developed in order to provide guidance to all types of organizations and their enterprises in managing the life cycles of man-made systems resulting in products or services or as enabling infrastructure systems (ISO/IEC 15288 2002 and 2008). Thus, the standard can be applied for the management of defined physical, defined abstract as well as human activity systems.

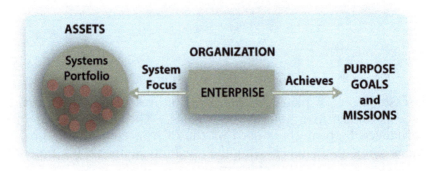

Figure 9: Achieving Purpose, Mission and Goals

The Enterprise System Aggregate

It is important for public, private and even non-profit organizations and their enterprises to understand and agree upon what their institutionalized system portfolio assets are and how they are related to each other. For this purpose, a categorization is useful. While the set of specific assets varies amongst private and public organizations and their enterprises, the categories of defined systems assets portrayed Figure 10 is representative for many enterprise. Note: in this portrayal and enterprise is viewed as a system that is an aggregate of systems.

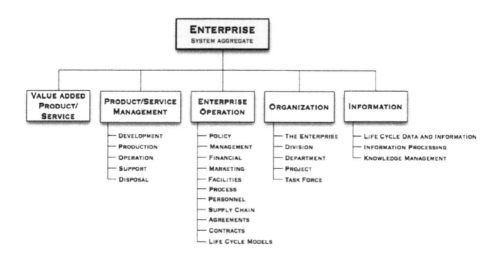

Figure 10: The Enterprise as a System of Interest

All public and private enterprises exist in order to provide some form of value added product(s) and/or service(s). These systems along with the systems for product/service management are typically the main (narrow) NSOI focus of an enterprise. However, in the wider WSOI context, all of the other systems are "enablers" for the provisioning of system products and/or system services as described in the first section of this presentation.

Even though not necessarily viewed by enterprise personnel in an explicit manner each one of these institutionalized assets forms a system composed of system elements and relationships that must, in some manner, be life cycle managed. Formally life cycle managing these systems according to appropriate life cycle models makes them explicit and leads to an improved understanding of the nature of systems and their role in the enterprise (ISO/IEC 15288 2002 and 2008). That is, those responsible for an asset as well as those influenced by the system asset develop a shared view of systems with other enterprise asset responsible parties. Such clear understanding and assignment of system asset responsibilities is a prerequisite to the effective operation of private, public and even non-profit enterprises. This should form the basis for the enterprise architecture.

Ownership of Systems

In taking a system's view of an organization, the more traditional definition of management functions is replaced by (or is defined to include) a system owner role. Ownership can involve system definitions, ownership of production, or ownership of one or more instances of a produced system. Based upon the type of system involved, system ownership can involve a wide variety of management roles as illustrated in Table 2. The reader can substitute "Manager of the X System" to identify the human who owns the corresponding system.

Asset System	*Business System*
Change Management System	*Configuration System*
Contract System	*Data System*
Engineering System	*Facilities System*
Financial System	*Human Resource System*
Information System	*Intellectual Property System*
Investment System	*IT System*
Knowledge System	*Life Cycle Process System*
Logistics System	*Marketing System*
Policy System	*Process System*
Product System	*Production System*
Program System	*Proposal System*
Public Relations System	*Quality System*
Requirements System	*Resource System*
Risk System	*Sales System*
Security System	*Service System*
Strategic System	*Supply Chain System*
Technology System	*Waste System*

Table 2: System Management Roles

Trading in System Products and Services

For instances of systems that are acquired by an enterprise for utilization (operation) as an asset, the system description is owned by the supplying organization. In such cases, the acquirer owns or licenses an instance of the system as a product or service for which rights of utilization are provided via an explicit or implicit acquirer-supplier agreement (in some cases in the form of a contract). To illustrate this acquirer-supplier relationship, consider Figure 11.

The figure indicates how a supplying enterprise from a system description template generates instances of the product or service for delivery to an acquiring enterprise. The acquiring enterprise then utilizes the system instance as an asset in achieving its purpose, goals and missions.

Naturally, the supplying enterprise has infrastructure system assets in their own portfolio that assist them in achieving their purpose, missions and goals of product and/or service development, production and support.

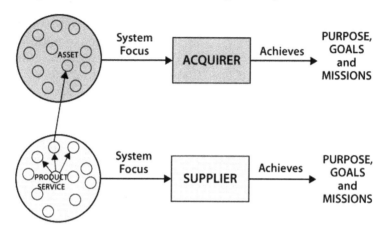

Figure 11: Trading in and Ownership of Systems

The enterprises are involved in making decisions related to the life cycle management of the system description, respective instances. In cases where the supplier provides a unique product and/or service to the acquiring organization, an agreement can be established in which both enterprises participate in the ownership and life cycle management of the system description. Whereas, for mass-produced products supplied to a variety of acquirers (consumers), the ownership of the system description typically remains with the supplying organization.

The ISO/IEC 15288 Agreement Processes are provided to assist in structuring relationships between acquirers and suppliers in a supply chain. The two processes are as follows:

Acquisition
obtain a product or service in accordance with the acquirer's requirements

Supply
provide an acquirer with a product or service that meets agreed requirements

The processes are to be used for enterprise external as well as internal acquisition and supply relationships. The outcomes of the processes as well as the activities are to be tailored in order to meet the specific needs of the enterprise and its agreements.

Figure 11 portrays one link in a supply chain. The supplier in turn can well be an acquirer of system products and services delivered by other suppliers that are assets in their system portfolio and used in the process of providing their products and/or services. For complex systems the supply chain for suppliers providing products and services can be rather long. Some examples include the supply chains related to various life cycle stages of an automobile System of Interest or health care information System of Interest. In such cases the products and services delivered by suppliers may become part of the life cycle management of a system description owned by the supplier. These outsourcing relationships and their impact upon the three fundamental transformations of systems are portrayed in Figure 12.

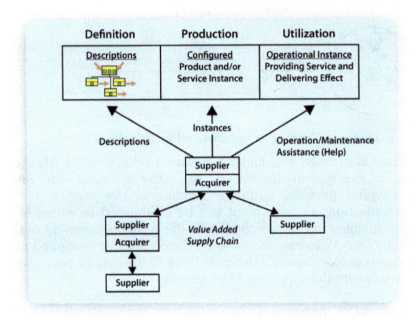

Figure 12: Outsourcing Relationships (Supply Chain)

In this figure, it is important to observe in respect to Definition that in an agreement with a supplier the outsourcing can involve delivering complete system description solutions or portions thereof. For example, a supplier could, given a system of stakeholder requirements developed by the acquirer, develop and supply a system for the functional or object based architectural design solution. The supplier in turn can be an acquirer of portions of their delivered results by outsourcing to other suppliers.

In respect to Production, the outsourcing agreement with a supplier can vary from total production responsibility to the supply of instances of system elements to be integrated by the acquirer. Once again these suppliers can be acquirers of portions of their delivery from outsourcing to other suppliers.

In respect to Utilization, for non-trivial systems, outsourcing agreements can be made with a supplier to provide for operational services, for example, operating a health care information system. Further agreements with suppliers can involve various forms of logistics aimed at sustaining a system product or service or for supplying assistance in the form of help desks. Once again suppliers that agree to provide services related to utilization can be acquirers of the services of other suppliers.

Important to all supply chains is that supplying parties contribute some form of added value to the life cycle of a System-of-Interest. The proper management of a supply chain system asset is a vital part of the operations of an enterprise. In fact, the supply chain itself is a System of Interest that is composed of acquirers and suppliers as system elements. There definitely is a structure tied together by agreement relationships. Further, the operation of the supply chain definitely results in an emergent behavior. The supply chain system becomes a vital infrastructure asset in the system portfolios of enterprises and forms the basis for extended enterprises.

With the background provided through the System Survival Kit, learning to Think and Act in Terms of Systems as well as the Enterprise System Properties, the reader is now positioned to consider how to architect enterprise systems. However first let us consider some important aspects of architecting any system.

Architecting Systems

In establishing system architectures it is vital to understand the importance of achieving balance between multiple key aspects of developing the System of Interest. These key aspects include architecture, processes, methods and tools, models and modeling, organization, and competence as described by (Bendz and Lawson 2001).

Balancing Architecture, Processes, Methods and Tools

A significant portion of the problems in dealing with complex systems is related to the fact that poor architectural underpinnings complicate virtually all process, method, and tool-related aspects of the system life cycle. This relationship of architectures to processes, methods, and tools was first identified by (Lawson 1994). Strong architectures can be characterized as being based upon a small number of driving concepts and principles and are typically developed by a small number of competent people with a shared vision leading to what is called organized simplicity as defined in the complexity concepts in the System Survival Kit.

In addition, a strong architecture only provides a minimal but sufficient set of interface standards and mechanisms. The effect of a strong architecture as portrayed in Figure 11 will tip the balance so that dependencies upon processes and related methods and tools become lighter. On the other hand, a weak architecture will tip the balance in the opposite direction so that processes, methods, and tools become heavy in order to compensate for weak architecture complexities. Unfortunately, since the mid-1970s, there has been a continued growth in complexities of computer-based systems leading to an emphasis upon heavy processes, methods, and tools. That is, emphasis has been placed upon how to do the job instead of doing a good job. A conclusion that can be drawn from this relationship is that it is worthwhile to expend efforts to develop proper architecture underpinnings. Further, it is useful to note that this relationship is a vital aspect of agility in process development and the modeling of enterprises as presented by (Bider, et. al. 2013).

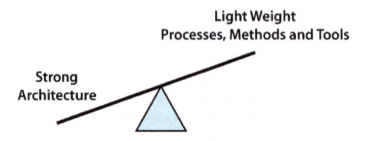

Figure 11: Balancing Architecture, Processes, Methods and Tools

Early Stages of the Life Cycle

The following ISO/IEC 15288 Technical Processes are utilized in defining a viable system solution:

Stakeholder Requirements Definition
define the requirements for a system that can provide the services needed by users and other stakeholders in a defined environment

Requirements Analysis
transform the stakeholder, requirement-driven view of desired services into a technical view of a required product that could deliver those services

Architectural Design
synthesize a solution that satisfies system requirements

The processes are tailored to meet the specific needs of various types of systems, various development strategies as well as the specific needs of organizations (enterprises) and their projects. Various forms of descriptions are produced as outcomes of applying the processes. As noted, with the system perspective provided above, it is useful to view each description as a version of the system. That is, from a System of Capabilities reflecting the need, a requirements document is an early version of the system. As a result of analyzing the requirements, the services to be provided by the system, often described as functions represent another version of the system. The architectural design leads to an identification of system elements and their interrelationships as a viable system design solution. These descriptions provide another version of the system.

The various versions reflect various concerns of stakeholders resulting in a variety of views of the system. A common classification of some useful views is as follows:

capability view – Describes the capabilities that need to be provided in order to achieve the desired system services.

operational view - Describes how the system will be utilized. Various "use cases" are identified that represent the different means of system utilization.

functional view - Describes the functions that will be required in order to provide the required system services.

object view – Describes the objects and their interactions that will be required in order to provide the required system services.

physical view - For defined physical systems, this view describes the structure of the system elements and interrelationships that will be utilized in the realization of the physical system.

activity view – Defines concrete activities of processes or procedures to be carried out in providing a service.

For non-trivial systems, there are typically multiple versions of requirement documents, functional and/or capability descriptions, and alternative architecture solutions that reflect the various views. This is the result of a development strategy involving iteration in the early stages of the life cycle until a satisfactory solution is obtained.

Note: The processes performed during the early "front-end" stages of the life cycle lead to a System Architecture. A companion standard to ISO/IEC

15288 is ISO/IEC 42010 (ISO/IEC 42010, 2011) that is concerned with Architecture Description. Since architecture has such a strong influence on eventual System Products and System Services, some of the important aspects of this standard are now considered.

Architecture Description

An international standard ISO/IEC 42010 (Architecture Description) that has been developed in order to provide guidance in architecting systems. This standard is based upon a previously successful standard IEEE 1471 that provided guidance for architecting software intensive systems (Maier, Emory and Hilliard 2004).

The standard provides a good summary of the relationship between systems, stakeholders, architecture and environment. An important aspect of describing System(s) of Interest is the differentiation between views and viewpoints.

> **architecture view** - work product expressing the architecture of a system from the perspective of system concerns

> **architecture viewpoint** - work product establishing the conventions for the construction, interpretation and use of architecture views

It can be noted that both are work products where in the case of a viewpoint it relates to the selection of the means of description used in producing views that are related to stakeholder concerns. Later we will observe that this is a central aspect of the Light-Weight Architectural Framework (LAF).

Architecture Frameworks

Architecture frameworks are defined and described in the ISO/IEC 42010 standard as follows:

architecture framework - conventions, principles and practices of architecture description established within a specific domain of application or community of stakeholders

> "An architecture framework establishes a common practice for creating, interpreting, analyzing and using architecture descriptions within a particular domain of application or stakeholder community. An architecture framework serves as a basis for creating architecture descriptions; a basis for developing architecture modelling tools and architecting methods; and as a

300

basis for processes to facilitate communication, commitments and interoperation across multiple projects and/or organizations."

The establishment of rules and conventions for viewpoints and the views is a valuable unifying factor in for example, managing a product line, organizing a group of related projects or establishing acquirer-supplier relationships for acquisition of system products and/or services. Architecture frameworks have also become popular as a means of collectively describing systems that are or interest to an enterprise that is, the enterprise architectures that is a subject of focus in this presentation.

A growing number of architecture frameworks have been established with the goal of assisting various communities of stakeholders in describing system architectures. One of the first frameworks was developed by John Zachman and bares his name, the Zachman Framework for Information Systems. (Zachman, 1987 and 2008) As a response to disorderly and costly acquisition activities, the US Department of Defense successively developed a Framework called DoDAF. In the United Kingdom, the MoDAF (Ministry of Defence) framework was created. There also exists a NATO framework called NAF. On the non-military side, there have arisen architecture frameworks for US Federal Enterprises (FEAF) and The Open Group consortium created TOGAF that instead of focusing upon system products provides a framework for processes. There are several others as well. A web search on Architecture Frameworks or any of these individual frameworks will yield many references.

Many of the frameworks have been developed by committees and consortiums and have become quite complex. One can even question the viability of the frameworks when it takes more time to learn about the framework (several hundred pages of description) than it takes to describe the system architectures that are of interest.

It is also interesting to note that several of the frameworks including DoDAF and MoDAF are now trying to retrofit the guidance provided by the ISO/IEC 15288 and ISO/IEC 42010 standards into their framework approaches. This retrofit will most likely add to the complexities to the already complex frameworks.

A Light-Weight Architecture Framework

In face of the growing complexity of architectural frameworks, there have arisen new framework approaches that reduce the complexity. Your author has been developing such an approach to architectural frameworks that builds upon an integration of the concepts and principles established in the ISO/IEC 15288 and ISO/IEC 42010 standards as well as the concrete system semantics that has been presented in the System Survival Kit.

Thus, in a manner similar to the balancing aspects of architecture, processes, methods, and tools portrayed in Figure 11, a better balance is sought in producing a Light-Weight Architecture Framework (LAF) as portrayed in Figure 12.

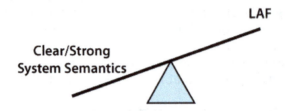

Figure 12: Balance System Semantics and Architecture Framework

Your author claims that via the establishment of the limited set of clear and strong system concepts and principles of the System Survival Kit that a Light-Weight Architecture Framework according to the balance shown in Figure 12 is feasible and desirable. One can consider the opposite situation where system concepts and principles are not well established or there exist a large number of concepts and principles that become difficult to understand and utilize result in a heavy architecture framework.

Life Cycle Actors and Their Viewpoints

LAF, in an ISO/IEC 15288 consistent manner, builds upon the fact that as a system progresses through its life cycle stages the concerns of various stakeholders are made evident. Thus, definition, development, utilization and eventual retirement of systems gives rise to a variety of views held by diverse life cycle related stakeholders as their concerns.

Thus work products produced by processes that are executed in projects during the life cycle stages are related to concerns and views that describe capabilities, requirements, functions/objects, products, services and lessons learned. The views expressed via viewpoints, correspond to system descriptions representing the togetherness (relationship and connection) properties of elements of the view. For example togetherness can be represented by text, structured text, or models such as system maps showing static groupings of related elements, diagrammatical or pictorial representations of elements and flows of material, data, information and/or energy or control of sequencing in the case of activities carried out by machines or humans. With this perspective, we can constitute that an architecture description is based upon a collection of described systems representing different life cycle related views of a System of Interest developed according to viewpoints as enumerated in Table 3.

Stakeholder	Views	Potential Viewpoints – Model Kinds
Owner	Capabilities	System Maps, Rich Pictures, Entity-Relationship, Systemigram
Conceiver	Requirements	Requirements Structured Text, Entity-Relationship, Influence Diagrams, Use Cases, Systemigram
Developer	Functions/Objects	Functions/Objects IDEF, Class Diagrams, UML, SysML
Producer	Product/Service	Product/Service Parts List
User/Maintainer	Service Delivered	Service Delivered Behavior Diagrams, Use Cases, Entity-Relationship, Systemigram
All	Lessons Learned	Stories, Archetypes, Metrics

Table 3: Stakeholder Views and Potential Viewpoint Description Methodologies

There are a variety of modeling methodologies that can be used to produce the various system descriptions as work products as indicated in Table 3. The following briefly describes some of the methodologies:

System maps – Systems maps are essentially structure diagrams. Each element or sub-system is contained in a circle or oval and a line is drawn round a group of elements or sub-systems to show that the things outside the line are part of the environment while those inside the line are part of the system. There are NO lines connecting elements, sub-systems or systems in a systems map; it is purely a statement of the structure as you see it in your mind.

Influence diagrams – These are developed from systems maps and indicate where one element in the situation has some influence over another. Arrows indicate the direction of the influence and the lines between elements may be of different thickness, shading or color in order to distinguish strong and weak influence. Strictly speaking, influence should only be shown from elements at a higher or at the same level in the system; that is to say, subsystems cannot influence systems and sub-systems and systems cannot influence the environment.

Entity Relationship Model (ERM) – ERM in software engineering is an abstract and conceptual representation of data. Entity-relationship modeling is a relational schema database modeling method, used to produce a type of conceptual schema or semantic data model of a system, often a relational database, and its requirements in a top-down fashion.

Systemigrams – is a word derived from "systemic" and "diagram"' and portrays a System-of-Interest which is described by text that is structured according to systemic principles. A Systemigram should not be constructed in attempt to capture first thoughts, but rather as a translation of the words and meanings that appertain to a piece of structured writing.

Unified Modeling Language (UML) – UML is a standardized general-purpose modeling language in the field of software engineering. UML includes a set of graphical notation techniques to create abstract models of specific systems.

Systems Modeling Language (SysML) – SysML is a Domain-Specific Modeling language for systems engineering. It supports the specification, analysis, design, verification and validation of a broad range of systems and System-of-Systems. SysML was originally developed by an open source specification project, and includes an open source license for distribution and use. SysML is defined as an extension of a subset of the Unified Modeling Language (UML) using UML's profile mechanism.

Integration DEFinition (IDEF) – IDEF is a family of modeling languages in the field of systems and software engineering. They cover a range of uses from function modeling to information, simulation, object-oriented analysis and design and knowledge acquisition. These "definition languages" have become standard modeling techniques.

Class diagrams – In the Unified Modeling Language (UML), a class diagram is a type of static structure diagram that describes the structure of a system by showing the system's classes, their attributes, and the relationships between the classes.

Rich pictures – Rich pictures were developed as part of Peter Checkland's Soft Systems Methodology as an approach to help capture appreciation and understanding of messy complex situations.

The selection of the viewpoint description methodologies and model kinds is central to systems life cycle management. In fact, since the methodologies are systems themselves, they become a part of the Enterprise systems portfolio. That is, they become the standards for predefined views that indicate what type of viewpoint definition is to be deployed for the work products related to processes applied during the various stages. Ideally, the set of viewpoints can become an enterprise standard for all system assets or for classes of system assets as well as Respondent Systems that are to be life cycle managed. As mentioned earlier the framework can support those systems that are relevant for development of a product line or support the parties involved in an acquirer-supplier relationship concerning standards for description and communication. On a broader scale, an architecture framework such as LAF can be used in an organizational or enterprise wide context thus providing standards for description and communication to all enterprise stakeholders.

Enterprise Intellectual Capital

During the life cycle of the sustained value-added and infrastructure system assets that are managed by an enterprise, data, information and knowledge is gathered. In respect to the Fundamental Life Cycle transformations identified earlier, the collection of data, interpretation as information, potential measurement and assimilation as knowledge is portrayed in Figure 13.

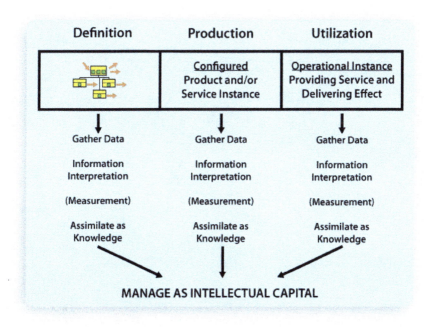

Figure 13: Assimilating Knowledge as Intellectual Capital

The data, information and knowledge gained during the life cycle are of various types. It can be related to system definition, to the production of instances as products or services or to the services provided during utilization. It can also be process knowledge related to the performance of the processes leading to the system definition and/or to a product or service in various life cycle stages. A prerequisite is of course the definition of an information model for the system.

Unified Data and Information Management

In building the enterprise information model, it is useful to use as concepts the terminology established by the ISO/IEC 15288 as a basis for classification. It could be done according to the data and information generated from processes that are to be implemented for the various stages of the life cycle; it could be also more generally based only upon the stages. An illustrative information model classification is portrayed in Figure 14. In this model a hierarchy of information classes is established where the leaves (end nodes) of the hierarchy identify classes into which data and information is to be gathered. Do not forget that the information may well be based upon models (textual or graphic) and can include voice and video media.

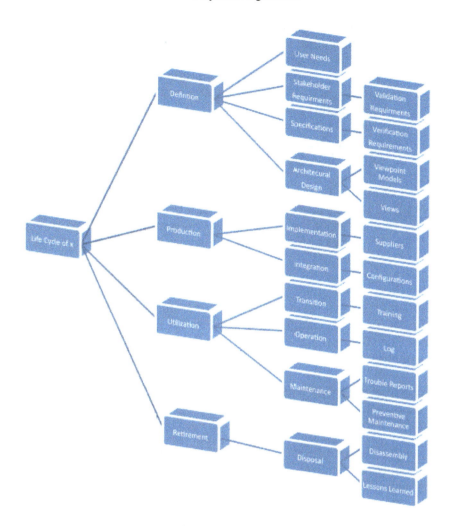

Figure 14: An Illustrative Life Cycle Information Model

The figure illustrates data and information collected for technical processes; however it can and should be extended with data and information related to the other ISO/IEC 15288 standard categories; namely Agreements, Organizational Project-Enabling and Project. The collections of data, information, measurements and knowledge associated with baselines and configurations are very germane and must be taken into account in organizing the data and information. Baselines can be associated with project information (scope, cost, schedule) or system product and/or service. Furthermore, some baselines actually represent a configuration in respect to descriptions and or product/service instances. As systems progress through the establishment of baselines and the creation of configurations, the knowledge gathered about the system, product, service, and processes is vital in the decision making of the CCB as well as in providing guidance in making changes.

As indicated in Figures 13 and 14, the assimilated knowledge becomes part of the intellectual capital of the enterprise, its groups, teams and individuals. Thus, enterprises are wise to formalize the structure of and the processes related to the gathering of knowledge in a Knowledge Management System. Naturally, this system like all others has a life cycle that must be managed (Herald, Berkemeyer, and Lawson 2004).

Within the domain of a Knowledge Management System, the Life Cycle Models as well as the sets of Processes that are used in the management of Systems of Interest from the system portfolio is true enterprise intellectual capital. They must be captured in the information model of the Knowledge Management System.

With intellectual capital that assists in understanding the dynamic operations of systems as well as in understanding how to effectively structure and operate change management and life cycle management, an enterprise is well equipped with the wisdom required to "Think" and "Act" in terms of systems.

Implementing Management Systems

Many enterprises and the organizations they belong to utilize management systems in their operation. In addition to Quality Management Systems defined in (ISO 9001 2008), a number of other management system standards may be required within an organization. The (ISO 14001 2004) Environmental Management System standard is one of them; however there are standards for information security, product safety, occupational health and other areas that also place requirements on management systems.

As mentioned in the introduction, the ISO 9001 standard refers to the use of system approach to managing processes. Given the background on systems presented in this presentation, we can now consider viewing the implementation of management systems from a unified system perspective.

Both ISO 9001 and ISO 14001 promote the utilization of a system approach to the management of quality, respectively of environmental factors. Being systems, they themselves must be life cycle managed by the organization and enterprise and, hopefully, through some form of Change Control Board. An organization planning to implement a management system according to ISO 9001 and/or ISO 14001 can utilize ISO/IEC 15288 as the basis for managing the life cycles of their management systems. The

308

reflection of this life cycle need and the encapsulation of the system elements of an ISO 9001 management system are portrayed in Figures 15.

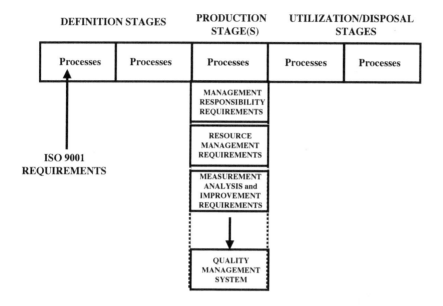

Figure 15: Quality Management System Life Cycle and Composition

Note: This is called a T-diagram (Lawson 2010) where the life cycle of a system composed of stages and the processes used in the stages are portrayed horizontally; whereas the system product or service composed of system elements integrated into a System of Interest is portrayed vertically as a result of some form of "production."

The relationships between the system elements are portrayed and defined in the system models provided in the ISO 9001 standard. The concrete product of the quality management system is documents (i.e. manuals) that are utilized in placing requirements on organization/enterprise activities, products and services. The life cycle management of these management systems provides a structured means of customizing (tailoring) and integrating the requirements of the standards with the realities of an organization. A vital part of this tailoring is the development of policies and procedures. The Enterprise then must assure, via policy and procedures, that system life cycles stages and their constituent processes incorporate, at appropriate places, the requirements of the Quality Management System via the utilization of the manuals.

The deployment (Utilization) of the ISO 9001 as well as other management systems such as ISO 14001 involves their use as stakeholder requirement inputs to all other systems that the organization produces in the form of products and/or services or uses as institutionalized system assets for their own business management and infrastructure needs. This utilization is portrayed in Figure 16.

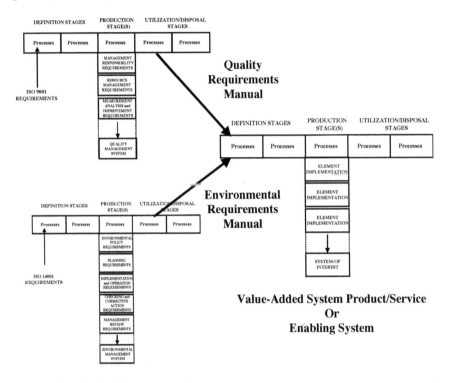

Figure 16: Applying Quality and Environment System Requirements

The quality and environmental aspects are taken into account in planning for systems related work that results in successive versions of a System of Interest. In particular, in the early stages of the life cycle the requirements are analyzed and then distributed to appropriate stages, processes and activities. Furthermore, the requirements related to product and service properties are provided to Respondent System projects that will perform the actual transformations on system definitions, produce the products and services, operate (perhaps via a line organization) and then potentially dispose of the system product or service.

Through the distribution of requirements into life cycles, their verification and validation for customer satisfaction, the framework of ISO/IEC 15288 provides an expedient mechanism for the implementation of ISO 9001 and ISO 14001 as well as other management system standards. Continual management review of the achievement of requirements by CCBs is provided in stage decision gates. Further, when the stages of the life cycle are iterated in the refinement of a system product or service or in producing new versions, the framework continues to provide decision points so that quality and/or environmental requirements remain in focus.

Conclusions

Understanding the operation of an enterprise is a prerequisite to being able to develop and utilize enterprise architectures. In this presentation, we have considered how a unified system perspective could be developed and utilized in providing the enterprise architecture as well as in operating an enterprise.

By consistently following a standards based approach as well as the concepts and principles of the System Survival Kit, the Light-Weight Architectural Framework (LAF) provides a unifying approach to systems within an enterprise. This is the hypothesis provided in this presentation that is in the research stage and needs to be further developed, applied and analyzed. Your assistance in this activity is sincerely appreciated.

About the Author

Harold (Bud) Lawson has been active in the systems arena since 1958 in both industrial and academic environments. He has been involved in several pioneering efforts in hardware and software technologies including being the inventor of the pointer variable concept for programming languages. He has contributed to of a variety of successful computer-based systems including high voltage power dispatching, automatic train control and automotive components. Dr. Lawson has held professorial appointments at several universities including the Polytechnic Institute of Brooklyn, University of California, Irvine, Universidad Politecnica de Barcelona, Linköping University, Royal Technical University, University of Malaya and Keio University. Since 1988, he has been a full-time independent consultant in the systems engineering of computer-based systems. He was the Head of the Swedish Delegation to ISO/IEC JTC1 SC7 WG7 as well as being the elected architect of the ISO/IEC 15288 standard. He received the Bachelor of Science degree from Temple University and the PhD at the Royal Technical University, Stockholm. He is a Fellow of the ACM, Fellow and Life Member of the IEEE, Fellow of INCOSE and IEEE Charles Babbage Award Computer Pioneer.

References

Ackoff, R. L. 1971. "Towards a System of Systems Concepts." Management Science, 17(11).

Arnold, S., and Lawson, H. 2004. "Viewing Systems from a Business Management Perspective, Systems Engineering." The Journal of The International Council on Systems Engineering, Vol. 7, No. 3, pp 229-242.

Beer, S. 1985. Diagnosing the System for Organisations, Wiley, Chichester and New York.

Bendz, J. and Lawson, H. 2001. "A Model for Deploying Life-Cycle Process Standards in the Change Management of Complex Systems, Systems Engineering." The Journal of The International Council on Systems Engineering, Vol. 4, No. 2, pp 107-117.

Bilder, I., Bellinger, G. and Perjons, E. 2013. "Modeling an Agile Enterprise: Reconciling Systems and Process Thinking." appearing in this book.

Boardman, J. and Sauser, B. 2008. Systems Thinking – Coping with 21st Century Problems, CRC Press, Boca Raton, FL.

Boyd, J. R. 1987. "An Organic Design for Command and Control, A Discourse on Winning and Losing." Unpublished lecture notes (Maxwell AFB, Ala. Air University).

Checkland, P. 1993. Systems Thinking, Systems Practice, John Wiley, Chichester, UK.

Checkland, P. 1999. Systems Thinking, Systems Practice – Includes a 30 year Retrospective, JohnWiley, Chichester, UK.

Checkland, P. and Sholes, J. 1990. Soft System Methodology in Action, Wiley, New York.

Flood, R.L. and Carson, E.R. 1998. Dealing with Complexity: An Introduction to the Theory and Application of Systems Science, Second Edition, Penum Press, London and New York.

Flood, R.L. 1998. Rethinking the Fifth Discipline: Learning within the unknowable, Routledge, London and New York.

Fornell, C. 2001. "The Science of Satisfaction." Harvard Business Review, 79, 3, March 120-121.

Forrester, J.W. 1975. Collected Papers of Jay W. Forrester, Pegasus Communications.

Herald, T., Berkemeyer, W. and Lawson, H. 2004. "A Knowledge Management System Life Cycle Description Using the ISO/IEC 15288 Standard" Proceedings of the INCOSE Conference, Toulouse, France.

ISO 9001 2008. Quality Management Systems, International Standardization Organization, 1, rue de Varembe, CH-1211 Geneve 20, Switzerland.

ISO 14001 2004. Environmental Management Systems -- Requirements with Guidance for Use, International Standardization Organization, 1, rue de Varembe, CH-1211 Geneve 20, Switzerland.

ISO/IEC 42010 2011. Architecture description – International Standardization Organization, 1, rue de Varembe, CH-1211 Geneve 20, Switzerland.

ISO/IEC 15288 2002. Information technology – System life cycle processes, International Standardization Organization/International Electrotechnical Commission, 1, rue de Varembe, CH-1211 Geneve 20, Switzerland.

ISO/IEC 15288 2008. Systems and software engineering - System life cycle processes, International Standardization Organization/International Electrotechnical Commission, 1, rue de Varembe, CH-1211 Geneve 20, Switzerland.

ISO/IEC/IEEE 15939 Measurement Process, International Standardization Organization/International Electrotechnical Commission, 1, rue de Varembe, CH-1211 Geneve 20, Switzerland.

Kaplan, R.S. Norton, D.P. 1996. The Balanced Scorecard: Translating Strategy into Action, Harvard Business School Press, Boston, MA.

Lawson, H., and Martin, J. N. 2008. "On the Use of Concepts and Principles for Improving Systems Engineering Practice.", Proceedings of the INCOSE International Conference, Utrecht.

Lawson, H. 2010. A Journey Through the Systems Landscape, College Publications, Kings College, UK.

Maeir, M., Emory, D., Hilliard, R. 2004. "ANSI/IEEE 1471 and Systems Engineering." The Journal of The International Council on Systems Engineering, Vol. 7, No. 3.

Pyster, A. and D.H. Olwell (eds). 2013. The Guide to the Systems Engineering Body of Knowledge (SEBoK), v. 1.1.1. Hoboken, NJ: The Trustees of the Stevens Institute of Technology.

Roedler, G., Rhodes, D., Jones, C., Schimmoller, H. 2010. Systems Engineering Leading Indicators Guide, Version 2.0, INCOSE-TP-2005-001-03. International Council on Systems Engineering (INCOSE), San Diego, CA.

Senge, P.M. 1990. The Fifth Discipline: The Art & Practice of The Learning Organization, Currency Doubleday, New York.

Senge, P.M., Klieiner, A., Roberts, C., Ross, R.B., and Smith, B.J. 1994. The Fifth Discipline Fieldbook: Strategies and Tools for Building a Learning Organization, Currency Doubleday, New York.

von Bertalanffy, L. 1968. General system theory: foundations, development, applications (Rev. ed.). New York: Braziller.

Weaver, W. 1948. "Science and Complexity." American Science, 36 pp 536-544.

Zachman, J.A. 1987. "A Framework for Information Systems Architecture." IBM Systems Journal, 26(3).

Zachman, J. A. 2008. The Zachman Framework™: A Concise Definition, Zachman International.

Transforming the Enterprise Using a Systems Approach

James N. Martin

Abstract

Enterprise Systems Engineering (ESE) is an emerging discipline that can be used to more confidently and rapidly create the essential changes for the modern enterprise to survive in these days of enormous economic and social uncertainty. Systems Engineering (SE) could have much to offer in enabling this transformation, but significant enhancements to traditional SE tools and methods must be brought to bear. This chapter describes a set of ESE principles and concepts that enables greater benefits when using the systems approach for enterprise transformation. These enhancements include technical activities, of course, but they also address the substantial leadership and managerial challenges at the enterprise level. We need to start applying more systems thinking when architecting the enterprise.

Keywords

Systems Thinking, Systems Engineering, Enterprise transformation

Introduction

This chapter provides an introduction to systems engineering (SE) at the enterprise level as compared to "traditional" SE (TSE) (sometimes called "conventional" or "classical" SE) performed in a development project. The concept of *enterprise* was instrumental in the great expansion of world trade in the 17th century[1] and again during the Industrial Revolution of the 18th and 19th centuries. The world may be at the cusp of another global revolution enabled by the Information Age and the technologies and cultures of the Internet.[2]

The discipline of SE now has the unique opportunity of providing the tools and methods for the next round of enterprise transformations. (Rouse 2006) Enterprise systems engineering (ESE) is an emerging discipline that focuses on frameworks, tools, and problem-solving approaches for dealing with the inherent complexities of the enterprise (Rebovich and White 2010).

ESE, for the purpose of this chapter, is defined as the application of SE principles, concepts, and methods to the planning, design, improvement, and operation of an enterprise. To enable more efficient and effective enterprise transformation, the enterprise needs to be looked at "as a system," rather than as a collection of functions connected solely by information systems and shared facilities (Rouse 2009). While a systems perspective is required for dealing with the enterprise, this is rarely the task or responsibility of people who call themselves systems engineers.

Creating Value

The basic concepts that drive the enterprise context of SE are shown in Figure 1. There are three types of organization of interest to ESE – businesses, projects, and teams.

---

[1] "The Dutch East India Company... was a chartered company established in 1602, when the States-General of the Netherlands granted it a 21-year monopoly to carry out colonial activities in Asia. It was the first multinational corporation in the world and the first company to issue stock. It was also arguably the world's first megacorporation, possessing quasi-governmental powers, including the ability to wage war, negotiate treaties, coin money, and establish colonies." (emphasis added, en.wikipedia.org/wiki/Dutch_East_India_Company)

[2] This new revolution is being enabled by cheap and easily usable technology, global availability of information and knowledge, and increased mobility and adaptability of human capital. The enterprise level of analysis is only feasible now because organizations can work together to form enterprises in a much more fluid manner.

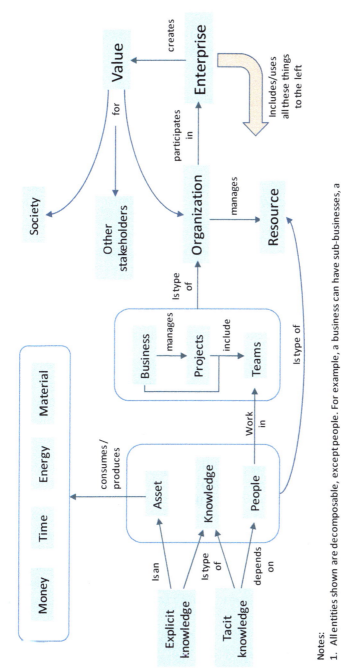

Figure 1. Organizations Manage Resources to Create Enterprise Value

Notes:

1. All entities shown are decomposable, except people. For example, a business can have sub-businesses, a project can have subprojects, a resource can have sub-resources, an enterprise can have sub-enterprises.

2. All entities have other names. For example, a program can be a project comprising several subprojects (often called merely projects). Business can be an agency, team can be group, value can be utility, etc.

3. There is no attempt to be prescriptive in the names chosen for this diagram. The main goal of this is to show how this chapter uses these terms and how they are related to each other in a conceptual manner.

A typical business[3] participates in multiple enterprises through its portfolio of projects. Large SE projects can be enterprises in their own right, with participation by many different businesses, and may be organized as a number of sub-projects.

A key choice for businesses that conduct SE is to what extent, if at all, they seek to optimize their use of resources – people, knowledge, assets – across teams, projects, and business units. (Optimization of resources is not the goal in itself, but rather a means to achieve the goal of maximizing value for the enterprise and its stakeholders.) At one extreme in a product-oriented organization, projects may be responsible for hiring, training, and firing their own staff, and managing all assets required for their delivery of products or services.

At the other extreme in a functional organization, the projects delegate almost all their work to functional groups. In between these two extremes is a matrix organization that is used to give functional specialists a "home" between project assignments. A full discussion of organizational approaches and situations along with their applicability in enabling SE for the organization is provided in the SEBOK (Sillitto 2012).

SE skills, techniques, and resources are relevant to many enterprise functions, and a well-founded SE capability can make a substantial contribution at the enterprise level as well as at the project level. Sillitto (2012) discusses enabling SE in the organization, while this chapter focuses on the cross-organizational functions at the enterprise level.

Knowledge is a key resource for SE. There are generally two kinds of knowledge: explicit and tacit. Explicit knowledge can be written down or incorporated in computer codes. Much of the relevant SE and systems knowledge, however, is "tacit knowledge" that only exists within the heads of people and in the context of relationships that people form with each other (e.g., team, project, and business level knowledge). The ability of an organization to create value is critically dependent on the people it chooses to employ, on what they know, how they work together, and how well they are organized and motivated to contribute to the organization's purpose.

Organizational Design

The competencies of individuals are important to the overall organizational capability. The organizational capability is also a function of

---

[3] Our use of the word "business" is not intended to mean only for-profit commercial ventures. As used here it also includes government agencies and not-for-profit organizations. Business is the activity of providing goods and services involving financial, commercial, and industrial aspects.

how the people, teams, projects, and businesses are organized. The organizational design should specify the roles, authorities, responsibilities, and accountabilities (RARA) of the organizational units to ensure more efficient and effective operations.

Effectiveness of enterprise operations is certainly driven by management principles, concepts, and approaches, but it is also largely driven by its leadership principles, concepts, and approaches. Sillitto (2012) discusses how to organize for effective performance of SE.

Organizational structure is tightly tied to creating value for the enterprise's various stakeholders. Since the enterprise is made up of various elements including people, processes, technologies, and assets, then the organizational structure of the people and the allocation of responsibilities for executing portions of the value stream is a "design decision" for the enterprise and hence is a key element of properly performing ESE. This organizational design should be based on organizational design patterns and their tradeoffs.

Capabilities and Competencies

The word "capability" is used in SE in the sense of "the ability to do something useful under a particular set of conditions." This chapter discusses three different kinds of capability: organizational capability, system capability, and operational capability. The relationships among these elements are illustrated in Figure 2, which connects to the previous figure at "people," "organization," and "enterprise." New systems (with new or enhanced system capabilities) are developed to enhance enterprise operational capability in response to stakeholder's concerns about a problem situation.

These stakeholders are the ultimate arbiters of value for the system to be delivered. Organizational, system, and operational capabilities cannot be designed, improved and implemented independently. The key to understanding the dependencies between capabilities is through architecture modeling and analysis as part of the overall Enterprise Capability-Based Planning Analysis activities described later in this chapter.

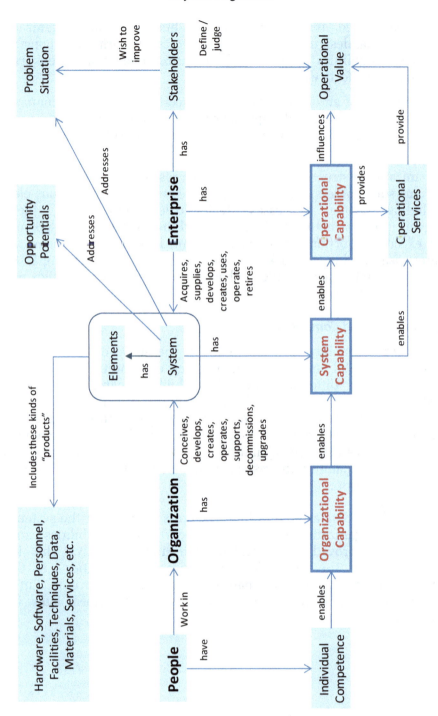

**Figure 2. Individual Competence Enables Organizational,
System & Operational Capabilities**

Organizational capabilities are addressed in (Sillitto 2012), and individual competencies are addressed in (Davidz et al. 2012). This chapter, however, focuses on the operational capabilities of an enterprise and the contribution of these capabilities to stakeholder value. Notice that the organization or enterprise will deal with either the system as a whole or with only one or a few of its elements. These elements are not necessarily hard items, like hardware and software, but can also include "soft" items, like people, processes, principles, policies, practices, organizations, doctrine, theories, beliefs, and so on.

Overview of the Chapter

This chapter will first provide some background on the scope of Enterprise Systems Engineering (ESE), imperatives for enterprise transformation, and potential SE enablers for the enterprise. It will then discuss how ESE relates to systems of systems (SoS). Next it will describe related business activities and necessary extensions of Traditional SE (TSE) that enable ESE activities. Each of the ESE process activities is discussed in the overall context of the unique circumstances in the operation of a large and complex enterprise.

Although some would say that the discipline of Enterprise Architecture (EA) already addresses the key challenges of transforming an enterprise, it is the considered opinion of this author as well as many others that EA is a necessary but not sufficient tool in the ESE toolbox. EA, however, is still considered to be one of the key activities of ESE, along with enterprise requirements engineering.

Fundamentals

Scope of Enterprise SE

Computer and communications technologies make it easier to integrate activities across the enterprise, but this does not necessarily make the enterprise more effective and efficient. To enable this to happen, one needs to look at the whole enterprise as a system, rather than as a collection of functions connected solely by information systems and shared facilities. (Ring 2004b; Valerdi, Nightingale, and Blackburn 2009)

Essential Challenges. Enterprises face strategic challenges (Rouse 2009) that are essential to address in order to ensure that the enterprise will succeed:

- Growth: Increasing impact, perhaps in saturated or declining "markets"

- Value: Enhancing relationships of processes to benefits and costs
- Focus: Pursuing opportunities and avoiding diversions
- Change: Competing creatively while maintaining continuity
- Future: Investing in inherently unpredictable outcomes
- Knowledge: Transforming information to insights to programs
- Time: Carefully allocating the organization's scarcest resource

To address these challenges, one recognizes that the central source of value in the enterprise is in its people. "Understanding and supporting the interests of an enterprise's diverse stakeholders—and finding the 'sweet spot' among the many competing interests—is a central aspect of discerning the work of the enterprise as a system and creating mechanisms to enhance this work." (Rouse 2009) The enterprise should be treated as "intelligent" in order to maximize the gains achieved through enterprise transformation. (Ring 2004a)

Enterprise Transformation. Enterprises are constantly transforming, whether at the individual level (wherein individuals alter their work practices) or at the enterprise level (large-scale planned strategic changes). (Srinivasan 2010) These changes are a response on the part of the enterprise to evolving opportunities and emerging threats. It is not merely a matter of doing work better, but sometimes doing different work instead (which is often a more important result). Value is created through the execution of business processes. However, not all processes necessarily contribute to overall value. (Rouse 2005, 138-150) It is important to focus on process to determine how it contributes to the overall value stream.

After gaining a good understanding of business processes, the next main concern is how best to deploy and manage the enterprise's assets: human, financial, and physical. The key challenge in transforming an enterprise is, in the midst of all this change, continuing to satisfice[4] key stakeholders. (Nightingale and Srinivasan 2011)

Transformation Context. Enterprise transformation occurs in the external context of the *economy* and *markets*[5] as shown in Figure 3 (Rouse 2009). The term "intraprise" is used here to denote the collection of many

---

[4] "Satisfice" means to decide on and pursue a course of action satisfying the minimum requirements to achieve a goal. For the enterprise as a whole, it is often impossible to completely satisfy all stakeholders all the time given their competing and conflicting concerns and interests. Therefore, the concept of "satisficing" is a very necessary and important element used for the effective execution of ESE practices.

[5] Of course, in the public sector the enterprise's "market" is commonly known as its "constituency."

systems internal to the enterprise. The intraprise includes more than just the information systems—it also includes the social and cultural systems in the enterprise.[6]

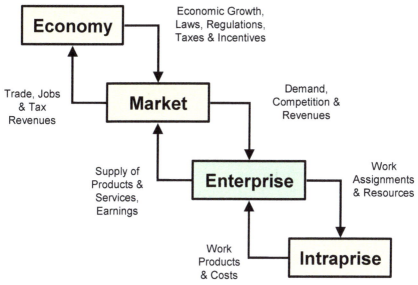

Figure 3. Context for Enterprise Transformation
(Source: Rouse, 2009)

Modeling the Enterprise. Models of the enterprise can serve as the basis for understanding the enterprise in its context of markets and economies. Figure 4 shows the various drivers (or inputs) of an enterprise and its potential outcomes (or outputs). (Rouse 2009) Work processes within (and outside) the enterprise serve to create useful outcomes for customers, end users, and other stakeholders. External drivers can cause enterprise state changes as well as influence the operations of these processes.

Enterprise architecture can be a key enabler for modeling and can serve as a basis for transformation. (Vernadat 1996; Bernus, Nemes and Schmidt 2003; Nightingale and Rhodes 2004) Enterprise architecture can be used to provide a set of models and views to help understand how the parts of the enterprise fit together (or don't). (Giachetti 2010)

---

[6] See (Sillitto 2012) for more details on how the social and cultural aspects of the organization impact the performance of SE on projects.

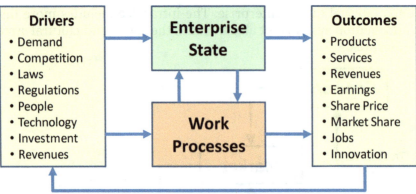

Figure 4. Drivers and Outcomes for the Enterprise
(Source: Rouse, 2009)

Treating the Enterprise as a System. To enable more efficient and effective enterprise transformation, the enterprise needs to be looked at "as a system," rather than as a collection of functions connected solely by information systems and shared facilities (Rouse 2009). What distinguishes the design of enterprise systems from product/service systems is the inclusion of people as a component of the system, not merely as a user/operator of the system.

> The term "enterprise system" has taken on a narrow meaning of only the information system an organization uses. Research and project experience has taught us that to design a good enterprise system, we need to adopt a much broader understanding of enterprise systems. The greater view of enterprise systems is inclusive of the processes the system supports, the people who work in the system, and the information [and knowledge] content of the system. (Giachetti 2010)

Enterprise Engineering. Another distinction is that "enterprise design does not occur at a single point in time like the design of most systems. Instead, enterprises evolve over time and are constantly changing, or are constantly being designed." [emphasis in original] (Giachetti 2010) Giachetti calls this new discipline "enterprise engineering." We consider the enterprise engineering set of practices to be equivalent to what we call ESE in this chapter.

> The body of knowledge for enterprise engineering is evolving under such titles as enterprise engineering, business engineering, and enterprise architecture.... Many systems and software engineering principles are applicable to enterprise engineering, but enterprise engineering's unique complexities require additional principles.... Enterprise engineering's intent is to deliver a targeted level of enterprise performance in terms of shareholder value or customer satisfaction.... Enterprise engineering methods include modeling;

simulation; total quality management; change management; and bottleneck, cost, workflow, and value-added analysis. (Joannou 2007)

In Pursuit of Value

Based on his theory of enterprise transformation, Rouse (2005, 279-295) has identified four alternative perspectives that tend to drive the need for transformation:

- Value Opportunities: The lure of greater success via market and/or technology opportunities prompts transformation initiatives.

- Value Threats: The danger of anticipated failure due to market and/or technology threats prompts transformation initiatives.

- Value Competition: Other players' transformation initiatives prompt recognition that transformation is necessary to continued success.

- Value Crises: Steadily declining market performance, cash flow problems, etc., prompt recognition that transformation is necessary for the enterprise to survive.

Work processes can be enhanced, streamlined, eliminated, and invented to help in the pursuit of enhanced value. These process changes should be aligned with enterprise strategy to maximize value produced by the enterprise. (Hammer and Champy 1993)

Enabling the Enterprise

ESE, by virtue of its inherent transdisciplinarity (Sage 2000, 158-169) in dealing with problems that are large in scale and scope, can better enable the enterprise to become more effective and efficient. The complex nature of many enterprise problems and situations usually goes beyond the abilities of standard tools and techniques provided to business school graduates and certified project managers. ESE can augment the standard business management methods using the tools and methods from the SE discipline to more robustly analyze and evaluate the enterprise as a holistic system. A more general perspective for dealing with the enterprise as consisting of scale, granularity, mindset, and timeframe, is provided in (White 2007) and (White and McCarter 2009, 71-105).

ESE can provide the enablers to address the concerns of enterprise executives as shown in Table 1. (Rouse 2009) The methods for dealing with, and the special characteristics of, complex adaptive systems must be properly considered when adapting TSE practices for use at the enterprise level. (von Bertalanffy 1968; Weinberg and Weinberg 1988; Miller and Page 2007; Rouse 2008, 17-25) For an approach to complex adaptive systems engineering (CASE), refer to (White 2008, 1-16) and (White and McCarter 2009, 71-105).

Table 1. Executive Concerns and SE Enablers (Source: (Rouse 2009))

Executive Concerns	SE Enablers
Identifying ends, means, and scope and candidate changes	System complexity analysis to compare "as is" and "to be" enterprises
Evaluating changes in terms of process behaviors and performance	Organizational simulation of process flows and relationships
Assessing economics in terms of investments, operating costs, and returns	Economic modeling in terms of cash flows, volatility, and options
Defining the new enterprise in terms of processes and their integration	Enterprise architecting in terms of workflow, processes, and levels of maturity
Designing a strategy to change the culture for selected changes	Organizational and cultural change via leadership, vision, strategy, and incentives
Developing transformation action plans in terms of what, when, and who	Implementation planning in terms of tasks, schedule, people, and information

The Enterprise Level

Agility and Robustness

For a large enterprise to survive in the 21st century, it must be agile and robust (Dove 1999 and 2001). The enterprise needs agile information systems to enable agile decision making. (Rouse 2006a) Handy (1992, 59-67) describes a federalist approach called "New Federalism" that identifies the need for structuring of loosely coupled organizations to help them adapt to the rapid changes inherent in the Information Age.

This leads to the need for virtual organizations where alliances can be quickly formed to handle the challenges of newly identified threats and a rapidly changing marketplace. (Handy 1995, 2-8) Handy sets out to define a number of federalist political principles that could be applicable to both SoS and Families of Systems (FOS). Handy's principles have been tailored to the domain of SE and management by Sage and Cuppan (2001, 325-345):

- Subsidiarity
- Interdependence

- Uniform and standardized way of doing business
- Separation of powers
- Dual citizenship

Scales of SE

One purpose of an enterprise is to explicitly establish operational dependence between systems that the enterprise owns and/or operates in order to maximize the efficiency and effectiveness of the enterprise as a whole. Therefore, it is usually more effective to treat an Enterprise System and an SoS as different types of things, with different properties and characteristics. This distinction is illustrated in Figure 5, where three corresponding categories of SE are shown. (DeRosa 2005) Details regarding this concept of ESE can be found in (Rebovich and White 2010, 477).

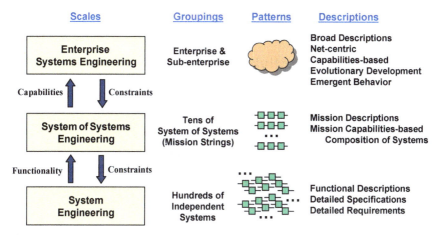

Figure 5. Different Groupings and Patterns Revealed at Different Scales (Source: (DeRosa 2005))

Relationships between Enterprise and SoS

An enterprise may require a particular operational capability that is brought into being by connecting together a chain of systems that together achieve that capability. Any one of these systems in the chain cannot by itself provide this capability. The desired capability is the emergent property of this chain of systems. This chain of systems is sometimes called an SoS. However the enterprise that requires this capability rarely has direct control over all the systems necessary to provide this full capability. This situation is illustrated in Figure 6. (Martin 2010)

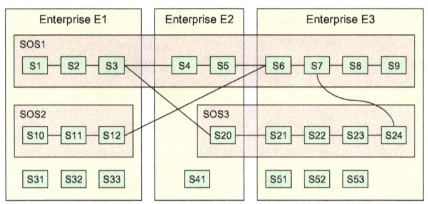

Figure 6. Relationships between an Enterprise and SoS's
(Source: (Martin 2010))

Enterprise E1 (in the example shown above) has full control over SoS2 but not full control over SoS1. TSE can be readily applied to the individual systems (S1, S2, ..., S53) shown within each enterprise, but it needs to be augmented with additional activities to handle SoS and enterprise kinds of issues. These activities are identified and described later in this chapter.

Related Business Activities

The following business management activities can be supported by ESE activities:

- Mission & Strategic Planning
- Business Processes & Information Management
- Performance Management
- Portfolio Management
- Resource Allocation & Budgeting
- Program & Project Management

Within the enterprise, TSE is typically applied inside a Project to engineer a single system (or perhaps a small number of related systems). If there is a SoS to be engineered then this might be handled at the Program level, but is sometimes handled at the Project level, depending on the size and complexity of the SoS. Figure 7 shows how these business activities relate to each other as well as the relative scope of ESE and product SE (Martin 2010).

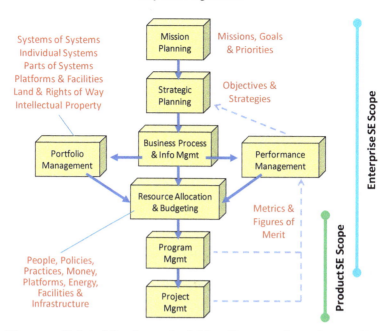

Figure 7. Related Business Activities (Source: (Martin 2010))

Shown in this manner, these business activities can be considered to be separate processes with a clear precedence in terms of which process drives other processes. TSE often uses "requirements" to specify the essential features and functions of a product system. An enterprise, on the other hand, typically uses goals and objectives to specify the fundamental characteristics of desired enterprise operational capabilities. The enterprise objectives and strategies are used in portfolio management to discriminate between options and to select the appropriate balanced portfolio of systems and other enterprise resources.

Business Management Cycles

PDCA stands for plan-do-check-act and is a commonly used iterative management process as seen in Figure 8. It is also known as the Deming circle or the Shewhart cycle after its two key proponents. (Deming 1986; Shewhart 1939) ESE inherently uses the PDCA cycle as one it fundamental tenets. After ESE develops the enterprise transformation plan, the planned improvements are monitored (i.e., "checked" in the PDCA cycle) to ensure they achieve the targeted performance levels. If not, then action needs to be taken (i.e., "act" in the PDCA cycle) to correct the situation and replanning may be required.

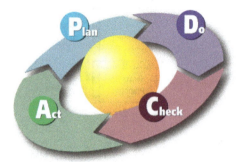

Figure 8. Shewhart's PDCA Cycle

Portfolio Management

Program and Project Managers direct their activities as they relate to the systems under their control. Enterprise management, on the other hand, is involved with directing the portfolio of items that are necessary to achieving the enterprise goals and objectives. The enterprise may not actually own these portfolio items. They could rent or lease these items, or they could have permission to use them through licensing or assignment.

The enterprise may only need part of a system (e.g., one bank of switching circuits in a system) or may need an entire SoS (e.g., switching systems, distribution systems, billing systems, provisioning systems, etc.). Notice that the portfolio items are not just those items related to the systems that SE traditionally deals with. These could also include platforms (like ships and oil drilling derricks), facilities (like warehouses and airports), land and rights of way (like railroad property easements and municipal covenants), and intellectual property (like patents and trademarks).

The investment community has been using portfolio management for a long time to manage a set of investments to maximize return for a given level of acceptable risk. These techniques have also been applied to a portfolio of "projects" within the enterprise. (Kaplan 2009) However, it should be noted that an enterprise is not merely a portfolio of projects. The enterprise portfolio consists of whatever systems, organizations, facilities, intellectual property, and other resources that help it achieve its goals and objectives.

Resource Allocation and Budgeting

The resource allocation activity is driven by the portfolio management definition of the optimal (or balanced) set of portfolio elements. Capability gaps are mapped to the elements of the portfolio, and resources are assigned to programs (or other organizational elements) based on the criticality of these gaps. Resources come in the form of people and facilities, policies and practices, money and energy, and platforms and infrastructure, among other things.

Allocation of resources could also involve the distribution or assignment of corporate assets like communication bandwidth, manufacturing floor space, computing power, intellectual property licenses, and so on. Resource allocation and budgeting is typically done on an annual basis, but more agile enterprises will usually do this on a more frequent basis.

Program and Project Management

There are commonly three basic types of projects in an enterprise. A *development project* takes a conceptual notion of a system and turns this into a realizable design. A *production project* takes the realizable design for a system and turns this into physical copies (or instantiations). An *operations "project"* directly operates each system or supports the operation by others. (Base operations are not typically called projects per se, but should nonetheless be considered as key elements to be considered when adjusting the enterprise portfolio.) The operations project can also be involved in maintaining the system or supporting maintenance by others. A program can have all three types of projects active simultaneously for the same system, as in this example:

- Project A is developing System X version 3.
- Project B is operating and maintaining System X version 2.
- Project C is maintaining System X version 1 in a warehouse facility as backup in case of emergencies.

Project management uses TSE as a tool to ensure a well-structured project and to help identify and mitigate cost, schedule, and technical risks involved with system development and implementation. The project level is where the TSE process is most often employed. (Martin 1997; Wasson 2006; ISO/IEC 2008; INCOSE 2010; Blanchard and Fabrycky 2010)

Enterprise Systems Engineering

The purpose of TSE is to bring together a diversity of discipline experts to address a wide range of problems inherent in the development of a large, complex "single" system. (Blanchard and Fabrycky 2010; Hall 1989; Sage and Rouse 2009) ESE expands beyond this traditional basis to "consider the full range of SE services increasingly needed in a modern organization where information-intensive systems are becoming central elements of the organization's business strategy." (Carlock and Fenton 2001, 242-261) The traditional role of SE is heavily involved in system acquisition and implementation, especially in the context of government acquisition of very large, complex military and civil systems (e.g., F22 fighter jet and air traffic control system).

ESE encompasses this traditional role in system acquisition, but also incorporates enterprise strategic planning and enterprise investment analysis. These two additional roles for SE at the enterprise level are "shared with the organization's senior line management, and tend to be more entrepreneurial, business-driven, and economic in nature in comparison to the more technical nature of classical systems engineering." (Carlock and Fenton 2001, 242-261)

Closing the Gap

Rebovich (2006) says there are "new and emerging modes of thought that are increasingly being recognized as essential to successful systems engineering in enterprises." The following process areas may be included in the ESE approach (DeRosa 2005) to close the gap between ESE and product SE:

- Strategic Technical Planning
- Enterprise Architecture
- Capabilities-Based Planning Analysis
- Technology Planning
- Enterprise Analysis and Assessment

These ESE processes are shown in the context of the entire enterprise in Figure 9. (DeRosa 2006) The ESE processes are shown in the middle with business processes on the left and TSE processes on the right.

SE is viewed by many organizations and depicted in many process definitions as bounded by the beginning and end of a system development project. Many have taken a wider view seeking to apply SE to the "whole system" and "whole life cycle." For example, Hitchins (1993) sets out a holistic, whole-life, wider system view of SE centered on operational purpose. Elliott and Deasley (2007) discuss the differences between development phase SE and in-service SE.

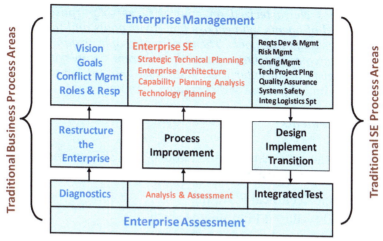

**Figure 9. Enterprise SE Process Areas in the Context of the Entire Enterprise
(Source: (DeRosa 2006))**

In contrast to TSE, ESE is more like a "regimen" (Kuras and White 2005) that is responsible for identifying "outcome spaces," shaping the development environment, coupling development to operations, and rewarding results rather than perceived promises (DeRosa 2005). ESE must continually characterize the operational environmental and the results of enterprise or SoS interventions to stimulate further actions within and among various systems in the enterprise portfolio.

Outcome spaces are characterized by a set of desired capabilities that help meet enterprise objectives, as opposed to definitive "user requirements" based on near-term needs. Enterprise capabilities must be robust enough to handle unknown threats and situations in the future. A detailed description of ESE can be found in (Rebovich and White 2010, 477).

Role of Requirements in ESE

TSE typically translates user needs into system requirements that drive the design of system elements. The system requirements must be "frozen" long enough for the system components to be designed, developed, tested, built, and delivered to the end users (which can sometimes take years, and in the case of very large, complicated systems like spacecraft and fighter jets, more than a decade).

ESE, on the other hand, must account for the fact that the enterprise must be driven not by requirements (that rarely can even be defined, let alone made stable) but instead by continually changing organizational visions, goals, governance priorities, evolving technologies, and user expectations. An enterprise consists of people, processes, and technology where the people act as "agents" of the enterprise:

Ackoff has characterized an enterprise as a "purposeful system" composed of agents who choose both their goals and the means for accomplishing those goals. The variety of people, organizations, and their strategies is what creates the inherent complexity and non-determinism in an enterprise. ESE must account for the concerns, interests and objectives of these agents. (DeRosa 2006)

ESE Process Elements

As a result of the synthesis outlined above, the ESE process elements to be used at the enterprise scale are as follows:

1. Strategic Technical Planning
2. Capability-Based Planning Analysis
3. Technology and Standards Planning
4. Enterprise Evaluation and Assessment
5. Enterprise Architecture and Conceptual Design
6. Enterprise Requirements Definition and Management
7. Opportunity and Risk Assessment and Management
8. Program and Project Detailed Design and Implementation
9. Program Integration and Interfaces
10. Program Validation and Verification
11. Portfolio and Program Deployment and Post Deployment
12. Portfolio and Program Life Cycle Support

The first six of these elements are described in some detail below. White (2006) discusses Opportunity Management in detail and how it differs from Risk Management. The others are more self-evident and will not be discussed in this chapter.

Enterprise Management

Enabling Systematic Enterprise Change. The SE process as applied to the enterprise as a whole could be used as the "means for producing change in the enterprise ... [where the] ... Seven Levels of change in an organization [are defined] as effectiveness, efficiency, improving, cutting, copying, differentiating and achieving the impossible." (McCaughin and DeRosa 2006). Ackoff tells us that:

Data, information, knowledge and understanding enable us to increase efficiency, not effectiveness. The value of the objective pursued is not relevant in determining efficiency, but it is relevant in determining effectiveness. Effectiveness is evaluated efficiency. It is efficiency multiplied by value. Intelligence is the ability to increase efficiency; wisdom is the ability to increase effectiveness.

The difference between efficiency and effectiveness is reflected in the difference between development and growth. Growth does not require an increase in value; development does. Therefore, development requires an increase in <u>wisdom as well as understanding, knowledge and information</u>. ((Ackoff 1989, 3-9), emphasis added)

Effectiveness vs. Efficiency. The essential nature of ESE is that it "determines the balance between complexity and order and in turn the balance between effectiveness and efficiency. When viewed as the fundamental mechanism for change, it goes beyond efficiency and drives adaptation of the enterprise." (McCaughin and DeRosa 2006) They provide a reasonably good definition for an enterprise that captures well this notion of balance:

> **Enterprise:** *People, processes and technology interacting with other people, processes and technology, serving some combination of their own objectives, those of their individual organizations and those of the enterprise as a whole.*

Key elements of the Enterprise Management process that oversees the "SE" of the enterprise as a whole are as follows:

- Strategic Technical Planning
- Capability-Based Planning Analysis
- Technology and Standards Planning
- Enterprise Evaluation and Assessment

The interactions between these four processes are illustrated in Figure 10, along with their interactions with other processes that deal with architecture, requirements, risk, and opportunity.

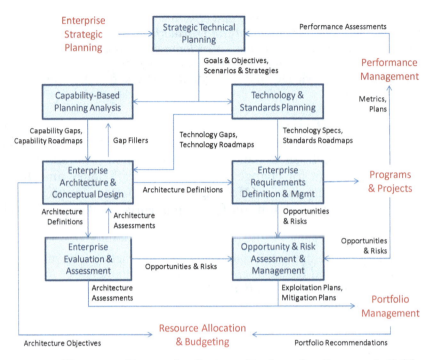

Figure 10. Enterprise Systems Engineering Process Activities

Strategic Technical Planning

The purpose of strategic technical planning is to establish the overall technical strategy for the enterprise. It creates the balance between adoption of standards and the use of new technologies, along with consideration of the people aspects driven by the relevant transdisciplinary technical principles and practices from psychology, sociology, organizational change management, etc.

This process uses the roadmaps developed during technology and standards planning. It then maps these technologies and standards against the capabilities roadmap to determine potential alignment and synergy. Furthermore, lack of alignment and synergy is identified as a risk to avoid or an opportunity to pursue in the technical strategy. The technical strategy is defined in terms of implementation guidance for the programs and projects.

Capability-Based Planning Analysis

The purpose of capability-based planning analysis is to translate the enterprise vision and goals into a set of current and future capabilities that helps achieve those goals. Current missions are analyzed to determine their suitability in supporting the enterprise goals. Potential future missions are examined to determine how they can help achieve the vision.

Current and projected capabilities are assessed to identify capability gaps that prevent the vision and technical strategy from being achieved. These capability gaps are then used to assess program, project, and system opportunities that should be pursued by the enterprise. This is defined in terms of success criteria of what the enterprise is desired to achieve.

There are different types of capabilities as shown in Figure 11. It is common practice to describe capabilities in the form of capability hierarchies and capability roadmaps. Technology roadmaps (discussed below under Technology Planning) are usually related to the system capabilities while business capability roadmaps (BCRMs) are related the operational capabilities of the enterprise as a whole.

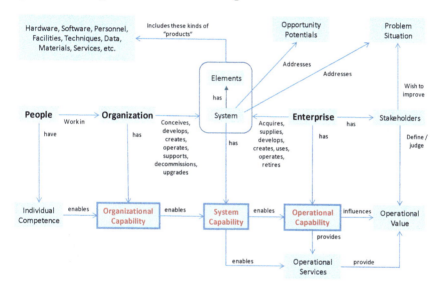

Figure 11. Different Kinds of Capabilities (Organizational, Systems, Operational) are Needed to Produce Operational Value

The BCRM development is usually done as part of Enterprise Strategic Planning, which is one level higher than, and a key driver for, the Strategic Technical Planning activity described above.

In some domains there may be competency roadmaps dealing with organizational capabilities, with perhaps the desired competency levels of individuals mapped out in terms of the jobs or roles used in the enterprise or perhaps in terms of the knowledge and skills required for certain activities. (Davidz et al. 2012)

Technology and Standards Planning

The purpose of technology planning is to characterize technology trends in the commercial marketplace and the research community. This activity covers not just trend identification and analysis, but also technology development and transition of technology into programs and projects. It identifies current and predicts future technology readiness levels for the key technologies of interest. Using this information, it defines technology roadmaps and technology insertion plans.

This activity helps establish the technical strategy and implementation guidance in the strategic technical plan. The Business Capabilities Roadmap (BCRM) from the Strategic Planning activity is used to identify which technologies can contribute to achieved targeted levels of performance improvements.

The purpose of standards planning is to assess technical standards to determine how they inhibit or enhance the incorporation of new technologies into systems development projects. The future of key standards is forecast to determine where they are headed and the alignment of these new standards with the life cycles for the systems in the enterprise's current and projected future portfolios. The needs for new or updated standards are defined and resources are identified that can address these needs. Standardization activities that can support development of new or updated standards are identified and initiated.

Enterprise Evaluation and Assessment

The purpose of enterprise evaluation and assessment (EE&A) is to determine if the enterprise is heading in the right direction. It does this by measuring progress towards realizing the enterprise vision. This process helps to "shape the environment" and to select among the program, project, and system opportunities. This is the primary means by which the technical dimensions of the enterprise are integrated into the business decisions.

This process establishes a measurement program as the means for collecting data for use in the evaluation and assessment of the enterprise. These measures help determine whether the strategy and its implementation are working as intended. Measures are projected into the future as the basis for determining discrepancies between what is observed and what had been predicted to occur. This process helps to identify risks and opportunities, diagnose problems, and prescribe appropriate actions. Sensitivity analysis is performed to determine the degree of robustness and agility of the enterprise.

Roberts states that EE&A must go beyond traditional system evaluation and assessment practices. (Roberts 2006) He says that this process area:

> ...*must de-emphasize the utility of comparing detailed metrics against specific individual requirement values, whether the metrics are derived from measurement, simulation or estimation... [it] must instead look for break points where capabilities are either significantly enhanced or totally disabled. Key characteristics of this activity are the following:*
>
> a) *Multi-scale analysis*
> b) *Early and continuous operational involvement*
> c) *Lightweight command and control (C2) capability representations*
> d) *Developmental versions available for assessment*
> e) *Minimal infrastructure*
> f) *Flexible modeling and simulation (M&S), operator-in-the-loop (OITL), and hardware-in-the-loop (HWIL) capabilities*
> g) *In-line, continuous performance monitoring and selective forensics.* (Roberts 2006)

Enterprise architecture can be used as a primary tool in support of evaluation and assessment. The structure and contents of the enterprise architecture should be driven by the key business decisions (or, as shown in the six-step process in (Martin 2005), the architecture should be driven by the "business questions" to be addressed by the architecture).

The evaluation and assessment success measures can be put into the enterprise architecture models and views directly and mapped to the elements that are being measured. An example of this can be seen in the NOAA Enterprise Architecture shown in (Martin 2003a and 2003b). The measures are shown, in this example, as success factors, key performance indicators, and information needs in the business strategy layer of the architecture.

Enterprise architecture can be viewed as either the set of artifacts developed as "views" of the enterprise, or as a set of activities that create, use and maintain these artifacts. In other words, enterprise architecture can be viewed as either the "noun" (i.e., things) or the "verb" (i.e., actions). The literature uses these terms in both senses and it is not always clear in each case which sense is intended.

Enterprise Architecture and Requirements

Enterprise architecture (EA) goes above and beyond the technical components of product systems to include additional items such as

339

strategic goals and objectives, operators and users, organizations and other stakeholders, funding sources and methods, policies and practices, processes and procedures, facilities and platforms, infrastructure, and real estate. The EA is not strictly the province of the chief information officer (CIO), and is not only concerned with information technology.

Likewise, enterprise requirements need to focus on the cross-cutting measures necessary to ensure overall enterprise success. Some of these enterprise requirements will apply to product systems, but they may also apply to business processes, inter-organizational commitments, hiring practices, investment directions, and so on (Bernus, Nemes and Schmidt 2003).

Architecture descriptions following the guidelines of an architecture framework have been used to standardize the views and models used in architecting efforts. (Zachman 1987, 276-292; Spewak 1992; Zachman 1992, 590-616) Architecture descriptions have also been developed using a business-question based approach. (Martin 2003b; Martin 2006) The ISO/IEC 42010 standard (ISO/IEC 2007) is expanding its scope to include requirements on architecture frameworks.

Government agencies have been increasingly turning to SE to solve some of their agency-level (i.e., enterprise) problems. This has sometimes led to the use of an architecture-based investment process, especially for information technology procurements. This approach imposes a requirement for linking business strategies to the development of enterprise architectures. The Federal Enterprise Architecture Framework (CIO Council 1999) and the DOD Architecture Framework (DODAF) (DoD 2009) were developed to support such an architecture-based investment process. There have been several other architecture frameworks also developed for this purpose. (ISO 2000; ISO/IEC 1998; NATO 2004; MOD 2004; Wikipedia 2010, 1)

Practical Considerations

When it comes to performing SE at the enterprise level there are several good practices to keep in mind (Rebovich and White 2010, 477):

- Set enterprise fitness as the key measure of system success. Leverage game theory and ecology, along with the practices of *satisficing* and governing the *commons*.
- Deal with uncertainty and conflict in the enterprise though *adaptation*: variety, selection, exploration, and experimentation.

- Leverage the practice of layered architectures with *loose couplers* and the *theory of order and chaos* in networks.

Enterprise governance involves shaping the political, operational, economic, and technical (POET) landscape. You shouldn't try to control the enterprise like you might do in a traditional SE effort at the project level.

Key Publications for Enterprise Systems Engineering

There are a few publications that serve as key references for the emerging discipline of ESE:

- Enterprise Systems Engineering: Advances in the Theory and Practice, Rebovich and White (eds.), 2010

- Engineering the Enterprise as a System, Rouse, Chapter 10 in the Handbook of Systems Engineering and Management, Sage and Rouse (eds.), 2009

- Handbook on Enterprise Architecture, Bernus, Nemes and Schmidt, 2003

- Complex Adaptive Systems Engineering (CASE), White, 2008

- A Theory of Enterprise Transformation, Rouse, 2005

- Journal of Enterprise Transformation, Nightingale and Valerdi (eds.), 2010

Conclusions

ESE as an emerging discipline can be used to more confidently and rapidly create the necessary changes for the modern enterprise to survive in these days of enormous economic and social uncertainty. The key elements of ESE were described in this chapter and areas for improvement were noted. The traditional methods and tools are necessary but not sufficient in using the systems approach to enable transformation of the enterprise. This new discipline is in the early stages of growth and maturation and will only have significant impact if we first recognize the required enhancements beyond the traditional SE approach.

About the Author

James Martin is an enterprise architect and systems engineer affiliated with The Aerospace Corporation developing solutions for information systems and space systems. He is a key author on the BKCASE project in development of the SE Body of Knowledge (SEBOK). Dr. Martin led the working group responsible for developing ANSI/EIA 632, a US national standard that defines the processes for engineering a system. He previously worked for Raytheon Systems Company as a lead systems engineer and architect on airborne and satellite communications networks. He has also worked at AT&T Bell Labs on wireless telecommunications products and underwater fiber optic transmission products. His book, Systems Engineering Guidebook, was published by CRC Press in 1996. Dr. Martin is an INCOSE Fellow and for eight years was leader of the Standards Technical Committee. He received from INCOSE the Founders Award for his long and distinguished achievements in the field.

References

Ackoff, R. L. 1989. From data to wisdom. Journal of Applied Systems Analysis 16 : 3-9.

Bernus, P., Nemes, L. and G. Schmidt (Eds) (2003) Handbook on Enterprise Architecture. Berlin : Springer.

Blanchard, B. S., and W. J. Fabrycky. 2010. Systems engineering and analysis. Prentice-hall international series in industrial and systems engineering. 5th ed. Englewood Cliffs, NJ, USA: Prentice-Hall.

Carlock, Paul and Robert Fenton. 2001. "System of Systems (SoS) Enterprise Systems Engineering for Information-Intensive Organizations," Systems Engineering Journal, Vol 4, No 4, 242-261.

CIO Council. 1999. Federal enterprise architecture framework (FEAF). Washington, DC: Chief Information Officer (CIO) Council.

Davidz, H. 2012. Systems Engineering Competency Knowledge Area. Article in the Systems Engineering Body of Knowledge (SEBOK). Published by the Body of Knowledge and Curriculum to Advance Systems Engineering (BKASE). www.bkcase.org.

Deming, W. E. 1986. Out of the crisis. MIT Center for Advance Engineering Study.

DeRosa, J. K. 2006. "An Enterprise Systems Engineering Model," INCOSE Symposium Proceedings.

———. 2005. "Enterprise Systems Engineering," Air Force Association, Industry Day, Day 1, Danvers, MA, 4 August 2005, https://www.paulrevereafa.org/IndustryDay/05/presentations/index.asp

DoD. 2004. DoD architecture framework (DODAF), version 1.0. Washington, DC: U.S. Department of Defense (DoD).

Dove, R. 2001. Response ability: The language, structure, and culture of the agile organization. New York, NY: John Wiley & Sons.

———. Knowledge management, response ability, and the agile enterprise. in Paradigm Shift International [database online]. Questa, NM, USA, 1999Available from http://www.parshift.com/docs/KmRaAeX.htm (accessed 2010).

Elliott, C., and P. Deasley. 2007. Creating systems that work--principles of engineering systems for the 21st century. Vol. (n/a). London, England: Royal Academy of Engineering.

Giachetti, R. E. 2010. Design of enterprise systems: theory, architecture, and methods. Boca Raton, FL, USA: CRC Press.

Hall, A. D. 1989. Metasystems methodology: A new synthesis and unification. International series on systems science and engineering. 1st ed. Vol. 3. Oxford, UK: Pergamon.

Hammer, M., and J. Champy. 1993. Reengineering the corporation: A manifesto for business revolution. New York, NY: Harper Business.

Handy, C. 1995. Trust and the virtual organization. Harvard Business Review (May-June): 2-8.

———. 1992. Balancing corporate power: A new federalist paper. Harvard Business Review 70 (6) (November/December): 59-67.

Hines, P. and N. Rich. 1997. The seven value stream mapping tools. Intl J of Ops & Prod Mgmt, Vol 17, No 1, 1997.

Hitchins, D. 1993. Putting systems to work. New York, NY: John Wiley & Sons.

INCOSE. 2010. INCOSE systems engineering handbook, version 3.2. San Diego, CA, USA: International Council on Systems Engineering (INCOSE), INCOSE-TP-2003-002-03.2.

ISO. 2000. Industrial automation systems -- requirements for enterprise-reference architectures and methodologies. Geneva, Switzerland: International Organization for Standardization (ISO), ISO 15704:2000.

ISO/IEC. 2008. Systems and software engineering - system life cycle processes. Geneva, Switzerland: International Organization for Standardization (ISO)/International Electrotechnical Commission (IEC), ISO/IEC 15288:2008 (E).

———. 2007. Systems and software engineering -- recommended practice for architectural description of software-intensive systems. Geneva, Switzerland: International Organization for Standards (ISO)/International Electrotechnical Commission (IEC), ISO/IEC 42010:2007.

———. 1998. Information technology -- open distributed processing -- reference model: Architecture. Geneva, Switzerland: International Organization for Standardization (ISO)/International Electrotechnical Commission (IEC), ISO/IEC 10746:1998.

Joannou, P. 2007. Enterprise, systems, and software—the need for integration. Computer, IEEE, May 2007.

Kaplan, J. 2009. Strategic IT portfolio management: Governing enterprise transformation. Washington, DC: Jeffrey Kaplan PRTM.

Kuras, M. L., and B. E. White. 2005. Engineering enterprises using complex-systems engineering. Paper presented at 15th Annual International Council on Systems Engineering (INCOSE) International Symposium, 10-15 July, 2010, Rochester, NY, USA.

Martin, J. N. 2012. Enterprise Systems Engineering Knowledge Area. Article in the Systems Engineering Body of Knowledge (SEBOK). Published by the Body of

Knowledge and Curriculum to Advance Systems Engineering (BKASE). www.bkcase.org.

———. 2010. An enterprise systems engineering framework. Paper presented at 20th Anniversary International Council on Systems Engineering (INCOSE) International Symposium, 12-15 July, 2010, Chicago, IL, USA.

———. 2006. An enterprise architecture process incorporating knowledge modeling methods. PhD., George Mason University.

———. 2005. Using an enterprise architecture to assess the societal benefits of earth science research. Paper presented at 15th Annual International Council on Systems Engineering (INCOSE) International Symposium, Rochester, NY, USA.

———. 2004. The seven samurai of systems engineering: Dealing with the complexity of 7 interrelated systems. Paper presented at 14th Annual International Council on Systems Engineering (INCOSE) International Symposium, 20-24 June, 2004, Toulouse, France.

———. 2003. An integrated tool suite for the NOAA observing system architecture. Paper presented at 13th Annual International Council on Systems Engineering (INCOSE) International Symposium, Arlington, VA, USA.

———. 2003. On the use of knowledge modeling tools and techniques to characterize the NOAA observing system architecture. Paper presented at 13th Annual International Council on Systems Engineering (INCOSE) International Symposium, Arlington, VA, USA.

———. 1997. Systems engineering guidebook: A process for developing systems and products. 1st ed. Boca Raton, FL, USA: CRC Press.

McCaughin, K., and J. K. DeRosa. 2006. Process in enterprise systems engineering. Paper presented at 16th Annual International Council on Systems Engineering (INCOSE) International Symposium, 9-13 July, 2006, Orlando, FL, USA.

Miller, J., and S. Page. 2007. Complex adaptive systems: An introduction to computational models of social life. Princeton, NJ, USA: Princeton University Press.

MOD. 2004. Ministry of defence architecture framework (MODAF), version 2. UK: U.K. Ministry of Defence.

NATO. 2004. NATO architecture framework (NAF), version 2. Brussels, Belgium: North Atlantic Treaty Organization.

Nightingale, D., and D. Rhodes. 2004. Enterprise systems architecting: Emerging art and science within engineering systems. Paper presented at Engineering Systems Symposium, Massachusetts Institute of Technology (MIT), 29-31 March, 2004, Boston, MA, USA.

Nightingale, D., and J. Srinivasan. 2011. Lean enterprise thinking: Driving enterprise transformation. New York, NY: AMACOM Press.

Nightingale, D., and R. Valerdi. 2011. Journal of enterprise transformation. Taylor and Francis.

Rebovich, G. 2006. Systems thinking for the enterprise: New & emerging perspectives. Paper presented at IEEE/SMC International Conference on System of Systems Engineering, April 2006, Los Angeles, CA, USA.

Rebovich, G., and B. E. White, eds. 2010. Enterprise systems engineering: Advances in the theory and practice. Boca Raton, FL, USA: CRC Press.

Ring, J. 2004. Intelligent enterprises. INSIGHT, A Publication of the International Council on Systems Engineering (INCOSE) 6 (2) (January 2004).

———. 2004. Seeing an enterprise as a system. INSIGHT, A Publication of the International Council on Systems Engineering (INCOSE) 6 (2) (January 2004).

Roberts, J. L. 2006. Enterprise analysis and assessment. Paper presented at 16th Annual International Council on Systems Engineering (INCOSE) International Symposium, 9-13 July, 2006, Orlando, FL, USA.

Rouse, W. B. 2009. Engineering the enterprise as a system. In Handbook of systems engineering and management., eds. A. P. Sage, W. B. Rouse. 2nd ed. New York, NY: Wiley and Sons, Inc.

———. 2008. Health care as a complex adaptive system: Implications for design and management. The Bridge, National Academy of Engineering 38 (1) (Spring 2008): 17-25.

———. 2006. Agile information systems for agile decision making. In Agile information systems., ed. K. C. Desouza. Woburn, MA, USA: Butterworth-Heinemann.

———. 2006. Enterprise transformation: Understanding and enabling fundamental change. New York, NY: Wiley and Sons, Inc.

———. 2005. Enterprise as systems: Essential challenges and enterprise transformation. Systems Engineering, the Journal of the International Council on Systems Engineering (INCOSE) 8 (2): 138-50.

———. 2005. A theory of enterprise information. Systems Engineering, the Journal of the International Council on Systems Engineering (INCOSE) 8 (4): 279-95.

Sage, A., and C. Cuppan. 2001. On the systems engineering and management of systems of systems and federations of systems. Information-Knowledge-Systems Management Journal 2 (4) (December 2001): 325-45.

Sage, A. P. 2000. Transdisciplinarity perspectives in systems engineering and management. In Transdisciplinarity: Recreating integrated knowledge., eds. M. A. Somerville, D. Rappaport, 158-169. Oxford, UK: EOLSS Publishers.

Sage, A. P., and W. B. Rouse, eds. 2009. Handbook of system engineering and management. 2nd ed. New York, NY: John Wiley & Sons.

Shewhart, W. A. 1939. Statistical method from the viewpoint of quality control. New York: Dover.

Sillitto, H. 2012. Enabling Systems Engineering in the Organization Knowledge Area. Article in the Systems Engineering Body of Knowledge (SEBOK). Published by the Body of Knowledge and Curriculum to Advance Systems Engineering (BKASE). www.bkcase.org.

Spewak, S. H. 1992. Enterprise architecture planning: Developing a blueprint for data, applications and technology. New York, NY: Wiley and Sons, Inc.

Srinivasan, J. 2010. Towards a theory sensitive approach to planning enterprise transformation. Paper presented at 5th European Institute for Advanced

Studies in Management (EIASM) Workshop on Organizational Change and Development, September 23-24, 2010, Vienna, Austria.

Valerdi, R., D. Nightingale, and C. Blackburn. 2009. Enterprises as systems: Context, boundaries, and practical implications. Information-Knowledge-Systems Management Journal 7 (4) (December 2008): 377-99.

Vernadat, F. B. 1996. Enterprise modelling and integration - principles and applications. London, UK: Chapman and Hall.

von Bertalanffy, L. 1968. General system theory: Foundations, development, applications. Revised ed. New York, nY: Braziller.

Wasson, C. S. 2006. System analysis, design and development. Hoboken, NJ: John Wiley and Sons Ltd.

Weinberg, G., and D. Weinberg. 1988. General principles of systems design. New York, NY: Dorset House Publishing Company.

White, B. E. 2007. On interpreting scale (or view) and emergence in complex systems engineering. Paper presented at 1st Annual IEEE Systems Conference, 9-12 April, 2007, Honolulu, HI, USA.

———. 2006. Enterprise opportunity and risk. Paper presented at 16th Annual International Council on Systems Engineering (INCOSE) International Symposium, 9-13 July, 2010, Orlando, FL, USA.

White, B. E. 2008. Complex adaptive systems engineering (CASE). Paper presented at Understanding Complex Systems Symposium, 12-15 May 2008, University of Illinois at Urbana Champaign.

White, B. E., and B. G. McCarter. 2009. Emergence of SoS, sociocognitive aspects. In Systems of systems engineering: Principles and applications., ed. M. Jamshidi, 71-105. Boca Raton, FL, USA: CRC Press.

Wikipedia. TRAK Architecture Framework [article]. in Wikimedia Foundation, Inc. [database online]. San Francisco, CA, USA, 2010Available from http://en.wikipedia.org/wiki/TRAK (accessed 2010).

Zachman, J. A. 1992. Extending and formalizing the framework for information systems architecture. IBM Systems Journal 31 (3): 590-616.

———. 1987. A framework for information systems architectures. IBM Systems Journal 26 (3): 276-92.

The Wise Doctor and the Foolish Consultant
A Fairy Tale for Our Times

(With thanks, and apologies, to H. C. Andersen!)

Dennis Sherwood

Der var en gang...

...once upon a time, not so long ago, in a small country town, not so far away, there lived a young doctor. She was happy. Not because the sun was always shining, for on many days, it rained; not because the birds were singing, although they were; not because she was in love with a handsome prince, for the handsome prince had just married her best friend Kate. But because she loved what she was doing. Ever since she had been a young girl, she had dreamed of being a doctor, of curing the sick, of healing the wounded. So she had worked hard at school, and even harder at university, until now she had become a junior partner in a small practice in a small country town. Every day, she rejoiced in successfully diagnosing her patients' needs, and using her skilled professional judgment to provide just the right remedies to achieve successful results. She was indeed happy.

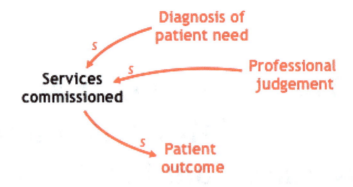

One bright morning, when the sun was shining and the birds singing, there was a knock on her door.

"Come in!" she said, not really expecting to see a handsome prince.

Nor was it, for when the door opened, in walked a tall, very, very, young-looking man.

"Hello" she said, with a smile. "Please sit down. How can I help?"

"On the contrary," replied Man-boy. "I'm here to help *you*!"

"Help me? But I don't need any help today, thank you."

"Ah! Yes you do, but you might not know it!"

"But if I think that I don't need help, how is it that you, a stranger, and one so young too, knows, with such self-assurance, that I do?"

"Let me explain. I am a Management Consultant!"

"Mmm. I see..." mused Young Doctor. "Then it is surely you, not I, who could do with some help. But your problem is not one I'm qualified to treat."

"You didn't let me finish," replied Man-boy somewhat peevishly. "I'm a Management Consultant, working for the Great Minister, and I'm here to help you budget!"

"Help me budget?" queried Young Doctor. "I can assure you I can budget quite well, thank you. I am very careful how much I spend on food and clothes; I regularly send some money to my aged mother; and I can usually find just a little to put away for a rainy day."

"Not *that* budget, silly!" retorted Man-boy. "I'm talking about your *clinical* budget!"

"Clinical budget? What's that?"

"That's the budget you have for providing clinical services."

"But I don't have a budget for providing clinical services. I just treat my patients. Which I do rather well. And that makes me happy."

"Well, that's why I'm here to help: for when the clock strikes twelve tonight, you will have your own, your very own, clinical budget! And one which the Great Minister has chosen to be just the right size for you!"

"That's very nice of the Great Minister. But I'm sure I can do just as well without it. So please thank the Great Minister for me, but let him know that I won't be taking up his kind offer."

"I'm not sure you quite understand. All doctors are being given the blessing of their own budgets, which will not only make them happier, but also make them better managers too."

"But I don't want to be a better manager, thank you. I would like to be a better doctor though..."

"I'm sure you want to be a better manager too, for we all want to ensure we don't overspend the Nation's resources dedicated to health care, don't we?" replied Man-boy, with rather more than just a hint of condescension in his voice. "Let me show you what I mean using this diagram..."

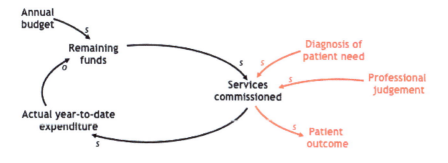

Young Doctor looked puzzled.

"Let me explain," said Man-boy. "This is called a negative feedback loop. What it means is that you will always want to make sure you have enough funds remaining for the rest of the year. And what that means is that you will constantly be modifying your clinical decisions accordingly to stay within your annual budget. It's all very simple."

"That loop looks pretty negative to me," replied Young Doctor despondently. "I don't want to be bothered with all this. My job is to treat patients."

"I understand. One of my higher degrees is in Change Manipulation, and I appreciate your apprehension. It is the first of four stages you will go through – you'll get angry soon."

"You might be right there," responded Young Doctor, feeling the anger rise. "Anyway, I really do have to treat some patients now, so you have to go."

Man-boy rose from his chair, and before leaving, made sure he had left his business card, including his four email addresses, his Twitter hashtag, his Facebook link, and the numbers for his business fax, business phone, home fax, home phone and of course both his business and his personal mobile phones too. "You may reach me twenty-four seven on any of these," Man-boy said reassuringly.

For the next few days, Young Doctor was happy, treating her patients. But she couldn't forget the strange conversation she'd had with Man-boy. Somewhere, in the back of her mind, she kept thinking about how on earth a budget would 'help' her. And every evening, as she lay on her bed, her thoughts continued, like a pea under her mattress, disturbing her rest. "No," she thought, "I'm not a 'manager'. I don't even know what a 'manager' is. And I'm sure I don't think like one. After all, had I wanted to be a manager, I would have chosen to become one. But I didn't. I wanted to become a doctor..." Eventually, she drifted into unquiet sleep...

And as she slept, she dreamt. She dreamt of doctors and managers, of manager-doctors and doctor-managers, of manators and docagers... And she dreamt of diagrams with curious curly arrows going backwards and forwards, of S's and O's, and... suddenly she awoke! Yes! That was it! That was what was troubling her! She had stumbled across the flaw in Man-boy's diagram. A mistake. Surely a mistake. The diagram Man-boy had shown her was wrong. Wrong in two ways. Firstly, psychologically. The diagram might represent the mental model of a 'manager', a bureaucrat, a slave to being controlled by budgets. But it didn't, just didn't, represent what she knew so many doctors felt like. And that led to the second error:

something was missing. In her mind, her clear, clear mind, Young Doctor saw what was clearly the right diagram:

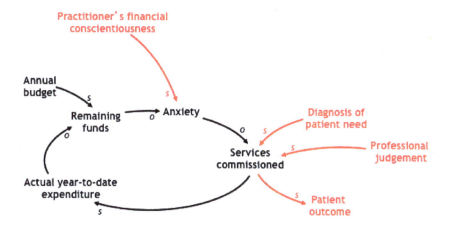

Yes, that's much better. The mind of the bureaucrat, she thought, was totally driven by a sense of financial anxiety that there wouldn't be enough money left in the budget in the future, and that it's therefore necessary to be prudent as regards what gets spent today. That's how the bureaucrat's mind works. But not the doctor's. Suppose, for example, that a doctor just doesn't give a monkey's about whatever the remaining funds might be. That doctor will just spend anyway – there could be nothing left, but the doctor just doesn't care. In fact, one of Young Doctor's partners - Profligate – was just like that. Profligate was indeed a good doctor, but he did spend money with consummate ease. And come to think about it, Worried, Young Doctor's other partner, was exactly the other way. Although he was, in no sense, a 'manager', he was in a permanent state of anxiety, and being a given a budget would just give him more to worry about...

And her own style? She was somewhere in the middle: not a couldn't-give-a-damn spendthrift like Profligate, nor a quivering neurotic jelly like Worried. She just wanted to get on with her job, which made her happy.

Days passed. But, try as she might, she couldn't get Man-boy's 'offer to help', or those writhing diagrams, out of her head. And she'd just received an email – time stamped 03:42 that morning – 'asking' if Man-boy could visit her 'to see how things were getting along' the next day. Apparently, he was due to meet Profligate then, too. So Man-boy will be in for one big shock, she thought.

And as she thought, she thought about how Profligate would be likely to behave. The concept of 'financial conscientiousness' was not, for sure, part of his consciousness, but he was a good doctor, and he was clever too – clever, perhaps, in a way in which she wasn't. For he understood how the bureaucracy worked, and how to get things done. She remembered a story he had told her once, a story about when he was a Houseman in a large general hospital. A children's ward he was working on was in a poor state of repair – crumbling plaster, peeling paintwork, that sort of thing. Nothing dangerous, but it looked a mess. He told her how for months he had been complaining through the 'normal channels', and trying to get the ward redecorated. Nothing happened. But then he had an idea. One of the children in the ward was the daughter of a local politician. One day, when the politician was visiting, he'd had a 'quiet word', resulting in a letter from the politician to the Chairman of the hospital's Board of Governors describing how his daughter was having nightmares because of the crumbly walls. Very soon thereafter, the plaster was fixed, and the walls repainted...

Yes, Profligate knew how to get things done. And he knows that if he scrimps on, for example, doing all the recommended diagnostics – even those that don't appear at first sight to be necessary – then there is the risk of a bad outcome for the patient. This is bad news indeed for the poor patient, but not just the patient – the Health Service gets a bad press too. "Aha! That's it..." she thought. "Profligate will use the *threat* of a disaster to squeeze more money..."

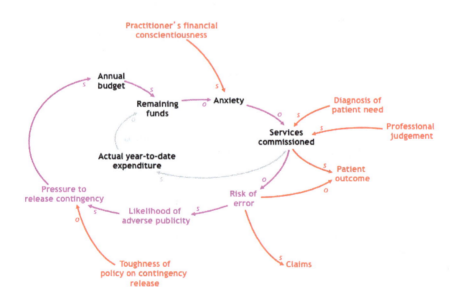

Young Doctor was feeling quite confident in drawing causal loop diagrams now – she'd just finished reading quite a good book on it* - and she noticed some interesting features of this one. The original balancing loop, with 'annual budget' as the target dangle, had now been subsumed in a larger balancing loop, so that the 'annual budget' was no longer a target dangle, but a variable inside a larger system. Clever. That strips the controlling power of the budget away. The larger system, though, has four dangles – 'diagnosis of patient need', 'professional judgment', 'practitioner's financial conscientiousness' and 'toughness of policy on contingency release'. Which of these would 'win', and so act as the true control?

From Young Doctor's point of view, of course, this was a no-brainer: to her, the twin dangles of 'diagnosis of patient need' and 'professional judgment' would always win, and she would argue with whoever held the purse strings until, as the saying goes in her part of the country, the ducklings grow into swans. But what about Profligate? What would happen with him?

As she thought about this, she realized that the system was being *designed* – probably unintentionally - to bring about a stand-off between Profligate, and those like him, and whoever has ultimate authority over money. Suppose, for example, that Profligate comes up against Kind Lord Pussy Cat, someone so soft – and so scared of bad publicity – that as soon as Profligate drops even the slightest hint that he needs more money ("or else something really bad might happen!"), he gets it. The original budget will be blown, and Profligate will win. But if he comes up against Old Miss Hard-as-Nails, then battle will rage, and something disastrous could well happen.

The system works most sensibly, of course, when a practitioner who is reasonably financially conscientious interacts with a purse-holder who is tough but sensible, not releasing contingency on a whim, but recognizing that sometimes something happens – like a virulent flu outbreak in the winter – that genuinely warrants extra funds.

And there's a fourth possibility too: one that probably applies within a given practice, where one partner is a spender, and another very careful. Oh dear! Profligate and Worried! If Worried sees Profligate 'getting away with financial murder', that could lead to all sorts of tension within the partnership...

---

* *Seeing the Forest for the Trees – A manager's guide to applying systems thinking*, by Dennis Sherwood (Nicholas Brealey Publishing 2002, with translations available in German and Mandarin).

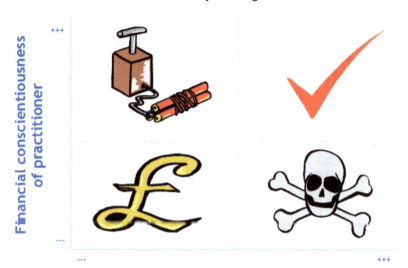

Toughness of contingency release

The practitioner is conscientious, and the policy on contingency release is tough (top right). This situation is stable, as the practitioner is 'sensible', and will not precipitate 'difficult' situations. The holder of the contingency know this, and so will be 'sensible' in return.

The practitioner is not conscientious, and the policy on contingency release is weak (bottom left). This situation is will haemorrhage money, as the profligate practitioner will exploit every opportunity to benefit from the weak policy.

The practitioner is not conscientious, and the policy on contingency release is tough (bottom right). This situation is very difficult, as the tough holder of contingency seeks to bring the profligate practitioner 'into line'. Each will be testing the limits of the other.

The practitioner is conscientious, and the policy on contingency release is weak (top left). This situation is more complex. In the case of a sole practitioner, the system should be stable, for the practitioner will 'police' him or herself. But in the case of a professional partnership or close-knit clinical team, the situation could become quite difficult: for example, there could be one profligate partner who is seen by the others partners, as a result of the weak policy, to be 'getting away with it'. In this case, there is likely to be tension within the partnership itself, which will test the extent to which the partners can exert peer pressure on one another without the situation becoming explosive.

And while she was thinking about Worried, she realized something else too...

354

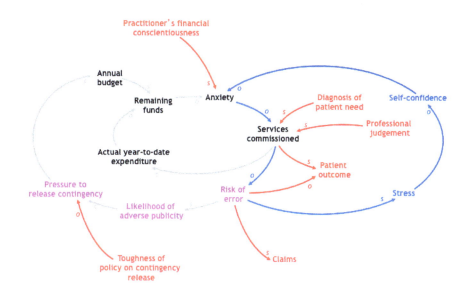

Poor Worried. He was stressed out enough already. From his point of view, being worried about overspending his budget is only a small part of it. In addition, he'll go frantic at the possibility of making a mistake resulting from under-diagnosis, which will only add to his anxiety. That reinforcing loop is nasty, really nasty.

So, the next day, when Man-boy, arrogant as ever, arrived to 'help', he got one hell of a surprise.

"What sort of consultant designs a system like this?" challenged Young Doctor, thrusting her most recent causal loop diagram before Man-boy's startled face. "Surely, if you're designing a system, shouldn't you make sure the design actually works, with no 'unintended consequences', driving the right, not the wrong, behaviors?"

"Well…you don't understand the bigger picture…" Man-boy spluttered.

"Don't I?" responded Young Doctor, looking at him right in the eye.

Whether or not Young Doctor lived happily ever after, time will tell…

But we do know that Man-boy didn't learn. People like that never do.

Explanatory Note

At the time of writing, early June 2011, the National Health Service in England is undergoing an unprecedented upheaval. Following the change of Government in the UK resulting from the election of May 2010, plans were tabled to change dramatically the way in which the annual expenditure of some £100 billion is managed. Very briefly, a key feature of the proposed new system is that local doctors – 'General Practitioners' – should take direct managerial responsibility for about 80% of the total budget.

About the Author

Managing Director, The Silver Bullet Machine Manufacturing Company Limited.

Systems Thinking in Healthcare IT in Denmark

Rasmus Fischer Frost
and
Linda Clod Præstholm

Abstract

In this chapter, we present an idea of how the Danish healthcare sector could anchor cooperation at all levels in the regions most efficiently, which serves to ensure success for all of the IT development processes in the healthcare sector of Denmark.

Keywords

Healthcare IT, Systems Thinking

The Development of Healthcare IT
- A Historical Fragmentation

In many countries, healthcare IT is an area under great development and subsequently also an area that lacks innovation and growth in different areas. Only a few countries can pride themselves with having fully digitized all of the important data surrounding the healthcare sector. This is particularly significant compared to the numerous larger organizations of different character, which enjoy communication and between actors more easily. The reason for the lack of this data digitization is in part to be found in the complexity of the healthcare sector, because hospitals in previous years (earlier municipalities, regions) had been viewed as separate entities. It is only within the last decade that the Danish government has begun considering the hospital sector in a larger perspective, where both the medical facilities are gradually being consolidated which has led to a greater involvement of sharing and communicating amongst patients and the data is tied together with them.

The digitization of these patient data along with the internal communication aspect have also been run as separate entities, at first as smaller units, where very passionate people have taken the responsibility of developing electronic healthcare records and similar initiatives locally. These initiatives have later spread to include clinics and then later to the hospital level and finally on a regional government level.

The hospital healthcare departments find themselves in a situation where they have been under great economic limitations and strains and have as a result not been able to do potential and required research, development and implementation of the optimal healthcare IT solutions. The subsequent introduction of healthcare IT further heightens the complexity of the data format perspective that is created due to the various electronic devices that produce data (scanners, x-ray devices, blood analysis devices, tissue analyses etc.). This complexity is supported by the fact that each department produces different types of data from different types of devices and system supplies. The use of paper is therefore still in most places the pivotal emphasis of patient treatment.

It has not been many years since the demand for a shared goal and a shared strategy for the digitization of the healthcare sector was established. Several organizations were established including the *Sammenhængende Digital Sundhed i Danmark* ("Coherent Digital Health Initiative in Denmark") agency (SDSD), which was founded by an agreement between the Government and Danish Regions. SDSD started its operations in the mid 2007 and subsequently released a strategy for the digitization of the healthcare sector that year. A later strategic outlet from SDSD was based on a report made by Deloitte Management Consulting, where the two most prevalent recommendations had been the guiding principles for the governance and execution of this strategy. It revolved around the recommendation of a consolidation of the IT operations in the regions of Denmark along with a denial of the demand for a national electronic patient health record service. This recommendation saw the establishment of IT-administrative units for each region together and in accordance with the founding of the regions. The five IT departments of the regions would not be required to work against a shared goal of a electronic healthcare record system, but "just" work to improve the exchange of data first and foremost within regions themselves and later in the terms across the country and in the healthcare facilities.

At the same time the Regional IT administrative departments also developed strategies for IT development for the hospitals within each region. IT development and administration became centralized in each of the five regions, including *Koncern-IT* (KIT) in the Capital Region, and local IT departments of the hospitals came to serve more in resemblance of a service desk unit.

Through projects, we have worked with the analysis of the IT architecture maturity and IT governance at a local hospital and at a regional IT management department. This was done to explore how the new administrative approach to IT has been executed. In our studies, we found conditions that could indicate a stronger need of development within areas of: overview of enterprise architecture (which may lead to give more consolidation opportunities), awareness and interaction within actual business processes at hospitals in conjunction with the cooperation and implementation of new IT solutions, including ownership of new IT solutions at the IT departments of local hospitals.

New Structure - New Context?

Since our work on the projects, there has been made substantial organizational changes, which may possibly provide even greater challenges for the IT strategic and administrative and collaborative areas. In early 2010, the Government and the Danish Regions chose to close the SDSD by the end of 2010. Instead, to facilitate the initiative of Connected Digital Health in Denmark and develop overall strategies, the Regions of Denmark proclaimed and instated a new organization: The Regional Healthcare IT Organization (in Danish abbreviated as RSI). RSI is headed by a steering committee, where all five regions and Danish Regions participate at the board level. Regional CIOs participate as observers in RSIs steering group meetings in order to provide the steering committee with professional competent advice.

Quoting RSIs website about the organization:

> *"The strong link between the RSIs steering committee and regional*
> *IT managers is important, because there must be assurance that the*
> *regional IT organizations can lead RSIs decisions into practice."*

This sounds fairly reasonable, but if you closer at the quote one will find two vague hypotheses, namely: 1) RSI makes decisions that must be carried out accordingly, and 2) the regional IT managers are accountable for the success of the decision process.

Additionally, it remains vague how this role ties in with the RSI's so-called *pejlemærker*, "points of orientation", which have the characteristics of a mixture of both concrete goals and loosely based visions. Are these recommendations something that should guide the cooperative strategic development or are they concrete goals to be followed?

In an attempt to understand how to create the best opportunities for the development of healthcare IT in Denmark at an organizational level, it has been our desire to be understand and analyze the organizational terms and function of RSI.

Understanding Complexity
- A Systemic Approach

When trying to understand an organization's structure, one often understands the organization in retrospect. One looks for what decisions and reasons that underlie the current structure. This includes questions such as: How has it evolved? What determines and influences what? This usually leads to a traditional organization chart with a tree-like structure. If you try to analyze the decision processes and workflows, it is often made from this hierarchical framework of understanding. Looking for the optimization of the workflow and collaborative techniques, such an organizational understanding does not offer much in terms of actual benefit of analysis. To understand the complexity and the immediate lack of coherence we will therefore use a different organizational framework of understanding and analysis.

Systemic Thinking

An approach to a broader understanding of the organization around healthcare IT in Denmark could be in the ways of systemic thinking. Systemic thinking provides a more nuanced and holistic picture on the organizations' structure and ensemble. Systemic thinking describes how there is a consistency across organizations, so that the actions and effects cannot be considered in isolation, but must always be viewed in context within the context they serve to function. A system is a set of interrelated things encompassed by a well defined and permeable boundary, interacting with one another and an external environment, forming a complex but unitary whole and working toward a common overall goal (Saha, 2010).

Systemic thinking can be used as a method to understand something very complex. The organization of healthcare IT in Denmark is a very complex matter and therefore an equally diverse conceptual framework is needed. A systemic approach offers a more cyclical mind-set than the one-tier approach that exists today, where strategy and development are expected to run as a series of dominoes, in which one piece after another fall into place.

The Viable Systems Model

One can first try to understand the organization itself. According to Patrick Hoverstadt, this understanding can be approached from two angles: either one can start with mapping the entire organization one step at a time or one can start at any given problem and thus quickly gain an understanding of a more efficient way to organize the enterprise. It would be a useful exercise to map the entire organizational structure of health care, not just in terms of IT organization, because if we look at the definition of system, we see that it is something that works together towards a common goal. In SDSD's strategy and KIT's approach, we see that their overall goal is linked to the Ministry of Health Authority's overall objectives, and healthcare IT is thus not a detached system, but must be viewed in a larger system, namely the healthcare sector as a whole. Hoverstadt applies the Viable System Model (VSM) developed by Stafford Beer, and has subsequently tailored a set of theories capable of better understanding how large complex enterprises operate and develop themselves.

An interesting characteristic of VSM is that it is very different from a traditional organizational chart, which is usually very hierarchical in its structure. VSM offers a different view of the organization, which also makes the architectural structures visible along with, workflows, decision processes, communication pathways, knowledge and performance management initiatives. VSM is applied by considering the many small organizational units, the total organization or system is composed of in a larger perspective. As one sets out to document and examine the organization according to VSM, many fractal structures of systems used in the organization unfolds. VSM is constructed of 7 systems:

- System 1: Operations

- System 2: Coordination
- System 3: Delivery management
- System 3*: Monitoring
- System 4: Development management and
- System 5: policy.
- The seventh system is the surrounding environment in which the system finds itself in and interacts with.

System 1: Operations contains the primary activities which the organization produces, and is what constitutes the organizations' very existence. At Rigshospitalet, one of the biggest and most complex hospitals in the Capital Region, this primary activity is represented by the care and treatment of patients. KITs primary activity is the administrative decisions and implementation of IT-investments and planning for all the 13 hospitals in the Capital Region. For RSI this representation of activity would arguably be the coordination of the IT-administrative tasks that KIT and many other IT-departments in the regions are undertaking.

System 2: Coordination is the system concerned with coordination that happens in regards to the primary activities so that they will not conflict with each other. In terms of the hospital, Rigshospitalet, one such activity of coordination is how the health personnel coordinate patient intake, hospital release and shift duty coordination. Regarding KIT, it would amount to project management to prevent redundant work but also avoid divided and separate work efforts on projects. The coordination of RSI would be expected to perform coordination similarly to KIT by coordinating the projects the projects in which RSI is involved.

System 3: Delivery Management spans the entire management processes coordinating primary activities in the sub-systems of the organization as a whole. This system consolidates and captures an overview of the production/or wares that the organization produce. In terms of Rigshospitalet, these management processes correspond to the different clinical management departments but also for the broader management of the entire hospital. Regarding KIT, this corresponds to the CEO or the executive management responsibility. Lastly for RSI, these processes are particularly interesting, depending on how RSI chooses to organize itself internally to the organization. This is because RSI itself might be overarching as corresponding to System 3: delivery management, which is responsible for coordinating and facilitating the entire healthcare IT organization and all of its outputs. These outputs are connected to the overall success of having to coordinate, plan and decide upon the IT-architecture and strategy of the healthcare sector. It raises questions, firstly, about how RSI views itself as an organization and secondly if they have the required political backing to accomplish the intended work.

System 4: Monitoring is concerned with the monitoring of managerial decisions or the production of activities seen from System 1: Operations. This means that System3: Delivery Management, circumvents the local System 2: Coordination in an attempt to monitor the primary activities of System 1: Operations. Firstly, this has in part to do with establishing trust amongst the stakeholders' awareness of how the flow of activities are going, and secondly to establish a comfort and relief amongst the co-workers from System 1, of knowing that their superiors know how and what the organization is producing in terms of activities. In light of the situation at Rigshospitalet, this corresponds to a situation where the stakeholder committee on top executive level or at the clinical level, went out to the different departments of treatment to examine the needs and potential shortages of personnel, time and space. This results in an examination of how the goals of a better healthcare sector are managed and achieved. In terms of KIT, this implies that the board of executives should visit the local IT departments of each hospital but also the clinical departments involved with treatment in order to establish how well IT has been implemented, how it works and performs in everyday operations and lastly how well it supports the needs of clinicians and ultimately the primary activity of the hospital: the treatment of patients. In terms of RSI, it would mean a monitoring of the regional IT-development, investment, implementation if one assumes that RSI corresponds to System 3: Delivery Management. One of the main tasks of RSI would then be to develop a method or a tool for monitoring all of these activities.

System 4: Development Management, similar to System 3, is a monitoring activity in System 3: Delivery management. If the purpose of System 3s * was monitoring activity via monitoring with the intent of establishing a current AS-IS picture, then System 4: Development Management is to create a TO-BE picture that incorporates the planning of development, determining budgets, developing strategies and lastly to determine and predict strategic risks. This view demands a broader distinction from the organization in order to be able to view it from the outside and in accordance with the surrounding environment. This is again in accordance with the responsibilities of RSI, however, the challenge would prevent itself from discouraging this development activity from also happening in local regional IT organizations such as KIT. Thus, RSI should transfer the strategic development from the regions and establish ownership at their organization if redundancies in terms of strategic, IT and operational development are not to occur locally and in a business silo.

System 5: Policy has tree functions attached which serve to consolidate the functions from System 3: Delivery management. These functions include:

- To determine a viable structure and strategy of the organization
- To secure essential values and the livelihood of the organization.
- To offset the role of the organization within the surrounding environment and the rest of the organization.

Summary and Recommendations for Further Analysis

Even by a very broad and general analysis of the identification of the various functions of the parts of the organization in relation to VSM, one is be able to expose organizational functions and structures that are wholly new information about the organization itself including more concrete knowledge of business processes.

Patrick Hoverstadt presents different ideas in his book on how one is able to optimize the different process levels within each system. In terms of optimizing the work of RSI for the rest of the organization it would arguably be relevant to examine especially how to improve the coherence, integrity and trust of the organization but also the development of the strategy. It serves part and parcel to underline the importance of the ability to be able to measure goals and decisions. This should be supported to give a personal responsibility of delivering something in return, so that the flow of management and strategy is not one-sided, but as a continuous loop of understanding. Given the complexity of the IT/enterprise architecture, it is our assumption that it would be valuable and interesting to examine how methods and tools within the Enterprise Architecture discipline would serve to support some of the monitoring processes which Patrick Hoverstadt finds important. Thus, one of RSIs main assignments should be the work of monitoring the IT-processes in Hospitals that span across the entire IT of the Regions of Denmark. In implementing this monitoring process, different methods could be employed, though they are not explained in detail in this article. Briefly, some of the methods could include KPI's, maturity assessments frameworks, BPM and BPMN. This will allow the stakeholders of the organization to get an overview and a clear picture of how Healthcare IT is utilized in the daily course of the work in the healthcare sector of Denmark.

In light of the systemic thinking approach, it would also be wise to look at how the organization fits in an enterprise architectural mind-set. With RSI's new management structure, Enterprise Architecture will most likely become an essential necessity to create insight, overview and coherence in the work that RSIs is set to accomplish. In other words, a requirement of a massive mapping of the systems catalogue along with all communication streams, both up and down-stream, would best be accompanied by an EA-tool as a supportive and attached element.

About the Authors

Rasmus is a digitalization consultant at the Municipality of Odense. He holds a BA in Media Sciences from University of Copenhagen, and a MSc in IT and Business from the IT University of Copenhagen.

Linda is an IT-strategy consultant at Region Sjælland. She is a professional nurse and radiation therapist, and holds a MSc in IT and Business from the IT University of Copenhagen.

References

Bestyrelsen for den nationale EPJ-organisation (2007) Strategiske udviklingsveje for EPJ, Deloitte.

Danske Regioner (2010) Pejlemærker for Sundheds-IT 2010.

Hoverstadt, Patrick, (2008) The Fractal Organization.

Koncern IT, Region Hovedstaden (2009) Ledelsesstrategi for Regionens sundheds-it.

Region Hovedstaden (2007) Koncern IT's Værdier.

Regionernes Sundheds-it Organisation (2010) En fælles regional samarbejdsmodel på sundheds-it området.

Regionernes Sundheds-it Organisation, website: http://www.regioner.dk/sundhed/sundheds-it/rsi/organisering

Rigshospitalet (2008) Rigshospitalets it-strategi 2008 – 2010, Region Hovedstaden

Saha, Pallab (2010) Advancing the Whole-of-Government Enterprise Architecture Adoption with Strategic (Systems) Thinking. NUS – Government Enterprise Architecture Research Project Report.

Sammenhængende digital sundhed i Danmark (2008) National strategi for digitalisering af sundhedsvæsenet 2008 – 2012, Danske Regioner.

Part 4

Systems Thinking in the Enterprise

Capability Formation Architecture for Provincial Reconstruction in Afghanistan

*Olov Östberg, Per Johannisson
and Per-Arne Persson*

Abstract

A Swedish national audit in 2011 reported serious shortcomings with regard to Sweden's contributions to international efforts, not least the participation in the UN-mandated NATO presence in Afghanistan, where Sweden was in charge of one of the 25 PRTs (Provincial Reconstruction Teams). A review of this engagement makes it undoubtedly clear that there are interoperability problems between and within the various communities of interests at play. These problems boil down to Sweden's century-old, self-imposed subsidiary doctrine that the Government only will tell the state agencies what to do, not how to do it, and that ministers as a result are using a hands-off approaches towards agencies. There is no comprehensive architecture for Sweden's declared comprehensive approach of the PRT engagement. A list of remedial action lines is presented. Recommended keywords for the future are High level architecture and Systems thinking, areas in which the experiences from the Swedish Armed Forces should be reused.

Keywords

Civil-military interoperability- systems thinking, change management, Sweden, Afghanistan, NATO

Preamble

In 2004, The Swedish National Audit Office (2004) found that there were serious shortcomings in the Government's management of the state agencies' use of information and communication technology – *eGov* – a fact which was hurting citizens and industry, as well as the agencies themselves. This was not news to present authors, who for a number of years before and after 2004 had been engaged in the promotion of a modern approach to the Swedish eGov struggle (Charas et al, 2007; Lind et al, 2009; Östberg, 2010).

Then, in 2011, The Swedish National Audit Office (2011) again found that there were serious shortcomings in the Government's capacity management, this time with regard to Swedish contributions to international efforts. And so, in the light of eGov experiences, the present paper sets out to follow up on one such international effort: Sweden's participation in the Provincial Reconstruction Teams – *PRTs* – in Afghanistan.

In both cases, the focal point is that the Government of Sweden is using is an extreme version of management via state agencies. The group of central offices is itself an agency, and every single contact between the government and citizens, industry, and society at large, take place at the perimeters of the 500+ independent agencies ('islands'); some very big and some very small. Unless the agencies are specifically instructed to team up with other agencies — and are provided with a team-up-budget — cross-agency projects and services are few and far apart. Swedish participation in international efforts is an area where cross-agency involvement is a necessity, but, as pointed out by the aforementioned 2011 audit, has yet to be implemented. Figure 1 is graphical interpretation of the state-of-the-art regarding Sweden's participation in Afghanistan.

Sweden in Afghanistan

Sweden's operations in Afghanistan consist of several
interacting parts – diplomacy, military operations,
civilian operations and development assistance.

Figure 1: There is no hub proper for the spokes at the Swedish Central Government Offices, no 'PRT Office of Comprehensive Approach'.

The UN-mandated NATO presence in Afghanistan

Osama bin Laden and the al-Qaeda network were believed responsible for the September 11, 2001 massive terror attacks in the United States. Following the Taliban's repeated refusal to expel bin Laden and his group and end its support for international terrorism, the United States and its partners launched an invasion of Afghanistan on October 7, 2001 (Operation Enduring Freedom, OEF). This invasion was a 'modernized' version of the invasion in Iraq, where CIMIC, the Civil-Military Cooperation concept, was used to emphasize the capability to achieve Tactical Consent from individuals and groups in the areas of importance. Today's popular notion of Winning Hearts and Minds implies a level of ideological communication with and control of the population, and thus goes far beyond CIMIC. Winning hearts and minds is however a phrase that has become associated with today's international civil-military presence in Afghanistan. Parallel to the OEF, the International Security

Assistance Force in Afghanistan (ISAF) under NATO command also has a regular military involvement in Afghanistan. ISAF is based on a UN peace-enforcement mandate and, as of 6 January 2012, engages 50 nations and 130,386 personnel. To this should be added the increasing national NGO contingent, i.e., along with the phasing out of the national troops (including some 700 from Sweden).

In form of the November 2010 Kabul Declaration, ISAF and the Government of the Islamic Republic of Afghanistan entered a new phase of joint effort, and set up the conditions for irreversible transition to full Afghan security responsibility and leadership in all provinces by the end of 2014. It was furthermore recognized that ISAF's mission is part of a wider international community effort, the success of which cannot be achieved by military means alone, and is intended to be consistent with a broader comprehensive approach involving both civilian and military actors under UN leadership. The New Face Transition (from enforced peace to mentorship for sustained peace) will be conditions-based, not calendar-driven, and will not equate to withdrawal of ISAF-troops. The international civilian effort, including the work done in nationally-led Provincial Reconstruction Teams (PRTs), should also continue to evolve and enable greater Afghan capacity and leadership and prepare for longer-term development assistance. As from the 2014 final withdrawal, the PRT division will however be discontinued.

It is a gigantic undertaking to bring about coherence in such a massed plethora of different types of capabilities and actors, especially when taking the security situation into consideration. One can even question if it is actually possible to establish inter- and intra-operability dealing with so many hearts, minds and structures; nations, politics, agendas, industry, military, the UN, the International Committee of the Red Cross (ICRC), etc. To this should be added that most of the ISAF member states supplement their respective peace-keeping agenda with rebuilding and development aid, and with democracy and human rights programs from Government and civil society. Not to mention that Afghanistan is a kaleidoscope of geography, religion, clans, insurgents, criminal networks, politics, and fights for power – a picture that is not facilitated by the lack of a capable centralized government in the war torn and poverty stricken nation.

Multidimensional interoperability comes to mind and so does Kurt Lewin's (1951) aphorism that "nothing is as practical as a good theory". A far-reaching conceptualization may on the other hand be met by approval, yet will prove to be overly difficult to implement.

Interoperability in Civil-Military Operations

The aforementioned difference between Winning Hearts and Minds (non-military efforts) and Tactical Consent (military efforts) indicates that there are interoperability issues in joint missions that need to be addressed.

In layman terminology, interoperability is a property referring to the ability of diverse systems and organizations to work together (inter-operate). The term is often used in a technical systems engineering sense, or alternatively in a broader sense, taking into account personal social, political, and organizational factors that impact system-to-system performance. If the system in question is the family of more or less independent government agencies, interoperability in the final analysis is the sine qua non for comprehensive Governmental capability. It requires Government leaders to take responsibility for improving the capabilities of Government agencies to effectively partner with other agencies and Governments as well as the private sector, non-profit groups, and research institutions. Governance is a foundational enabler for creating and improving Government interoperability/capability. That same governance was the focal point in the 2011 critique by the Swedish National Audit Office.

Addressing these foundational needs, and acknowledging that citizens and businesses expect efficient public services across Europe, the European Commission (2010) has initiated the 2010-2015 program on the Interoperability Solutions for European Public Administrations (ISA). The program addresses this need by facilitating efficient and effective cross-border electronic collaboration between European public administrations. ISA has a budget of 164.1 Million Euros. In the ISA context, interoperability means facilitated cross-border and cross-sector information exchange, taking into account legal, organizational, semantic (tactical), and syntactical (technical) aspects. It should be observed that ISA addresses service output (efficiency) rather than service uptake (effectiveness).

A similar dichotomy can be observed in military arenas, and in particular with regard to the use of computer technology. Operational headquarters needs to have in place a robust and efficient C3 agenda; Command, Control & Communications. By way of example, as a member of the NATO Partnership for Peace framework, Sweden invited NATO to participate in the development of such a "framework" to allow better interoperability between NATO and Sweden in civil-military settings. The ensuing joint project team consisted of the Swedish Armed Forces, the Swedish Defense Material Administration, the Swedish Emergency Agency, the NATO C3 Agency, and the city of Gothenburg. The overall objective for this Swedish agency initiated project was to test if a "service oriented architecture"

(SOA) in the form of many-to-one information sharing could facilitate the linking together of sensors, decision makers, and weapon systems, as well as multinational military, governmental, and non-Governmental agencies in a seamless, collaborative, planning, assessment and execution environment. Among the lessons learned, worthy of mention is that the military community must learn to speak "civilian" and that military resources can, from a civilian perspective, look enormous and can hamper collaboration on equal terms. Over all, the reported results were highly appreciative of the SOA approach (Arnell 2009):

> "As the project progressed the use of SOA turned out to be facilitator for the experiment's success. It is hard to conceive how the project could have been able to integrate such a variety of Swedish military and civilian systems together with NATO systems and actually, in such a short time span, get them to interact with each other, have we not chosen a SOA-environment. Even though the emphasis in this project was to demonstrate the technical benefits of a SOA-approach, essential operational questions of how to operate in a SOA-environment have been identified."

An ongoing reality test of civil-military interoperability & capability is taking place in Afghanistan in the form of ISAF, and its semi autonomous Provincial Reconstruction Teams (PRTs). They started as military installations with just thin guidance on the use and reuse of civilian resources. Since then, the PRTs have developed more towards civil-military cooperation on a more equal basis. Initially ISAF was charged to oversee the country's progression into democracy in just the Kabul capital and province, but it has steadily increased its mandate, through United Nations Security Council Resolutions, to cover the entire country. The ISAF lessons-learning process has placed the integration of participating nations' products high on the agenda, recognizing that "embeddedness" is not enough (Eronen 2008):

> "The bulk of the criticism is directed to the military's tendency to forget the realities outside its own camp. With only loose external and internal guidelines, the PRTs are 'left to their own devices' to organize their mission."

This should not come as a surprise; the PRTs were given a free rein to conduct themselves as they saw fit in their own provinces. The PRT Terms of Reference actually recognizes that PRT commanders, whilst following the general intent and spirit of these Terms of Reference, will be bound to follow operational priorities set by their respective military chains of command. This may require them to assign 'functions not listed', or carry out functions listed in a less prescriptive manner.

One example of 'functions not listed' is how to deal with the oftentimes stark culture of corruption. Local Afghanistan politicians are seen to want to get rid of the PRTs, so there can be more unfettered opportunities for corruption or stealing the aid money that comes with foreign peacekeepers (Strategy Page, 2011).

However complex the PRT system may be, the Afghanistan ISAF member states have to live with it for several years to come. According to the ISAF PRT Handbook, PRTs are interim structures to be dismantled when they have fulfilled their missions: to build up the capacity of a district or province, then leave or hand off to the Afghans when the Afghans are capable of managing for themselves. Easier and quicker said than done. The present paper therefore looks into the possibility of getting closer to a good theory in support of the practical work the PRTs have been tasked to carry out. The practical work will not be less complex after the PRT system has been discontinued in connection with the 2014 military withdrawal. Tomorrow's practical work can however be improved by attending to today's concerns.

That seems also to be the view of Godsave (2007). Based on the debate of how the PRT model is fairing in Afghanistan, she addressed the genuine concerns and issues which are rectifiable and suggested that the model might be more effective with clearer guidelines, an infrastructure project focus and advanced civilian training. With these improvements addressed, the model could be of future use in other post-conflict situations.

Reviewing the PRT concept, Abbaszade et al. (2008) concluded that the ISAF partners should continue to use PRTs and fund their activities. Some of the listed recommendations for improvements are that (1) a 'whole of Government' approach should be strengthened by means of dedicated appropriations, (2) the PRTs should eventually be civilian-led, yet fully supported by the military, and (3) deployments should be synchronized across agencies.

Re-Visiting the Concept 'Civil-Military'

By using the term 'Comprehensive Approach', EU has stressed the civil part of the PRTs. Norheim-Martinsen (2009) concluded that such a Eurocentric approach broadened the perspective to the extent that broad (civil-military) interoperability reduced the significance of traditional military interoperability. Such developments might however be dealt with by means of aforementioned 'good theory'.

Assessing the degree of (broad) civil-military interoperability, Svensson (2011) found that the differences in attitude within Swedish PRT mission were not primarily between civilian and military actors, but rather between the field level and the national level. Contributing to the civil-military field alignment, i.e. broad interoperability, was that the civil and military leadership was on par. Such observations are valuable for the design of a national Swedish comprehensive approach.

It is commonplace to associate Human Rights with Peace Building, especially since Peace Building usually takes place on a UN mandate; and since UN and its agencies are central in upholding and implementing the principles enshrined in the Universal Declaration of Human Rights. Based on five world-wide field studies Gunner and Nordquist (2011) found that agendas of Human Rights and Peace-Building, respectively, were in need of a new partnership approach, recognizing that there are built-in conflicts. This conflict is amply recognized in the October 2011 NATO Standards (Allied Joint Civil-Military Medical Interface Doctrine, AJMedP-6) that have been agreed by civilian humanitarian actors on the use of military assets. The most important standards are (emphasis added):

> *"(1) Military will only be employed on request of a civilian "Humanitarian Co-coordinator".*
>
> *(2) Engagement of military assets is a "means of last resort", only considered in the absence of adequate civilian assets to achieve a certain task.*
>
> *(3) All humanitarian engagement has to retain a "Civilian Character", so military assets will only be in a supporting role.*
>
> *(4) All military effort has to be limited in time and scope, providing a clear "exit strategy" for the handover to civilian actors.*
>
> *(5) All military assets have to respect the UN code of conduct.*
>
> ***These standards cannot be entirely accepted by the military, as operational planning is driven by differing imperatives.** But these standards need to be known to the military medical planners and recognized as a primary guide to civilian attitudes towards the military."*

Different standards may come into play at different development phases. These are the acknowledged phases for the International Security Assistance Forces (ISAF) operating in Afghanistan:

Peacemaking (PM) involves the diplomat-led activities aimed at establishing a cease-fire or a rapid peaceful settlement and is conducted after a conflict has started. Through comprehensive approaches, the activities can include the provision of good offices, mediation, conciliation, and such actions as diplomatic pressure, isolation, sanctions, or other activities. Peacemaking is accomplished primarily by diplomatic means; however, military support to peacemaking can be made either indirectly, through the threat of intervention, or in the form of direct involvement of military assets, matured into peacemaking.

Peace Enforcement (PE) operations normally take place under the principles of Chapter VII of the UN Charter. The difference between PE and other Peace support operations (PSOs) is that the Chapter VII mandate allows more freedom of action for the commander concerning the use of force without losing legitimacy, with a wider set of options being open. Even in a PE operation, consent should be pursued through persuasion prior to using force, with coercion through force being an option at any time without altering the original mandate. These operations are coercive in nature and are conducted when the consent of all parties to the conflict has not been achieved or might be uncertain. They are designed to maintain or re-establish peace or enforce the terms specified in the mandate. In the conduct of PE, the link between political and military objectives must be extremely close. It is important to emphasize that the aim of the PE operation will not be the defeat or destruction of an adversary, but rather to compel, coerce, and persuade the parties to comply with a particular desired outcome and the established rules and regulations.

Peace Building (PB) involves actions that support political, economic, military, and social measures through comprehensive approaches and that are aimed at strengthening political settlements of a conflict. Thus, for a society to regenerate and become self-sustaining, it must address the constituents of a functioning society. Peace Building includes mechanisms to identify and support structures that will consolidate peace, foster a sense of confidence and well-being, and support economic reconstruction. Peace Building therefore requires the commitment of political, humanitarian and development resources to a long-term political process.

Peacekeeping (PK) operations are generally undertaken in accordance with the principles of Chapter VI of the UN Charter in order to monitor and facilitate the implementation of a peace agreement. The loss of consent or the development of a non-compliant party may limit the freedom of action of the PK force and even threaten the continuation of the mission or cause it to evolve into a PE operation. Thus, the conduct of PK is driven by the requirement to build and retain perceived legitimacy. Peace Keepers, will then become Sustainable Peace Builders, and will eventually withdraw into roles as true Partners and Advisers.

The PRT capability mix-up will have to shift along with this moving PRT target, a fact which will be a hindrance to full interoperability: Central

Government vs. Field Personnel, Military vs. Civil approach, Society Build-up vs. Human Rights, Rotation #n vs Rotation #n+1, and so forth. To this should be added that the 50 ISAF nations and their 25 PRTs to a certain degree have different goals and compositions, not to mention the vast number of different Communities of Interests (COIs) that make up the Islamic Republic of Afghanistan. In general terminology, COI means sharing agreement as to goals. NATO has a more strict definition:

> *"A Community of Interest (COI) is a collaborative grouping of users who share and exchange information in the pursuit of common goals or missions." NATO Architecture Framework; NAF113_Ann3_APP07 (2007).*

This self-organized group collaborates by sharing information, ideas, common practices and other resources to pursue and enhance achievement of common interests, processes, goals, or missions. Communities of Interest span institutional structures and hierarchies and are not bound by organizational affiliation. A shared vocabulary enables information exchanges.

The ISAF PRTs is a COI made up of swarms of nested sub COIs that are not stable over time, and when operating in Afghanistan they are tasked to interoperate with an even more complex plethora of COIs. An oversimplified graphic description of the resulting COI playing ground is shown in Figure 2 on the next page.

This illustration[9] was created by PA Consulting Group on behalf of the U.S. Office of the Joint Chiefs of Staff, and shows the U.S. military's plan for "Afghanistan Stability/COIN Dynamics – Security." COIN stands for Counter-Insurgency.

---

[9] The picture was widely circulated in 2009, after having been distributed at a press conference (see e.g. http://nbcnews.to/13RXO1J)

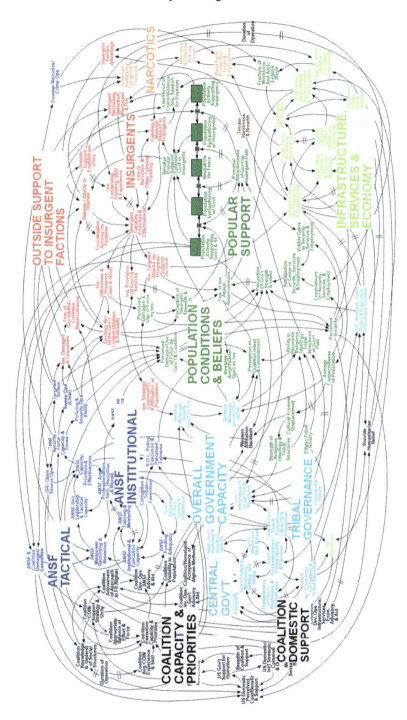

Figure 2. PA Consulting Group on behalf of the U.S. Office of the Joint Chiefs of Staff. Reproduced with permission from the US-based Project on Defense Alternatives (2012)

As clearly illustrated in Figure 2, the interplay characteristics in Afghanistan are extremely complex. At a summer 2009 briefing in Kabul, Stanley McChrystal (2011), former US commander of allied occupation force, commented that very figure with the words: "When we understand that slide, we'll have won the war". And two years later, reflecting on the 10 years of US presence in Afghanistan: "We didn't know enough and we still don't know enough. Most of us, me included, had a very superficial understanding of the situation and history, and we had a frighteningly simplistic view of recent history, the last 50 years".

It should be noted, however, that Figure 2 has a Counter Insurgence (COIN) perspective, i.e., a military rather than civil perspective. What would then a civil-military PRT perspective be?

It has been argued that the ISAF PRT concept, as introduced by UN, will be "a crucible of civil-military relations in the future" (Frerks et al 2006). For the time being there are 25 PRTs, of which e.g. the one operated by the U.S. is located in a hostile area whereas the ones operated by Sweden and Germany, respectively, are located in more peaceful areas. The U.S. views seem to prevail, and as earlier noted, CIMIC, the Civil-Military Cooperation concept, was used to emphasize the capability to achieve Tactical Consent from individuals and groups in the areas of importance.

From a humanitarian point of view, "PRTs are hybrid structures which have contributed to the blurring if not altogether erasing the distinction between humanitarian aid and military objectives" (Runge 2009). Many civil and non-government organization are therefore distancing themselves from civil-military cooperation (subdues conflicts) and would rather use the phrase civil-military relations (accepts conflicts). For example, for a key organization like the ICRC, the conducting of neutral, independent and impartial humanitarian action in situations of armed conflict and internal violence is at the heart of its mandate and a fundamental part of its identity. The ICRC seeks dialogue with *all* actors involved in a situation of armed conflict or internal violence as well as with the people suffering the consequences to gain their acceptance and respect. This approach is chosen to give them the widest possible access both to the victims of the violence and to the actors involved. It also helps to ensure the safety of the staff on mission. In relation to these key principles of the ICRC, close co-operation with the military entities of one side is therefore problematic.

Interoperability Makes Sense

If the mission commander is unable to make sense of the big and small pictures beaming up from the mission arena — see Figure 2 — then surely the individual actors may have grounds for feeling like being part of a senseless mission. The individuals have to make sense of what trickles down from 'higher levels': the mission objectives, the strategy and tactics implemented in their own units and those of other units, and, of outmost importance, the actions and reactions of the Afghan society.

Not being able to make sense of 'something' can be phrased as not being interoperable with this 'something', be it organizations, people, signals, tools, or environments. Sense making and situational awareness can be viewed as concepts that enable us to investigate and improve the interaction between people, systems, and technology artifacts. The present paper will however use the more established concepts interoperability and community of interest (COI).

Interoperability is a hallmark for a community of interest (COI), i.e. units sharing and exchanging information in the pursuit of common goals or missions. The units may in turn consist of sub units, etc. ISAF is made up of PRTs, which have military and civil branches, which in turn make up COIs that have to be interoperable vis-a-vis Afghan soil and society as indicated in Figure 2.

A look at the Swedish PRT engagement reveals some interoperability anomalies believed to be present in most of the 25 PRTs at work in Afghanistan.

Mazar-e-Sharif (led by Sweden); 1 out of 25 PRTs

Sweden has a military presence in Afghanistan as from 2002, and as a PRT actor as from 2006. In March 2011, in an audit report, the Swedish National Audit Office (2011) published findings and recommendations regarding Sweden's contributions to the international efforts in Afghanistan:

> *The Government's political statements and policies concerning international engagements have not been manifested in instructions to the concerned agencies.*
>
> *FBA (Folke Bernadotte Academy) the agency tasked to functions as a platform for cooperation between Swedish agencies and organizations, and their international partners, has not been provided with any means to bring about coordination and cooperation, and has to rely on 'management by education'.*
>
> *FM (the Swedish Armed Forces) has a next to zero civil/military capacity of relevance for international engagements; the Government has not issued a single requirement as to how such a capability shall come about and for what tasks it shall be used.*

As a response to this audit critique, the Government tasked FOI, Swedish Defense Research Agency, for a more detailed account of the Swedish presence in Afghanistan. The telling title of the report is Chasing Synergy (Tham et al 2011), which starts by rephrasing what the Government wants the targeted agencies to deliver:

> *A new PRT model – a Transition Support Team – shall be introduced that is expected to be developed to the extent that by 2012 that there will be a civilian command-and-control of the entire Swedish engagement (civilian as well as military) in the Mazar-e-Sharif region.*

> *The Swedish PRT shall be targeted toward supporting the capacity build-up of the Afghan security forces. And the new model, planning, management, and implementation, shall take place in a conjoint manner.*

> *It is nevertheless of outmost importance that the roles are clearly separated. Humanitarian aid and international military presence must be separated. Yet, there must be synergy between said two efforts.*

The second part of the report is to some extent the result of a field study tailored toward providing information on the most crucial aspect of what the Government had instructed its PRT actor to do:

> *The PRTs approaches have over the years continued to have a strong military component as prescribed in the ISAF doctrines on operational control (OPCON) and counter-insurgency (COIN) respectively. As a result Sweden's comprehensive and balanced civil-military approach has been compromised. The problem is that Sweden has not made it clear how its PRT shall relate to ISAF's doctrines*

> *Advised by the Swedish Defense Research Agency (FOI), Sweden in 2010 established a civil PRT office co-located with the Swedish military forces. The office is headed by an ambassador from the Ministry of Foreign Affairs, and rest the staff are advisers from various Governmental agencies (including FOI). Formally, and contrary to the military office, the civil office reports to the Embassy in Kabul. One negative consequence of this organization is that the advisers don't know if they 'belong' to the embassy or to their respective agencies in Sweden. The general view is that this is a hindrance to synergy between the agency capabilities. Another often-voiced view is that the civil office was established too late and is understaffed.*

As to the civil-military synergy, a major drawback is that there are no common Terms of Reference for the two co-located offices and their meetings. Besides the valued informal information exchange at the meetings, the primary function of the meetings is that the military side can ask the civil side on its views on the military planning and can ask for support for ongoing and planned operations.

With regard to Chasing Civil-Military Synergy, the primary obstacles are (i) that there is no formal synergy-enhancing structure in place, and (ii) that there are at least two different chains of command in place. Synergies often evolve on a person-to-person base, but now and then agencies change their PRT representatives. An even more problematic situation is the Swedish International Development Cooperation Agency (SIDA), the most important civil agency in Sweden's PRT, does not have a seat at the PRT ISAF table – nor does SIDA want their aid projects to be militarily 'tainted'.

A companion to the lack of Swedish civil-military synergy is the existence of a stark Civil-Military Resource Asymmetry (Egnell and Nilsson 2011). The military part oftentimes has had a long preparation time, comes well equipped and well staffed, and hereby sets the agenda. The military part further more has a tradition of quick and forceful actions, whereas the civil side has a low intensive and protracted agenda. Contributing to the evolvement of biased agenda settings is the fact that the Swedish Government never made it clear what was meant by Coordination Gains (Lackenbauer 2011) and Synergy, respectively.

PRTs in General

In his capacity as special advisor on development for UNAMA – the U.N. Assistance Mission in Afghanistan – Mark Ward (2010) summarized the over-all development of the PRTs:

The Afghan Government now has a presence in many districts and provinces. They are managing small development projects themselves, as they should. And they are getting better all the time. And funds available to PRTs to do projects have grown significantly.

The problem is that many PRTs are still doing short term local projects when the Afghans can do them for themselves, quite often, without being fully coordinated with local Governmental representatives. And many of the PRTs have more funds than the local Afghan authorities. So in many provinces, the PRT is now competing with the local Afghan authorities to deliver services to the communities.

So what should the PRTs be doing differently? A few practical suggestions:

First, the PRTs should start providing some of their funding to the Government, such as through the National Solidarity Program, so the people see their Government getting things done. The PRTs may be able to play a supporting role, but the Afghans have to lead and be seen in the lead.

Second, stop competing with the Afghans and direct PRT funds to those longer term projects which the Afghans do not yet have the capacity to manage. Take on a coordinated multi-year project instead. Don't insist on starting and finishing the project during your short rotation. PRT commanders should not be rewarded for cutting ribbons on short term projects during their rotations. They should be rewarded for standing back and letting the Afghans do the work, or for starting complex multi-year projects that the local Afghans can't manage themselves.

Third, search for and use locally produced items and services whenever possible, be it bottled water, furniture, cement or construction services. When you procure locally you are spending your dollars twice by keeping funds in this country, and within local markets.

Fourth, think about a transition plan for your PRT in your region. In some parts of the country, we may be able to turn the PRTs over to the Afghans relatively soon. They need local infrastructure and might welcome the facility you have built. In other parts of the country, where Afghan capacity is not yet far enough along, maybe there is a role for an international civilian organization in the interim. Or your Government may want to use the PRT in the future as a base for civilian diplomatic and development work. The important thing is to start thinking about where you are going.

Managing the Swedish PRT Presence in Afghanistan: To-Do List

Today's PRT system is based on military considerations and will eventually be replaced by a new model when all civil/military support in 2014 will be fully civil. The Swedish capacity building for the unknown future must be a truly forward looking 'lessons learned' approach:

1. Accept that a PRT is a dynamic concept that needs agile attention and tuning.
2. The comprehensive approach used in Afghanistan should be based on a comprehensive approach originating from Sweden.

3.   A 'PRT Office of Comprehensive Approach', at the Central Government Offices, should have decision power across stove-piped ministries and agencies.
4.   The PRT Office should be the 'owner', guardian, and implementer of a basic PRT architecture for concepts, missions, and capabilities.
5.   Swedish adaptation of the ISAF PRT Handbook.
6.   The transition from an all-military to an all-civil mission should be based on reality (facts), and thus should not be calendar driven.
7.   The structures and protocols for meetings in Afghanistan, and reporting back to Sweden, should be formalized.
8.   Field personnel recruited from state agencies should report to the PRT Office, and not to their respective base agencies.
9.   Field personnel from state agencies and civil society (public) alike should be 'PRT Certified' by the FBA Agency tasked to provide PRT capability training.
10.   Training should include "How to separate roles, yet work as a team."

Outline of a Basic PRT Architecture for Sweden's PRT Presence in Afghanistan

Returning to Figure 2, there are actually 13 different interoperability domains at the ISAF Counter Insurgent (COIN) side, i.e. 13 different Communities of Interest (COIs). The insurgent side have their own COIs and interoperability domains.

When the figure was released in 2009, it was met with comments such as i) this is the ultimate command and control architecture make believe dream in which all aspect of a war situation is under `control´ and can be addressed, or ii) this only shows how far removed the Pentagon gang has become from the Main street pedestrian view that the `project´ of occupying a foreign nation to protect security at home is incomprehensible, expensive, time consuming, ineffective and ultimately leads us to be lost in a hopeless `spaghetti logic´.

It is a fact that Sweden is one out of 50 nations participating in an UN-mandated NATO presence in Afghanistan named ISAF PRT, based on civil-military cooperation, and that Sweden is the lead nation in one of the 25 PRTs. A conclusion is that Sweden does need some sort of interoperability & capacity map / architecture to transform from being helpful soldiers fighting insurgents into civil advisors in the (re)building of the institutions of the Afghanistan society.

Let's give it a try!

Let's suppose that there is a sufficient degree of interoperability within the 13 COIs discernible in Figure 2. But we know for a fact that there is a serious lack of interoperability in-between various PRT COIs. When two

COIs are trying to make sense of each other, at least two interactions are needed. A complete interoperability sensing-out in-between 13 COIs means 169 time-consuming and costly interactions. There is, however, no need for an all-embracing PRT interoperability, and so a system or architecture for task-selective (service oriented) interoperability building would be an extremely useful tool. It should be stressed that interoperability building is a generic concept that incorporates not only vocabularies but more importantly e.g. capability building. And a COI can be a federation of systems.

Now let's move to Sweden.

UN, EU, and NATO are calling!

This is not news to the generals and diplomats. The Swedish Armed Forces have in fact been working on this for quite some time, and presents a structured overview of what it takes for Sweden to participate in the multi-national effort in Afghanistan. The military part of the requested task force, based on civil-military cooperation, seems to be in good shape, so the Government appoints an ad hoc cross-agency advisory group to provide advice, primarily to the ministry of Foreign Affairs, on the softer part of the Afghanistan 'troop'.

Time goes on. Not much is heard in Sweden on the developments in Afghanistan, except for occasional information flares in connection with rare Swedish casualties. The politicians in charge are awaiting the 2014 election. The state-of-the-year-2012-art is that the Ministry for Foreign Affairs without any defined method struggles with the delivery of *civil-military* capacity in Afghanistan, and has a hands-off (or gloves on) approach to civil-*military* capacity.

Figures 3 and 4 are diagrams of the present authors' views on a Swedish agile, modern structure for addressing international efforts. No such comprehensive approach is in place today. With regard to security matters, including the management of a PRT in Afghanistan, an Inquiry (SOU 2011) in March 2011 concluded that:

> *The security concept has been broadened over the years and the Ministry of Foreign Affairs (MFA) has a responsibility that has been expanded without this being defined or the division of responsibilities between ministries being clarified. The Inquiry proposes that this be done. The MFA must actively take the lead and provide support for the rest of the Government Offices.*

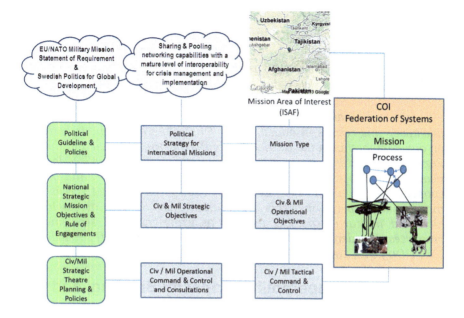

Figure 3. Proposed diagram for future mission networking capabilities.

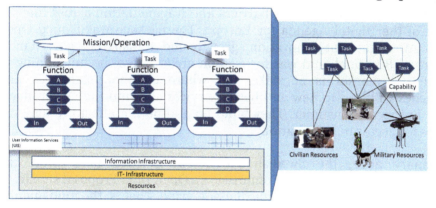

Figure 4. Complementary view of the 'engine box' (see Figure 3). Information services cater for the needed information exchange between mission actors. This takes place by means of infrastructural channels and product.

Components of the 'engine box' (Figures 3 and 4) are already up and running at the Swedish Armed Forces. In line with #3 in aforementioned "To-do List" – and in response to the Inquiry – the Government should take charge of this 'box' and turn it into a Comprehensive PRT Office of sort. Standardized operational procedures should be used for achievements to be delivered.

Information infrastructure (Figure 4) is a socio-technical concept emphasizing that service takes place within existing infrastructures, including the whole network of technology, vendors and customers

(Bygstad 2010). It is not an easy task to bring together military and civil into such a joint planning environment. But it must be done, especially as the PRTs are required to develop from fully military to fully civil. Some of the merging issues are illustrated in Figure 5. The Swedish Government has on the other hand acknowledged that support is available:

> *Sweden shall make use of the civil-military dimension, a least whenever this results in added value. This cooperation builds both on our Partnership in the Euro-Atlantic Partnership Council and the Partnership for Peace, including our participation in NATO- led peace-support operations in the Balkans and Afghanistan, and on cooperation between the EU and NATO on EU-led crisis-management operations. This cooperation gives Sweden access to civil and military expertise, as well as experience and strategic resources. Sweden's cooperation with NATO in EAPC/PfP, Article No.: UD05.018, 2005*

An Engine for Interoperability, Capacity Building, and Change Management

In December 2011, the European Commission presented a package of measures to overcome existing barriers and fragmentation across the EU, as part of the Digital Agenda for Europe. The package was named Open data -- An engine for innovation, growth and transparent governance, COM(2011) 882 final, and was focused on areas where the functioning of the internal market is at stake and where common standards and approaches will lead to new and better services and information products for the European consumer. They build on and do not affect the national regimes for access to information.

In January 2012, the Swedish Parliament decided to support the Government position that the Commission's Open Data Proposal should be rejected with reference to the subsidiary doctrine. That is, the fundamental doctrine that policy making decisions should be made at the most decentralized level, in which a centralized governing body would not take action unless it is more effective than action taken at a lower government level. Reference to this principle is often used by EU Member States which for one reason or other are unhappy with decisions from the European Commission. Such requests are rarely successful beside from the benefit of some 4-6 years of leeway. With respect to the `open data engine´, this means that Swedish Public Authorities can keep charging for public data for several more years.

A subsidiary doctrine of sorts has been used in Sweden for hundreds of years, to the effect that the Government only (can) tell the state agencies what to do, not how to do it, and that ministers as a result are using hands-off approaches towards agencies.

That very self-applied doctrine is the explanation for the lack of a central Government PRT engine, see Figure 1. The doctrine should, however, NOT be applied in this case. More effective actions can NOT be taken at a lower government level, be it civil, military or civil-military.

Let there be an Engine for Interoperability, Capacity Building, and Change Management, as symbolically depicted in Figure 5.

And let it be fully understood that said engine is a generic concept for handling any kind of knowledge in any kind of Community of Interest:

- people
- skills
- missions
- software

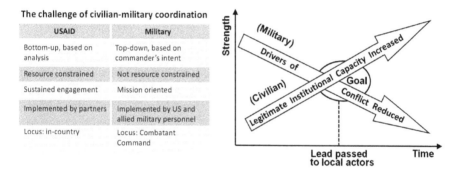

Figure 5. Left: The planning environments for civilian vs. military efforts [Civilian-Military Operations Guide, USAID's Office of Military Affairs, Ver. 1, 2010]. Right: Spectrum of conflict transformation [ISAF PRT Handbook, Ed. 4, 2010]

The envisaged Engine for Interoperability, Capacity Building, and Change Management is a major administrative undertaking. Niccolò Machiavelli (1469-1532), the founder of modern political science, had this to say about such undertakings (Machiavelli 1532):

It must be considered that there is nothing more difficult to carry out, nor more doubtful of success, nor more dangerous to handle, than to initiate a new order of things. For the reformer has enemies in all those who profit by the old order, and only lukewarm defenders in all those who would profit by the new order, this lukewarmness arising partly from fear of their adversaries, who have the laws in their favor; and partly from the incredulity of mankind, who do not truly believe in anything new until they have had the actual experience of it.

Systems Thinking is Mandatory

On March 12, 2012, the Swedish PRT was officially declared as a civil mission headed by an ambassador reporting to the Swedish Foreign Service (SFS) the military troop will probably not be reduced until late 2014. Earlier, on February 2011, a Government Expert Group on Public Economics (Murray 2011) called for a thorough SFS modernization with regard to efficiency and effectiveness, because:

> Besides SFS, several ministries — e.g. defenso, finance, environment, industry, and justice — have equally as important Foreign relations issues as do Foreign aid and trade. The general mechanism for coordinating Government policy is joint preparation based on the collective decision-making of the ministers in the Cabinet. Indeed a complicated matrix organization with entangled administrations and politics, and as a result there is no defined business case but a business characterized by "one damned thing after another." The solution must be to have three separate ministries, for Foreign Policy, Foreign Trade, and Foreign Aid and Development, respectively.

Niccolò Machiavelli would probably have advised Sweden not to split SFS into three ministries. OK, says the report from The Government Expert Group on Public Economics, it may possibly work without a split, but here are some of the must-haves in relation to e.g. the Swedish presence in Afghanistan:

- Develop a mission and business idea
- Introduce a clear line of command
- Clarify that missions are part of the Government Offices
- Establish a project organization
- Develop a "learning organization"
- Develop information technology for the needs both of the Ministry for Foreign Affairs, as well as for the Government Offices as a whole
- Establish a position as administrative head of the entire SFS
- Concentrate and strengthen the control of the agencies involved
- Strengthen the control of the ministry by both the Parliament and by the Government
- Broaden recruitment to the FS
- Make personnel administration a joint function for the Ministry for Foreign Affairs and the Government Offices
- Develop business data, monitoring and evaluation

- Summon the staff of the Ministry for Foreign Affairs into one, modern office

The common denominator for the above bullets is that there must be a Framework in the form of a High Level Architecture and an analysis according to Systems Thinking.

In the hard, concrete, physical world, a framework is a structure for supporting or enclosing something else, especially a skeletal support used as the basis for something being constructed. In the soft, cognitive, management world, a framework is a set of assumptions, concepts, values, and practices that constitutes a way of viewing reality and providing core directions.

Architecture is, within systems engineering, defined as "fundamental concepts or properties of a system in its environment embodied in its elements, relationships, and in the principles of its design and evolution" (ISO 42010). Consequently, in a social system "fundamental" concepts and properties refer to people-elements and inter-human relations, formal and informal power positions, objectives, preferences and law. Originally the High Level Architecture (HLA) concept was developed in the US Department of Defense and later applied in the Swedish Network-Based Defence Initiative (Wang et al 2008). A HLA provides the specification of a common technical architecture for use across all classes of simulations. It provides the structural basis for simulation interoperability. It is likely to be useful when planning and preparing for missions, new as well as ongoing, in order to test equipment and procedures.

A system is a set of elements that are interrelated or interact with one another for a certain purpose within a larger whole – the system. A system has emergent properties which ideally mean that the whole is more than the parts.

Systems thinking can mean two different approaches. The first is the seemingly attractive and applied but not suitable type of systems thinking in terms of engineering, modeling, design and construction (Checkland 1999). It dominates the political and military thinking and acting but it is not enough, instead opening for negligence towards the abundant social, cultural and political PRT-issues we have described. Worse, the concepts involved in the architectural foundation for this kind of systems approach do not allow for making sense of the operational theatre (What is going on? What to do?). The underpinning ontology may become corrupt.

Therefore, in accordance with our previous statements when applied on a social system, the second kind of systems thinking is a way to apply a unique perspective on (the social) reality, which sharpens the awareness of the whole (i.e. the system in focus) and its inter-related parts (subsystems). This way of systems thinking aims at discovery, learning, diagnosis and dialog for better understanding, definition and work with systems, possibly through modeling (Haskins 2007). It is through communication, a suitable hierarchy and control that this whole can demonstrate the previously mentioned and desired emergent properties as a system, and survive in a changing environment. This is applicable on any organization, whether it is a ministry, a Non-Governmental Organization (NGO) or a PRT/TST. Those in command or in office should understand these fundamentals which actually are possible to track back to Machiavelli's principles that we have referred to.

Unfortunately, the record of PRT-deployment indicates that the first type of systems thinking dominates, possibly because it legitimates impaired and detached managerial control in favor of an all too political control system which prioritizes its own endurance at the cost of the PRT-survival. Another explanation to the current situation is a common lack of organizing competence and system insight, something that can be cured however.

There will be an opportunity to apply the outlined type of systems thinking in the next phase of the Afghanistan mission. Sweden and Finland have been partners in the Swedish led PRT in Mazar-e-Sharif. It will be business as usual in the near future, but the PRTs (Provincial Reconstruction Teams) will be renamed TSTs (Transitional Support Teams). The military TST component will gradually disappear, but it is doubtful if the Swedish civil support to Afghanistan will be channeled via the TST in Mazar-e-Sharif. There is however no doubt about the Swedish commitment; as from 2013 Afghanistan will be number 1 recipient of Swedish Foreign aid.

Lessons Learned

The above bullets on developing a learning organization are addressed by The Centre for Army Lessons Learned, and in particular by its US Afghanistan PRT Handbook. The published lessons learned and best practices are actions that PRT members have employed to overcome situation-specific obstacles and achieve a desired outcome; and they have been shared with the US allied ISAF partners (including Sweden). "These should not be interpreted as `one-size-fits-all´ solutions or doctrines. What works in one place and time may not work in another place and time. Rather, these are actions that have been effective in the past and that should be considered by future PRT members. Deployed personnel must use their own discretion to determine whether such actions or suggestions would be useful in their particular circumstances."

The PRT Handbook is not a doctrinal product. The information provided is written by US Government employees for those individuals who will serve in a stability and reconstruction environment. The handbook describes an architecture framework in the form of an analysis and program management process specifically designed to help practitioners improve stability in a local area. The framework's four steps are i) Situational awareness, ii) Analysis, iii) Design, and iv) Monitoring and evaluation. It encourages unity of effort by providing field implementers from various organizations with a common framework to:

- Understand the environment from a stability-focused perspective.
- Maintain focus on the local population and its perceptions.
- Identify the root causes (sources) of instability in a specific local area.
- Design activities that specifically address the identified sources of instability.
- Monitor and evaluate activity outputs and impacts, as well as changes in overall stability.

It is of outmost interest that The International Council of Swedish Industry together with the non-profit Swedish Institute of International Affairs has published a report (Andersson, 2011) calling for such a framework for analysis with regard to corporate activity in sensitive markets characterized by conflicts.

Sweden has contributed troops to ISAF as from 2001. On June 1, 2012, the Swedish military personnel rotation #23 was on duty, amounting to a troop of 500. As informally agreed at the NATO Lisbon Summit in November 2011, the ISAF mission withdrawal would begin in 2011 and would be completed by the end of 2014. Sweden's gradual withdrawal will be carefully planned, starting with troop rotation #24. Some of the 50 nations contributing to ISAF have political problems with the proposed gradual withdrawal agenda. By way of example, after an Afghan soldier in January 2012 shot and killed four French soldiers on a base in eastern Afghanistan, France immediately suspended military training and assistance for Afghan forces and set its national final withdrawal date to the end of 2013.

France is not the only ISAF nation setting an agenda of its own. Such behavior is to be expected when 28 NATO members and 22 other ISAF nations join forces in a dangerous multiyear mission. In such an environment there will always be a degree of non-interoperability between nations, between military the civil and operations, and between actors within operation.

These events witness of the need for careful analysis and measures to be taken.

Conclusions

The problems and frustrations experienced by Sweden in connection with participating in the UN-mandated NATO presence in Afghanistan are by and large shared with other nations. Recent Swedish investigation have pointed out that the Government is in need of modern tools and management structures, not just with regard to Afghanistan but for Sweden's ever increasing international engagement, in public as well as private sector. Recommended keywords for the future are High level architecture (for simulation during design and planning) and Systems thinking (adjusted for social systems), areas in which the experiences from the Swedish Armed Forces should be reused. It is necessary, however, to realize what the system is before pure engineering principles are applied, and that politics includes risk-taking and responsibility, not only political survival. Specifically, crucial systems aspects to consider are about hierarchy, distribution of authority, communication and control in order to make different organizational elements form a well-functioning whole. Just chasing synergy is not enough – it should be calculated in the design and planning phase of a mission.

During the NATO Summit in Chicago, May 20–21, 2012, Sweden and Finland jointly pushed for increased ISAF attention to interoperability and capacity building during the orderly withdrawal process. This is in line with the smart defense concept introduced by NATO Secretary General Anders Fogh Rasmussen; ISAF members are facing fiscal restraints and NATO must see to it that resources should not be wasted as a result of capability and interoperability insufficiencies. We believe that an analysis based on systems thinking will clarify the practical requirements to achieve proper interoperability because communication is a crucial capacity, not only in technical terms.

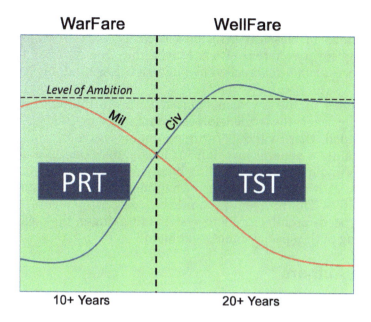

WarFare   **WellFare**

Level of Ambition

Mil   *Civ*

PRT   TST

10+ Years   20+ Years

Figure 6. A GamePad view of the military/civilian dynamics as outlined at the NATO Summit in Chicago, May 20–21, 2012.

The 'smooth' view in Figure 6 should be compared to the more chaotic (realistic?) view in Figure 2. What cannot be contested however is the urgent need for a smart foreign support architecture focusing on interoperability and capacity building.

Finally, there is also no doubt about the need for a Swedish 'smart' Foreign support architecture focusing on interoperability and capacity building. By 'smart' is meant that one should pick up elements from the rapid Internet development regarding e.g. Open Government Data and Social Media (Klang & Nolin, 2011). The uncovered central government shortcomings when handling the PRT issues must not continue in the TST era and beyond, be it Swedish civil, military, or civil-military activities at foreign soil.

We feel it necessary to remind that interoperability is more than technical connections, and that capability building exceeds systems engineering but can rely and presuppose it. The examples and lessons learned demonstrate the need for tailoring missions and teams to actual conditions, and to share experiences between nation states.

We point at the need for joint training and education of policy makers, civilian and military officials, the adaption of objectives to circumstances and to realize that capability is not an object or machine. It grows from commitment and motivation. Properly used, systems thinking can counter the tendency to execute faceless, anonymous political control of missions abroad by admitting too many cooks around the kettles letting each one get a spoon instead of classical principles such as unity of command and accountability for a coherent effort. Maybe the "one damned thing after another"-process can be succeeded by one that is less random.

The weaknesses in the Swedish approach was further uncoiled to the general public when the armed forces commander-in-chief in December 2012 concluded that without further funding Sweden could not be defended against a general invasion for longer than one week (O'Dwyer, 2013). The prime minister responding by saying that defense was a special interest area with no higher priority than any other of the state's many areas of politics. The problem is, however, as seen in Figure 1, that the government needs architecture and systems thinking in the balancing and interoperating of the special interests at hand.

About the Authors

Olov Östberg is Professor emeritus at Mid Sweden University. Olov has held professor positions in Sweden, Japan, USA and UK. He has been granted four patents. The present paper is #238 in his CV, which covers areas such as Occupational Safety and Health, Industrial Engineering and Psychology, Human Factors, Human Computer Interaction, and Circadian Rhythm. Interspersed with research, he has spent 25 years with Public Administration Agencies providing advice on the role of eGovernment.

Per Johannisson is a Senior Technical Expert of Architecture from the Swedish Defense Material Administration, and a retired technical officer from the Swedish Royal Navy with specialties in underwater technology and communication. He is currently running the Nii Enterprise Architecture Company providing tactical & technical functions as a service (FaaS) for governmental agencies and civilian commercial and industrial life.

Per-Arne Persson, PhD, LtCol (Ret.) is a former Army officer. His dissertation in 2000 at Linköping University dealt with Information Systems Design for Command Work. After working in a transformation program for the Swedish defense, he got a research position at the Swedish National Defense College in 2004. He became responsible for a development project for the lower level military intelligence function, spanning strategic planning, organizational design, and tools for intelligence analysis.

References

Abbaszadeh, N., Crow, M., El-Khoury, M., Gandomi, J., Kuwayama, D., MacPherson, C., Nutting, M., Parker, N, and Weiss; T., Provincial

Reconstruction Teams: Lessons and Recommendations. Woodrow Wilson School of Public & International Affairs, Princeton University, 2008.

Andersson, J., Evers, T., and Sjöstedt, G. (2011) Private Sector Actors & Peacebuilding. Stockholm: Swedish Institute of International Affairs.

Arnell, K et al (2009) NATO and Sweden Joint Live Experiment on NEC: A First Step Towards a NEC Realization. Reference Document DOP-D125-09. NATO Consultation, Command and Control Agency.

Bygstad, B. (2010), Generative mechanisms for innovation in information infrastructures. Journal of Information and Organization, 20:3-4, Pp. 156-168.

Charas, P., Johannisson, P., & Ostberg, O., A Philosophy of Public Service - Architectural Principles for Digital Democracy. International Journal of Public Information Systems, 2007:2, Pp. 89-99.

Checkland, P, Systems Thinking, Systems Practice, John Wiley & Sons, Chichester 1999.

Egnell, R., and Nilsson, C., Swedish civil-military cooperation in international efforts: From promising concept to concrete action. The Royal Swedish Academy of War Sciences Proceedings and Journal, 2011:1, 75-93 (In Swedish, English summary).

Eronen, O. (2008) PRT Models in Afghanistan. Approaches to Civil-Military Integration. CMC. Finland Civilian Crisis Management Studies, 1(5).

European Commission (2010) Towards interoperability for European public services. COM(2010) 744.

Frerks, G., Klem, B., Laar, S. van, and Klingeren, M. van. Principles and pragmatism: civil-military action in Afghanistan and Liberia. Utrecht: University of Utrecht, Bart Kleim Research Report, 2006.

Godsave, H., The Provincial Reconstruction Team (PRT) model of post-conflict intervention: progress in Afghanistan and future Prospects. MA Dissertation. Conflict, security and development programme. London: King's College, 2007.

Gunner, G, and Nordquist, K.-A. (2011), An Unlikely Dilemma – Constructing a partnership between human rights and peace building. Church of Sweden Research Series No 4

Haskins, C. (ed.) (2007) INCOSE Systems Engineering Handbook, a Guide for Life Cycle Processes and Activities (Version 3.1)

ISO/IEC/IEEE 42010:2011 – Systems and software engineering – Architecture description

Klang, M. & Nolin, J. To Inform or to Interact, that is the question: The role of Freedom of Information. Social Media Policies, Information Science and Social Media – International Conference, Åbo/Turku, Finland, 2011.

Lackenbauer, H. (2011). Reflections on civil-military cooperation in Afghanistan – Experiences from a political adviser 2009-2010. Swedish Defense Research Agency. FOI Memo 37093 (in Swedish).

Lewin, K. (1951) Field theory in social science; selected theoretical papers. D. Cartwright (Ed.). New York: Harper & Row.

Lind, M., Ostberg, O., & Johannisson, P., Acting Out the Swedish e-Government Action plan - Mind and Mend the Gaps. International Journal of Public Information System, Vol.2009:2, Pp. 37-60.

Machiavelli, N., The Prince. Chapter VI. Florence, 1532.

McChrystal, S. (2011) after 10 years, Afghan war only half done. The Guardian, 7 October 2011

Murray, R., (2011) A New Situation for the Foreign Service. Stockholm: The Government Expert Group on Public Economics, ESO 2011:1

Norheim-Martinsen, P. M., EU capabilities for a Comprehensive Approach: Broad Interoperability as a Comparative Advantage. Norwegian Defence Research Establishment, FFI-rapport 2009/01300.

O'Dwyer, G. (2013) Sweden's Military Spending To Rise? DefenseNews, Feb. 1, 2013.

Runge, P., The Provincial Reconstruction Teams in Afghanistan: Role model for civil-military relations? Bonn: International Center For Conversion, Occasional Paper IV, 2009.

SOU (2011) A World-class Ministry of Foreign Affairs. Stockholm: Government Central Offices, SOU 2011:21

Strategy Page (2011) Afghanistan and the impossible scheme, Murphy's Law Article Index June 7, 2011. (http://www.strategypage.com/htmw/htmurph/articles/20110607.aspx)

Svensson, S., Lessons Still to be Learned – Interoperability Between Swedish Authorities in Northern Afghanistan. Bachelor Thesis, Global Development Studies, School of Global Studies, University of Gothenburg, 2011.

Swedish National Audit Office (2004) Who is in charge of the electronic administration? (In Swedish) Stockholm: Swedish National Audit Office, RiR 2004:19.

Swedish National Audit Office (2011) Swedish Contributions to International Efforts. (In Swedish) Stockholm: Swedish National Audit Office, RiR 2011:14.

Tham, M. Lindell, M., and Hull Wiklund, C. (2011), Chasing Synergies: Civil-Military Relations in PRT Mazar-e Sharif, FOI-R--3356--SE (in Swedish, English summary).

The Centre for Army Lessons Learned (2011) Afghanistan Provincial Reconstruction Team Handbook 11-16. U.S. Army Combined Arms Center, Feb. 2011

Wang, W., Yu W., Li, Q., Wang W., and Liu, X. Service-Oriented High Level Architecture, European Simulation Interoperability Workshop. Edinburgh, Scotland: Simulation Interoperability Standards Organization. 08E-SIW-022. 2008

Ward, M. (2010),The Future of PRTs. A speech available at https://www.cimicweb.org/Documents/ PRT%20CONFERENCE%202010/The%20Future%20of%20PRTs%20new.pd f

Östberg, O., Swedish e-gov 2010 – Where is it coming from and where is it going. International Journal of Public Information Systems, Vol. 2010:2, Pp.149-169.

Holistic Management, Sense-Making and Intelligent Business

Peter Sjølin

Abstract

The increasing complexity at all levels of scale renders the traditional approach to Enterprise Architecture and its governance inadequate. In this chapter, an alternative approach, based on a stratified system approach, is suggested. It is argued that Enterprise Architecture should be conceived as an integral aspect-system of the enterprise, which, holistically and systemically governed, enables more strategic, more effective and more resilient enterprise engineering.

Keywords

Enterprise Architecture, holistic management, sense-making

Introduction

There are probably many different ways to make sense of each of the many different enterprises and organizations across the planet. This particular paper investigates one particular approach by questioning the validity of the data and the selected methods of articulating strategies and plans. This should give the reader an idea on how to develop better plans that in turn would improve an enterprise's ability to obtain competitive advantages. Competitive advantages can apply to both organizations in the private sector and in the public sector. In the case of the public sector competitive advantage can be understood as the ability to make use of resources in a way that ensures that organization is able to provide its stakeholders with services of the expected service level.

In order to make proper decisions on how to develop the enterprise's competitive advantages, it becomes a necessity for the enterprise to deal with the question of sense making. In regards to sense making questions like how the enterprise architects can make use of the frameworks to deal with information gleaned from the enterprise's environment? And how often well the social and technical systems of the enterprise adapts to trends in the enterprise's environment? And how do the enterprise architects interpret the collected data.

This chapter makes use of a three step approach to organizational learning and data collection that essentially was based on Weick's (2000) approach to organizational sense-making. Ultimately the focus for collecting the information from the organization's environment is to facilitate enterprise engineering whereas the decision-makers can design the future state of the organization's enterprise in order to ensure competitive advantages (Porter 1985).

Interpretation of Data

The enterprise architects will through their work with frameworks that are designed to encompass business architecture, application architectures and the technical architecture work with interpretation of existing data in to artifacts which the organization can make use of. The enterprise architects are through their working collecting data from various internal sources such as interview with stakeholders on how the infrastructure works, or through collecting data from various sources on how the business strategy is or for that matter interviewing various programmers who have in depth knowledge of how the applications works. The enterprise architects are through scanning the organizations markets and environments for disruptions and new technologies that can enable new combinations of business processes and technologies that could enable the organization to gain competitive advantages. This knowledge should enable what is known as informed governance. Informed governance is roughly conducted by the chief architect (or other leading figure in the enterprise architecture department) engage the various decision-makers e.g. the Chief Information Officer, Chief Financial Officer, the Chief Operating Officer, or the Chief Executive Officer and through his meetings with the decision-making profiles he can influence them. The decision-makers are articulating the business strategy. Impact comes through the social systems of management. What is important in this stage is to avoid falling into to the black hole, which is named the planning school by Henry Mintzberg (2009). The planning school is characterized by the decision-makers are decoupled from the formulation of the business strategy and the technocrats who is in charge of the formulation of the business strategy are not fully aligned with the in depth knowledge of the organization's day to day operation. The process of developing a business strategy cannot be prioritized over implementation of the strategies.

The chief architect is not the owner of the strategy formulation process, but he has the opportunity to impact various decisions-makers and through that lay a foundation for informed governance.

Learning

The enterprise architects have to learn from the social systems that the decision-makers take part and adapt to these systems in order to learn how to influence them. In particular should the enterprise architects work with adapting to the process of formulation of business strategies. Failing to do so will lead to the enterprise architects cannot enable the organization to make informed decisions and as such not support business outcomes or competitive advantages.

The chief architect has to ensure that the models that the enterprise architects apply in their approach to analyze and making compatible to support the process for formulating the business processes would have to be adapted to incorporate information from the organization's external environments.

The input that the chief architect would base his analysis on would have to integrate as many aspects of how the organization's operation as possible. Usually the information in the framework would be biased towards the perspectives of the IT department since most organizations have installed their enterprise architecture programs in the IT department. In order ensure sense making that the enterprise architects collect would have to be compared to information from other sources. Where it is possible the enterprise architects should support their information with sources that originates from the organizations external environments.

The enterprise architects and the decision-makers are a part of a social-technical system. A social-technical system consists of a social structure where the employees, middle managers and executives interact with one another with the purpose to achieve objectives. The technical part of the socio-technical system is build upon the fact that the IT department and for that matter the operations of the organization usually posses technical systems of which the employees, middle managers and executives interact with in order obtain their objectives.

The enterprise architects and the decision-makers would have to learn from how the business and it-strategies are articulated in the past and how they act upon the business strategies. The findings from the learning phase will enable the enterprise architects to foresee how the various decision-makers in the socio-technical system will react when a new information technology strategy is formulated and when it is executed. The findings will have to be taken into account and applied properly in the framework the enterprise architects make use of. The enterprise architects would usually make use of a central repository to store information that has been through a sense-making process about how the organization works; however there can be many different perspectives on who interacts with the information and interpreter the meaning of it. As a consequence there can be especially need for specific layer in the enterprise architecture repository that is packed especially with information for the middle managers and the executives. Likewise would it become a necessity to ensure that the middle managers and the executives have the opportunity to fill information in the repository through a web-browser or similar tool. This can enrich the information that can help the decision-makers to make decisions that can ensure that the organization will achieve competitive advantages.

In order for the enterprise architects to gain an in depth understanding of how the organization's enterprise can create value planning it is a necessity to document the strategic planning cycle. Likewise is it important that the strategy planning cycle is transparent for the decision-makers.

The Cycle

The process is cyclic and it is essential that it is built upon a cyclic structure in order to make their predictions more reliable. More reliable plans can be made by the decision-makers to enable the enterprise to achieve its goals. Furthermore the cycle can be enhanced with the enterprise, if an Enterprise Architecture Program is established and the decision makers makes use of the data produced by the enterprise architecture program.

The illustration below illustrates how the enterprises can make use of the sense-making process to achieve a more coherent, better-aligned and more agile enterprise. As it is illustrated, the Enterprise Architecture program is used to enable the decision-makers to align the various conceptual sections of the enterprise. The scope of the model is to illustrate how coherent leadership based on sense-making can lead to projects that enable change.

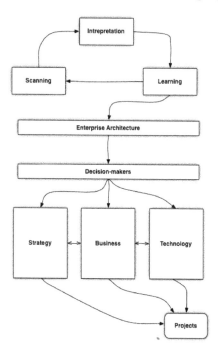

Figure 1. Sense-making and Enterprise Architecure

The experienced reader will note that the model above applies the same definition as Bernard (2005) that states that enterprise architecture is the sum of strategy + business + technology (p.33). Bernard operates with an assumption that the enterprise architecture program can draw up a blueprint, which the chief architect can communicate, to the decision-makers that can use it to take decisions about how the organization should develop in order to achieve its objectives. Bernard defines two concepts when it comes to enterprise architecture. The current enterprise architecture (As-Is) and the future state architecture (To-Be). The blueprint shows how the various business processes, information systems and IT- infrastructure have to be designed.

Assuming that enterprise architecture as a part of the sense-making process and enabling design of the enterprise through influencing the various decision-makers can be noted as enterprise engineering. Through the sense making process it becomes a necessity that the chief architect works with the assessing the business processes since they essentially will be the driver for business transformation. Furthermore should the chief architect work with the organization's operating model (Ross et al 2006) and especially focus on the platform for execution.

Primary processes refer to processes that are essential for the enterprise to deliver value to its customers. The chief architect should naturally apply a multi-perspective analysis understand the underlying principles of the enterprise and the socio-technical. For this the chief architect and his associates (the enterprise architects, solution architects and business architects) should investigate the operating models and business models of the organization's enterprise in order to gain an understanding of how the enterprise's internal environment will in the near future. The scanning of the internal environment should uncover the processes that are not fully supported by IT and also those by which the enterprise would gain advantages by investing in IT and organizational. The chief architect could make use of inspiration from Hammer (2000) that speaks of obliteration of the organization's current business processes and redefine them in order to capture the benefits of newer and more modern information technologies and information systems, and the overhaul should be based upon the blueprint that the chief architect and enterprise architects have drawn through usage of the enterprise architecture framework.

The blueprint should ensure that the business processes have to be grouped in the framework as either support processes or primary processes. The focus of this activity is to identify how connecting them with the proper processes in order to give the customers the best possible support to ensure continuous improvement can optimize the businesses processes. Likewise is it important that the chief architect and the enterprise architects understand that in an organization-wide transformation process it is a necessity for some domains to transform with different paces than others.

Connecting the Business Processes and the Information Systems

As earlier mentioned enterprise architecture is a tool that enables the decision-makers to understand how the organization's enterprise architecture works. In order to gain the needed overview the enterprise architects has to make use of a structured methodology (e.g. a business process framework and an information technology framework or an enterprise architecture framework like ArchiMate).

The role of the framework is to set of standards that dictate how the various artifacts that would be documented and stored in the repository are to be defined. In other words the framework is the alpha and the omega for building the foundation for an organization's enterprise ontology. The framework will eventually give the chief architect a series of artifacts that can be combined in numerous ways and explored and new perspectives on problems and challenges that the organization experience and faces. The framework and enterprise architecture repository has to be easy to understand and the various perspectives should tell a story which has to be designed in a way that enables the stakeholders to easily understand what challenges and problems and how the organization can overcome them. This will lead to specification of business and IT projects.

The As-Is scan of the business processes and IT rarely generate synergies due to the lack of obliteration of processes that were designed for the pre-computer and pre-Internet age. It is necessary for the chief architect and his associates to investigate the enterprise's current usage of information technology and information systems.

They should be working with a methodology that documents the various information systems, platforms, applications, and devices that the enterprise applies in order to provide the various stakeholders (executives, middle managers and employees) with proper information for understanding how the social system works. Before the transformation program is started, the chief architect or his associates should benchmark the business processes so it is possible for the decision-makers to evaluate how the changes have impacted in the organization. It can be benefit for the organization to view information technologies and processes as investments (Potts 2008) since it enables a coherent business development.

The investment process is essentially the embodiment of the corporate strategy, the IT strategy, the financial strategy, etc. After the chief architect and his associates have completed their analysis of the enterprise's corporate strategy, a road map should be articulated so the focus could be shared among the members of the Enterprise Architecture group, and later on among the various decision-makers in this said enterprise.

It is the author's opinion that the investment approach would have to be connected with the enterprise's program management. It will become a necessity for the enterprise to deal with its approach to enterprise investments and program management since it is the decision-makers who are responsible for the allocation of resources to the projects and systems in which the enterprise is able to invest for its own benefit. Ross et al (2006) works with an approach that the platform for execution should be built project by project. Each project adds a bit more maturity to the organization's enterprise architecture.

The future state architecture (To-Be architecture) should be described in a transition plan to facilitate communication with the stakeholders and the decision-makers in order to evaluate projects to which resources are to be allocated and which are to be implemented. The transition itself has to be guided by the principles articulated by the chief architect and the decision makers. As mentioned earlier in this chapter, the complexity is a barrier that can't be ignored if the synergies of enterprise architecture and enterprise governance are to be harvested.

Grouping Processes and Information Systems

The social systems have to be identified, and as such it becomes a necessity to group the systems into various specialized domains. Each of these domains would have to generate synergy among the social systems and the information systems in order to justify their existence. The domains are necessary for coping with the question of complexity.

Complex organizations can very well own processes and departments that are specialized to the degree that it constitutes a silo. In those cases, the silos can't be viewed as negative issue, as long as the employees, middle managers and executives in charge of the various processes communicate and interact with one another on regular basis.

In order to ensure advantageous changes by grouping the various information systems and social systems, the managers would have to allocate resources in order to facilitate communities of practices that would enable the stakeholders in the enterprise to understand and adapt to the new situation in the enterprise. It is pivotal that the decision-makers allow the various members of the enterprise to make use of their time at work and in the change process to form such social networks.

A community of practice is defined by Wenger (1999, p. 47) as:

> *"Such a concept of practice includes both the explicit and the tacit. It includes what is said and what is left unsaid; what is represented and what is assumed. It includes the language, tools, documents, images, symbols well-defined roles, specified criteria, codified procedures, regulations, and contracts that various practices make explicit for a variety of purposes."*

It is a necessity to make use of the social networks to create an understanding of how the enterprise works since it will add an extra and necessary level of information to the information that is stored in the enterprise architecture repository used to give sense-making to the decision-makers since it help the decision-makers understand why the As-Is situation is for the organization and what needs to be done in order to achieve the perfect To-Be state. The social networks are likewise pivotal in order to enable the change process that occurs within the enterprise, and as such the chief architect and the decision-makers who are in charge of the enterprise have to identify change agents and motivate the various social networks to adapt to the changes and work alongside the goals that they have articulated for the enterprise. In this light the decision takers would have to trust that the members of the enterprise work for the best of the enterprise and to some extent allow the employees to self-organize and prioritize the various tasks at hand.

Value Through Combining IS and Processes

The chief architect and his associates would have to investigate how the enterprise can generate value through grouping the social systems and information systems. The scope of this endeavor is to select the projects that will have the greatest impact on the overall enterprise's architecture, operating model and platform for execution.

Progress in each of the projects will impact the enterprise's architecture and thereby transform the architecture from the As – Is architecture (Bernard 2005) to the To-Be architecture. From an architecture perspective it seems like the enterprise architecture program will when executed enable maturation of the enterprise's architecture. It can be considered a process. It is very likely that the stakeholders will be easier won over if they can see a logical plan that includes economical estimations of how the plan impacts the enterprise's financial situation. It is needless to say that the enterprise's decision makers would have to have an insight on how well the enterprise can process the various resources it has at hand and thereby produce the products and services that its customers want to purchase.

To gain an overview of what the organization's current applications it is a necessity to scan the internal environment and the cash flow can be an enabler to gain an insight into the As-Is application landscape. The chief architect and his associations should work with identifying which applications that are the most costly for the organization in terms of licenses and from their start a classification. Compiling a list of the top 30 applications in regards of cost and engaging those who are using them to find out what they think of them in terms of quality, stability and efficiency. Likewise should the questions like the complexity of design of the application and how hard it is to maintain the application, and how hard it is to alter the application when needed. The enterprise architects with these data evaluate the applications in a matrix similar to the Boston Matrix (Bente 2012) and from that provide the decision-makers on what to be done with the information systems. With this in mind a technology strategy can be articulated and application management plans for how to deal with in efficiencies of the information systems and how to enable the true potentials that can lead to the foundation of the competitive advantages.

The evaluation process is likewise a part of scanning an enterprise's internal and external environment and as such the enterprise architecture program should work as the platform for the construction of a shared ontology across the enterprise. The chief architect should keep in mind that in business units, departments or segments that can be characterized as complex, it is rather likely that their particular views cannot be generalized into an enterprise's ontology or add their views to the technology strategy or application management plans. In this light the chief architect and his associates would have to decide if they should apply a top-down or a bottom-up approach. The approach chosen would eventually become a part of the strategic dialogue on what has to be done. Will the decision-makers tolerate increased autonomy or would they prefer increased centralization? As earlier mentioned, it seems to be the tendencies of the development organizations to deal with such predicaments.

Changing the Enterprise

The chief architect and the decision-makers would have to go further with the change of the enterprise. The change process would have to be a part of the overall enterprise architecture program and it will certainly impact the enterprise and how it works. In order to do so, the chief architect would have to influence the stakeholders (decision makers, the middle managers and the employees). The first step to initiate the changes is through questioning how the enterprise is able to collect the data needed for better decision-making. The data can be used to derive applications management plans that can enable a starting point for analyzing the application architecture and IT infrastructure. The decision-makers will have a better opportunity to understand and act upon the need for change if the various business units and information systems can be organized into clusters of which different projects can stimulate to change into the desired state as describe in the blueprint for the To-Be architecture.

The combination of information systems and social systems is necessary for harvesting the synergies within each system and each of the clusters. The clusters can most likely produce synergies for each of the areas that demonstrate the possession of the kind of gravity needed to produce a barrier of complexity.

Before the chief architect and the decision-makers commit themselves to changing the enterprise, they would have to understand how the enterprise and its architecture work. In order to achieve this, the chief architect would have to choose an enterprise architecture framework, adapt the framework to the particular organization's enterprise and implement the framework. Thereafter the chief architect and the enterprise architects should work on identifying the various artifacts and organizing them in an enterprise architecture repository. While working with the identification of artifacts and organization of artifacts in the EA repository, it is important that the chief architects understands that there might be barriers to define an unified ontology and that as a result of that there might be a necessity to create several different sub-units of the EA repository. The chief architect works with an assumption that each of the specialized operations of the enterprise should be mapped as a separated entity and as a separate mini-architecture of the enterprise.

It is possible to convert extremely specialized knowledge for each of the specialized processes to other parts of the enterprise without much loss of the meaning of each of the artifacts. It is better that there is a platform for informed governance for each of the segments than a system that does not adapt to the entire enterprise. The managers of each of these segments should in the long run participate in the community of practice that shares knowledge and know-how with one another. The chief architect can to some extent work as the change manager by convincing the various stakeholders in the enterprise to support the changes and at the same time enable them to take the changes even further.

The change manager would have to ensure that the office of internal communication is located and positioned as a part of management for it symbolizes the foundation of management for all other segments of the enterprise. It is pivotal that the middle-level managers support the change efforts since they act as the approvers of each of the employees' time and effort to commit to the particular change system. If the middle-level managers ignore the call for change and disapprove of the changes that the employees suggest then it is very likely that the changes will come to a standstill and eventually fail. The commitment of the employees would also be of great importance since it is likely that each of the employees has specialized knowledge of how the work processes interacts.

Conclusions

The organization has to work with several different approaches to challenge their particular views on how the enterprise collects the data that are used by the decision-makers. It is also likely that the various decision-makers of the enterprise would have to deal with identifying segments of the enterprise that are too complex to be adapted to generalized business processes. The chief architect and his associates would have to deal with the challenges of adding value to the enterprise by organizing standardized business activities and facilitating business processes, but at the same time be able to identify where it would not make sense to apply standardized systems.

The focus of the members of the enterprise architecture team would have to include the concept of complexity and the concept of enterprise ontology, and so should the repositories, in order that they be able to connect the various sections of the enterprise and communicate the meaning of how the enterprise works to the decision-makers and other stakeholders who would have to make use of the knowledge that is presented in the repositories.

It is a necessity for the decision makers and the chief architect to investigate the various elements of the enterprise in order to achieve better insight into how the enterprise works, and from that enable better decision-making in order to achieve the objectives for the enterprise. The more information that the chief architect and his associates can collect the more need there is for sense-making and for that the chief architect would have to design and apply an enterprise architecture framework and ensure that the artifacts that the framework exposes to the decision-makers are easy to understand and gives the decision-makers an idea of what challenges that the organization faces and how to overcome them. Essentially the scope has to be on organization transformation that are focuses on a coherent approach to business development so the organization makes better use of its investments in information technologies to enable innovation that in turn can enable competitive advantages.

The primary function of the enterprise architecture program is to enable sense-making meaning that it actively scans the internal and external environments of the organization's enterprise in order to enable a form of learning that can be made use of in strategic planning.

About the Author

Peter Sjølin is an enterprise architect at PFA Pension in Copenhagen. He holds a bachelor degree in business administration and computer science from Copenhagen Business School and a MSc in Business and IT from the IT University of Copenhagen.

References

Bernard, S., A., 2005. An Introduction To Enterprise Architecture: Second Edition 2nd ed., AuthorHouse.

Bente, Stefan. Collaborative Enterprise Architecture. Morgan Kaufmann, 2012.

Dietz, J.L.G., 2006. Enterprise Ontology: Theory and Methodology, Springer.

Hamel, G., 2007. The Future of Management, Harvard Business School Press.

Hammer, M., 1990. Reengineering Work: Don't Automate, Obliterate. , Harvard Business Review no. 68.

Hoogervorst, J.A.P., 2009. Enterprise Governance and Enterprise Engineering, Springer.

Kotter, J.P., 1995. Leading Change: Why Transformation Efforts Fail. Harvard Business Review, (March - April 1995), p.9.

Wenger, E., 1999. Communities of Practice: Learning, Meaning, and Identity New Ed., Cambridge University Press.

Mintzberg, H., Ahlstrand, P.B. & Lampel, J.B., 2008. Strategy Safari: The Complete Guide Through the Wilds of Strategic Management 2nd ed., Financial Times/ Prentice Hall.

Porter, M.E., 1985. Competitive Advantage: Creating and Sustaining Superior Performance, New York: Free Press.

Potts, C., 2008. fruITion: Creating the Ultimate Corporate Strategy for Information Technology illustrated edition., Technics Publications, LLC.

Ross, J.W., Weill, P. & Robertson, D.C., 2006. Enterprise Architecture as Strategy: Creating a Foundation for Business Execution illustrated edition., Harvard Business School Press.

Weill, P. & Ross, J., 2009. IT Savvy: What Top Executives Must Know to Go from Pain to Gain, Harvard Business School Press.

Weill, P. & Ross, J.W., 2004. IT Governance: How Top Performers Manage IT Decision Rights for Superior Results, Harvard Business School Press.

Weick, K.E., 2000. Making Sense of the Organization, Wiley Blackwell.

Balancing Agility with Stability:
Systemic View on Business Processes

*Ilia Bider, Gene Bellinger
and Erik Perjons*

Abstract

On the first glance, the concept of enterprise/business agility and business process management (BPM) seems to be in conflict. Enterprise/business agility means an enterprise's ability to react on changes in the surrounding business world as well as discover new opportunities constantly appearing in the market for launching new products and services. BPM is, normally, considered as a tool for achieving high efficiency through standardization, specialization, and automation. By taking a systemic view on business processes this paper shows that BPM can serve as a way of achieving agility rather than being a barrier to it. The presented systemic view on business processes is based on an enterprise model consisting of three types of components: assets, sensors and business process instances. These components can be recursively decomposed, which allows for different levels of details when modeling an enterprise. The paper shows how the Assets-Sensors-Processes model can be used for finding new ways of achieving enterprise/business agility, e.g. through cross-manning of business processes. It also discusses changes that need to be introduced in the contemporary theory and practice of BPM in order to make BPM a tool for achieving agility as well as the role that Systems Thinking should play in achieving this goal.

Keywords

Business Process Management, Systems Thinking, Systemic View, Enterprise Agility, Enterprise Modeling, Enterprise Architecture

Introduction

Enterprise/business agility is a property of an enterprise to function in the highly dynamic world (Sherehiy et al. 2007). The agility concerns both being able to adjust the enterprise to changes in the surrounding environment, and discovering new opportunities constantly appearing in the dynamic world for launching new products/services. Agility requires leadership, motivation, organizational learning, inventiveness, and open eyes on what is happening outside and inside the enterprise. Agility is not possible to achieve by having very strict rules of how to handle business situations, and strict, hierarchical line of command.

On the other hand, always working in the ad hoc manner in order to give way to creativity will consume too much energy and can make the enterprise inefficient and, thus, loose its competitive advantages of being creative. Therefore, some rules/guidelines on how to handle often occurring business situations should exist, which leads to the needs of having "standardized" business processes even in an agile enterprise. An enterprise without standardized processes can be compared with a person that needs to think how to make each next step when walking along the street.

Summarizing the above we can rephrase the first Law of Regulatory Compromise from (Weingber and Weingberg 1988) as follows:

> *Agility gives protection against unknown;*
>
> *Business processes against known;*
>
> *and the use of each sacrifices some opportunities to use the other.*

In order to be agile and efficient the right balance between creativity and standardization should be achieved. The latter cannot be done based on the mainstream directions in Business Process Management (BPM), e.g. Six Sigma and Lean, which is mostly preoccupied with standardization, specialization, and automation in order to optimize the performance of the enterprise (Harmon 2007; Weske 2010). The mainstream BPM continues exploring the ideas with the roots in the industrial revolution, i.e. the ones developed by Frederick Winslow Taylor, and Henry Ford. These ideas are quite feasible when we want to have only one make of product, like Ford's black model T, manufactured year after year. These ideas are hardly compatible with agility. The more optimized a process is, the more difficult it will be to change it; at least, there is a great risk that it will be so. A less optimal process that is easier to change can be much more "optimal" in the long run.

This chapter is devoted to investigating the concept of business processes with a view to make them a tool for obtaining *agility* rather than be a barrier for creativity and inventiveness. Our objective is to obtain agility without loosing stability of the whole enterprise. To achieve this objective we take a systemic view on business processes which allows having processes with any degree of strictness, as well as use business processes as a tool of discovering changes in the environment and new opportunities in the market.

Informal View on Business Processes

The term business process encompasses two concepts (which often confuses outsiders), business process type and business process instance. We give both concepts the following pragmatic definitions:

- Business process type (BPT) is a plan/template for handling business situations of a certain type
- Business process instance/case (BPI) is a situation (being) handled according to the plan/template

The plan/template can include information on the following:

- Situation that requires application of the plan, i.e. what triggers the plan
- Goal to reach
- Sub-goals and an order in which they could/should be achieved (goal decomposition)
- Operations/activities that should be completed for achieving goals/sub-goals and their order of execution (operational decomposition)
- Rules of responsibility/participation (both for sub-goals and operations)
- Rules of collaboration/communication between participants pursuing common goals/sub-goals (communication/collaboration channels)

For example, consider a situation of developing a software system customized for a specific customer. Then, the general plan for handling this situation can be shown as a simplified flow diagram as in Fig. 1.

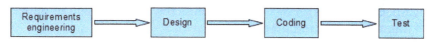

Fig.1. A plan/template for handling a situation when there is a need to develop a customized software system

To this flow, many details can be added, e.g. the first step in Fig. 1 should be carried out by requirements engineers, the second step should result in use-case diagrams, or the third step requires using Java as a programming language. The more details are added, the more rigid the process will be. For example, setting a requirement that all programming should be done in Java will force the developers using this language even in cases where it does not fit, e.g. for development of operating systems.

The plan/template can reside in any or a combination of all of the following:

- In the heads of members of staff used to participate in the process instances of the given type (tacit knowledge). This knowledge guides the process participants what can/should be done or/and what is prohibited, without them concisely thinking about it.
- As information artifacts, e.g. written documents, process maps and other kinds of process descriptions (explicit knowledge) that reside on paper or inside a computer, e.g. as web-based hypertext. These artifacts contain explicit instructions on what can/should be done or/and what is prohibited.
- In software systems used to support running process instances (built in knowledge). The usage of such systems forces process participants to do some actions in a certain way and/or in a certain order, or/and prohibit to do it in other ways.

In other words, the knowledge on the rules (and the processes themselves) can range from being completely tacit (e.g. resides in the heads of the process participants) to being partly or totally explicit (e.g. depicted in detailed process maps).

Systemic View on Business Processes

According to Systems Thinking (ST) (Checkland 1999; Jackson 2003), an enterprise is regarded as a whole, i.e. a system. Such a system maintains its existence through constant interaction between its parts, i.e. people, departments, teams, etc. The system interacts also with its environment, a bigger whole. Furthermore, the system manifests a unique behavior that cannot be derived from the sum of its parts. According to business process management perspective (Harmon 2007; Weske 2010), an enterprise is regarded as a number of repeatable business processes. These two perspectives looks on the surface completely different and to integrate both of them we need, first, to reconcile them.

The reconciliation is done via considering processes as a special type of systems. To do this we use the idea of system-coupling diagrams that comes from (Lawson 2010) and is represented in Fig. 2. The diagram describes a general case when a particular situation in the system's environment, on the left-hand side of the diagram, causes a larger system, e.g. an enterprise, to create a respondent system, e.g. a project, to handle the situation. The respondent system is built from the assets that the larger system already has. Some of these assets are people, or other actors (e.g. robots). Other assets are control elements, e.g. policy documents, that define the behavior of the respondent system. The latter are   denoted as black dots in Fig. 2.

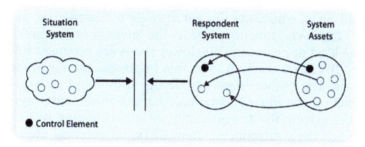

Fig. 2. System coupling diagrams from (Lawson 2010)

As we mentioned in the previous section, the term business process encompasses two concepts Business Process Type (BPT), and Business Process Instance (BPI). Actually, a BPI corresponds to the idea of respondent system from (Lawson 2010). Such system has a short lifespan, it can be minutes, hours, days, month or years, but its lifespan is always (considerably) shorter than the lifetime of the whole enterprise. A BPI system is created to deal with a situation and achieve some (operational) goal, e.g. to deliver services or goods ordered by a given customer and get paid. This system is disbanded after the goal has been reached. A BPI system includes parts of the whole enterprise system, e.g. people, departments, and some elements of the environment, e.g. customers or/and investors. At any moment of time, an enterprise has numerous BPIs in progress providing the majority of the interactions between the system's components and the system and the environment.

A BPT can be seen as a set of rules that describes the dynamic behavior of BPIs aimed at dealing with certain type of situations. For the sake of this paper, we consider BPT as consisting of two parts:

- Start conditions that defines a situation when a new BPI system of the given type should be created
- Execution rules that define what should be its goal, who should be included in it, how the job is to be done, how components interact, etc. (see more on this in the previous section). Execution rules function as a control element of a respondent BPI system.

The execution rules can be prescriptive or imperative (e.g. what should be done), restrictive (e.g. what should not be done), recommended (e.g. how normally things are done but it is allowed to do it differently), or a combination of all three categories. BPT rules are "imprinted" in manuals, process maps, employees handbooks, computer systems, heads of employees (oral tradition), or a combination of the above.

BPTs work as business DNA creating BPIs based on the needs, e.g. impulses or changes in the environment or inside the enterprise itself. BPTs plus tools used in BPIs, e.g. telephone lines, computers, production lines, paper and pens, constitute the enterprise's infrastructure, allow the enterprise to effectively function inside the given environment. BPTs constitute some kind of hierarchy. The lower levels are occupied BPTs that should produce BPIs as a reaction to simple impulses, like incoming order from a customer. The higher levels are occupied by more strategic BPTs that should react on the more substantial changes in the environment by reconfiguring the system itself, which may include changing BPTs (a kind of genetic engineering), introducing new BPTs, or deleting the obsolete ones.

The Assets-Sensors-Processes Model

Based on the systemic view on business, we can consider an enterprise as consisting of three types of components: assets, sensors and BPIs as depicted in Fig. 3, and explained below.

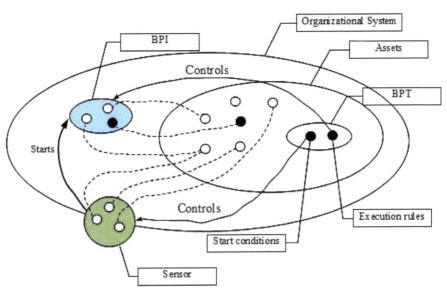

Fig. 3. An enterprise model consisting of three types of components: assets, sensors and BPIs

1.   Assets (tangible and intangible) are:

- People with their knowledge and practical experiences, beliefs, culture, sets of values, etc.
- Physical artifacts, such as computers, telephone lines, production lines, etc.
- Organizational artifacts, formal as well as informal, such as departments, teams, networks, roles, etc.
- Informational artifacts, such as policy documents, manuals, process descriptions (BPTs), etc. To information artifacts belong both written (documented) artifacts, and tacit artifacts, the ones that are imprinted in the people's heads (e.g. culture.)

The assets are relatively static, which means that by themselves they cannot change anything. Assets are activated when they are included in the other two types of components. Assets themselves can be changed by other types of components when the assets are set in motion for achieving some goals. Note that assets here are not regarded in pure mechanical terms. All "soft" assets, like sense of common goals, degree of collaborativeness, shared vision, etc., belong to the organizational assets. Note also that having organizational artifacts does not imply a traditional function oriented structure. Any kind of informal network or resource oriented structural units are considered as organizational artifacts.

2.   Sensors are a set of (sub)systems, the goal of which is to watch the state of the enterprise itself and its environment and catch impulses and changes (trends) that require firing of BPIs of certain types. We need a sensor (which might be a distributed one) for each BPT. The work of a sensor is governed by the Start Conditions of the BPT description (which is an informational artifact). A sensor can be fully automatic for some processes (e.g. an order placed by a customer in a web-based shop), or require human participation to detect changes in the system or its surroundings.

3.   BPIs are a set of respondent systems initiated by sensors for reaching certain goals and disbanded when these goals are achieved. The behavior of a BPI system is governed by the Execution Rules of the corresponding BPT. Dependent on the type, BPIs can lead to changes being made in the assets. New people are hired or fired, departments are reorganized, roles are changed, new policies are adopted, BPT descriptions are changed, new BPTs are introduced, and obsolete ones are removed.

Classification of Business Processes

We can roughly differentiate three categories of business processes dependent on the complexity of the sensor, and the nature of the process itself:

1.   The first category encompasses *operational* processes, like sales, production, HR (e.g. hiring), etc. A sensor discovers the need (e.g. customer needs - sales, or internal needs - HR), and initiates a relatively structured BPI to attain the operational goal (making a deal, or hiring a new employee). To operational processes belong what, usually, is regarded as core processes, and support processes.

2.   The second category encompasses *process improvement* (optimization) processes. A sensor here is based on the performance indicators established for measuring efficiency, productivity, or other parameters of a given operational process. If the performance of this operational process is not according to the expectations, a process improvement (re-engineering) BPI starts with the goal to change the BPT of the operational processes. The BPT of the process improvement processes can be based on some known methods (like Six Sigma, or Lean). As a rule, the improvement processes are less structured than the operational ones.

3.   The third category encompasses *strategic* processes. A sensor here is based on the macro view on the whole organizations. If the overall performance is below expectation, a strategic BPI is fired with the goal of considerably changing the assets. This can include radical changes in BPTs of all kinds of processes, removing obsolete processes, introducing new ones, rearranging departments, substituting key managers, introducing new technology, etc. These are the processes where Systems Thinking is (though may be too seldom) applied as guidelines for finding the best places to make changes (i.e. leverage points). The process here may be completely ad hoc, or use some loose structure, e.g. a serious of brainstorming sessions.

An example of a strategic process based on Systems Thinking is presented in section "Demonstrating the model".

Interplay between the Processes and Components

Due to the interplay between the different categories of processes, an enterprise behaves as an adaptive system. It constantly interacts with the environment based on the BPTs of operational processes, optimizes itself to the current environment through the improvement processes, and can reconfigure itself when the environment changes based on the strategic processes (after which it can start optimization to the new environment). Graphically this interplay is depicted in Fig. 4.

Basic interconnections between the components of different types are depicted in Fig. 3. We list and explain them below adding the interconnections that are not explicitly shown in the figure.

A BPI is started by the corresponding sensor and it uses organizational assets such as people, machines, etc. to produce the result, i.e. reach some goal. In particular, the execution rules of the BPT controls the behavior of each BPI that belongs to this process type.

As was already mentioned, a BPI can be started in order to intentionally change the organizational assets fire or hire people, change policies, change BPTs, reorganize departments, etc. But even when a BPI does none of the above, it does make a change just because it was running for some period of time. During its run, a BPI creates a trace either on paper, or inside the organizational database, or just in the heads of people participating in this process instance. Depending on the type of organizational memory, the trace may stay in memory a very short period of time, or last "forever". All remembered traces of BPIs constitute the experience based knowledge of the organization, which, as an information artifact, adds to the set of organizational assets.

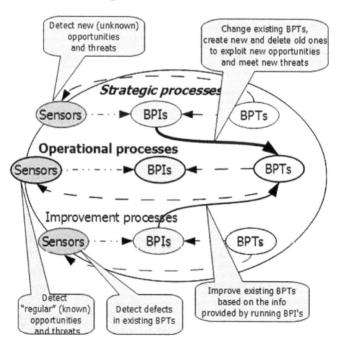

Fig. 4. Interplay between three different categories of processes

A sensor starts a BPI each time it detects that its start conditions are satisfied, and it uses assets such as people, machines, etc. to detect this situation. In particular, the start conditions of the BPT controls the behavior of the sensor (see Fig. 3).

For a sensor to identify when a BPI is to be started, it needs access to the relevant information in order to test the start conditions. This information is usually delivered by some already finished BPIs and can be found in their traces. The information that sensors need can be provided by operational BPIs aimed at practical goals (as their side effects). However, in many cases, just having standard operational processes is not enough to provide all information needed for the sensors. Special "information gathering" BPTs need to be designed with the only goal of obtaining relevant information for the sensors. The start condition for such a BPT could be very simple, a BPI should run each year, month, week, day, or hour. Information gathering processes are especially needed for the sensors belonging to the categories 2 and 3 of the process classification from previous section. A periodical survey of the customers to determine their level of satisfaction is a typical example of an information gathering BPT.

Another way of obtaining information needed for sensors is to enhance the standard operational processes in order to gather this information during turns of the BPIs. This can be done by adding to them steps (operations) that are not important for these processes as such, but can provide information for sensors belonging to other business processes. An example of such enhancement could be a set of questions to the potential customer who has chosen not to buy a product or service, just to find out the reason for his/her decision (e.g. wrong price range, wrong service).

Decomposition

Both a sensor and a BPI are systems, and thus in its own turn could be, if necessary, decomposed. Consider an example of a compound sensor. Let us have a fast growing enterprise that wants to keep the pace of its expansion for a number of years ahead. Let this enterprise be a consulting business, the growth of which depends on the number of employees. The management decides to run a strategic overview BPI according to a BPT as soon as there is a danger for growth or decline (start condition of the BPT). One of the parameter that reflects pace of growth is the rate of consultants hiring minus the rate of losing them, e.g. to competitors. A sensor needs to evaluate this data against some threshold value and start a strategic overview when the value is below the threshold. There could be two possibilities to create such sensor:

- Ensure that all needed information is available in real-time, then the sensor just needs to do some calculation and issue a start signal if necessary
- Make a periodical, say once a month, information gathering, and only then make some calculation, and issue a start signal if necessary

The second case represents a compound sensor as in Fig. 5, which consists of a simple Sensor1 that "watches" the clock and starts an information gathering BPI on the 1st of each month. The BPI gathers information and produces a report (informational artifact). Another sensor, Sensor2 in Fig. 5, reacts to a new report, makes comparisons and starts a new strategic overview BPI if necessary.

A similar decomposition can be done for a complex BPI, for example, when it represents a complex processes instance, e.g. a project. Complex sensors/BPIs are more typical for the improvement and strategic processes than for the operational ones.

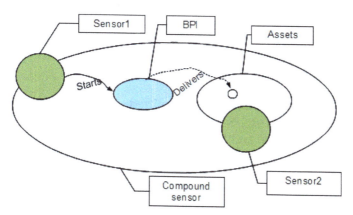

Fig 5. Compound censor

Demonstrating the Model

Analysis of the Internet Bubble

Consider a simplified example of an IT consulting company with a sales department, a consulting department, and a HR department. The company uses a "usual" business model of charging per hour based on the expert level of its consultants.

The sales department conducts sales BPIs according to the sales BPT, part of which is hourly pricing of consulting services according to the level of the consultants expertise. The HR department is hiring consultants according to the rules of hiring BPT, part of which is salary ranges according to the experience and education of the consultants. Hiring is done to ensure growth or just compensate natural lost.

Suppose management discovers that HR hires fewer consultants than expected. An investigation shows that the reason for this is that the company offering less competitive salaries than their competitors. The rules of hiring BPT are revised and salary offers is becoming higher. The rate of hiring returns to normal (i.e. expected hiring rate).

Suppose that at the same time new sales is starting to decline. An investigation shows that the company chargers the customers more per hour than their competitors. The rules of the sales BPT are revised and the company starts charging less per hour. The rate of getting new consulting assignments return to normal (i.e. expected sales).

The above adjustment can go through several cycles until the "strategic sensor" catches a new trend: the revenues from new assignments do not cover costs for their completion. A strategic BPI is fired to find the best leverage point(s) to solve the problem.

What happens if the strategic sensor discovers the above situation too late, or there is no such strategic BPT at all, or the fired BPI is unsuccessful? Well, bad luck, the company goes out of business.

Does the example above sounds too simplified? It might be so, but in the late 1990s a lot of start-up Swedish IT consultancies operated in this manner until most of them went out of business when the IT bubble burst. We are not stating here that the management of these companies did not know what they were doing, some of them knew. Their actions might have a more rational behavior, like dumping prices in hope to get rid of the competitors while having enough of risk capital. This, however, did not matter much in the end, the unsustainable behavior resulted in a crush independently of the reasons behind it.

The artificial example above shows that the absence of a proper sensor may result in a complete demise of an enterprise working in a highly dynamic environment. This example reveals the weakness of the traditional enterprise structure, in which each process type engages a separate set of people. Sales BPIs are manned with sales staff, hiring BPIs are manned with HR staff, process improvement BPIs are manned with the Process Office staff, strategic BPIs are manned with high-level management. An example of such structure is schematically shown in Fig. 6.

There are two weaknesses in the traditional organization that are revealed by the example above:

- Parts of the systems are separated from each other and thus may easily drift apart totally destroying the system (as was shown in the example above).
- The traditionally built enterprise is vulnerable if it operates in a highly dynamic competitive environment. The whole structure will work fine provided that sensors discover emerging situations fast enough so that organization have time to adjust. In a highly dynamic environment, the costs of creating sensitive sensors might be too high to make the whole idea sustainable.

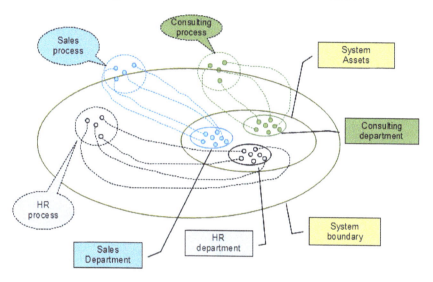

Fig. 6. Traditional enterprise structure from the process perspective. This picture is less detailed than the one in Fig. 3, a process circle here encompasses both a BPI and a sensor.

Selling IT Consultants and Hire a Friend Principles

As a reaction on what happened during the IT bubble the Swedish IT consulting industry adopted two new principles: "selling IT consultants" (which means a consultant who also function as a salesperson), and "hire a friend" (which means convincing your friends to work for your company). On the conceptual level, both principles mean removing the rule that different operational processes, e.g. sales, service delivery, hiring, are manned by different categories of people. It is not clear whether every IT consultant can be a good sales person, or a good HR person, but in the most cases due to his/her positioning in the outer world, a consultant can greatly contribute to the sales and HR processes. For example, a BPT of the sales process can include a consultant serving as:

- a part of the process "sensor" by creating leads,
- a provider of information during the process, and

- as promoter of the company's line of products and services.

It does not mean that the sales staff should disappear and all sales should be conducted by consultants. It means active engagement of other categories of professionals in the sales process on a regular (not ad hoc) basis. Expected results are more sensitive, and less expensive sensors which will make the enterprise more efficient on the whole.

Selling consultants and hiring a friend represent examples of so-called cross-manning of business processes. A schematic representation of this concept is given in Fig. 7, which is a modification of Fig. 6.

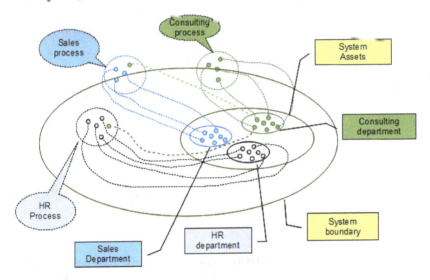

Fig. 7. Cross-manning of business processes

Discussion

Examples above show that the Assets-Sensors-Processes enterprise model can be applied on the conceptual level to discover and explain strong sides and weaknesses of different ways of organizing business. For example, it helps to understand and explain the essence of cross-manning. Cross-manning can be applied not only to the operational processes (category 1), but also to the process improvement processes (category 2). Instead of letting specially assigned process re-engineers make detailed process designs, we can let people engaged in these processes make, at least, part of the BPTs design themselves? Let process specialists and management devise basic guidelines, and let professionals on the floor fill in the details. After all, it is the professionals on the floor who work inside the processes that are in a better position to arrange how to do things in a smooth way. The advantages are as following:

- People on the floor will know sooner when the old BPTs stop to satisfy the internal or external environment (more sensitive sensor for the improvement process)
- As people on the floor know better not only the business, but also each other's capabilities, they are in a better position to adjust BPTs not only to the abstract goals but also to particular people that manage the operational processes.

Implications for Business Process Management

In the previous sections, we have presented an enterprise model that is based on a systemic view to business processes. Applying the model to practice requires rethinking the traditional view on business processes. This issue is shortly discussed in the following sub-sections.

Objectives with Business Process Management

The focus on optimization should be dropped. Business processes can be used for many goals, where optimization is only one of them, e.g.:

- Saving time and effort through having a ready-made template/plan (i.e. BPT) instead of devising a new one for each case (i.e. for each BPI).
- Ensure identity of the enterprise by treating similar cases equally and independently of which members of staff that are handling them, e.g. ensure same quality (good or bad) of service for all customers.
- Ensure compliance with external rules and regulations or internal policies
- Setting a framework for improvement of efficiency, quality, or other parameters. The plan/template can be evaluated based on the experience of its application, critically analyzed and tuned.
- Ensure stability and predictability when average costs and time for handling various situations is known and can be used for longer-terms planning.
- Acquiring other specific properties, like transparency, higher level of cooperation between members of staff, agility, etc.

More Attention to Sensors

When designing business processes, more attention should be paid to having good sensors than having best possible processes. There is no need to have an optimal process for handling a customer order if we do not have a sensitive sensor that identifies who might need our products. In the same way, it does not make much sense to have a perfect product development process if we do not have a good sensor that can discover the needs for a new product earlier than our competitors. The concept of cross-manning discussed earlier seems to be one of the ideas that could be useful in creating sensitive sensors.

New Business Process Modeling Techniques

The ways of defining business processes should be changed. The preoccupation with optimization has lead to the view on the process as a flow of operations. This view has been cemented by creation of the workflow modeling techniques and standards. In essence, the workflow view is nothing else than the conveyor belt concept transferred from the production to administration and service.

The problem with rigidness of workflows is well known, and a number of solutions, like exception handling, have been proposed to introduce flexibility. However, following the saying "we can't solve problems by using the same kind of thinking we used when we created them" attributed to Einstein, continuing usage of the workflow paradigm does not make much sense.

From a practical point of view, we need to move from the totally prescriptive (imperative) definitions of the process execution rules to the constraint-based definitions, which is a combination of guidelines and restrictions.

From a scientific point of view, we need to abandon the idea of a process as a flow of operation or events, and start considering it as a trajectory in a multidimensional state space, which is standard in other fields where the process concept is used, e.g. mathematical systems theory. Fig. 8 represents a simplified example of a state space for the order delivery process taken from (Khomyakov and Bider 2000; Bider 2002). The state space here consists of two sets of product dimensions (*ordered* and *delivered*) and two financial dimensions (*invoiced* and *paid*). At any time the state of the affairs in the order delivery process can be represented as a point in this state space.

Under the state-oriented view, the process type is defined as a set of restrictions on the trajectory of the process instance in the state space, including the requirement that the trajectory should lead to the goal. Such view can facilitate creation of execution rules that would permit creativity without breaking the enterprise policies or rules mutually agreed by the process participants themselves.

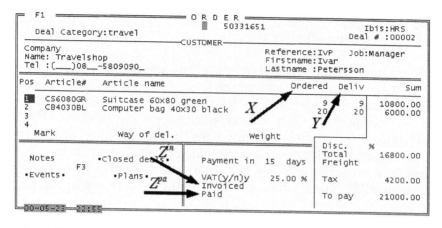

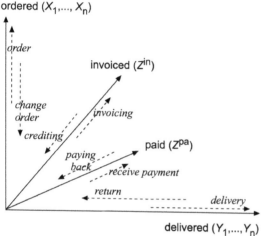

Fig. 8. Multidimensional state space for order delivery process: above a screen shot from a system that supports the process; below a simplified state space that can be used for describing the process. Pictures are from (Andersson et al., 2005)

New Types of Business Process Support

In the era of total computerization, the implementation of business processes in the organizational practice is, usually, connected to the introduction of business process support systems. Following the tradition of modeling business processes as workflows, the most wide-spread systems to support business processes are based on workflow engines. Transition from totally prescriptive process definitions to the constraint-based ones, which gives more space for creativity, requires rethinking the architectural principles on which business process support systems are being built. Instead of serving as a hard regulator, such systems should facilitate communication/collaboration between the members of the process team. The conveyor belt metaphor built in workflows should be abandon in favor of the construction site metaphor of the shared spaces as suggested in (Bider, Perjons, and Johannesson 2010,   2011; Bider, Johannesson, and Schmidt 2011).

In a business process support system with the shared spaces architecture, the process map is used not to define the flow of operation, but as a way of structuring a shared space used by participants of a bushiness process instance for coordinating their efforts and reports the progress. Shared spaces are typical for social software where they are used as an effective channel of communication between people. Properly structured, shared spaces can be used for supporting communication/collaboration between participants of a BPI. An example of such structuring is shown in Fig. 9.

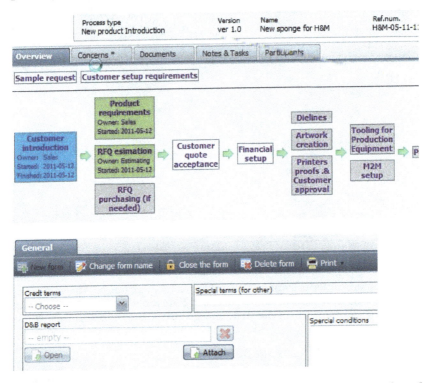

Fig. 9. A shared space for a process instance: above – a map that shows the overall structure of the shared space; below – a form that shows the detailed structure for a particular step

New Ways of Developing Business Processes and Support Systems

Achieving agility requires introducing changes in BPTs as soon as the need for this is discovered. As suggested earlier, discovering the needs and implementing the adjustments are to be entrusted to the process participants themselves. The adjustment should be made in a timely manner, which is critical to obtaining the overall agility of the enterprise. The standard way of developing business processes shown on the left-hand side of Fig. 10 may not be suitable for this end. The cycle of first modeling a process to-be, and then building a new system to support it, or recoding the existing one may be too long, not counting the time needed to learn how to use the new/updated system in practice. By the time the new process is implemented in the enterprise, it may very well be outdated.

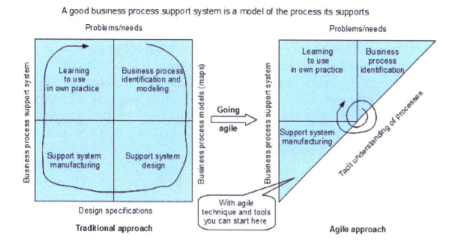

Fig. 10. Standard vs. agile development of business processes

Introducing changes in BPTs can be accelerated by adopting an agile method of system development where manufacturing of the support system is merged with the process design/redesign, as shown on the right-hand side of Fig. 10. To make the agile development of business process possible, there should be a tool that allows the process team to develop/change their process support system without engaging IT people. In case the system is based on the shared spaces architecture, as in Fig. 9, such a tool should facilitate process participants to draw/redraw the overall structure of the shared space, as well as to draw/redraw the detailed structure attached to each step. An example of such tool is presented in (iPB, 2008).

Implications for Systems Thinking

The model suggested in this paper is based on the systemic view on business processes. The idea of cross-manning of business processes discussed earlier is directly related to Systems Thinking (ST), as it improves the cooperation between the systems components (people) divided by specialization introduced via business processes. The role of ST in the suggested model is not limited to these two considerations. The strongest side of ST is its ability to deal with systems dynamics (in mathematical sense, on the level higher than the first derivatives). This feature is most important for strategic processes, where ST can help with the following:

- Designing sensors that initiate strategic BPIs in advance, i.e. before the situation becomes unmanageable.
- Providing methods to be used in the analytical phase of a strategic process to understand the system behavior. This can be done by discovering positive feedback loops that exaggerate a problem, negative feedback loops that function as barriers to growth, or lack of negative or positive loops in places where they are needed.
- Providing methods to be incorporated in the corrective action of a strategic process, like removing undesirable positive or negative loops, or adding desirable ones. This can be done by changing the assets, including making changes in the existing BPTs, adding new BPTs, or removing some of them.

To be of use in the above, the ST ideas need to be incorporated in strategic processes. Below, we present an example of such incorporation in the form of a Systemic Perspective process. This process can be used as a generalized template of applying ST as soon as there is a sign that something goes wrong/not as expected. The main concepts used in this process and the relationships between them are depicted in Fig. 11. The shared space, similar to Fig. 9, of a business process support system to facilitate this process is presented in Fig. 12. The Systemic Perspective (Bellinger 2011) represents an iterative unfolding of understanding intended to provide the basis for developing a strategy. This strategy, when implemented, is highly likely to address the situation of interest as intended while minimizing the likelihood of unintended consequences.

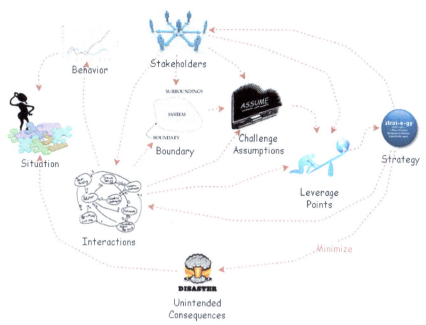

Fig.11. Main concepts behind the Systemic Perspective process

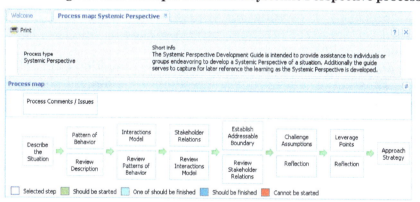

Fig.12. The structure of a shared space for the Systemic Perspective process

The following description will provide clarification of the main concepts and relationships between them from Fig. 11.

- *Situation*. A situation of interest considered warranting attention, along with an assessment of the implications of not acting, and a definition of the preferred alternative situation, forms the basis for developing understanding. The situation as-is is a result of unfolding pattern of *behavior*.
- *Behavior*. The patterns of behavior represent an unfolding of some aspects of a network of interactions. As such we endeavor to

433

understand the network of *interactions* responsible for creating the patterns of behavior.

- *Interactions.* The network of interactions is the result of some set of actions by one or more *stakeholders.* As such we endeavor to understand the mental models and motivations of the stakeholders responsible for the situation.
- *Stakeholders.* We seek to understand the motivations and the mental models of the stakeholders and the motivations and mental models of those stakeholders who are influenced by the network of interactions.
- *Boundary.* Based on an understanding of the network of interactions and stakeholders boundaries are established to keep track of which stakeholders are responsible for which aspects of the network of interactions, and which set of interactions are considered to be part of the addressable network of interaction.
- *Challenge Assumptions.* Though all the segments to this point assumptions have been made. It is essential that we challenge those assumptions because decisions made on invalid assumptions are unlikely to support the intended results.
- *Leverage Points.* Once we understand the network of interaction addressable it is essential to identify those leverage points which are likely to transform the current situation into the desired alternative situation.
- *Strategy.* The strategy is developed with the intention of migrating the situation of interest in the direction of the desired alternative situation and at the same time ensuring the minimization of *unintended consequences.*
- *Unintended Consequences.* Unintended consequences are typically the result of actions taken without appropriate systemic consideration. And, unintended consequences are seldom beneficial and as such the intent of the strategy is to minimize them.

A more in depth introduction to this model is provided in (Bellinger 2011).

Concluding Remark

In this chapter, we have presented an enterprise model that is based on the systemic view on business processes. The model is aimed at showing the ways of achieving enterprise/business agility without loosing stability. For now, the Assets-Sensors-Processes structure is just an idea of a new modeling technique. More research and practical work is needed to convert our theoretical model into a practical methodology. The promising thing here is that this can be done stepwise. The underlying thinking can already be applied for understanding some situations. The first step in creating a methodology can be quite simple, i.e. design a technique that helps to list all enterprise processes, classify them according to the three categories introduced, and describe what kind of a sensor each of them has. A step forward towards such a methodology has been done in (Bider, Perjons, and Elias 2012). Based on this list, one can start debating the presence, efficiency and sensitivity of existing sensors before raising the issue of optimization of the processes themselves. An example of how each element on the process list can be informally described is given in Table 1, which contains a template of what we can call a process signature.

Process property	Description
Process name	Put a name under which the process is known
Process type	☐ Operational ☐ Improvement ☐ Strategic
Objective with having the process	List objectives in the manner described in section 9.1
Start conditions	Describe the situation which requires firing the process
Sensor	Describe how the start situation is discovered
Goal	Describe the goal the BPI should achieved
Sub-goals	Describe sub-goals to be achieved before the goal can be achieved
Level of explicitness of BPT	Evaluate the explicitness based on the 10 points scale, where 0 means everything is in the heads of process participants (oral tradition), 10 – process rules are fully documented and are strictly followed, or/and they are built in a process support system
Level of prescriptiveness of BPT	Evaluate the prescriptiveness based on the 10 points scale, where 0 means that there are no mandatory rules on how to reach the instance goal/sub-goals, i.e. participants are free to do their best, 10 – all operations on how to reach the instance goal/sub-goals and the order in which they should be completed and fully determined

Table 1. Example of a process signature

Acknowledgments

The work on the material presented in this paper was supported by the LinkedIn group "Systems Thinking World" (http://www.linkedin.com/groups/Systems-Thinking-World-2639211). The authors are grateful to all members of the group who participated in the discussions, as their comments helped us to considerably improve the material.

The material discussed in this chapter was first presented at PoEM 2011.Working Conference on the Practice of Enterprise Modeling (Oslo Norway, 2-3 November, 2011) and published in the proceedings of this conference (Bider, Bellinger, and Perjons 2011) by Springer. This chapter is a revised and substantially extended version of the conference proceedings.

About the Authors

Dr. Ilia Bider - researcher, software engineer and business analyst - is a co-founder and Director R&D of IbisSoft and a researcher at the Department of Computers and Systems Sciences of Stockholm University. He has MS in Electronic Engineering and PhD in Computer and Systems Sciences, and combined experience of over 30 years of research, and practical work.

Gene Bellinger – Knowledge Management and Systems Thinking expert with a long industrial experience in these fields. He spent most of his time on promoting the usage of Systems Thinking by being the host of Systems Thinking World and developing SystemsWiki.org

Dr. Erik Perjons – researcher at the Department of Computer and Systems Sciences of Stockholm University. He has a PhD in Computer and Systems Sciences, and has participated in several international and national research projects in areas such as business process management, service oriented architecture, system integration and knowledge management.

References

Andersson, B., Bider, I., Johannesson, P. and Perjons, E., 2005. "Towards a Formal Definition of Goal-Oriented Business Process Patterns", BPMJ, Emerald, Vol. 11, No 6, pp. 650-652.

Bellinger, G., 2011. Systemic Perspective , Volume I. Foundations.

Bider, I., 2002. State-oriented business process modeling: principles, theory and practice, PhD thesis, KTH, Stockholm.

Bider, I., Bellinger, G., and Perjons, E., 2011. "Modeling an Agile Enterprise: Reconciling Systems and Process Thinking". Lecture Notes in Business Information Processing (LNBIP), Vol. 92, Springer, pp. 238-252.

Bider, I., Johannesson, P., and Schmidt, R., 2011. "Experiences of Using Different Communication Styles in Business Process Support Systems with the Shared Spaces Architecture", Lecture Notes in Computer Science (LNCS), Vol. 6741, Springer, pp. 299-313.

Bider I., Perjons E. and Elias M., 2012. "Untangling the Dynamic Structure of an Enterprise by Applying a Fractal Approach to Business Processes", Lecture Notes in Business Information Processing (LNBIP), Vol. 134, Springer, pp. 61-76.

Bider, I., Perjons, E., and Johannesson, P., 2010. "In Search of the Holy Grail: Integrating social software with BPM. Experience report", Lecture Notes in Business Information Processing (LNBIP), Vol. 50, Springer, pp. 1-13.

Bider, I., Perjons, E., and Johannesson, P., 2011. "A strategy for merging social software with business process support", Lecture Notes in Business Information Processing (LNBIP), Vol. 66, Part 4, Springer, pp.372-383.

Checkland, P., 1999. Systems Thinking, Systems Practice, Wiley.

Jackson, M. C., 2003. Systems Thinking: Creative Holism for Managers, Wiley.

Harmon, P., 2007. Business Process Change. A Guide for Business Managers and BPM and Six Sigma Professionals, Morgan Kaufmann Publishers.

iPB, 2009. iPB Reference Manual (on-line documentation), IbisSoft, http://docs.ibissoft.se/node/3.

Khomyakov M., and Bider, I., 2000. "Achieving Workflow Flexibility through Taming the Chaos". In. Patel D., Choudhury I., Patel S., de Cesare S. (Eds.) OOIS 2000 - 6th international conference on object oriented information systems, Springer, pp.85-92.

Lawson, H., 2010. A Journey Through the Systems Landscape, College Publications.

Sherehiy, B., Karwowski, W., and Layer, J.K.., 2007 "A review of enterprise agility: Concepts, frameworks, and attributes". International Journal of Industrial Economics, Vol. 37, 445-460.

Weingberg G.M., and Weingberg D., 1988. General Principles of Systems Design, New York, NY: Dorset House Publishing.

Weske, M., 2010. Business Process Management. Concepts, Languages, Architecture, Springer.

Intelligent Enterprise Systemics and Pragmatics

Jack Ring

Abstract

This chapter discusses what makes an intelligent enterprise. It argues that by using systemics as an approach, enterprise limits can be expanded by engaging the participants in modeling and simulating the enterprise while it is engaged in acknowledging requests, producing responses, and prudently investing rewards. Often not done or considered to be 'management's job', modeling and simulation throughout the enterprise is one of the better ways to make the enterprise more effective and sustainable.

Keywords

Intelligent Enterprise, responsiveness

Introduction[1]

An enterprise exists to facilitate commerce between a marketplace and supplier-place. An enterprise consists of two or more people taking action with limited resources to produce result(s) that trigger rewards from stakeholders. This description applies not only to commercial enterprises but also to governments (or departments, agencies, or bureaus thereof), schools, charities, street gangs, missionaries, perpetrators of money laundering/ fraud, a church, or parents raising a child, as well as to a helicopter crew rescuing stranded boat people.

Enterprise does not mean the IT system as in Enterprise Resource Planning, or Enterprise Search. We stress that enterprises are far more than sequences of computer programs. An enterprise breathes, perspires, inspires, laughs, co-learns, etc., by systemizing frontal lobes, the sources of abstractions, chunking, subsumptions, intuition, induction, abduction, deduction, etc., then, because choice-making is laden with unrecognized errors, the intelligent enterprise continually and vigorously vets its knowns as well as its unknowns.

Likewise, enterprise does not mean the partial view of an enterprise as afforded by Enterprise Architecture Frameworks. The static, impersonal model of an enterprise fostered by such frameworks does not reveal behavior, the basis of value generated for enterprise beneficiaries. Enterprises strive to achieve Big Hairy Audacious Goals. Enterprises stumble, recover, learn, celebrate, etc.

An enterprise is intelligent when it exhibits four behaviors:

> Measures the worth of its results to its customers and suppliers.
>
> Is continuously, accurately aware of enterprise situation with respect to enterprise goals,
>
> Adapts and aligns the enterprise to changes in enterprise context and capabilities so as to improve goal achievement, and
>
> Sustains enterprise integrity and enterprise value to stakeholders even when all factors are changing unpredictably.

Context is that externality with which a System interacts. Environment is that which is neither System nor Context.

Although each intelligent enterprise may be seen as a system, no intelligent enterprise stands alone. Each is a member of one or more supply chains, or

---

[1] Presented at International Conference on (Inter-) Enterprise Systems Theory and Theory in Action, October 15-17, 2007.

value webs, simultaneously. Each has multiple customers and suppliers. Each of those serve many other enterprises, even competitors.

Few intelligent enterprises exist today. The globalization of expropriation, damage, pollution, and waste suggests a growing need for enterprises to become intelligent. This highlights the growing need for personnel who are qualified to initialize and evolve intelligent enterprises. These are dual practitioners – of systems and of leadership. In fact, every participant is expected to become a co-leader when purpose and scope calls for their specific talents.

Co-leadership is not a location or a position but an emergent characteristic. Co-leadership applies to ideas, to finding ways and means, and to caretaking as well as to stimulating and guiding people. Co-leadership in intelligent enterprises devises and applies policies, principles, practices, and infrastructures. Some call this management but others call it organization development, strategic planning, marketing, product planning, supply chain management, composing, screen writing, lawmaking, practicing medicine, etc.

When Enterprise ⇔ System

About Systemics

Systemics includes both descriptive modeling of perceived systems and prescriptive modeling of intended systems in operation (Warfield, 2006). Models depict context, content, structure as well as behavior. The praxis of systemics, the elaboration of information punctuated by decision, is performed by humans. System management is seen as a system in operation. The dimensions of a systems management activity include purpose, passion, policies, principles, personnel competencies, practices, and prosthetics (intellectual and informational). The latter are the aids and tools that enable productivity and innovation during information elaboration and decision.

We note that the current prescriptions and recipes for doing systems engineering do not contain the requisites for an intelligent enterprise.

The Three Rs of Commerce

A transactional view of an enterprise shows the three R's of commerce, Request, Response and Reward. This behaviorist view is used in the interest of communicating with readers of an engineering mindset. Practitioners of psychology and social science may find this view too machine-like thus prefer other characterizations. As illustrated in Figure 1 Request, labeled [1] in the figure, occurs because the enterprise has established Relationships with the Marketplace. These foster information exchange with each part of the Marketplace, despite Competitors' interference, in order to understand their characteristics. Request [1] prompts the enterprise to assess its situation, plan projects, and update its enterprise model. In many enterprises the enterprise model is quite informal and distributed throughout the enterprise only in the heads of the participants. This is what Senge (1999) referred to as "common mental model." We note, however, the mental models in many enterprises are more diverse and conflicting than common.

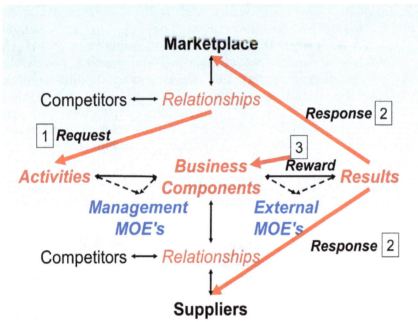

Figure 1.

Transactional View Of An Enterprise

The enterprise invokes activities, typically as one or more projects. These apply Business Components to produce Results. Business Components include[2]:

Products – one vehicle for transmitting value to customers. Includes hardware products, software products and information products.

Services – the other vehicle for transmitting value to customers. Services include planning, executing and assessing.

---

[2] This list was adapted in 1981 by the author from various works by Steven Wheelwright, Harvard, Arnaldo Hax, MIT, and members of Advanced Projects, Manufacturing Systems Division, Honeywell.

Resources – Cash and other real assets including real estate, and inventory (properly discounted). Also, knowledge (models) and relationships. Does not include People. People are the reason for the enterprise, not the resources. A Human Resources subsystem is not a useful concept in an intelligent enterprise.

Projects – the set and sequence of activities by which People apply information, time and other resources to honor all inputs, add value, and generate all outputs.

Systems – the mechanisms that store, process, and move both materials and data throughout an organization as well as support decisions.

People – the total roster of the enterprise. Includes the Board of Directors and any other group whose decisions directly influence enterprise achievement.

Information – the usable part of the enterprise's knowledge base. The knowledge base includes the technology (know how) base. Includes the data stored in the people, information system, library and other places.

Policies – articulation of strategy in the form of rules by which the enterprise allocates resources, conforms to norms and standards and controls its politics. Used to bound the permissible forms of processes and cultural behavior.

Culture – "the way things are done around here." The beliefs and values, the rituals, the symbols, the recognitions and rewards. Includes the political power patterns and dances.

Mission – The statement of enterprise purpose. Justifies the existence of the enterprise. Clearly explains the role the enterprise will play relative to its context.

Vision – Describes the enterprise meaning. An expression of what the effort is all about. Sufficiently vague to be inclusive and inviting. Often uses metaphor to communicate meaning.

The Results comprise Response, labeled [2] in Figure 1. Response, [2], represents the deliverables – the value carriers to both Marketplace and Supplier-place. Reward, [3], represents the benefits to the enterprise that are triggered by the Response. Rewards may be monetary, informational, aspirational, inspirational, and/or intangible (trust and loyalty as well as increased image or prestige).

McDavid (1999) describes a complementary view of 'enterprise as system.'

443

Enterprise Measures of Effectiveness

According to Drucker (1954) the four key indicators of enterprise effectiveness are Market Standing, Productivity, Innovation, and Liquidity. These are lagging indicators. Complementary leading indicators focus on enterprise leadership effectiveness. These are; Incidence of Conflicting Goals, Cost of Quality, Model Fidelity, Change Proficiency, Results of Employee Climate Surveys, and Benchmarks.

Enterprise Failure Symptoms

An enterprise exhibits an etiology that may be familiar to those grounded in basic psychology.

If each information/direction item listed in the left column of the table is not produced or not communicated in an adequate, accurate, and timely manner, then the enterprise participants and stakeholders exhibit the emergent behavior listed in the rightmost column. Especially pernicious is the last behavior, sabotage. This includes self-sabotage that manifests as the lack of interest in learning anything.

Absence of:	Leads to Participant:
Mission/Vision	Ambiguity
Strategy	Disorientation
Intent/Objective	Ambivalence
Goals	Alienation
Plans	Dissonance
Commitments	Distrust
Competencies	Dismay/Futility
Energy/Automation	Malaise
Teambuilding	Isolation
Collaboration	Dread
Tenacity	Apathy
Achievement	Depression
Recognition	Negative Rumors
Co-celebration	Sabotage

Scanning an existing enterprise for such participant behaviors can quickly reveal the likely sources from the leftmost column. As will be addressed later this is especially true of enterprises intended to accomplish systems management.

The Intelligent Enterprise

Meaning of Intelligent Enterprise

Enterprise means two or more persons, applying (necessarily limited) resources through actions to achieve mutual purposes. Because the human mind cannot discern reality from thought, a minimum of two human minds must be engaged; the presence of two minds does not guarantee intelligent behavior, but is a prerequisite.

Intelligent means that the purpose maximizes stakeholder value while conforming to systems and societal principles, all while unpredictable change occurs in any factors. Acknowledgement of systems and societal principles precludes the enterprise from pursuing illegal, alleviate, and unethical desires of any persons involved.

Intelligent enterprise does not mean that the enterprise staff has a high IQ. Intelligent refers to the presence of specific capabilities or behaviors, notably, situation awareness and goal pursuit.

An intelligent enterprise exhibits modes of intelligent behavior. Like modes of an automobile automatic transmission, enterprise intelligence may vary over time and situation depending on the mode in which the enterprise is operating.

When comparing two intelligent enterprises the one with greater abilities and/or orchestration can accommodate a greater rate and range of change without loss of stability or integrity. Rate of change means the velocity at which an enterprise must adapt and align, also called its change proficiency. Range of change means the variety of stimuli to which the enterprise can respond and garner rewards. In the literature, Range is variously referred to as viable performance envelope, repertoire of capabilities, or ability to learn.

All enterprises have the opportunity to improve and those that fare best apply systems thinking, feeling, and doing to arrange the enterprise assets and activities for best results in the given situation. An enterprise does not exhibit a continuum of asset and activity patterns. Rather, certain arrangements are more stable than are others. These are called modes of enterprise operation.

An enterprise exhibits various modes of intelligence over time and in comparison to other enterprises. An enterprise's mode of intelligence is influenced by how well its architecture harmonizes its size and technological proficiency. The latter includes not only thermodynamics and informatics technologies but also the know how of teleonomics (Gilbert, 1996) and social dynamics.

The need for initializing enterprises and continuously improving each intelligent enterprise is pervasive. Intelligent enterprises are initialized and evolved by qualified personnel using policies, principles, practices, techniques and tools which some call systems management but others call organization development, strategic planning, marketing, product planning, supply chain management, composing, screen writing, lawmaking, practicing medicine, etc.

Two or More People

People are the key ingredient. There need be no upper limit on the size of an enterprise, however the range and rate capabilities of an enterprise may diminish significantly as size increases.

Each person in or associated with the enterprise has a mental model of a) purpose and intended outcomes, b) what behaviors are and are not acceptable and c) ways their enterprise can pursue purpose. In the intelligent enterprise, these mental models are coherent. In the intelligent enterprise with a high mode of intelligence, the mental models reinforce and amplify one another. Likewise, each person has a sufficient level of enthusiasm to help one another overcome fear, ideally transforming that energy into more enthusiasm thus innovation.

Limited Resources

An intelligent enterprise must never have more resources than it needs, otherwise it cannot maximize Return on Resources while achieving best parsimony. Accordingly, each new Request will likely put the intelligent enterprise into a resource-limited state thereby triggering innovative adaptation. Ideally, the mix of resources matches the resource implications of incoming Requests. Otherwise, new resources must be seized while idle ones must be shed.

When the marketplace and/or supplier place gets highly competitive, thus fickle, one important ramification is that the intelligent enterprises break-even capacity must be well below maximum capacity. This is not reserve capacity (incurring cost even when not applied). It is the lower limit of the ability to shed capacity to match demand while paying only for actual capacity employed. A break-even point in the range of 50% to as low as

30% of maximum capacity is indicated for intelligent enterprises operating in highly uncertain contexts. In contrast, most current enterprises seem to have a break-even point at 70% to 90% of their maximum capacity.

Actions

An intelligent enterprise plans and executes three kinds of actions: fulfilling commitments, gaining new commitments and improving the ability to do both – better, faster, cheaper.

Purpose

The Purpose, maximizing value for stakeholders while conforming to systems and societal principles, is not a single valued objective function. The two or more people must be clear on the purpose of the enterprise and capable of making difficult choices regarding intended results and consistent activities. Although prevailing 'theories of the firm' taught in business schools presume that enterprise purpose is profit, Dr. Novak suggests that the purpose of an intelligent enterprise should be learning – by the two or more people – and jointly with customers and suppliers. The previously mentioned 'Drucker measures' indicate that the enterprise decision makers must seek the balance point between profit and learning and always be alert to a shifting balance point.

Stakeholders

Stakeholders include all relevant and affected parties, both positive and negative, regarding the enterprise. One of the strategic decisions is deciding which stakeholders the intelligent enterprise will serve and which it will purposefully ignore.

Principles of Systems and Society

System principles highlight the presence of quality, requisite variety, parsimony and harmony. Crosby (1992) defines quality as conformance to requirements, no more no less; not a scalar as in high quality or low quality.

Societal principles vary with the scope of the stakeholder community. The scope can range from a nearly philosophical set often attributed to Marilyn vos Savant, as the Absence vs. Presence of:

> Humility instead of Pride, knowing that we are not alone in the world.
>
> Generosity instead of Covetousness, allowing others to have what they deserve.

447

Restraint instead of Lust, controlling our compulsions and impulses.

Kindness instead of Anger, tolerating our fellow humans' mistakes.

Moderation instead of Gluttony, satisfying ourselves with necessities.

Charity instead of Envy, helping those who cannot help themselves.

Diligence instead of Sloth, making ourselves useful in the world.

A less abstract view (Hock, 1999) of societal principles emphasizes interoperability among the 'two or more people' engaged in the enterprise. This model maximizes synergy when the respective parties commit to,

Being open to interactions with any other enterprise that subscribes to the principles.

Having the right to self-organize at any time, on any scale or around any activity consistent with the Purpose of the enterprise.

Making deliberations and decisions by bodies and methods that reasonably represent all relevant and affected parties and are dominated by none.

Vest authority in, and make choices to perform functions and use resources, at the smallest or most local part that includes all relevant and affected parties.

Exchanging information related to achieving the Purpose in accordance with the Principles, freely and fully unless doing so violates legal constraints.

Resolving conflict creatively and cooperatively without social, ecological, or physical violence.

Educe, not compel, behavior to the maximum degree possible.

Respecting, protecting, and encouraging individual, cultural, and societal diversity.

Unpredictable Change

An important nuance is Unpredictable Change. This applies to inputs and capabilities and to the Goal. A Goal-seeking System must have the Competency and Energy to sustain Convergence on system integrity as both Situation and Goal change asynchronously. Depending on the frequency and magnitude of the 'stochastic shocks' of change, this unpredictability can be near moot or can become the central factor in enterprise sustainability.

The copious literature about strategy can be boiled down to choosing a set point on the continuum from an offensive type (striving to maximize gain) to a defensive type (striving to minimize loss). This choice field is sufficient when perceived uncertainty is low. When perceived uncertainty is high, the focus inevitably shifts from serving the customer to preserving the institution (bureaucrat thinking). In the case where perceived uncertainty is low while actual uncertainty is high the enterprise incurs "restructuring costs." A review of annual reports of U.S. enterprises indicates that restructuring costs are in the range of a trillion dollars annually. Often a strategy of 'muddling through' is adopted. In contrast is the strategy of Generating Opportunities while not leading the enterprise into a blind alley. The Intelligent Enterprise generally applies Generating Opportunities.

Problem System Dynamics

The Market place and Supplier-place consist of enterprises that interact with the enterprise of interest. All are changing. Even when change is largely unpredictable, patterns of change are discernable and can inform the intelligent enterprise regarding co-alignment challenges and opportunities. Each intelligent enterprise must be thought of and treated as one variable in a multi-variable, implicit differential equation. In simple cases, the pattern of interaction can be explicit. However, because of the interactions of people the pattern is implicit and second order. People have thresholds of expectations and sense changes in/by another person. "He came on too strong" is a familiar expression. This kind of relationship is prevalent in systems of humans. It is similar to discontinuous, compressible flow as studied in fluid dynamics.

Similarly, the Marketplace and Supplier-place will change in dimensions of variety (ever larger and more 'complex' systems), ambiguity (ever more abstract and vague, even tacit, needs) and scope or strangeness (challenging the bounds of knowledge and technology).

Inevitably, neither Marketplace nor Supplier-place is ever satisfied. Better, faster, cheaper is their persistent demand and any enterprise not responsive to the demands soon experiences the apathy of its stakeholders. Of course the goal, here, is not 100% customer satisfaction. One could go broke chasing that goal. The real goal is "just a little bit better than competition."

Enterprise System Dynamics

Limits of Scale

An intelligent enterprise may need to scale in size from two to 250 employees and beyond. A human has limits in some aspects, physical and social being apparent. A human may be limitless in other aspects such as abstraction and thinking... Acting locally while thinking globally is one recipe for meaningful growth and the key to this recipe is a model of the enterprise including its dynamics. Recent cases are demonstrating that cellular organizations with less than 50 persons per unit, abiding by common purpose and principles as their orchestrating framework (Hock, 1999) have proven quite effective. Opposing examples are hierarchical piles based on the presumption of economy of scale. Although Learning Curve slope is important during production doubling episodes 1 – 6, it becomes less so as the product nears commodity status, approximately after the seventh doubling of production. Meanwhile interference with innovation increases with enterprise size, particularly in hierarchical enterprises.

Limits to Responsiveness

As noted previously, intelligent enterprises must respond to rate of change and range of change. Dove (2001) describes key considerations as Enterprise Architecture, Knowledge Base, and Decision style. Limits to responsiveness are manifested in the physical realities of legacy systems, logical realities of institutionalized practices and policies, and emotional realities of participants and their patterns of interrelationships and styles of interrelation.

Expanding the Limits

Enterprise limits can be expanded by engaging the participants in modeling and simulating the enterprise while it is engaged in acknowledging Requests, producing responses, and prudently investing rewards. Often not done or considered to be 'management's job', modeling and simulation throughout the enterprise is one of the better ways to make the enterprise more effective and sustainable. Once the participants perceive that the name of the game is pursuit (Ring, 2000a) then the level of enthusiasm and innovation in the enterprise rises considerably.

Executives as Systemists

At this point it should not need to be said but is too important to leave unsaid. The dynamic and integrity limits of an enterprise thereby the limits of stakeholder value it may cause will be directly proportional to the ability of its executives to think, feel and act as systemists.

About the Author

Jack Ring applies systems principles and systems engineering practices to the evolution of people systems such as business enterprises, and he mentors high tech organizations regarding strategy, innovation, organization, business process and growth. He is experienced in a variety of markets and businesses including industrial, commercial, aerospace, intelligence and the public sector. Jack learned management competencies at General Electric.

References

Crosby, P., (1992) The Eternally Successful Organization, Signet, Reprint Edition.

Dove, R., (2001) Response Ability; The Language, Structure, and Culture of the Agile Enterprise, Wiley and Sons.

Drucker, P. (1954) The Practice of Management, Harper.

Gilbert, T., (1996) Human Competence; Engineering Worthy Performance, HRD Press. Rev&Updtd edition.

Hock, D. (1999) Birth of the Chaordic Age, Berrett-Koehler Publishers.

McDavid, D. (1999) Discovering the User's Ontology in a Living Enterprise, Proceedings of the International Conference on Systems Engineering, Las Vegas, NV.

Madni, A. et al, (2001) IDEON™: An extensible ontology for designing, integrating, and managing collaborative distributed enterprises, Systems Engineering, Volume 4, Issue 1, 2001, Pages: 35-48.

Novak, J., (1998) Learning, Creating and Using Knowledge, Earlbaum, pg 90.

Ring, J., (2000a) The Chaordic Form of Collaborative Commerce, Presentation to Delphi Group Summit, San Diego, CA.

Ring, J. (2000b) Effective Control in Peopled Systems, INCOSE Proceedings of International Symposium 2000.

Ring, J. (2001a) Systems Engineering the Agile enterprise, Tutorial conducted at International Council on Systems Engineering Symposium, Melbourne, AUS, 2001. CD available from author.

Ring, J. (2001b) The Next Venue for Systems Engineering, INCOSE Proceedings of International Symposium 2001, Melbourne, Australia.

Ring, J., (2001c) Discovering the Architecture of Product X, INCOSE Proceedings of International Symposium 2001, Melbourne, Australia.

Ring, J. (2002) E-Business Infrastructure Capability Assessment, INCOSE Proceedings of International Symposium 2002, Las Vegas, NV, USA.

Ring, J., (2004) Xtreme Project Management; Another 12-step Process? International Conference on Systems Engineering, ICSE04 Conference Proceedings, Las Vegas, NV, USA.

Ring, J. (2004b) Factors Influencing SE Practices by 2010, INCOSE Proceedings of International Symposium 2004. Toulouse, FR.

Rouse, W. (2005) Enterprises as systems: Essential challenges and approaches to transformation, Systems Engineering, Volume 8, Issue 2, Pages: 138-150.

Senge, P. (1999) The Fifth Discipline: The Art & Practice of The Learning Organization, Doubleday/Currency.

Starkermann, R., (2003) Amity and Enmity Editions a la Carte' Zurich, ISBN 3-908730-29-5.

Ullman, D., (2001) 12 Steps to Robust Decisions, Trafford Publishing, Victoria, BC.

Warfield, J. (2006) Introduction to Systems Science, World Scientific Press, 2006.

Weinberg, G., (2001) An Introduction to General Systems Thinking, Dorset House, Reprinted 2001.

Wymore, A. W. (1998) Subsystem Optimization Implies System Suboptimization: Not! at http://www.sie.arizona.edu/sysengr/wymore/optimal.html.

Wymore, A. W., (1993) Model-based Systems Engineering, CRC Press

Modelling and Simulating Firm Performance with System Dynamics

John Morecroft

Abstract

Why do some firms consistently outperform rivals? The resource-based view (RBV) offers an approach to analyzing this fundamental question that is amenable to modeling and simulation. Firms are conceived as collections of strategic resources that create products and services. High-performing firms are those which possess unique and difficult-to-imitate resources from which they derive competitive advantage. This proposition is easy to apply and understand if uniqueness is concentrated in a single static resource. But usually the situation is much more complex. A firm comprises many interrelated resources that are changing over time. In these situations modeling and simulation can help to explain differential performance. The model-based approach is illustrated with a system dynamics model of an international radio broadcaster. The broadcaster possesses tangible resources such as staff, studios, languages, and transmitters, as well as intangibles such as program quality and editorial reputation. The model reveals the structure of the resource system. Analysis of the structure (including simulations) can help to isolate the reasons for high (or low) performance. An important conclusion is that uniqueness often lies in the information network that coordinates resource building rather than in the resources themselves.

Keywords

System dynamics, modeling, simulation, high-performing firm

Where Does Competitive Advantage Come From?

Resource-based theory suggests that competitive advantage stems from differences in firms' resources (Wernerfelt 1984, Barney 1991). Here resources can be tangible and measureable such as employees and equipment or they can be intangible such as reputation and employee motivation. The literature identifies several characteristics that resources must possess if they are to provide sustainable advantage (Grant 1991). Strategically important resources must be durable and they should not be mobile or tradable. Moreover, they should not be easy for rivals to replicate or substitute with alternatives. It is also assumed that these inimitable resources can be acquired at no additional cost to the resources used by other firms competing in the same industry. These criteria ensure that unique resources remain unique without the firm incurring additional costs. Finally, strategic resources should be complementary, in other words capable of working well together with the other resources that go to make-up the business.

Nevertheless there is a lot more to be said. Where exactly does uniqueness stem from? Is it concentrated in one resource or somehow distributed among all resources? And how are rival organizations able to build distinctive resource positions as the basis for a sustainable competitive advantage without being copied? This particular question is of obvious practical significance.

Modeling a Resource System

It is straightforward in principle to say that strategic resources should work well together, but how can you be certain, or at least confident that they will? One approach is to build a model of the resource system (the network of the firm's interlocking strategic assets) and see how it actually works by simulating it.

This approach represents the firm as a collection of tangible and intangible resources, entirely compatible with the resource-based view. But in addition it uses principles of system dynamics and information feedback to realistically represent how resources are interlinked in the firm (Morecroft 2002). These basic principles are explained in more detail later. Through careful quantification and simulation it is then possible to understand experimentally how performance depends on resources and more specifically how performance evolves over time according to the way resources accumulate under the guidance of management. The links between system dynamics and the resource-based view RBV continue to be developed as an active research thread within the strategy area. Reviews can be found in Gary et al 2008 and in Maritan and Peteraf 2010.

Publications by Kunc and Morecroft 2010, Repenning and Henderson 2011, and by Warren 2002 and 2008, further illustrate the ideas in action.

Modeling an International Radio Broadcaster

The best way to understand the approach is with a practical example. Here we model an international radio broadcaster, BBC World Service and its potential sources of competitive advantage over rival broadcasters. This, broadly speaking, was the challenge posed by the Directorate Secretary of BBC World Service in the mid-1990s, faced with an array of changes in the business including intensifying competition from broadcasters such as Voice of America and Deutsche Welle, advances in broadcasting technology and cuts in funding from central government. The resource-based view gives a natural starting point for the model. What are the key resources that enable an international broadcaster to offer a differentiated service and so achieve superior performance? Here practical measures of performance widely used in the industry include number of listeners, cost per listener, geographical reach and impact on opinion leaders.

Figure 1 shows a simple resource list that arose in a series of meetings with an experienced management team at BBC World Service. These resources underpin a broadcast business covering 65% of the earth and 80% of the world's population with over 1,200 hours of programming per week in English and 43 other languages, listened to by 143 million people every week. Assets are supported by funding shown on the left of the figure and, in combination, the assets attract listeners shown on the right. As resource-based theory would suggest there is a rich mix of tangibles and intangibles to contemplate. The tangibles include staff and studios located at Bush House, which is the headquarters of World Service on the Strand in London. There are also foreign correspondents stationed in the numerous countries that receive World Service broadcasts, and an international network of more than fifty transmitters (short-wave, medium-wave and FM) that beam programs to listeners across the globe. The intangibles include the portfolio of languages as well as soft yet vital factors such as program quality, program mix and editorial reputation.

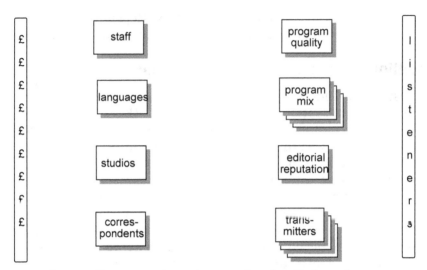

Figure 1. Resources in an international radio broadcaster.
A list of tangibles and intangibles.

The next step in creating a simulation model of World Service is to depict each resource as a stock accumulation complete with inflows and outflows. Levels or stocks are basic building blocks of system dynamics models portraying fundamental and universal processes of accumulation and depletion that govern the build-up of any enduring asset.

Figure 2 is the resource list of figure 1 re-drawn to show resource accumulations. Consider a tangible resource like staff. The arrow on the left shows an inflow of new staff corresponding to hiring. The arrow on the right shows an outflow corresponding to attrition or staff turnover. The arithmetic governing a resource accumulation is commonsense yet also mathematically precise. If an organization is employing 100 staff at the start of a quarter, hires 10 new staff and loses 2 during the quarter then it starts the next quarter with 108 staff. The same symbols and arithmetic govern all other resources, both tangible and intangible. On the lower right, the number of transmitters is an accumulation of the difference between transmitters being commissioned (inflow) and transmitters being decommissioned (outflow). The number of languages in the language portfolio is the accumulation of new languages added and languages withdrawn. Similarly, program quality (measured say on an index from 0 to 100) is the accumulation of increases in quality and decreases in quality. Note that the depiction of stocks does not, in itself, say anything about what actually drives the inflows and outflows. It simply shows that accumulation is happening. The organizational drivers are added to the overall "resource map" later as will be explained below.

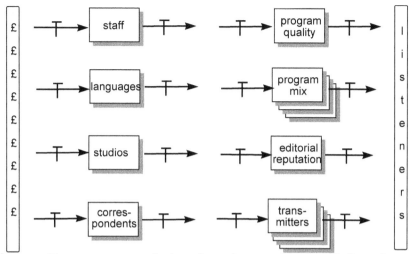

**Figure 2. Resource accumulations in an international radio broadcaster.
Evolving tangibles and intangibles.**

Stock accumulations are important to resource-based thinking because they introduce dynamics, by tracking how resources evolve over time as a result of management policies applied. So if we want to understand how an organization came to own a special configuration of resources, accumulations will allow us to trace how each resource was built, step-by-step over time, starting from an earlier resource endowment. Moreover, if we want to understand how an organization's resource position will change in the future (and the implications for dynamic competitive advantage) then accumulations will allow us to trace that too, starting from the current resource endowment.

Stock accumulations are also important to resource-based thinking because they capture the inertia that lies behind firms' competitive positions. This point has been made convincingly in the strategy literature by Dierickx and Cool (1989) in their widely cited paper 'Asset Stock Accumulation and Sustainability of Competitive Advantage'. They point out that strategic asset stocks are accumulated by choosing appropriate time paths of inflows and outflows over a period of time. Using the "bathtub" metaphor (which is also widely used in system dynamics) they point out a fundamental inertial constraint on strategy change - that while flows (of strategic resources) can be adjusted instantaneously, stocks cannot. It takes a consistent pattern of resource flows to accumulate a desired change in strategic asset stocks. From this observation they derive a number of dynamic characteristics governing the sustainability of privileged asset positions including time compression diseconomies, asset mass efficiencies, interconnectedness of asset stocks, asset erosion and causal ambiguity.

Dierickx and Cool's concept of asset stock accumulation breaks free from quasi-static equilibrium reasoning that has dominated much of classic resource-based theory. This equilibrium reasoning is encapsulated in the strategic factor markets argument developed by Barney (1986) which focuses on the cost of acquiring resources to implement strategies, and the relationship between these costs and the returns to a strategy once it is implemented. As Barney points out, when the cost of resource acquisition equals the value created by implementing a strategy, a strategy generates normal returns, even if it successfully creates imperfect competition in product markets. The point here is that in a rational world with perfect strategic factor markets, a firm that creates a differentiated product will have already paid an up-front resource acquisition cost that exactly offsets the extra value which can be reaped in the market from the product's uniqueness. Barney (1989) points out that, in principle, the same strategic factor markets argument applies even to "non tradable" assets accumulated by the firm over time because there is normally a cost to the firm in developing these assets, which is the cost of forgoing other opportunities. So stock accumulation does not inherently allow the creation of privileged asset positions, but rather opens-up the possibility of novel ways of acquiring resources cheaply that later turn out to be valuable. The implication is that resource based theory is able to shed light on such potentially advantageous situations by "examining the costs born by a firm in developing these assets over time" and comparing them to the benefits they yield. But this comparison is exceedingly difficult to carry out in advance for a realistic firm pursuing a new strategy. To make such a comparison a management team must not only specify its strategic resources and the costs of developing them, but also describe the policies that cause resources to change and then infer how the resulting resource system will evolve in the future. It is exactly in this area of visualizing, quantifying and rehearsing the dynamics of asset stock accumulation that modeling and simulation can offer both theoretical and practical insight to strategists. For example such a model-based approach can reliably handle dynamic phenomena in which advantageous stock accumulations such as R&D know-how vigorously reinforce themselves, or where potentially damaging intangible stock accumulations such as morale deplete to dangerously low levels that suddenly and unexpectedly destroy competitive advantage.

Linking Resources to Business Performance

Individual resources like a transmitter or a studio have no intrinsic value in isolation (except their sale price). Their value to the business derives from how they combine with other resources to deliver a distinctive product or service (Porter 1991). System dynamics enables the creation of resource maps that show how firms' resources interact. For example, in a radio broadcaster, audience size can be traced back to all eight resources shown in figures 1 and 2. A sample from this web of connections will illustrate the point. According to industry experts audience depends on a mixture of technical, language and programming capabilities. Let's consider each of these audience drivers:

1. The technical potential audience measures the number of people who could receive the broadcast signal, regardless of whether or not they wanted to listen. This measure of audience is a function of the number and type of transmitters, the footprint or area served per transmitter and the average population density in the regions served. Factors such as footprint and population density are known practical parameters in the broadcasting industry. The resource map in figure 3 shows the causal links by which these factors translate the strategic resource of transmitters into technical potential audience.

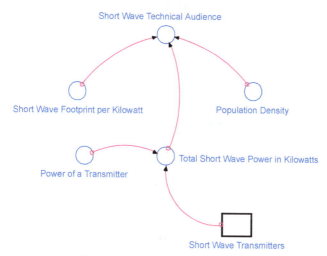

Figure 3: Visualising the link between transmitters and audience.

2. Potential language listeners measures the number of people with access to radios who could understand a radio program regardless of whether or not they can receive the broadcast signal. This number is a function of the current language portfolio and radio's share of language speakers. Broadly speaking, the more languages in the portfolio the more potential listeners, though of course some languages such as Mandarin, English or Spanish are much more widely spoken than other such as Greek, Finnish or Zulu.

3. Maximum audience measures the number of listeners who can understand at least one broadcast language, have access to a radio and can receive the signal. This number comes from combining technical potential audience and potential language listeners and is a practical example of the complementarity between transmitters and languages.

4. Indicated audience measures the number of listeners from the available pool who tune in to the programs offered by World Service. This number is a fraction of the maximum audience and depends in part on the convenience of program scheduling. Convenience can be traced through broadcast hours (how many hours per day the station is on the air) to staff hours available and ultimately to the number of staff.

Here among these drivers of audience size is a realistic portrayal of complementarity between three of the broadcaster's strategic resources: transmitters, language portfolio, and staff. The corresponding resource map shows how changes in any of these resources interact to influence audience size according to causal links and operating parameters supplied by industry experts. The map captures both obvious and subtle causality. For example, an increase in the number of transmitters will lead unambiguously to a proportional increase in technical potential audience. However, this increase may or may not translate into a commensurate increase in listeners depending on whether these extra transmitters reach previously unserved potential language listeners. Similarly, an increase in staff will lead unambiguously to a proportional increase in program hours (providing program mix remains constant). However, this increase may or may not translate into a commensurate increase in listeners depending on how the extra program hours are allocated across the language portfolio and how much unfilled airtime is still available.

Resource maps not only show the underlying business processes through which resources drive performance, but they also guide quantification of the model, allowing facts and figures about the business to enter the analysis. Resource complementarity arises from practical operating details of the business. These details are widely known, can often be quantified, and usually cannot be altered by management - they are operating constraints. For example in broadcasting the footprint of a short-wave transmitter is 7,500 square kilometers per kilowatt of short-wave power and that's a fact of transmission technology which partly determines the economics of audience size and cannot be changed. Similarly, the likelihood that a listener will find a World Service broadcast in an appropriate language at a convenient time depends on the ratio of broadcast hours per language per day and the number of hours in a day. Once again, facts determine the nature of the causality. Moreover, the greater the likelihood of finding a World Service broadcast, the more listeners will be attracted (assuming other factors such as program mix and quality remain unchanged). This particular relationship between convenience and listening is a behavioral assumption about listeners. It may not have the hard precision of transmitter footprint, but nevertheless there are logical bounds on the relationship. For example, if broadcast hours in a given language are zero, then obviously there will be no listeners in this language. On the other hand if a given language is broadcast for 24 hours per day then that's the most convenient schedule possible, so audience size in this language will then depend entirely on other factors such as program mix and quality. Between these extremes of convenience audience listening is governed by the familiar law of diminishing returns.

Resource Flows and Operating Policy - The Drivers of Accumulation

Resource stocks change over time by accumulating resource inflows and outflows. Moreover, these resource flows are governed by operating policies under the control of management. In system dynamics policies are represented as goal-seeking feedback processes. Figure 4 shows an operating policy for a single resource in isolation. The firm takes corrective action whenever there is a gap between desired resource (the amount of resource the management team is aiming for) and apparent resource (the amount of productive resource the firm currently possesses). The extent of corrective action depends on both the size of the resource gap and the time required to correct the gap.

Consider for example program staff in an international broadcaster. Staff planning begins with budgeting that allocates a fraction of annual operating funds to program making. Knowing the total budget available for staff and normal staff salary gives the desired number of program staff. This desired number is compared to the actual number of staff in drawing-up recruitment plans. If management chooses to correct staff discrepancies over a period of four months then, on average, the inflow of staff each month is one quarter of the staff gap.

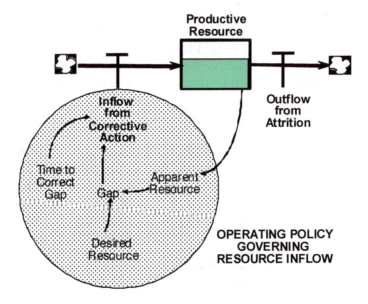

Figure 4. Operating policy and goal-seeking feedback. Resource adjustment in a purposive firm.

A similar rationale applies to investment in new transmitters. The overall budget is split between operating funds and capital funds. The capital budget is allocated to short-wave, medium-wave and FM transmitters according to established priorities. Once applied these priorities determine the desired number of transmitters the broadcaster can afford to purchase and operate. For example, the capital cost of a short-wave transmitter is around ten million pounds sterling, so a capital budget of forty million pounds will allow, at maximum, the purchase of four new transmitters The gap between desired and current number of transmitters then drives new investment. On average it takes six months to construct a new FM transmitter and 24 months to construct a new short-wave transmitter.

These examples show that goal seeking feedback is a realistic and versatile way to capture the practical organizational procedures, pressures and constraints that drive resource inflows and outflows.

Resource Coordination

In principle we could imagine goal-seeking feedback policies regulating the inflow and outflow of each and every resource in a firm. However, it is self evident that some kind of coordination is necessary among the different resources if a firm is to pursue a consistent strategy to achieve sustainable competitive advantage and to outperform rivals. In practice the degree of coordination depends crucially on the policies that control accumulation and more specifically on the composition of the decision rules: quantity and quality of information they use and the weight they give to this information.

One way to achieve coordination is through adaptive goal formation that links the desired level of a given resource to resource levels elsewhere in the organization. Figure 5 shows an adaptive policy. Here the desired resource is not simply a constant value but depends on the apparent level of other resources which are themselves accumulating and changing elsewhere in the organization.

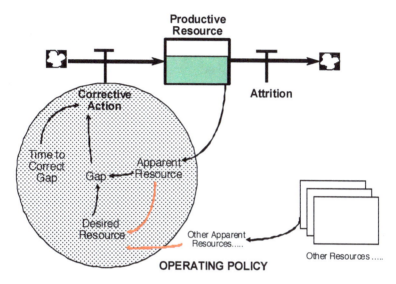

Figure 5. Adaptive goal formation.
Sophisticated purposive behavior and dynamic complexity.

Adaptive goals often arise in the routines of functional decision-making and these procedures can be modeled. A simple but parochial example of an adaptive goal is one that seeks to perpetuate the growth of a single resource - a policy of empire building. In this case the goal is equal to the current value of the resource enlarged by an expansion factor. For example, an adaptive goal for desired staff might be existing staff plus five percent. If it takes three months to acquire new staff then this goal will bring about corrective action to increase staff by five percent per quarter. Moreover, this rate of increase is sustained over time because whatever the current level of staff, the goal is always to have five percent more. A more sophisticated adaptive goal might arise from comparing an apparent resource with one or more resources elsewhere in the organization and seeking to achieve a specified balance between them. For example desired staff in an international radio broadcaster depends on program mix (the blend of news, current affairs, documentaries, music and repeats). It takes approximately 48 staff hours to produce one hour of documentary but 24 hours or less to produce one hour of music. So if management decides to

463

add a higher proportion of music then the total number of staff required to sustain a given broadcast schedule (desired staff) falls.

By contrast, budgeting contains more complex adaptive goals. In this case the desired resource is equal to the affordable resource within the constraints of the agreed budget allocation. So a broadcaster may divide-up its operating (non-capital) budget between program making, support and transmission. The fraction of the budget allocated to each of these categories will determine the amount that can be spent on program makers, support staff and maintenance of transmitters. The policy for allocating funds then becomes critical for understanding the consistency of resource building. In many organizations budget allocations are political, territorial, myopic and governed by precedent. For example if program making has traditionally received 70 percent of a broadcaster's operating budget then 70 percent will form the basis for future budget negotiations and is unlikely to change significantly without strong political pressure. A special case of policy coordination is optimal resource building. If a firm achieves this ideal it means that each guiding policy accumulates resource in a way that builds a privileged asset position consistent with the firms overall strategy. But what does it take to achieve such optimality? Information feedback theory provides some useful insight. An optimal policy requires information about every single resource stock in the firm in order to determine the best adjustment of any single resource. In a radio broadcaster such tight coordination means that an adaptive goal such as desired staff would depend not only on program mix but also languages, studios, correspondents, program quality, editorial reputation and transmitters. Clearly such complex criteria, if applied rigorously, would overload any practical hiring policy with too much information. Equally it would be impractical to link investment in new transmitters directly to staff, program mix and editorial reputation. Realistic operating policies are selective in their use of coordinating information (Morecroft 1985). They operate within the constraints of bounded rationality, falling short of the objective rationality of strategic factor markets.

It is tempting to think that "operating policy" as used in this paper is the same as "high performance routine" as used by Teece and Pisano. There are indeed strong parallels because both routines and policies describe firm specific coordination mechanisms. However, an operating policy treats an organizational routine as an information processing activity. It portrays managers as decision makers with bounded rationality (Morecroft 1985). A policy shows how managers select, prioritize and process business information when adjusting resource stocks (Forrester 1961 and 1992, Morecroft 2007 chapter 7, Sterman 1989 and 2000 chapter 15).

This feedback representation is important because it says that the uniqueness of firms derives from how they process information, as well as their endowment of resources. Moreover, the coordinating information network is conceptually distinct from a resource or even a set of linked resources. It is a web of discretionary connections that controls an array of accumulations. It is therefore possible to search for firm uniqueness and competitive advantage in the structure of the web (the information cues used by decision makers, the weight given to these cues, the resulting types of feedback loop) as well as in the array of resources.

Algebraic Equations from A Resource Map

To obtain a simulator it is necessary to convert a resource map into algebraic equations. To many people this step might seem impractical. How can one express algebraically the kind of organizational relationships implied by operating policies, or the impact of intangible resources, or the synergies to be gained from complementary resources?

To illustrate we examine the language portfolio of World Service and the corresponding equations. This fragment of the resource map is good sample because it shows representative equation formulations for an adaptive goal (the target number of languages) in a part of the organization which is steeped in history and tradition. Guidelines on how to formulate algebraic equations from a resource map are provided in Sterman 2000 and in Morecroft 2007[12].

Figure 6 is a visual model of the language portfolio using the mapping symbols and conventions of system dynamics. The current language portfolio accumulates the change of languages agreed by management. There are forty-four different languages being broadcast. This initial endowment contains the history of all previous changes to the portfolio. The operating policy which guides the change of languages is a goal seeking feedback process. The management team adjusts the portfolio whenever there is a gap between the required language portfolio and the current portfolio. Management has some discretion over how quickly to take corrective action which is represented by the time to adjust portfolio.

---

[12] Online courses in system dynamics are available from Worcester Polytechnic Institute WPI in Worcester Massachusetts www.online.wpi.edu. Further information about system dynamics can be obtained from the System Dynamics Society www.systemdynamics.org.

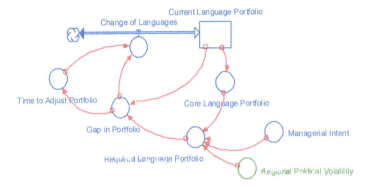

the language portfolio reflects the history and traditions of the
organisation as well as current operating pressures

Figure 6. Visual model of a changing language portfolio.

The required language portfolio is an adaptive goal anchored in the tradition of the core language portfolio and modified by short-term pressures from managerial intent and regional political volatility. Efficiency drives can lead to plans to cut languages. On the other hand, political unrest (such as conflict in the Balkans in recent years) can lead to calls to add languages. Underlying all debate about languages is a widely shared view of the need for a core language portfolio that should not be compromised. This core represents a deeply held belief about the number of broadcast languages necessary for World Service to achieve its mission.

The drivers of path dependency (resource endowments and operating policy) raise an important practical question about firm performance. How do you reliably infer the future behavior of a firm knowing its initial resources and its policies? System dynamics offers simulation as a rigorous way to infer the behavior of a resource system. However, there is a price to be paid for simulation. It is first necessary to convert resource maps of the kind shown in figures 3 and 6 into quantitative algebraic formulations.

For example, asset stock adjustment in figure 6 is captured in the four equations below. Equation 1 shows the algebra of stock accumulation. The current language portfolio at time t is equal to the language portfolio at time t-1 plus the change of languages over the time interval t-1 to t. To start there are 50 languages. Equation 2 expresses the change of languages as the gap in the portfolio divided by the time to adjust the portfolio. Equation 3 defines the time to adjust portfolio as 6 months. Equation 4 then shows the gap in portfolio as the difference between the required language portfolio and the core language portfolio.

1. Current_Language_Portfolio(t) = Current_Language_Portfolio(t - 1) + (Change_of_Languages)

INIT Current_Language_Portfolio = 50 {languages}

2. Change_of_Languages(t) = Gap_in_Portfolio(t)/Time_to_Adjust_Portfolio

3. Time_to_Adjust_Portfolio = 6 months

4. Gap_in_Portfolio(t) = Required_Language_Portfolio(t) - Core_Language_Portfolio(t)

Adaptive goal formation is captured in equations 5 through 7. Equation 5 shows how the required language portfolio is anchored to the core language portfolio and then modified by multiplicative influences from managerial intent and regional political volatility. Equation 6 shows the core language portfolio as a slowly adapting function of the current language portfolio. The formulation uses a special smoothing function SMTH1 to represent how the gradual embedding of languages in the organization comes to be recognized as the stable core of the portfolio which is not affected by short-term cuts or additions to the portfolio. Finally, equation 7 defines time to embed language as 36 months which is the time to achieve widespread acceptance of the composition of the portfolio.

5. Required_Language_Portfolio(t) = Core_Language_Portfolio(t) *Managerial_Intent(t) *Regional_Political_Volatility(t) {languages}

6. Core_Language_Portfolio = SMTH1(Current_Language_Portfolio,Time_to_Embed_Language) {languages}

7. Time_to_Embed_Language = 36 {months}

The reward for investing time in equation formulation is a simulation engine that can reliably show how path dependent strategies arise from resource endowments and operating policies. This ability to infer ex-ante how business performance arises from the structure and time evolution of a firm's resource system is missing from contemporary resource-based theory. Yet it is arguably the only way to escape the tautological trap that superior resources can only be recognized after they have produced superior performance.

Dynamic Complexity and Performance
- Scenarios from the World Service Microworld

This section presents scenarios generated by a gaming simulator called the World Service Microworld (Delauzun et al 1996) representing an imaginary international broadcaster competing in the same industry as BBC World Service. The simulator's graphical interface includes a decision screen that allows users to adjust staff size, transmission capacity, languages, and programs. Pull-down menus invoke a host of time charts and reports showing business performance.

The simulator can be initialized in many different ways, though it's cost structure, listener behavior and transmission options (type and range) are calibrated to the real business. For the purpose of this paper the simulator was set-up to represent a scaled-down and deliberately disguised version of World Service called Voice of the World. The opening scene is described below and was drawn-up in consultation with an industry expert.

Voice of the World (VOW) is an international radio broadcaster operating in ten languages which between them span 3,680 million people, a large proportion of the world's adult language speakers. The chosen languages are Arabic, Bengali, English, Hindi, Indonesian, Mandarin, Portuguese, Russian, Spanish and Urdu. VOW's mission is to offer convenient, high quality news and current affairs to its listeners and to influence opinion leaders around the globe. To achieve this end it offers a program schedule which includes 24 hours per day of continuous broadcasting in English and Arabic. It offers 5 hours per day in the other eight languages in the portfolio. This schedule translates into approximately 100 hours of programming per day or 700 hours of programming per week.

These 700 hours are delivered as 10 percent straight news, 60 percent news and current affairs, and 30 percent documentary. VOW does not broadcast music of any kind, and follows a policy of no repeat broadcasts. To develop this volume and mix of programs VOW employs professional staff including language experts. In the industry there is a rough rule of thumb that each hour of programming takes one staff-week to prepare. On this criterion VOW should employ around 700 staff. However, because the company attracts ambitious and hardworking individuals it has been able to operate with 500 staff, thereby achieving a cost advantage over rivals.

Given the language portfolio, the network of transmitters must have a global reach. VOW currently operates a combination of 80 short-wave and medium-wave transmitters which experts believe to be sufficient to beam a signal of adequate quality to most parts of the world. For flexibility and cash-flow reasons the company leases all its transmitters - the annual leasing cost is £175,000 per transmitter (averaged across the combination of short-wave and medium-wave) whereas the capital cost of a new transmitter is £ 3 million (averaged across the same combination).

This configuration of resources has provided VOW with an estimated audience of 45 million listeners at a cost per listener of £1.52 per person per year. This is good performance by industry standards, but perhaps it can be improved. We now use the simulator to explore three different scenarios for competing in the future.

Scenario 1: Business-as-Usual

VOW has established a strong position with its current configuration of resources. Scenario 1 explores the implications of business-as-usual over the next five years. To implement this plan the company retains its existing portfolio of 10 languages and a broadcast schedule of 700 hours of programming split 10 percent straight news, 60 percent news and current affairs and 30 percent documentary. It follows a no-growth policy for staff, simply replacing those who leave. It follows a similar no-growth policy for transmitters, renewing any leases that expire.

The results are shown in table 1 below for a selection of performance indicators generated by the microworld. In year 1 estimated audience continues to grow slowly reaching 46.05 million listeners and driving down the cost per listener to £1.42 per person per year. Program quality is 76 percent and growing (which explains the increase of listeners). However quality is lower than the industry average which is between 85 and 95 percent. This low quality is partly explainable by the long working week of 69 hours per person which in turn stem from a policy of lean staffing. Quality is also affected by the proportion of new recruits which is 17 percent.

	Estimated Audience	Cost per Listener	Program Quality	Proportion of New Recruits	Working Week
	millions	£ per person per year	percentage	percentage	hours per week
Year 1	46.05	1.42	76	17	69
Year 2	48.10	1.36	76	15	69
Year 3	49.65	1.31	77	15	69
Year 4	50.92	1.28	77	14	68
Year 5	52.01	1.25	77	14	68

Table 1: Results of Business-as-Usual Scenario

In subsequent years audience continues to rise slowly and grows to 52.01 million by year 5. Cost per listener falls still further, declining to a value of only £1.25 per person per week by the end of the simulation (not as good as the real World Service, but better than some rivals). This steady downward trend of cost against a backdrop of stable tangible resources (staff and transmitters) is interesting and is a dynamic phenomenon that the simulator helps to make clear. Listeners are rising because of positive lagged effects from the intangible resource of program quality. Moreover, staff costs are falling (albeit only slightly) because recruitment expenses are less in an organization with a declining proportion of new recruits (down from 17 percent of employees at the start of the scenario to 14 percent by the end). Quasi-static equilibrium thinking is unlikely to detect such effects. But they are real and important, amounting here to a 12 percent increase in cost efficiency over five years.

Scenario 2: Staff-Boost

Business-as-usual delivers incrementally better performance, but it doesn't really challenge the organization's view about how to best leverage complementary resources. Maybe rivals can find a better blend of resources that achieve a still lower cost per listener and attract even more listeners. Scenario 2 is an experiment in adding more staff. Such a policy change might be justified on the grounds that a working week of 68 hours is exceptionally long and is jeopardizing program quality. Higher program quality may attract many more listeners, more than enough to offset the cost of extra staff. The reasoning sounds plausible, but a simulation can help trace the implications over time (and draw attention to the assumptions that lie behind the results).

To implement this plan the company follows a policy of recruiting 20 percent more staff each year for a period of two years. Meanwhile executives retain the existing portfolio of 10 languages with a 700 hour broadcast schedule weighted to news and current affairs (remember the earlier argument that resources like languages and program mix are difficult to change because they are embedded in culture and tradition). The company maintains its network of 80 transmitters, renewing any leases that expire. After two years the staff growth policy reverts to no-growth, simply replacing those who leave.

The results are shown in table 2 below. The outcome is partly as expected, but there are some surprises. In particular the behavior of cost per listener is puzzling, at least in the short run. What the table reveals is an example of dynamic complexity where firm performance gets worse before it gets better. In year 1 estimated audience rises to 46.53 million, a slight improvement over business-as-usual, but not much. The length of the working week falls as expected. There is a slight increase in program quality, but the hoped-for advantage to quality from a less stressful work routine is offset by an influx of new recruits who make up 26 percent of total employees.

	Estimated Audience	Cost per Listener	Program Quality	Proportion of New Recruits	Working Week
	millions	*£ per person per year*	*percentage*	*percentage*	*hours per week*
Year 1	46.53	1.50	78	26	62
Year 2	50.59	1.50	85	30	53
Year 3	55.20	1.38	90	23	49
Year 4	58.87	1.29	92	17	48
Year 5	61.64	1.23	93	14	48

Table 2: Results of Staff-Boost Scenario

In year 2 recruitment continues apace and audience size grows encouragingly to more than 50 million listeners. The working week falls to 53 hours and program quality rises to 85 percent. But the proportion of new recruits grows to 30 percent and cost per listeners remains stubbornly high at £1.50 per person per year. This cost is much worse than the equivalent £1.36 for business-as-usual. After two years, the expectation that rising quality will attract more than enough listeners to offset the extra staff cost seems unfounded. However, the rest of the scenario shows that rewards really are there once the benefits of the staff boost work their way through to experienced staff. In year 3 the audience size grows by 10 percent to more than 55 million and cost per listener plummets to £1.38 per person per year - still not as good as business-as-usual, but fast approaching. Meanwhile the organization benefits from a simultaneous fall in the working week (down to 49 hours) and the proportion of new recruits (down to 23 percent). In years 4 and 5 more of the same advantageous changes play-out to yield an audience size of 61.64 million and program quality of 93 percent. Cost per listener ends at an impressive £1.23 per person per year, lower than business-as-usual and falling faster.

The staff-boost scenario shows that a broadcaster can outperform a business-as-usual rival by deliberately building-up staff in relation to other resources. Although this effect might seem plausible from an end-of-scenario perspective, causality is much more puzzling during implementation. Two years is a long time in business and a policy change that appears to damage competitive performance over such a prolonged period could easily be reversed.

Scenario 3: Transmission-Boost

Scenario 3 is an experiment in adding more transmitters. Such a policy change might be justified on the grounds that transmission capacity needs more attention. Normally it is a remote technical asset in the minds of broadcasters. They don't see and experience transmitters in the same way they do program making, studios and newsgathering. Therefore there may be a tendency to underspend on transmitters because the benefits are literally "in the ether". Interestingly this bias has been noted frequently among players of the World Service microworld, who, even after ten years or more of broadcasting experience, have no clear grasp of how much it costs to run short-wave transmitters (for example few are aware that the electricity bill alone for short-wave transmitters is 15 percent of the total operating budget).

To implement this capacity plan the company follows a policy of leasing 20 percent more transmitters each year for a period of two years. Meanwhile executives hold steady the level of all other resources under their control including languages, broadcast schedule, program mix and staff. Incidentally, in this scenario the number of staff is reduced back to 500, the same as in business-as-usual. After two years the company reverts to no-growth of transmitters.

The results are shown in table 3 below. This time the results are quite clear. There is less dynamic complexity than in scenario 2. In year 1 audience rises to 48.24 million, some 2 million more listeners than in business-as-usual. Cost per listener is slightly higher at £1.45 per person per year because the full cost of the rental is borne before the full benefit of new listeners materializes. There is a time-lag before new listeners tune-in. It takes time to realize that an adequate signal is available. Meanwhile, the figures for program quality (76 percent), proportion of new recruits (17 percent) and working week (69 hours per week) are identical to scenario 1, indicating that transmission is relatively independent of the rest of broadcast operations.

In year 2 there is a big gain in listeners which pushes cost per listener down to £1.35, below the equivalent cost in business-as-usual. The benefit continues to grow in years 3, 4 and 5. At the end of the scenario the audience size is 62.09 million and the cost per listener is £1.20, both of which are slightly better even than the results achieved in scenario 2, staff-boost. This performance improvement is achieved despite lower-than-normal program quality (77 percent) and a long working week (68 hours).

	Estimated Audience	Cost per Listener	Program Quality	Proportion of New Recruits	Working Week
	millions	*£ per person per year*	*percentage*	*percentage*	*hours per week*
Year 1	48.24	1.45	76	17	69
Year 2	55.27	1.35	76	15	69
Year 3	59.11	1.27	77	15	69
Year 4	61.08	1.22	77	14	68
Year 5	62.09	1.20	77	14	68

Conclusion

A dynamic resource-based view of the firm is a synthesis of resource-based theory and system dynamics[13]. It extends resource-based thinking in a number of ways. It provides a visual language for representing asset stock accumulations and resource complementarity. It resolves complementarity into two distinct components: 1. operating constraints that reflect how things really work together in practice; and 2. discretionary operating policy that managers use to guide and coordinate resource accumulation on the basis of feedback information. It is in the area of discretionary operating policy that firms can achieve competitive advantage by accumulating resources in a superior way to rivals.

Operating policy is not a resource of the system per se, rather it is a property of the decision-making and information network of the firm. However, there are well-defined rules and guidelines for representing operating policy and information flows drawing on principles of bounded rationality and information feedback systems. The rigor of algebraic modeling and simulation is available to tease-out the dynamic consequences of a resource map and to explain how behavior over time arises from the structure of the resource system and its coordinating policies.

The resulting framework is useful for visualizing and rehearsing competitive advantage and for analyzing the causes of superior firm performance. An application of the approach to an international radio broadcaster shows the basic principles of resource mapping and illustrates the value of simulation for interpreting path dependent strategy.

---

[13] Readers who would like a practical introduction to the spectrum of systems methodologies, including system dynamics, are referred to Systems Approaches to Managing Change (editors Holwell and Reynolds 2010).

About the Author

John Morecroft is a Senior Fellow in Management Science and Operations at London Business School, and an internationally recognized expert in the use of business modeling and simulation for strategy and scenario development. He has advised international organizations including Shell, BBC and Mars Inc. He holds a BSc (Bristol), a MSc (London) and a PhD (MIT).

References

Barney JB 1986. Strategic factor markets: Expectations, luck and business strategy, Management Science, 32 (10), 1986, pp 1231-1241.

Barney JB 1989. Asset stocks and sustained competitive advantage: A comment. Management Science, 35 (12), 1989, pp 1511-1513.

Barney JB 1991. Firm resources and sustained competitive advantage, Journal of Management, 17 (1), 1991, pp 99-120.

Delauzun F, Hobbs M, Langley P, Morecroft JDW, Morecroft LE 1996. The BBC world service microworld user guide, System Dynamics Group educational document ED-0003-A, Decision Technology Centre, London Business School, August 1996.

Dierickx I, Cool K 1989. Asset stock accumulation and sustainability of competitive advantage, Management Science, 35 (12), 1989, pp 1504-1510.

Forrester JW 1961. Industrial Dynamics, Pegasus Communications, Waltham, MA, 1961.

Forrester JW 1992. Policies, decisions and information sources for modeling, European Journal of Operational Research, 59 (1), 1992, pp 42-63.

Gary MS, Kunc M, Morecroft JDW, Rockart SF 2008. System Dynamics and Strategy, System Dynamics Review 24(4), 407-429, 2008.

Grant RM 1991. The resource-based theory of competitive advantage: Implications for strategy formulation, California Management Review, Spring 1991, pp 114-135.

Holwell S and Reynolds M (editors) 2010. Systems Approaches to Managing Change: A practitioner's guide for the Open University, Springer, 2010.

Kunc MH, Morecroft JDW 2010. Managerial Decision-Making and Firm Performance Under a Resource-Based Paradigm, Strategic Management Journal, 31(11), 1164-1180, 2010.

Maritan CA, Peteraf MA 2010. Building a bridge between resource acquisition and resource accumulation, Journal of Management 2010.

Mosakowski E, McKelvey W 1997. Predicting rent generation in competence-based competition, chapter 3, 65-85, in Competence-Based Strategic Management (Heene and Sanchez editors), John Wiley and Sons, Chichester, UK, 1997.

Morecroft JDW 1985. Rationality in the analysis of behavioral simulation models, Management Science, 31(7), 1985, pp 900-916.

Morecroft JDW 2002. Resource management under dynamic complexity, in A Systems View of Resources, Capabilities and Management Processes (Morecroft, Heene and Sanchez editors), Elsevier Pergamon, Oxford, 2002.

Morecroft JDW 2007. Strategic Modelling and Business Dynamics: A Feedback Systems View, Wiley 2007.

Porter ME 1991. Towards a dynamic theory of strategy, Strategic Management Review, 12, 1991, pp 95-117.

Repenning NP, Henderson RM 2011, Making the numbers? "Short-termism" and the puzzle of only occasional disaster, forthcoming in Management Science.

Sterman JD 1989. Modeling managerial behavior: Misperceptions of feedback in dynamic decisionmaking, Management Science, 35 (3), 1989, pp 321-339.

Sterman JD 2000. Business Dynamics: Systems Thinking and Modeling for a Complex World, Irwin/McGraw-Hill, 2000.

Teece D, Pisano G 1994. The dynamic capabilities of firms: an introduction, Industrial and Corporate Change, 3(3), 1994, pp 537-556.

Warren KD 2002. Competitive Strategy Dynamics. Wiley 2002.

Warren KD 2008. Strategic Management Dynamics, Wiley 2008.

Wernerfelt B 1984. A resource-based view of the firm, Strategic Management Journal, 5 (2), 1984, pp 171-180.

www.ingramcontent.com/pod-product-compliance
Lightning Source LLC
Chambersburg PA
CBHW071058050326
40690CB00008B/1059